Get the eBooks FREE!

(PDF, ePub, Kindle, and liveBook all included)

We believe that once you buy a book from us, you should be able to read it in any format we have available. To get electronic versions of this book at no additional cost to you, purchase and then register this book at the Manning website.

Go to https://www.manning.com/freebook and follow the instructions to complete your pBook registration.

That's it!
Thanks from Manning!

F# Deep Dives

F# Deep Dives

Edited by Tomas Petricek
Phillip Trelford

MANNING
SHELTER ISLAND

For online information and ordering of this and other Manning books, please visit
www.manning.com. The publisher offers discounts on this book when ordered in quantity.
For more information, please contact

    Special Sales Department
    Manning Publications Co.
    20 Baldwin Road
    PO Box 761
    Shelter Island, NY 11964
    Email: orders@manning.com

Manning Publications Co.   Development editor: Cynthia Kane
20 Baldwin Road   Copyeditor: Liz Welch
PO Box 761   Proofreader: Tiffany Taylor
Shelter Island, NY 11964   Typesetter: Dennis Dalinnik
                            Cover designer: Marija Tudor

ISBN 9781617291326
Printed in the United States of America

2 3 4 5 6 7 8 9 10 – SP – 23 22 21 20 19

brief contents

    1 ▪ Succeeding with functional-first languages in the industry   1

PART 1 INTRODUCTION **23**

    2 ▪ Calculating cumulative binomial distributions   25

    3 ▪ Parsing text-based languages   45

PART 2 DEVELOPING ANALYTICAL COMPONENTS **71**

    4 ▪ Numerical computing in the financial domain   73

    5 ▪ Understanding social networks   98

    6 ▪ Integrating stock data into the F# language   129

PART 3 DEVELOPING COMPLETE SYSTEMS **151**

    7 ▪ Developing rich user interfaces using the MVC pattern   153

    8 ▪ Asynchronous and agent-based programming   182

    9 ▪ Creating games using XNA   210

    10 ▪ Building social web applications   244

PART 4 F# IN THE LARGER CONTEXT **279**

    11 ▪ F# in the enterprise   281

    12 ▪ Software quality   299

contributors

Chris Ballard	chapter 11
Keith Battocchi	chapter 6
Colin Bull	chapter 8
Chao-Jen Chen	chapter 4
Yan Cui	chapter 10
Johann Deneux	chapter 9
Kit Eason	chapter 2
Evelina Gabasova	chapter 5
Dmitry Morozov	chapter 7
Tomas Petricek	chapters 1 and 3, appendix
Don Syme	chapter 1
Phillip Trelford	chapter 12

contents

preface xiii
acknowledgments xiv
about this book xvi

1 Succeeding with functional-first languages in the industry 1
TOMAS PETRICEK WITH DON SYME

F# as part of an ecosystem 2
    Reflecting industry trends 2 ▪ Building a healthy environment 4

F# from a business perspective 5

Understanding business problems and implications 7

Inferring business needs 9
    Writing correct software 10 ▪ Reducing time to market 11
    Managing complexity 14 ▪ Writing efficient and scalable software 15

Learning from case studies 17
    Balancing the power-generation schedule 17 ▪ Analyzing data
    at Kaggle 18 ▪ Scaling the server side of online games 19

Summary 20

PART 1   INTRODUCTION 23

2   *Calculating cumulative binomial distributions*   *25*
    KIT EASON

    Implementing the formula   26
        The formula for cumulative binomial distribution   26
        Coding the formula   28

    Adding tests   30
        Adding NUnit and FsUnit   30 • Generating test cases in Excel   30
        Exposing the Fact function to unit testing   33 • Returning large
        integers from the Fact function   34 • Processing large integers in
        the Binomial function   35

    Time for a rethink   36
        An alternative approach   37 • Implementing the Excel algorithm   38

    Refactoring   40
        Eliminating the cumulative flag   40 • Identifying common functions
        between the two while loops   41 • Eliminating duplication, mutables,
        and loops   42

    Summary   43

3   *Parsing text-based languages*   *45*
    TOMAS PETRICEK

    Introducing the Markdown format   46
        Formatting text with Markdown   46 • Why another
        Markdown parser?   47

    Representing Markdown documents   48
    Parsing spans using recursive functions   49
    Implementing the parser using active patterns   52
        Parsing spans using active patterns   52 • Parsing blocks using
        active patterns   56

    Turning Markdown into HTML   61
    Processing Markdown documents   63
        Implementing the tree-processing patterns   64 • Generating references
        from hyperlinks   66

    Summary   69

PART 2 DEVELOPING ANALYTICAL COMPONENTS 71

4 *Numerical computing in the financial domain* **73**
CHAO-JEN CHEN

Introducing financial derivatives and underlying assets 74
Non-dividend-paying stocks 74 ▪ European call options 74

Using probability functions of Math.NET 74
*Configuring F# Interactive 75 ▪ Downloading and setting up
Math.NET Numerics 75 ▪ Random variables, expectation,
and variance 76 ▪ Generating normal random samples 78*

Geometric Brownian motion and Monte Carlo estimates 79
*Modeling stock prices using geometric Brownian motion 79
Payoff function, discounted payoff, and Monte Carlo estimates 84
Analyzing Monte Carlo estimates using variance 88
Pricing path-dependent options 89 ▪ Variance reduction
using antithetic variates 92*

Summary 96

5 *Understanding social networks* **98**
EVELINA GABASOVA

Social networks on Twitter 99

Connecting to Twitter 100
*Downloading the social network around the F# Software Foundation 101
Nodes in the Twitter network 102 ▪ Links in the Twitter network 102
Network representation in the JSON format 103*

Visualization with D3.js 105

Exploring the social network 108
*Representing a network with an adjacency matrix 109 ▪ Reading JSON
files with type providers 109 ▪ In-degrees and out-degrees 112
Finding the most-connected users 114 ▪ Using the R provider to
visualize the degree distribution 115 ▪ Log degree distribution
and scale-free networks 116*

PageRank 119
*Mathematical formulation of PageRank 119 ▪ Calculating PageRank
with a damping factor 121 ▪ Using MapReduce to compute
PageRank 123 ▪ PageRank results 125 ▪ Visualizing
important nodes 126*

Summary 126

6   Integrating stock data into the F# language   129
KEITH BATTOCCHI

Introducing type providers   130

*Using the CSV type provider   130 ▪ How the CSV provider works   131
The philosophy behind type providers   132*

Designing and implementing the CSV type provider   133

*Design strategy   133 ▪ Inferring column types   135
Implementing the runtime and type provider   138*

Implementing the Yahoo! Finance type provider   143

*Getting company information using YQL   143 ▪ Implementing the
type provider   145 ▪ Generating company names lazily   146
Reusing the CSV provider   147 ▪ Yahoo! Finance provider
in action   149*

Summary   150

PART 3   DEVELOPING COMPLETE SYSTEMS 151

7   Developing rich user interfaces using the MVC pattern   153
DMITRY MOROZOV

Setting the scene   155

*The trading application   155 ▪ Introducing the MVC pattern   155
Defining the model   158 ▪ Implementing the main trading view   160
Handling interactions in the controller   161 ▪ Gluing together
the MVC pieces   164*

Living in an asynchronous world   166

Making data binding safer   169

*Are magic strings the only choice?   169 ▪ Introducing statically typed
data binding   170 ▪ Handling nullable values in data binding   171
Handling conversions   173 ▪ Adding transformations   174*

Summary   181

8   Asynchronous and agent-based programming   182
COLIN BULL

All about asynchronous workflows   182

What are asynchronous workflows?   183 ▪ Meet the agents   183

Extracting data from the world   190

*The extract, transform, and load (ETL) model   191 ▪ Scheduling
ETL work   195 ▪ Implementing ETL pipeline workers   197*

Putting a system together 201

*Introducing scalable systems 201 ▪ Building on event streams 201
Designing for scalability 202 ▪ Implementing the system 203
Going beyond simple agents 208*

Summary 208

9 Creating games using XNA 210
JOHANN DENEUX

Getting started 212

*Defending Europe against incoming missiles 212 ▪ Understanding the
execution flow of an XNA game 213 ▪ Structure of an XNA game in
Visual Studio 215*

Selecting the input device on the Press Start screen 217
Modeling and updating the game world 223
Rendering the game and the scoreboard 230

Rendering the game 230 ▪ Rendering the scoreboard 233

Performing I/O safely using async 237
Putting it all together 240
Summary 242

10 Building social web applications 244
YAN CUI

Designing a social game 245

Features 245 ▪ The UI 246 ▪ Client-server interaction 246

Prerequisites 248
Implementing the contracts 249

The model 249 ▪ Requests and response objects 250

Implementing the server 253

*Common utility functions 255 ▪ The data access layer 256
The game engine 260 ▪ The HTTP server 265*

Implementing the client 266

*The XAML 267 ▪ Representing the game state 268
Utility functions 270 ▪ The app 272*

Putting it together 276
Summary 278

PART 4 F# IN THE LARGER CONTEXT 279

11 F# in the enterprise 281
CHRIS BALLARD

Sample project   281

We'll start with some data   282

Creating the basic service implementation   287

Creating a client wrapper for the service   290

Giving your application a user interface   292
  *Creating the basic Prism shell   292 ▪ Creating a Prism WPF
  plug-in module in F#   294 ▪ Making your service available
  throughout the application   296*

Summary   297

12 Software quality 299
PHIL TRELFORD

What software quality really means   300
  *Understanding requirements   301 ▪ Avoiding defects early
  with types   303 ▪ Holistic approach to testing   304*

From exploratory to unit testing   305
  *Exploratory testing   306 ▪ Unit testing   308
  Parameterized tests   313*

Writing effective unit tests   314
  *Fuzz testing with FsCheck   315 ▪ Avoiding dependencies
  with test doubles   317*

Acceptance testing   320
  State of the art   321 ▪ Specifying behavior with TickSpec   322

Summary   326

appendix *F# walkthrough: looking under the covers   327*

index   350

preface

For the last two years, interest in F# and functional-first programming has been growing steadily. More than 10 books about F# are now on the market, more than one new user group has appeared somewhere in the world every month during the last year, and the number of members of and visitors to the F# Software Foundation has been increasing at a steady rate.

Many people become interested in F# because they hear about the benefits that functional-first programming gives you: the F# type system mostly removes the need for null checking and other invalid states; avoiding a mutable state and its declarative nature makes it easier to understand your programs; and the agent-based programming model simplifies concurrency. These are all nice facts about F#, but how do you put them into practice?

We provide the answer with this book. Rather than introducing F# language features using simple, toy examples, we worked with F# experts who have hands-on F# experience. We asked each of them to write a chapter based on a real scenario that they solved with F#. Each chapter is a case study documenting not just the source code written, but also the author's approach to solving the problem, how it integrates with the broader ecosystem, and the business benefits gained from using F#.

This means the narrative of the book isn't built along the technical aspects of the F# language. Instead, we focus on the business benefits you get from using F# in practice. Although we look at diverse domains ranging from game development to financial systems and social network analysis, there is still a common theme. The four key concepts you'll see repeated over and over are *time-to-market*, *taming complexity*, *correctness*, and *performance*. How these concepts fit with actual business problems is covered in detail in chapter 1, which was coauthored by lead F# language designer Don Syme.

acknowledgments

As the editor of this book, but author of only part of it, I feel slightly uncomfortable writing the acknowledgements section, because this book would not exist without the authors of the individual chapters, and they deserve most of the credit and thanks. In other words, if the book feels inconsistent, it's because of me; but if you like the content, you should thank the individual authors! You will find their names and bios at the end of each of the chapters. I would also like to thank my co-editor, Phil, who helped to shape the book and find an interesting group of contributors.

The main theme of this section is patience. I'm grateful to everyone at Manning for their continued support despite the numerous delays as we worked on this book. I would also like to thank all the readers of the MEAP (Manning Early Access Program) version of this book who did not ask for a refund and believed that they would eventually receive a finished book. It took a long time, but it's finally here!

As I said, most of the acknowledgments should be dedicated to the authors of the individual chapters and the great people around them who supported them while they were writing (and hopefully made my continuous nagging bearable!). Thank you all for letting your friends, husbands and wives, or fathers and mothers work on this book for so many nights and weekends!

I want to thank everyone at Manning who made this book possible: Mike Stephens, who helped start the project; Marjan Bace, who trusted us; Cynthia Kane, who kept the project alive during crucial times; and the many individuals who worked on the book during production, including copyeditor Liz Welch, proofreader Tiffany Taylor, typesetter Dennis Dalinnik, and many others who worked behind the scenes. Special thanks to Mark Seemann for his careful technical proofread of the book shortly before it went into production.

Finally, the book also benefited greatly from the feedback that was provided by the reviewers of early drafts. This includes Adrian Bilauca, Christopher Reed, Dave Arkell, David Castro Esteban, Dennis Sellinger, Jeff Smith, Jon Parish, Jonathan DeCarlo, Kostas Passadis, M Sheik Uduman, Mark Elston, and Pasquale Zirpoli. Thank you!

TOMAS PETRICEK

about this book

Have you looked into F# briefly, found it interesting, and felt that your business could benefit from using it—but you aren't sure how to best use F# in practice, how to approach problems from the functional-first perspective, and how to convince your colleagues that F# is the right choice? If you're nodding while reading these words, then you're holding the right book!

In this book, we've tried to answer many of the difficult questions that you have to answer when you learn F# and want to use it in practice. What does your business gain from adopting functional-first programming? What are some of the areas where people have succeeded with F#, and what is the best strategy for integrating F# with the rest of your ecosystem? And how do F# developers and architects think when they approach a problem?

These aren't easy questions, and there isn't a single answer. So rather than seeking just 1 answer, we collected 11 answers from different people who come from different backgrounds and different industries. If you're working in a particular industry, then you'll likely find a chapter that is close to what you're doing, and you can start reading the book from there, focusing on the topic(s) that are close to you. That said, none of the chapters is specific to a single industry or a single problem. Each chapter has a more general takeaway point that is interesting even if you're coming from elsewhere.

Although the chapters were written by different people and cover different topics, we tried to find a common narrative for the book. This link is provided by chapter 1, "Succeeding with Functional-First Languages in the Industry," which is based on Don Syme's talk from NDC 2013. As someone who has been in touch with many successful F# users since the first versions of F#, Don is the most qualified person to give the bigger picture. And you'll see that the points discussed in chapter 1 keep reappearing in the later chapters.

What will this book give you?

If you're still wondering whether this is the right book for you, here's what you'll get from reading it:

- *Industrial case studies*—Rather than focusing on toy examples to demonstrate language features, this book is based on real uses of F# in the industry. In other words, you won't see another naïve Fibonacci calculation, but rather a calculation of a cumulative binomial distribution used in a real-world life expectancy model, with unit tests and C# integration.

- *Functional-first thinking*—When explaining the implementation, each chapter offers a bigger picture and describes not just the finished code, but also the considerations that motivated the solution. This means you'll learn how experienced F# developers and architects approach the problem and how this differs from (and overlaps with) other methodologies, such as object-oriented and test-driven approaches.

- *Business value*—As developers, we often get carried away with interesting technical problems and forget that software is created to solve business problems and produce a unique business value. We tried to keep this in mind throughout the book. For more business-minded readers, this book explains what you gain by using F#. For more technical readers, we give you all you need to effectively explain the benefits of F# to your colleagues and managers.

Of course, no single book can be a great fit for all purposes, so it's worth saying what this book *isn't*, to avoid disappointment.

What won't this book give you?

This book is *not* an F# language introduction. Although it includes an appendix that gives a quick overview of the most important F# language features, it's probably not the first F# resource you should look at. You don't need to be an F# expert to read this book, but some basic familiarity with the language is useful if you want to understand all the technical content of the book.

The book includes 11 different case studies, but you probably won't find a ready-to-use solution to the problem you're currently solving (unless you're really lucky). We teach you how to use the functional-first approach to solve problems in the industry, and we demonstrate this using a number of examples from diverse domains, but in the end, you'll have to do the work on your own.

If there is a single rule in computing that always holds, it's the rule that there is no single rule in computing that always holds. Keep this in mind when reading this book and using the ideas described here!

How to read this book

Unfortunately, books these days still have to be organized in a sequential order, including this one. This is perhaps the best order to follow if you want to read the entire book, because it starts with more accessible chapters and continues to more advanced topics. But there are other options:

- *By problem domain*—Later chapters don't generally rely on earlier chapters, so if you're working in a specific industry (say, finance or gaming), you can start with the chapters that discuss topics that are closest to your domain.
- *By programming theme*—Similarly, you can look at the cross-cutting problems that interest you. For example, choose the chapters that talk about user-interface development, writing numerical calculations, testing, and enterprise or asynchronous and concurrent programming.
- *As a technology overview*—Finally, you can read parts of this book to get an overall idea about the business value that F# provides. If you're not interested in all the technical details but want to know why and how F# is used, you can read chapter 1 and then read the first few pages of the other chapters. Each chapter starts with the business perspective, so you get a good idea of the reasons to choose F# for different problems and tasks.

To help you find what you're interested in, let's quickly go through the table of contents.

Roadmap

The book starts with an introductory chapter, followed by four parts that group the content by theme. It ends with a brief F# overview in an appendix:

- Chapter 1 looks at the business motivations behind using functional-first programming languages. What are the problems faced by businesses when developing software (especially analytical components)? How does F# help to solve those?

Part 1 contains easier-to-read chapters that serve as a great starting point to refresh your F# knowledge. It also demonstrates how F# makes it possible to write code that corresponds to the description of a problem domain:

- Chapter 2 presents a relatively simple numerical problem that arises when modeling life expectancies. It shows how you can easily encode numerical computations in F# and goes into interesting details about making the implementation practical.
- Chapter 3 explores the power of pattern matching for encoding the logic of your code. The example used throughout the chapter is a simple Markdown parser, but the chapter also highlights the benefits of modeling domain using functional types.

Part 2 focuses on implementing advanced analytical components for calculations and data processing:

- Chapter 4 looks at using F# for financial simulations using Monte Carlo methods. Because of the nature of the problem, this chapter is more mathematical than the others, but the key point is easy to see: F# makes it easy to turn mathematical models into code.

- Chapter 5 uses F# to understand social networks—specifically, Twitter. It's a great example of end-to-end data analysis with F#, starting from data access, implementing algorithms such as Page Rank, and visualizing data using the D3 visualization library.

- Chapter 6 looks at writing *type providers*—a unique F# feature that makes it possible to integrate external data sources directly into the F# language. The chapter describes the implementation of a type provider for easy access to stock prices using Yahoo! Finance.

Part 3 discusses how to use F# for the development of complete systems:

- Chapter 7 is a myth buster. It shows not only that F# can be used for user interface programming, but also that using F#, you get additional safety and correctness that would be impossible in other languages. The chapter uses a simple trading application as an example.

- Chapter 8 discusses the development of scalable concurrent data processing using F# asynchronous workflows and the agent-based programming model. Along the way, it creates a simple agent-based framework and also an elegant computation expression for writing data-processing computations.

- Chapter 9 is about game development with F#. It incorporates topics that are important in pretty much any application: how to asynchronously handle user interactions and how to implement control-flow logic that is modeled using state machines.

- Chapter 10 is based on experience with developing the server-side part of social games using F#. It discusses the unique challenges of social gaming (like scalability) and develops a simple yet complete multiplayer farming game.

Part 4 describes how to integrate F# with the larger context:

- Chapter 11 takes a step back from the technical perspective and discusses how to succeed when introducing F# into the enterprise. It talks about using F# in a risk-free way and integrating F# components into larger C# solutions.

- Chapter 12 talks about one of the easiest ways of introducing F# into the enterprise: testing. It doesn't just talk about unit tests, but instead discusses what should be tested, how to write useful tests, and how F# simplifies this task through a number of great libraries.

Finally, the appendix is a quick overview (and reminder) of key F# features. Rather than going through language features one by one, it tries to show the bigger picture—the focus on compositionality that exists in all aspects of the language.

Online resources

As already mentioned, this book doesn't cover all aspects of the F# language. You may find it useful to read it with an internet connection available, so that you can find the F# details that didn't fit into the book.

The best starting point for finding information about F# is the F# Software Foundation (www.fsharp.org). Its learning page provides links to other great F# books, as well as a number of great free resources that cover most of F#:

- Try F# (www.tryfsharp.org) is a website with interactive tutorials that you can run in your web browser (using Silverlight). It includes tutorials that introduce F#, work with data, and also use F# in finance.
- F# for Fun and Profit (www.fsharpforfunandprofit.com) is a great website that includes tutorials on some of the most important F# features, such as understanding F# types.
- F# Wikibook (http://en.wikibooks.org/wiki/F_Sharp_Programming) is a detailed site that documents most of the F# language constructs, ranging from expressions to object-oriented features and advanced topics.

Code conventions and downloads

All the source code in the book, whether in code listings or snippets, is in a `fixed-width font like this`, which sets it off from the surrounding text. Output from F# Interactive appears in an *`italicized fixed-width font`*. In most listings, the code is annotated to point out the key concepts, and numbered bullets are sometimes used in the text to provide additional information about the code. We have tried to format the code so that it fits within the available page space in the book by adding line breaks and using indentation carefully.

The code examples in most of the chapters are self-contained, but we also maintain a repository where you can easily download all the samples and play with them without typing everything yourself. You can find all the links on the book website maintained by the authors at www.functional-programming.net/deepdives.

The code for the examples in the book can also be downloaded from the publisher's website at www.manning.com/FSharpDeepDives.

Author Online

Purchase of *F# Deep Dives* includes free access to a private web forum run by Manning Publications where you can make comments about the book, ask technical questions, and receive help from the authors and other users. To access the forum and subscribe to it, point your web browser to www.manning.com/FSharpDeepDives. This page provides information on how to get on the forum once you are registered, what kind of help is available, and the rules of conduct on the forum.

The Author Online forum and the archives of previous discussions will be accessible from the publisher's website as long as the book is in print.

Succeeding with functional-first languages in the industry

Tomas Petricek with Don Syme

Any other programming book would start by introducing the technology it's about, but we're going to do things differently. See, most of the time, you don't read programming books just because you want to learn about a technology. Of course you want to learn the technology, but that's secondary—you want to learn it because you face a practical problem that you need to solve, and you want to do this more rapidly, more reliably, and with fewer bugs than with the technologies you were using before. For that reason, this chapter isn't focused on the F# language, but instead on solving practical business problems.

When talking about programming languages, it's easy to lose this big picture—we programmers are often excited about interesting technical aspects, innovative language features, or elegant ideas. But the evolution of programming languages really does matter in practice, because it enables us to tackle more complex problems and build products that we couldn't even imagine a couple of years ago. For example, who would believe that computers would be able to instantly translate spoken English to spoken Chinese, while maintaining the style of the speaker's voice?[1]

In this chapter, we'll look at the business motivations behind using F#, drawing from a number of case studies made by existing F# users. The technical aspects of many of the case studies are explained in later chapters by the people who developed and successfully deployed them. We'll start with a business situation that many F# users share, and then we'll look at the business problems they faced and how they solved them.

---

[1] BBC News, "Microsoft demos instant English-Chinese translation," November 9, 2012, www.bbc.co.uk/news/technology-20266427.

But before discussing the main topic of this chapter—business motivations—we'll briefly look at how F# fits in with the current industry trends and at the rich F# ecosystem that combines commercial companies and an enthusiastic open source community.

F# as part of an ecosystem

Technologies never exist separately in themselves, and F# is no different. From an overall perspective, it fits perfectly with two important trends in the industry: functional and polyglot programming. At a closer look, there's a large and lively ecosystem around F# that's represented by the F# Software Foundation (www.fsharp.org). Let's look at what this means in practice.

Reflecting industry trends

In recent years, there have been two clear trends in the programming language world:

- *Functional programming* is now undeniably a trend in the industry. An increasing number of programming languages support the functional paradigm, including C++, C#, JavaScript, Python, and Java 8. Moreover, the functional approach underlies many successful libraries, including LINQ and Task Parallel Library (TPL) in the .NET world, and also jQuery and Node.js.
- *Polyglot programming* is the trend of combining multiple languages or paradigms in a single project to take advantage of their benefits where they can be of most use. At the same time, polyglot programming makes it easier to integrate existing stable components with new additions. When using multiple languages, you don't need to rewrite the entire system in a new language when you want to use it—it's perfectly possible to write new components in a different language and integrate them with the existing codebase.

How about F#? First, it's a *functional-first* language. This means F# encourages programmers to use the functional approach, but it fully supports other paradigms. You can use object-oriented style for integrating F# code in larger systems, and you can use imperative style to optimize performance-critical parts of your code.

Second, F# can integrate with a wide range of platforms and languages. It can be compiled to .NET and Mono, and also to iOS and Android (using Xamarin tools) or JavaScript (using WebSharper or FunScript). The type-provider mechanism allows integration with environments like R and MATLAB, as well as databases, WSDL and REST services, and Excel. Let's go a little bit deeper before moving on.

MAKING FUNCTIONAL-PROGRAMMING FIRST-CLASS

The About F# page on the F# Software Foundation website has the following tagline:

> *F# is a strongly-typed, functional-first programming language for writing simple code to solve complex problems.*

The *strongly typed* part refers to the fact that F# uses types to catch potential errors early and also to integrate diverse data sources and other programming environments into the language. As you'll see in later chapters, the types in F# feel different from those in languages like C++, C#, and Java. This is mainly thanks to type inference, which figures out most of the types for you.

The *functional-first* wording refers to F#'s support for immutable data types, higher-order functions, and other functional concepts. They're the easiest way to write F# code, but they're not the only way. As already mentioned, F# supports object-oriented and imperative but also concurrent and reactive programming paradigms.

Finally, the last part of the statement says that F# is a language that lets you solve complex problems with simple code. This is where we need to look at the broader business perspective. We encourage all readers, including developers, to continue reading this chapter; understanding the business perspective will help you succeed with F#.

MAKING POLYGLOT PROGRAMMING FIRST-CLASS

These days, polyglot programming goes well beyond combining F# and C# on a single .NET runtime. Applications consist of components written in multiple languages, using remote services via REST or WSDL. Scientific computations may call scripts written in R or MATLAB or use optimized FORTRAN or C/C++ libraries; web applications need to call JavaScript libraries; and so on.

As a language that can be compiled to .NET and Mono, F# easily interoperates with languages like C++, C#, and Visual Basic .NET, but that's just the beginning. Without going into the details, here are some of the options:

- *F# on iOS and Android*—Thanks to the Xamarin tools, it's possible to develop iPhone, iPad, and Android applications in F#. The tools come with full F# editor support, based on the community-developed open source MonoDevelop integration.
- *F# for the web and HTML5 apps*—WebSharper is a supported product that lets you develop cross-tier and client-side HTML5 applications using F#. An open source project called FunScript has similar aims and can also import JavaScript libraries using the type-provider mechanism.
- *F# for GPU programming*—F# can be compiled to GPU code using Alea.cuBase. There are also efficient GPU stats libraries like StatFactory FCore.
- *F# and R, MATLAB, and Excel*—F# 3.0 type providers enable integration with R and MATLAB. You can call R and MATLAB functions directly from F# in a typed way with auto-completion. Similarly, you can access Excel data or even run F# in Excel.
- *F# and web-scale data sources*—Type providers bring web-based knowledge to the language. They provide integration with Freebase (a knowledge database), World Bank data, and arbitrary web services and REST-based services.

The type-provider mechanism is explained in chapter 6, and we'll look at how you can write a provider that integrates stock data directly into the language. To understand the balance between different languages in an enterprise context, see chapter 11. For all the other topics, the F# Software Foundation website (http://fsharp.org) is the best starting point.

Before moving to the main topic of this chapter—the business perspective—let's switch from looking at general industry trends to the ecosystem that exists around the F# language and its commercial and open source contributors.

Building a healthy environment

F# is an open source, cross-platform language that has a number of industrial supporters as well as a lively open source community. The contributors work together through the F# Software Foundation, which also hosts the F# homepage at www.fsharp.org—a useful resource if you're looking for both technical and nontechnical information about F#.

F# Software Foundation (FSSF)

To quote the mission statement, "The mission of the F# Software Foundation is to promote, protect, and advance the F# programming language, and to support and facilitate the growth of a diverse and international community of F# programmers." This is achieved in a number of ways.

- FSSF maintains an open source repository for the F# source code and community projects (http://github.com/fsharp), and it manages contributions to key F# projects.
- FSSF seeks to expand the relevance of F# skills and the range of platforms and technologies that can be used with F# and to promote the adoption of F#. This is done, for example, by supporting conferences, training, and other events and collecting testimonials from existing users (http://fsharp.org/testimonials).
- FSSF provides room for affiliated groups, including F# user groups around the world (http://c4fsharp.net) and technical working groups that focus on developing F# in a specific direction, such as data science and machine learning or open engineering.

The F# Software Foundation is registered as a non-profit organization and allows those who agree with the mission statement to join. It also encourages members to join specific technical working groups where they can engage with the community and help to work toward FSSF's goals.

FSSF guarantees long-term support for F# and provides a collaboration platform for all the interested parties:

- MSR Cambridge contributes to the language design.
- The community develops open source extensions and tools.
- Xamarin provides support for iOS and Android.
- The Microsoft product group builds professional F# tooling for Windows.
- SkillsMatter provides F# training and conferences.
- BlueMountain Capital contributes to key data-science libraries.

And this is just the start of the list!

F# from a business perspective

The problem with understanding the business needs for F# (or any other programming language) is that programming languages are complex technologies. Their implications for business are indirect and can be hard to imagine. The "Learning from case studies" section later in this chapter will discuss concrete areas where F# is used, but first let's look at the problem more generally—what are the business motivations for adopting F#?

To deal with this question, we'll borrow ideas from SPIN,[2] which is a methodology for "selling complex products." But don't worry—this isn't a sales-pitch chapter! The methodology tells us that we need to ask four important questions to understand the business perspective for a complex technology. In this chapter, we'll go through some common answers from F# adopters (but, of course, the situation is different for every company).

SPIN selling

The idea of SPIN selling is to ask potential customers a series of questions that help them understand the business needs for the new technology (as illustrated in the figure):

- *Situation*—What is the customers' existing situation? In our context, what software are they developing, and what are their constraints?
- *Problem*—What problems do the customers face in their current situation? What do they struggle with during the development of their projects?
- *Implication*—What are the business implications of those problems? Do the problems mean projects aren't finished on time or that developers can't deliver products with all the required features?
- *Need*—What is needed to overcome these problems? How can a new technology, such as a programming language, help solve these problems?

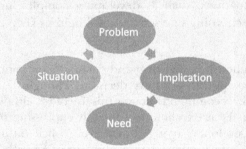

The SPIN selling methodology describes the situation, followed by a specific problem. It proceeds to implications of the problem and only then asks, "What is needed to solve the problem?"

You can probably imagine a lengthy sales call based on these questions, but also look at the positive side. It's all too easy for a technical person to skip the first and third questions and say something like, "Our trading system doesn't scale, so we need to rewrite it in F#." This might be true, but it's a difficult argument to make without understanding the business context.

---

[2] Neil Rackham, *SPIN Selling* (McGraw-Hill, 1988).

The business situations for each chapter in this book are different, ranging from companies developing financial systems or models to companies developing user interfaces in games and web applications. One of the most common situations for F# adopters is the development of *analytical* and *data-rich* components.

Analytical and data-rich components

Most applications contain a computational core that implements business logic, or a component that accesses a wide range of data sources. For some applications (such as CRUD user interfaces), the computational core may be simple, and most of the focus may be on data. For other applications (such as games), data access is minimal, but the computation matters.

Such analytical and data-rich components are what make the application valuable, but with such a general definition, the value may be hard to see. Here are some examples from later chapters:

- Financial models and insurance-calculation engines, such as those discussed in chapters 2 and 4, are examples of analytical components.
- Analytical components in games include artificial intelligence but also the component that's responsible for managing the flow of the gameplay (see chapter 9).
- Another example of an analytical component is an algorithm that analyzes social networks and tells you how to better target advertisements, or recommends people whom you might want to follow (see chapter 5).

So, what's the general business situation we're looking at? For the purposes of this chapter, let's imagine that you're leading a team developing analytical or data-rich components. Other business situations, such as developing complex user interfaces, are equally important, but choosing one scenario will help us keep the chapter focused.

> **TECHNOLOGY RADAR**   The choice of analytical and data-rich components as our motivating scenario isn't an arbitrary decision. ThoughtWorks' *Technology Radar* publication recommends exactly this use of F#, although using a different wording: "F# is excellent at concisely expressing business and domain logic. Developers trying to achieve explicit business logic in an application may opt to express their domain in F# with the majority of plumbing code in C#."[3]

The first task is to understand the business problems that you might have as a team leader for a company developing analytical and data-rich components.

---

[3] ThoughtWorks, *Technology Radar*, March 2012, http://mng.bz/wZvF.

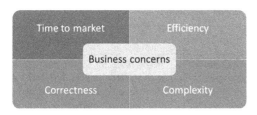

Figure 1 The key business concerns for developing analytical and data-rich components

Understanding business problems and implications

As already mentioned, we're focusing on analytical and data-rich components. Imagine a team developing financial or actuarial models, a team developing server-side components for a massive multiplayer game, or a team building machine-learning algorithms for a social network or ecommerce recommendation system.

There are a number of specific criteria for such systems. An important part of the development process is research or prototyping. Developers need to be able to quickly try multiple, often complex, algorithms and test them. These then have to be deployed to production as soon as possible; and for computationally heavy tasks, the algorithms need to be efficient.

The four most common problems are summarized in figure 1. Analytical applications typically implement more *complex* tasks than the rest of the system; they only deliver value if the implementation is *correct*, is delivered *in time*, and satisfies nonfunctional requirements such as *efficiency*. Table 1 revisits the problems and explores their business implications.

Table 1 Business problems and their implications

	Problems	Implications
Correctness	As computers become more efficient, financial and actuarial models grow increasingly complicated. The amount of available data grows equally quickly, so algorithms that process this data become more advanced.	If a user interface displays a picture incorrectly, your user will likely be annoyed, but they won't lose money. But money can easily be lost if something goes wrong in an analytical component of a financial system.
	Maintaining the correctness of such systems raises many problems. It becomes difficult to add new features without breaking existing code, and systems may break as data sources and formats evolve. In settings where models are developed by researchers and are later reimplemented by developers for production code, it's hard to keep the two in sync.	An infamous example of a correctness problem was the Mars Climate Orbiter probe launched by NASA in 1998. The probe failed during launch because one part of the system was using metric units (force measured in Newtons) and another was using imperial units (measured in pound force).
	An incorrect system that produces incorrect values can easily lead to wrong decisions being made.	Even when incorrect systems don't have such massive consequences, they may lead to buggy services and the loss of reputation for the company, or to buggy products and a loss of customers.

Table 1 Business problems and their implications *(continued)*

	Problems	Implications
Time to market	Another important consideration for analytical and data-rich components is the *time to market*—how much time is needed before an initial idea can be turned into production-quality code. For example, a financial company might have a research department that develops models in statistical or numerical environments like R and MATLAB. When a model is designed and tested, it's passed to developers who translate the models to C++ for deployment to production. Such translation can easily take six months. Consider another example from the social gaming domain. A quick release cycle is important to make sure that your players keep getting new features, or even new games, every few weeks.	In the financial sector, the inability to turn a new mathematical model into a system that can be used in production might mean the business loses an opportunity that exists only in a short timeframe. In the social gaming world, a company will quickly lose players if the games aren't rapidly updated or new features aren't added. The time to market is also important in the startup world, which is symbolized by the phrase "fail fast." You want to be able to develop initial prototypes quickly, so that you can immediately verify the viability of some idea. If the prototype does work, you should also be able to quickly turn it into a complete project.
Efficiency and scalability	Two related concerns are efficiency and scalability. Efficiency is mainly important for computationally heavy software such as financial models. For example, models that were originally developed by researchers in R or Python need to be translated to more efficient C++ code or optimized Python. If the researchers were able to write their models more efficiently, then the translation step wouldn't be needed. Scalability matters even for software that doesn't perform heavy computations. A server-side application (such as a social game backend) or UI (a game frontend) needs to handle multiple concurrent requests or user interactions.	Efficiency and scalability have varying importance in different contexts. A common case for efficiency in financial systems is that models need to be recalculated overnight, so there's a hard limit. Failure here means up-to-date information isn't available. Similarly, when serving a web page with ads, the ad service needs to choose an appropriate ad based on the user's information almost instantly. As for scalability, server-side code that doesn't scale will consume excessive resources and make maintenance costly. On the client side, nonscalable applications can hang and lead to a poor user experience.
Complexity	Analytical and data-centric components are usually the parts of an application that implement advanced logic. They provide value by implementing mathematical models, data analyses, or processing of concurrent events. In a poorly designed system, complexity can easily grow beyond a tractable level, most commonly because different features that should be independent interact in unexpected ways.	As a result of increasing complexity, your company might not be able to implement a desired financial model, AI behavior, or data analytical component, because it's too complex. As a result, you won't be able to provide the data that users and customers need (or not at the required quality), or an entire project or product may fail. In other words, without the right tools, you'll often have to settle for a suboptimal solution.

The business problems and implications outlined here are by no means complete, and they overlap. Handling efficiency or complexity often impacts time to market—you need to spend more time optimizing your system or tracking bugs. Efficiency and scalability are also often linked to correctness. In an attempt to make code more efficient, you could easily introduce bugs when trying to parallelize code that uses shared state.

The key takeaway from this section is that developing software is hard. Exactly where the difficulties lie will depend on the particular software you're developing. Understanding these difficulties and how they affect the business is crucial to finding the right way to tackle them, and one solution may be using a more appropriate programming language!

Inferring business needs

Many of the business problems discussed in the previous section are directly addressed by language features in functional-first programming languages or by their inherent aspects. We'll discuss F#-specific features, but many of these observations apply to other functional-first languages.

Functional-first programming languages

We use the term *functional-first* to distinguish between purely functional languages and those that combine functional aspects with other paradigms. As with any language classification, this is, to a large extent, a subjective measure.

In *traditional functional languages*, such as Miranda, Haskell, and ML, the only way to write programs is to fully adopt a functional style. There may be some exceptions (such as effects in ML), but the overall program structure has to be functional.

In *functional-first languages*, the functional approach is highly encouraged. This is done mainly by choosing the right defaults and using syntax that makes the functional style more convenient. But it's still possible to use other styles.

In languages like F# and Scala, you can write fully object-oriented and imperative code. This is sometimes needed for interoperability or efficiency—and it's an important aspect that makes such languages successful in practice. But most new code can be written in the functional style and can benefit from properties that make functional languages unique, encouraging correctness, a shorter time-to-market period, efficiency, and the ability to solve complex problems.

Let's now go over the four business problems again, but this time using a more developer-focused perspective. You'll see that functional-first languages have unique features that help you tackle the problems just discussed.

Writing correct software

As you'll see in the next section, a surprising number of F# users report that they can write software without any, or with a minimal number of, bugs. Where does this result come from? This is a difficult question to answer, because correctness follows from the nature of functional languages. The best way to understand it is to look at two concrete examples.

LIVING WITHOUT NULL REFERENCES

Tony Hoare introduced NULL references in 1965 in Algol. In a 2009 talk, he referred to this language feature as his "billion dollar mistake."[4] If you do a quick search through your bug database, you'll understand why. The number of bugs caused by NULL references is astonishing. To tackle this, F# doesn't allow you to use NULL with types defined in F#. When you want to represent the fact that a value may be unavailable, you have to do so explicitly using the option type.

Compare the following F# and C# code that finds a product by ID and prints its name:

F# code	C# code
Optional type indicates that a product may not be found	**Type doesn't tell you if the function always returns a valid product**
```let findId id : option<Product> = // Find product and return Some(p) // or return None if id is unknown```	```Product FindId(int id) { // Find product or return 'null'}```
```match findId 42 with| Some p -> printf "%s" p.Name| None -> printf "Not found!"```	```Product p = FindId(42);Console.Write(p.Name);```
Compiler checks that all cases are handled	**You can access properties without checking for nulls.**

Of course, the two snippets are different, and the C# version doesn't correctly handle null values. The point is that there's no indication that it should. The type option <Product> in F# is an explicit indication that the function may not return a value and that you have to handle that case. In other words, F# allows you to make invalid states non-representable. If you have a Product value, then you *always* have a product.

This ability to track information in types goes well beyond NULL values.

CALCULATING CORRECTLY USING UNITS OF MEASURE

Another area where F# uses types to guarantee correctness of code is numerical calculations. In the business implications discussed earlier, we mentioned the Mars Climate

---

[4] Tony Hoare, "Null References: The Billion-Dollar Mistake," QCon London, August 25, 2009, http://mng.bz/
   l2MC (video).

Orbiter. The project failed because one part of the system represented force in metric units and another used imperial pound force.

In F#, you can annotate numeric values with information about units, and the compiler ensures that units are used in a consistent way. Consider this F# Interactive session (with the F# Interactive output typeset in italic):

```
> let force1 = 15.0<kg m/sec^2>
  let force2 = 5.0<lbf>
;;
val force1 : float<kg m/sec ^ 2> = 15.0
val force2 : float<lbf> = 5.0

> force1 + force2;;
error FS0001: The unit of measure 'lbf' does not
match the unit of measure 'kg m/sec ^ 2'

> [<Measure>] type N = kg m/sec^2;;
(...)

> force1 + force2 * 4.4482<N/lbf>;;
val it : float<kg m/sec ^ 2> = 37.241
```

The two numerical values have different unit annotations and thus different types.

Adding two numbers with incompatible units generates a compile-time error.

Defines derived unit to make the code more readable

❶ Compiler checks that multiplication results in a value in Newtons

The purpose of this example isn't to show that F# is a perfect language for writing control systems for NASA probes. Units of measure can be used in ordinary business applications. For example, you can use them to distinguish between product prices (by defining *dollar*, or a *currency* unit) and ratios that are unit-less.

Also, the example demonstrates a more fundamental and prevailing aspect of statically typed functional-first languages: they use types to capture more about the domain that you're working with. In F#, this is enhanced by sophisticated type inference, so you don't usually have to write the types yourself. In this example, the compiler infers that the result has the kg m/sec^2 unit (or, in other words, is in Newtons) ❶.

It may seem that thinking about types and missing values will make the development process slower, but this isn't the case. You may need to spend more time when writing the initial implementation, but you'll spend much less time tracking bugs. Moreover, there are a number of other aspects that make the development process faster.

Reducing time to market

In the previous section, we discussed a scenario where a company uses mathematical software such as R or MATLAB to develop and test models, but then rewrites the software using another language, such as C++, for deployment. F# has also been dubbed "the language that both scientists and developers understand," which makes it a great language for such cases.

Another important aspect of F# is that it interoperates extremely well with the outside world. As a .NET language, it can access a wide range of .NET libraries and easily call efficient C/C++ code when needed. For other environments, such as R or MATLAB, the type-provider mechanism allows smooth integration. Let's first look at how F#

connects the research and development phases. Then we'll quickly look at the integration options.

FROM RESEARCH TO PRODUCTION

Developers and researchers often have different needs. As a researcher, you want to be able to quickly and easily load data from a local file (without worrying about deployment, because you're running the script locally). Then you want to run some analysis of the data, write algorithms to work with the data, and visualize the results. You don't need to worry about the structure of the code—you're just writing scripts that you'll probably rewrite when you realize that you need another algorithm.

On the other hand, as a developer, you need to create a project and package your algorithms nicely in types and modules that will be easily usable from F# or C#. You need to write unit tests for the algorithm and make sure the library can be integrated with an automated build system.

These two sets of requirements are different, but F# can be used both ways: as an interactive environment and also as a full programming language. This combination makes it possible to smoothly transition from the research phase to the developer phase. The typical process is outlined in figure 2.

INTEROPERATING WITH R

Another important aspect of F# that helps speed up the time to market is that it can interoperate with existing solutions. If you have an efficient library that does a calculation in C++, you don't want to rewrite it from scratch in another language and spend weeks optimizing it. Similarly, if you have a mathematical model or a useful function written in mathematical package like R or MATLAB, you want to be able to reuse such code and call it from your newly written code.

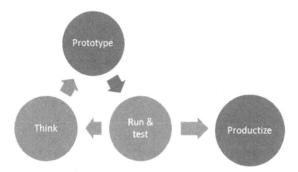

Figure 2   In a typical R&D process, you start with an interesting idea. F# makes it easy to translate the idea into an initial prototype that is a rough and incomplete implementation but that gives you enough so that you can quickly test it and see if the idea works. This is repeated a number of times until you reach a solution that works—at that point, the existing F# code can be cleaned up, documented, and properly tested and encapsulated, and it becomes part of the product.

As a .NET language, F# can easily interoperate with any .NET libraries and call C/C++ code through P/Invoke. But the type-provider mechanism takes these integration capabilities much further.

> **F# TYPE PROVIDERS** In a few words, type providers make it possible to write lightweight plug-ins for the F# compiler that generate types based on external information. A type provider can look at a local database and generate types to represent tables, and it can also analyze code in other languages like JavaScript and MATLAB and generate types for interoperating with such code. We'll look at implementing a type provider in chapter 6.

The following brief snippet demonstrates how the R type provider works. Understanding the details isn't important for the purpose of this chapter—the key thing is that you can easily combine data processing in F# and a call to an external function. Given a value `prices` that represents stock prices obtained earlier, you can pass the list easily to the `var` and `mean` functions that are available in the base package in R:

```
#r "RProvider.dll"                                References the R
open RDotNet                                       type provider
open RProvider
open RProvider.``base``                            R packages, such as base, become
                                                   automatically available, and you can
                                                   see them in autocomplete lists.
let divs =
  [ for prev, next in Seq.pairwise prices ->       Calculates a log of differences
      log (next / prev) ]                          between consecutive prices in F#

let var = R.var(divs).AsNumeric().First()          Calls an external library via automatically
let mean = R.mean(divs).AsNumeric().First()        provided functions R.var and R.mean
```

This example is slightly artificial, because there are F# functions for calculating variance and mean. But it demonstrates the idea—if you have a more complex function written in another language, the type-provider mechanism allows you to call it easily. An important aspect that can't be shown well in print is that you also get full development environment support. When you type R followed by a dot, the editor shows you a list of all available functions (based on the information provided by the R type-provider).

F# for data science and machine learning

One area where F# stands out is data science and machine learning. In fact, one of the first success stories for F# was an internal system created at Microsoft Research, which implemented a more sophisticated algorithm for ranking ads for Bing.

This is further supported by a wide range of libraries:

- *Deedle* is a library for manipulating structured data and time-series data. It supports grouping, automatic alignment, handling of missing values, and pretty much all you need to clean up your data and perform data analyses.

(continued)

- *F# Data* is a collection of type providers for accessing data from a wide range of data sources, including CSV, XML, and JSON files, as well as some online services such as the World Bank or Freebase.
- *F# Charting* makes it possible to create charts interactively with just a few lines of F# code, including multiple charts combined in a single chart area.
- *R type provider and MATLAB type provider* make it possible to call the two most widely used mathematical and statistical packages from F#.

In this section, we mostly focused on scientific and data analytical applications—F# is an excellent fit for this domain, and it's easy to demonstrate how it can help get your ideas to market more quickly. But the "Learning from case studies" section of this chapter looks at a number of case studies, and you'll see that time to market is an important aspect in pretty much every domain where F# is used. Before doing that, let's look at the next two business problems.

Managing complexity

Can a programming language make it easier to solve complex problems? The case studies on the F# Foundation website show that the answer to this question is yes. In this section, we'll look at a simple example that is explained more in chapter 3. You can also find additional experience reports in the "Learning from case studies" section, later in this chapter.

The key to managing complexity is finding the right abstractions for talking about problems. For example, when describing 3D models, you don't want to do that in terms of pixels—you want to use a language based on triangles, or perhaps basic 3D objects such as cubes and spheres.

This approach is sometimes called *domain-specific languages* (DSLs). The key idea is that you define a language that can easily be used to solve multiple instances of problems of the same class (such as creating various 3D objects or modeling prices of stock options). In functional languages, this concept is so prevalent that you can think of any well-designed library as a DSL.

PARSING MARKDOWN WITH DSLS

To demonstrate how F# lets you define appropriate abstractions for solving problems, we'll look at *pattern matching*. This is a fundamental idea in functional languages, where you specify rules for recognizing certain data structures (such as non-empty lists, lists starting with a date that's greater than today, and so on). F# makes the mechanism even more powerful by supporting *active patterns* that let you specify custom recognizers for such structures.

In chapter 3, we'll implement a parser for the Markdown document format. A document can contain formatting such as *hello* for italicized text or [F#](http://fsharp.org) for hyperlinks. Even without understanding the syntax, you can see that the following snippet encodes these two rules:

```
match chars with
| Bracketed '*' '*' (body, rest) ->
    // Create block of italicized text
| Bracketed '[' ']' (body, Bracketed '(' ')' (url, rest)) ->
    // Create hyperlink with body and url
| _ ->
    // Handle other cases
```

Case when chars starts with a substring containing a body bracketed with asterisks and followed by rest

Case when chars starts with a body bracketed using [...], followed by a URL delimited using (...) and then the rest of the text

The details of the snippet, as well as F# active patterns, are explained in chapter 3. The point of showing this example here is that there's a clear correspondence between our earlier description of the format and the code you write to implement it.

This is why functional-first languages can be so effective at managing complexity— they let you build abstractions (such as the Bracketed pattern) that you can then use to elegantly solve the problems at hand (such as recognizing formatting commands for italicized text and hyperlinks).

Writing efficient and scalable software

The last problem that can have a serious impact on your business is efficiency and scalability. We outlined the implications earlier—financial models need to complete in overnight batches, server-side applications need to handle an increasing number of concurrent clients, UIs should react promptly without blocking, and so on.

This group of problems is diverse. Most important, you need to distinguish between computationally intensive tasks (such as evaluating financial models) and tasks where the main issue is coordinating multiple requests and avoiding blocking.

COMPUTATIONALLY INTENSIVE TASKS

For computationally intensive tasks, F# provides an excellent balance between code that's easy to write and that runs efficiently. This means initial prototypes can be turned into production-quality implementations without complete rewrites.

This topic is too broad to be covered in a single section, so we'll just summarize the key observations here:

- *Strong typing and generics*—F# is a strongly typed language, which means calculations, array manipulations, and other primitive operations are compiled to native code (although this happens at startup using just-in-time (JIT) compilation). Moreover, the .NET approach to generics means none of this efficiency is lost when working with reusable types such as collections.
- *Performance profile similar to C#*—In general, most programs written in F# will have the same performance profile as C# programs. There are some differences: F# has a number of features, such as inlining, that can make F# code faster, and some functional constructs need to be used with care.
- *Parallelism*—As a .NET language, F# has full access to highly optimized libraries for parallel programming, such as the Task Parallel Library (TPL). Using these from F# is significantly easier than from imperative languages, thanks to the emphasis on immutable data types.

- *Ability to write better algorithms*—Perhaps more important, thanks to the language's expressivity, you can implement more complex algorithms. As a result, you can use more efficient (but complex) models and algorithms.

In summary, F# is efficient enough for any task that you could solve in C#. In many cases it will be faster, either because you can use some nice F# feature or, more important, because it allows you to write more sophisticated algorithms. But for highly optimized computations, you can easily call native C/C++ routines.

COORDINATION-INTENSIVE TASKS

In many domains, systems don't need to perform computationally intensive computations, but they do need to handle a large number of interactions, updates from other services, or concurrently running tasks. Consider two sample applications that inspired chapters 8 and 10:

- A trading system that concurrently receives updates from the stock exchange, or other such data sources, needs to display the current state on the screen, perform some simple visualizations, and display them and handle user interaction.
- The server side of a social game only needs to handle service calls from the client side, but it needs to do that for an enormously huge number of requests.

These problems don't just require better libraries or better locking primitives. Writing such applications using traditional concurrency primitives like threads or even tasks won't work because such applications have completely different interaction patterns (see figure 3):

- *Sequential model*—In traditional sequential applications, there's a single control flow. The application has one entry point that calls other components (objects or procedures), and the control proceeds until the result is returned.
- *Parallel model*—In parallel systems that use multiple threads or tasks, the control flow can be forked and then joined to perform more computations in parallel. Nevertheless, the coordination model is still similar to the sequential model.
- *Agent-based model*—The behavior of true concurrent systems is different. It's also called *agent-based*, because the system consists of multiple agents that can communicate by exchanging messages. The system can be structured as agents that solve individual aspects of the problem, like communicating with a stock exchange, handling user-interface requests, or keeping track of some state.

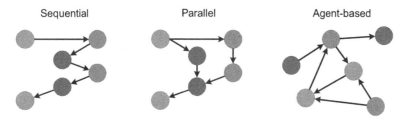

Figure 3   The control flow in sequential, parallel, and agent-based applications

The agent-based programming model (also called the *actor model*) is powerful for writing highly concurrent applications. One of its early adopters was Ericsson (using the Erlang language), which still uses it for many applications in telecommunication. The model is directly supported by F# libraries, and it has been used in many major software systems. We'll look at some of them, as well as other case studies, in the next section.

Learning from case studies

In the preceding three sections, we presented the business aspects of developing analytical and information-rich components. We started by looking at the business situation—what analytical and information-rich components are, and why they're important. Then we looked at common business problems associated with their development. We identified the four most common problems: complexity, efficiency, time to market, and correctness.

> **F# TESTIMONIALS** The F# Software Foundation collects user testimonials and links to detailed case studies at http://fsharp.org/testimonials. At the time of writing, there are some 50 testimonials from a wide range of domains, from DNA programming and modelling to financial and actuarial applications to games and teaching.

Then, in the more technical "Inferring business needs" section, we examined how F# can help in solving these business problems. As a last step, let's now examine existing F# systems and see how they use F# features to solve the problems outlined earlier.

Balancing the power-generation schedule

The first application that we'll look at is a system developed by a large UK-based energy company. The following is a brief summary of the system:

> *I have written an application to balance the national power-generation schedule for a portfolio of power stations to a trading position for an energy company. The client and server components were in C#, but the calculation engine was written in F#.*

The first important observation is that being able to interoperate with other .NET components is of great importance in this case. The F# portion of the code is relatively small (when measured by line count), but it implements the important and unique logic of the application. This exactly matches the "analytical component" pattern that we talked about earlier.

Now, let's look at three technical aspects that directly match the business problems of developing analytical components:

> *Working with script files and [F# Interactive] allowed me to explore the solution space more effectively before committing to an implementation ....*

This confirms our earlier discussion about integrating research and development. The ability to prototype solutions quickly (and fail fast if an approach doesn't work) is one of the main reasons behind reduced time to market.

The developer next states,

> *The equations I implemented ... dealt with units of time, power, and energy. Having the type system verify the correctness of the units of the inputs and outputs of functions ... eradicates a whole class of errors that previous systems were prone to.*

Units of measure address *complexity* and *correctness*. By annotating numeric values with their units, it's easier to write complex computations, because you get immediate feedback from the editor about the units of values that you work with. This leads us to the next point:

> *I can be ... trying hard to get the code to pass the type checker, but once the type checker is satisfied, that's it: it works. ... Weird edge-case errors are minimized, and recursion and higher-order functions remove a lot of book-keeping code that introduces edge-case errors.*

The author may be exaggerating slightly, but he has good reasons for making such claims:

> *I have now delivered three business-critical projects written in F#. I am still waiting for the first bug to come in.*

Of course, when developing applications in the functional style, you still need to test your code properly. We'll discuss this topic in chapter 12. But it's much easier to test software when the compiler already provides many guarantees, such as the lack of `NullReferenceException` errors.

Analyzing data at Kaggle

The next interesting user of F# is Kaggle, which is a Silicon Valley based start-up. Kaggle builds a platform for data analysis based on crowdsourcing. Companies and individuals can post their data to Kaggle, and users from all over the world compete to provide the best models:

> *We initially chose F# for our core data analysis algorithms because of its expressiveness. We've been so happy with the choice that we've found ourselves moving more and more of our application out of C# and into F#. The F# code is consistently shorter, easier to read, and easier to refactor, and, because of the strong typing, it contains far fewer bugs.*

Again, the initial usage of F# at Kaggle was for developing analytical components that process data. The company's experience confirms that the choice helped with correctness (fewer bugs) and time to market (shorter and easier to read code). As in the previous case study, the fact that F# interoperates well with the rest of the world is important:

> *The fact that F# targets the CLR was also critical—even though we have a large existing code base in C#, getting started with F# was an easy decision because we knew we could use new modules right away.*

An interesting observation that Kaggle makes about the use of F# is related to DSLs. We talked about them when looking at the Markdown parser in the earlier "Managing complexity" section. This is what the Kaggle developers have to say:

> *As our data analysis tools have developed, we've seen domain-specific constructs emerge naturally; as our codebase gets larger, we become more productive.*

The essence of this quote is that the developers were able to use the right abstractions without them interacting in unexpected ways. This is perhaps the most important aspect of the functional style for general-purpose programming. By providing the right means for building abstractions, a codebase can naturally grow and can be extended with more orthogonal useful functions; these can be composed to more easily solve problems from the domain of the system.

For our last case study, we'll turn our attention from data analytics to concurrency and gaming.

Scaling the server side of online games

GameSys is a company developing social, massively multiplayer online role-playing games (MMORPGs). The social gaming domain is unique in that games need to be developed and released extremely frequently. At the same time, the server side needs to be able to scale well—if a game becomes popular, this will cause a massive peak.

At GameSys, F# is used for both the implementation of some small analytical components (that define the behavior of a game) and, more interestingly, for efficient handling of concurrent requests:

> *F# first came to prominence in our technology stack in the implementation of the rules engine for our social slots games, which by now serve over 700,000 unique players and 150,000,000 requests per day at peaks of several thousand requests per second. The F# solution offers us an order of magnitude increase in productivity ... and is critical in supporting our agile approach and bi-weekly release cycles.*
>
> *The agent-based programming model ... allows us to build thread-safe components with high-concurrency requirements effortlessly ... These*

> *agent-based solutions also offer much-improved efficiency and latency while
> running at scale.*

Again, F# is used for two of the reasons that we discussed earlier. The first is increased productivity, which leads to shorter time to market. Because of the pressure for frequent game updates, this increased productivity can be a key business factor.

In addition to implementing game logic, the next aspect is building server-side components that handle coordination between computations and distribution of state. The server side of a social game is a typical example of coordination-intensive computation, as discussed in the earlier "Writing efficient and scalable software" section. We won't attempt to explain here why the agent-based programming model is so powerful; you can find the details in chapter 10, which is written by the author of the preceding quote.

Summary

In this chapter, we focused on topics that are probably more important than code—the business context in which software is developed. Our goal was to give you a conceptual framework that you can use to analyze business problems. When you read the later chapters in this book, you can remind yourself of the four business problems we discussed: time to market, complexity, efficiency, and correctness.

With these four keywords in mind, you'll see that each of the later chapters deals with solving an important business problem, and applying the ideas explained there will have a direct effect on your business. If you're a software developer interested in F#, we hope this chapter also gives you some useful hints that you can use to explain the benefits of F# not just to your technical colleagues, but also to your management.

About the authors

This chapter is based on Don Syme's talk, "Succeeding with Functional-First Programming in Industry," at NDC 2013.

Don Syme is a Principal Researcher at Microsoft and an F# community contributor. He is an advocate of data-rich, functional-first programming with a focus on simplicity, correctness, and robustness of code. Over the last 14 years at Microsoft, he's helped drag programming kicking and screaming into the modern era through technical contributions such as generics for C#, async programming in F# 2.0 and C# 5.0, and type providers in F# 3.0.

Tomas Petricek is a long-time F# enthusiast and author of the book *Real-World Functional Programming* (Manning, 2010), which explains functional programming concepts using C# 3.0 while teaching F# alongside. He is a frequent F# speaker and does F# and functional training in London, New York, and elsewhere worldwide.

Tomas has been a Microsoft MVP since 2004, writes a programming blog at http://tomasp.net, and is also a Stack Overflow addict.

He contributed to the development of F# during two internships at Microsoft Research in Cambridge. Before starting a PhD at the University of Cambridge, he studied in Prague and worked as an independent .NET consultant.

Introduction

In chapter 1, we looked at a number of business problems that people regularly face in the industry, and we discussed how F# can help you overcome those problems. But when professional software developers look at functional-first programming for the first time, they sometimes say that it looks difficult. In the first part of the book, we're going to look at a couple of examples that demonstrate that nothing could be further from the truth.

Functional-first programming may appear unfamiliar at first, but the ideas behind it are simple. The following two chapters demonstrate this well. In chapter 2, Kit Eason explains how to implement one mathematical task that his team faced when building a life-expectancy modeling system. You'll see that you can often solve problems by composing a couple of functions together in an easy way. At the same time, we'll begin diving into solid software engineering and unit testing.

Chapter 3 also doesn't require deep understanding of F#. We'll look at implementing a parser for the Markdown format in an extensible way. You'll see that by following a few basic principles, you can write code that is reusable and extensible. In this chapter, you'll learn about pattern matching in F#: one of the fundamental pieces that make it easy to express complex logic with simple code.

As mentioned in the preface, this book isn't an introduction to F#, but chapters 2 and 3, together with the appendix, cover some basic F# language features that may be useful if you haven't written much F# before. At the same time, these two chapters describe solutions to real-world problems. The takeaway is that you can achieve interesting things with just a little F# knowledge. Take this as encouragement to start playing with F# and do your next project with it!

Calculating cumulative binomial distributions

Kit Eason

As you learned in chapter 1, many development projects involve taking financial or statistical models that are specified in some other way (such as Microsoft Excel or MathWorks' MATLAB) and translating them into robust, scalable systems. This task can be arduous. This chapter is a detailed case study of how my colleagues and I used F# to solve a problem we encountered during this process. I could've chosen from many other examples from the same project, which involved a substantial F# calculation engine. But we went up several blind alleys to solve this one, and that gives me the opportunity to show you how a feature can be brought to market promptly using an experiment-and-fail-fast approach—something at which F# excels.

The case study involves applying statistical tests to a life-expectancy model. Actuaries often use such mathematical models to evaluate the future liabilities of a pension scheme (see, for example, figure 1). If the model suggests that the life expectancies of the members will be long, then the liabilities of the scheme will be higher, because it will be paying out to pensions for a longer period of time. Conversely, if the model suggests that life expectancies will be relatively short, the liabilities are lower. Therefore, the accuracy of the model is crucial to the projected solvency of the scheme: too few assets and long projected lifespans mean disaster! For this reason, actuaries periodically examine the fit between the models they've been using and the actuarial experience of pension scheme members. Have members lived longer than we predicted over the past few years or not as long?

One way to measure the quality of fit between the model and the *experience*, as it's called, is to calculate a cumulative binomial distribution. Because this is a book about F# and not actuarial mathematics, we won't delve any further into the significance of the test. As a developer, you need to ensure that the calculation is performed correctly.

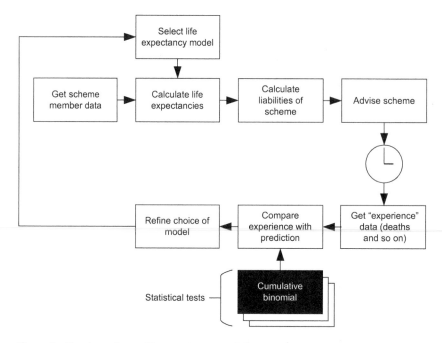

Figure 1   Pension scheme life expectancy modeling process

Our case study starts at the point where the binomial distribution test (and many other statistical tests) had already been implemented in a fairly large-scale project. We'd used the Math.NET Binomial.CumulativeDistribution method, and it worked perfectly for small datasets. But for any substantial dataset, we were getting a numerical overflow. So the task at hand, and the subject of this chapter, is to reimplement the calculation of this distribution in our own code.

Implementing the formula

In this section, you'll take the first steps in implementing the formula for cumulative binomial distribution. In doing so, you'll learn general lessons about coding calculations in F#, including how to perform iterative accumulation without loops, and how and when to use aliases and custom operators to simplify code.

The formula for cumulative binomial distribution

Figure 2 shows the mathematical formula for calculating cumulative binomial distribution. Although you don't need to understand the statistical subtleties, you do need to understand the notation used in the formula, and the next subsections explore this topic. If you're already familiar with the notation involved, skip to the section "Coding the formula."

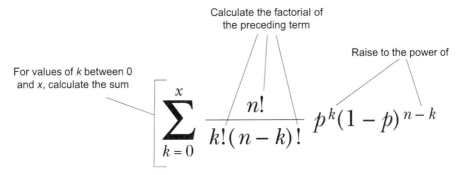

For values of *k* between 0 and *x*, calculate the sum

Calculate the factorial of the preceding term

Raise to the power of

Figure 2   Formula for cumulative binomial distribution

FACTORIALS

The exclamation marks in the formula mean *factorial*—that is, take all the numbers between 1 and the number in question (inclusive), and multiply them together. For instance, 2! is 2, 3! is 6 (1 × 2 × 3) and 4! is 24 (1 × 2 × 3 × 4). The interesting thing about factorials is that they get bigger rather quickly as *n* increases. For example, 10! is 3,628,800.

Calculating factorials is a great F# 101 example. The following listing shows the same calculation done in three different styles.

Listing 1   Three approaches to calculating the *n* factorial

```
let FactWithMutation n =
    let mutable result = 1
    for i in 1..n do
        result <- result * i
    result

let rec FactWithRecursion n =
    match n with
    | 0 -> 1
    | _ -> n * FactWithRecursion (n-1)

let FactWithFold n =
    [1..n] |> Seq.reduce (*)
```

Naturally, being an F# developer, I consider the third approach to be the most elegant, but that's a matter of personal style. All three work fine for modest values of *n*. (For clarity, I've omitted checks for unusual inputs like $n < 1$, which you'd need to handle correctly in practice.) In the spirit of "not optimizing prematurely," we won't worry at this point about which is fastest.

CAPITAL SIGMA

Going back to the formula, you have the construct shown in figure 3. As an imperative programmer (for example, in "classic" C#), you'd mentally translate this construct into a for loop and an accumulator variable. As a LINQ or F# programmer, you might be more inclined to interpret this as a .Sum() (LINQ) or Seq.sumBy (F#) operation.

- Take successive integers from 0 to *x*

- Call each value *k*

- Calculate the formula using that value of *k*

- Sum the results

Figure 3   Capital sigma

SUPERSCRIPTS AND MULTIPLICATION

The superscripts (as in p^k) mean that the first term is raised to the power of the second. Raising to a power can be expressed in F# using the ** operator. Finally, terms that are joined together without symbols between them are multiplied.

Coding the formula

You have all the mathematics you need to understand the formula. On to the code. I felt that a good way for you to get started would be to code a naïve version of the formula in F#, get some passing tests working for modest input values, and then investigate what happened for larger inputs.

Listing 2   First attempt at coding the cumulative binomial distribution

```
let Binomial x n p =                              ❶  Nested Fact
    let Fact n =                                      function
        match n with
        | _ when n <= 1 -> 1
        | _ -> [1..n] |> Seq.reduce (*)          ❷  Custom operator
    let (!) = Fact                                   for Fact
    let f = float
                                                 ❸  Alias for float
    [0..x]
    |> Seq.sumBy (fun k -> f(!n) /
                    (f(!k) * f(!(n - k))) *
                    p**(f(k) * (1. - p)**f(n-k)))
```

In this listing you nest the Seq.reduce version of the Fact function ❶ into the Binomial function and then improve it a bit to cope with inputs less than 1.

I have mixed feelings about nesting inner functions like this. On the plus side, you can simplify the logic of an algorithm with little helper functions without polluting the wider namespace with items that are only locally relevant. On the minus side, unit tests can't see these inner functions. For this reason, it's wise to keep them simple; and if they get complicated, you need to refactor them out to a location where they can be seen by unit-testing frameworks. I find that in practice I often use nested functions, but I always keep them simple. Or if I don't keep them simple, I soon come to regret it.

You'll also notice that you're creating a couple of simple aliases. The first of these ❷ is an alias for the Fact function that we just talked about. The alias is !, which allows you to nearly replicate the n! syntax used in the original formula, albeit as a prefix.

User-defined operators are a construct that F# developers view with considerable caution. I see one big advantage and one big disadvantage:

Advantage	Disadvantage
As in the example we're developing here, custom operators can help you keep your code concise and perhaps reflect some other notation system, such as the ! operator.	They can easily end up obfuscating your code. This problem has been relieved somewhat for users of Visual Studio 2013, which supports tooltips and "navigate to definition" for custom operators.

I tend to keep custom operators local to the point at which they're used so it's obvious from the context what's going on. I don't define many custom operators that are widely scoped across a substantial codebase. Having said that, there are examples, most notably WebSharper (www.websharper.com), that use custom operators extensively and to great effect. The exclamation point (!) is already used in F# to express dereferencing, so perhaps in this case it might have been better to use a different symbol for the factorial operator—one that doesn't mean anything else, such as ~~.

The next alias ❸ is f for float. It seems like a trivial alias, but it reflects one of the few real annoyances of using F# in a numerical and mathematical context: the fact that you can't freely intermix floating-point and integer values in operations such as addition and multiplication. Although you can understand why the language is designed this way (it prevents many bugs and simplifies the type inference process), in practical terms it's an impediment when coding calculations such as the one we're dealing with here. Aliasing the float cast operator to f mitigates this somewhat. For fairly obvious reasons related to naming, it's best to do this only locally.

An alternative to casting to float in the main calculation would have been to get the Fact function to return a floating-point value by casting at the end of its body. This approach would have worked, but it feels a little wrong to return a floating-point value from what's essentially an integer operation.

With the functions, aliases, and operators in place, the final two lines of the code end up reflecting, reasonably closely, the logic and even some of the notation of the original formula:

```
[0..x]
|> Seq.sumBy (fun k -> (f(!n) /
                (f(!k * !(n - k))) * (p**(f(k)) * ((1. - p)**f(n-k))))))
```

Figure 4 shows how the original formula maps to the code.

At this point, you've coded the formula without using loops, instead using higher-order functions such as Seq.reduce and Seq.sumBy. You've also used aliases and custom operators to make the code more concise—although you should keep in mind that custom operators in particular are to be used with caution and restraint.

You could now integrate this code into the wider project, replacing the Math.NET Binomial.CumulativeDistribution method that was failing. But because you're dealing with code you wrote yourself, it's probably time to think about adding some unit tests.

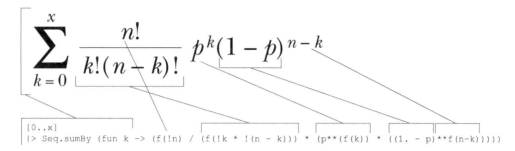

Figure 4   How the formula maps to the code

Adding tests

All significant code should have unit tests. Fortunately, unit testing in F# is a straight-forward, even pleasant process. In this section you'll add unit tests to the `Binomial` function to prove that it produces correct results across the range of values that the life expectancy project will be processing. In doing so, you'll learn how to use the open source libraries NUnit and FsUnit to simplify the unit-testing process, and you'll see how to use Excel to generate test cases. You can also find more about testing F# code in chapter 12.

Adding NUnit and FsUnit

NUnit is a widely used unit-testing framework for Microsoft .NET. FsUnit builds on NUnit to help you write unit tests in the most F#-idiomatic way possible.

   If you're using Visual Studio, you can use NuGet to add FsUnit to your project. In Visual Studio, select Project > Manage NuGet Packages. You can search online for *fsunit* and install it (figure 5). NuGet is aware that FsUnit requires NUnit and will install it as well.

   You'll also need some kind of test runner. This requirement isn't specific to F#—you'll need the same thing to run NUnit tests for a C# project. I favor NCrunch (www.ncrunch.net) or TestDriven.Net (www.testdriven.net). Another option is the NUnit Test Adapter (installable via the Visual Studio Gallery).

   To use the attributes and methods that FsUnit and NUnit provide, you must open the appropriate namespace above your tests:

```
open NUnit.Framework
open FsUnit
```

Having set up your test frameworks, the next step is to generate some test cases.

Generating test cases in Excel

For numerical programming, I find it useful to generate test cases in Excel. This approach has several advantages. Excel is an extensively used and trusted application. Also, when coding a mathematical or numerical system, you'll often find that either

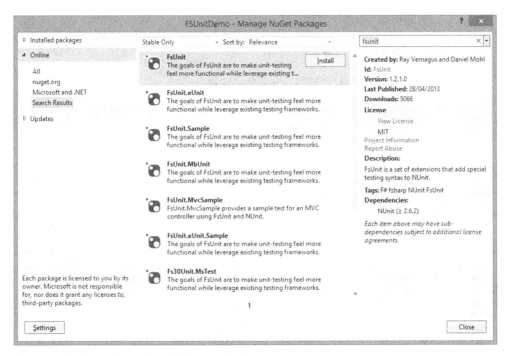

Figure 5   Finding and installing FsUnit using NuGet

your product is replacing a system that originally consisted of Excel spreadsheets, or whoever tests it uses Excel results as a comparison. Finally, you can make Excel do the work of getting your test case syntax right.

Excel already implements a BINOM.DIST function, which replicates the calculation you're trying to use here. You just need to set the final parameter of the function to TRUE because the distribution you're calculating is the cumulative version. So, start off your Excel spreadsheet with a few possible values of *x*, *n*, and *p*:

x	n	p
1	10	0.5
2	10	0.5
3	10	0.5
4	10	0.5
5	10	0.5

Then add a column for the BINOM.DIST formula, and enter the formula itself:

```
=BINOM.DIST(A2,B2,C2, TRUE)
```

Be sure to copy the formula for all your permutations.

As I mentioned, you can have Excel write the syntax of the test case attributes. This is a matter of concatenating some string literals and the relevant cell values together. Here's the formula for doing this:

```
="[<TestCase("&A2&","&B2&","&C2&","&D2&")>]"
```

This formula generates nicely formatted test case attributes like the following, which you can paste straight into your F# code:

```
[<TestCase(1,10,0.5,0.0107421875)>]
```

Now that you have a test case, you need a test! The following one is nice and minimal—and the code passes.

Listing 3   Unit test

Test case pasted straight from Excel

```
type ``Given the Binomial function``() =

    [<TestCase(1,10,0.5,0.0107421875)>]
    member t.``the result is calculated correctly``(x, n, p, expected) =
        let actual = Binomial x n p
        actual |> should equal expected
```

Back quotes, which let you use spaces

Flushed with your early success, add a few more cases to Excel and paste them into the code:

```
[<TestCase(1,10,0.5,0.0107421875)>]
[<TestCase(2,10,0.5,0.0546875)>]
[<TestCase(3,10,0.5,0.171875)>]
[<TestCase(4,10,0.5,0.376953125)>]
[<TestCase(5,10,0.5,0.623046875)>]
```

Four more tests, four more passes!

But when you start to permute the second parameter, you meet with disaster:

Fails when second parameter is 13

```
[<TestCase(5,13,0.5,0.29052734375)>]
Error   1    Test 'BookFactorial+Given the Binomial function.
the result is calculated correctly<Double>(5,13,0.5d,0.29052734375d)' failed:
   Expected: 0.29052734375d
   But was:  0.090225916781906362dat
       FsUnit.TopLevelOperators.should[a,a](FSharpFunc`2 f, a x, Object y)
at BookFactorial.Given the Binomial function.the result is calculated
correctly[a](Int32 x, Int32 n, Double p, a expected) in
C:\Code\VS2013\BookFactorial\BookFactorial\Library1.fs:line 58
C:\Code\VS2013\BookFactorial\BookFactorial\Library1.fs    58
```

Just when you were beginning to get confident! And these are modest-size inputs. In the real system that uses this code, the *n* input could easily be in the tens of thousands and beyond.

I'm sure at this point anyone who has had anything to do with factorial calculations will be screaming at the page—and sure enough, when you investigate a bit further, the simple Fact inner function is the culprit. Here are the values it produces for the first 15 positive integers, together with results produced by Wolfram|Alpha (www.wolframalpha.com):

n	Fact n	Wolfram|Alpha
0	1	1
1	1	1
2	2	2
3	6	6
4	24	24
5	120	120
6	720	720
7	5,040	5,040
8	40,320	40,320
9	362,880	362,880
10	3,628,800	3,628,800
11	39,916,800	39,916,800
12	479,001,600	479,001,600
13	1,932,053,504	6,227,020,800
14	1,278,945,280	87,178,291,200
15	2,004,310,016	1,307,674,368,000

The Fact function runs out of steam for inputs above 12. Not a great performance given the size of inputs it will be facing in real life. How are you to address this?

Exposing the Fact function to unit testing

Your next step is something I hinted at much earlier. If there's a nested function that has any risk of failure, you should consider moving it out so it's accessible to unit testing. Having de-nested Fact, you can generate the tests from the Wolfram|Alpha results earlier.

Listing 4 Unit tests for larger inputs, from Wolfram|Alpha

```
type ``Given the Fact function``() =

    [<TestCase(1,1)>]
    [<TestCase(2,2)>]
    [<TestCase(3,6)>]
    [<TestCase(4,24)>]
    [<TestCase(5,120)>]
    [<TestCase(6,720)>]
```

```
[<TestCase(7,5040)>]
[<TestCase(8,40320)>]
[<TestCase(9,362880)>]
[<TestCase(10,3628800)>]
[<TestCase(11,39916800)>]
[<TestCase(12,479001600)>]
[<TestCase(13,6227020800)>]
[<TestCase(14,87178291200)>]
[<TestCase(15,1307674368000)>]
member t.``the result is calculated correctly``(n, expected) =
    let actual = Fact n
    actual |> should equal expected
```

❶ **Won't compile: values too large for integers**

The results immediately give you a clue about what's going wrong—the test cases for 13, 14, and 15 ❶ don't even compile:

```
Error     1    This number is outside the allowable range for 32-bit signed
integers    C:\Code\VS2013\BookFactorial\BookFactorial\Library1.fs      56
19    BookFactorial
```

Clearly you're dealing with values that are too big to be held as integers.

Returning large integers from the Fact function

What happens if you alter the Fact function to return a large integer, as embodied in .NET's BigInteger type? You need to tweak the tests a bit because big integers can't be represented directly in [<TestCase()>] attributes. You'll represent them instead as strings and parse them in the body of the test.

Listing 5 Expressing big integers as strings

```
type ``Given the Fact function``() =
    [<TestCase(0,"1")>]
    [<TestCase(1,"1")>]
    [<TestCase(2,"2")>]
    [<TestCase(3,"6")>]
    [<TestCase(4,"24")>]
    [<TestCase(5,"120")>]
    [<TestCase(6,"720")>]
    [<TestCase(7,"5040")>]
    [<TestCase(8,"40320")>]
    [<TestCase(9,"362880")>]
    [<TestCase(10,"3628800")>]
    [<TestCase(11,"39916800")>]
    [<TestCase(12,"479001600")>]
    [<TestCase(13,"6227020800")>]
    [<TestCase(14,"87178291200")>]
    [<TestCase(15,"1307674368000")>]
    member t.``the result is calculated correctly``(n, expected : string) =
        let expected' = System.Numerics.BigInteger.Parse(expected)    ◁─── Parse
        let actual = Fact n                                                 BigInteger
        actual |> should equal expected'                                    from string
```

You can also amend the Fact function to return a big integer.

Listing 6 Version of the `Fact` function that returns a big integer

```
let Fact n =
    match n with
    | _ when n <= 1 -> 1I
    | _ -> [1I..System.Numerics.BigInteger(n)]
           |> Seq.reduce (*)
```

Note that although the range `1..n` doesn't need to consist of big integers (n won't be that large), making it do so using the I suffix and the `BigInteger` converter forces the `BigInteger` implementation of the multiplication operator to be used. This in turn causes `Seq.reduce` to return a `BigInteger` result.

With that change in place, the extra tests pass, so at least you've extended the reach of `Fact` a little. Although its result rapidly gets too large to represent in a test case even as a string, you can use F# Interactive to prove that it runs:

```
val Fact : n:int -> System.Numerics.BigInteger

> #time;;

--> Timing now on

> Fact 100000;;
Real: 00:00:16.844, CPU: 00:00:18.953, GC gen0: 1373, gen1: 161, gen2: 160
val it : System.Numerics.BigInteger =

282422940796034787429342157802453551847749492609122485057891808654297795090106301787255177l...
    {IsEven = true;
     IsOne = false;
     IsPowerOfTwo = false;
     IsZero = false;
     Sign = 1;}

>
```

For the moment let's gloss over the fact that this takes a few seconds, and a lot of garbage-collection activity, to run. It'll be faster in production, right?

Now let's return to the `Binomial` function and adjust it to use the new `Fact` function. At the moment, `Binomial` doesn't compile, because `Fact` is producing big integers that can't be freely multiplied, divided, and so forth with other types.

Processing large integers in the Binomial function

You're going to need a fair bit more casting to even begin to make the big integer approach work, which means reluctantly moving away from the style where you try to calculate the whole formula in a single line. Instead, you'll calculate sections of the formula separately. The following listing is my rough-and-ready attempt to do this.

Listing 7 Version of the `Binomial` function that supports the `BigInteger` type

```
let Binomial x n p =
    let (!) = Fact
    let f = float
```

```
[0..x]
|> Seq.sumBy (fun k -> let term1 = !n
                       let term2 = !k * !(n - k)
```

Dividing BigIntegers
returns BigInteger ➊
```
                       let term1over2 = term1 / term2
                       let term3 = p ** f(k)
                       let term4 = 1. - p
                       let term5 = n - k

                       term1over2 * term3 * (term4 ** term5)
```

If you paste this code into your editor, you'll see that it doesn't compile. The message you get relates to the final line ("The type float is not compatible with the type System.Numerics.BigInteger"), but if you hover around a bit you'll find that the real problem occurs earlier ➊: the value term1over2 is a big integer. The mathematics of the situation require you to have a floating-point value here, but the framework doesn't have a way of directly dividing one big integer by another to produce a floating-point value. The nearest you can get is BigRational (available as part of Math.NET Numerics), which will give you a genuine result for the division of two big integers. But this is put in rational form, and there's no straightforward way to recover a floating-point number from the rational.

We could go down a few other paths here. One of these, suggested by a colleague, is to add up the logarithms of 1..n and take the exponential of the resulting sum (see the next listing). This code works well and is fast—but for *n* greater than 170, it produces a result of infinity.

Listing 8   Calculating factorials using logarithms
```
let LogFact n =
    if (n<1) then
        1.0
    else
        [|1..n|] |> Seq.map float |> Seq.map log |> Seq.sum |> exp
```

Time for a rethink

Up to now, we've taken the approach of blindly translating the original, canonical formula into code. Although the final results are modest numbers, following the formula means calculating intermediate results that are somewhat colossal. For example, if your calculation requires you to calculate 100! (9.332621544e+157), this is a number that greatly exceeds the number of protons in the universe: a mere 10^{80}. You can play around with the mechanics all you like, but calculations involving numbers this big are always slow and unmanageable.

At this point I often find myself having an imaginary conversation with that great scourge of the software developer, the Astute User. Here's how the conversation might go:

> *Me: "I'm not sure this is even possible. The intermediate results we have to calculate are gigantic."*

> *Astute user: "Then how is Excel doing this? And that's presumably coded in C++. You're telling me your fancy new language can't do something that Excel has been doing (fast) for years."*
>
> *Me: "Umm."*

An alternative approach

After I had that conversation with myself, I returned to my favorite search engine and looked for "cumulative binomial distribution Excel overflow." I got lucky—there's a detailed blog post on that topic ats http://support.microsoft.com/kb/827459.

This blog post outlines how earlier versions of Excel hit this overflow problem when calculating cumulative binomial distributions—and, more important, how it was solved. Don't worry too much about the mathematical justification for the technique; instead let's focus on the pseudocode that Microsoft was good enough to publish. Here it is in full.

Listing 9   Excel's algorithm

```
TotalUnscaledProbability = TotalUnscaledProbability + 1;
If (m == x) then UnscaledResult = UnscaledResult + 1;
If (cumulative && m < x) then UnscaledResult = UnscaledResult + 1;
PreviousValue = 1;
Done = FALSE;
k = m + 1;
While (not Done && k <= n)
   {
     CurrentValue = PreviousValue * (n - k + 1) * p / (k * (1 - p));
     TotalUnscaledProbability = TotalUnscaledProbability + CurrentValue;
     If (k == x) then UnscaledResult = UnscaledResult + CurrentValue;
     If (cumulative && k < x) then UnscaledResult = UnscaledResult +
        CurrentValue;
     If (CurrentValue <= EssentiallyZero) then Done = TRUE;
     PreviousValue = CurrentValue;
     k = k+1;
   }
end While;
PreviousValue = 1;
Done = FALSE;
k = m - 1;
While (not Done && k >= 0)
   {
     CurrentValue = PreviousValue * k+1 * (1-p) / ((n - k) * p);
     TotalUnscaledProbability = TotalUnscaledProbability + CurrentValue;
     If (k == x) then UnscaledResult = UnscaledResult + CurrentValue;
     If (cumulative && k < x) then UnscaledResult = UnscaledResult +
        CurrentValue;
     If (CurrentValue <= EssentiallyZero) then Done = TRUE;
     PreviousValue = CurrentValue;
     k = k-1;
   }
end While;
```

Step 1: Find $n*p$ and round down to the nearest whole number, m.

Step 2: Calculate the unscaled probabilities for $k > m$.

Step 3: Calculate the unscaled probabilities for $k < m$.

```
Return UnscaledResult/TotalUnscaledProbability;
```
Step 4: Combine the unscaled results.

Implementing the Excel algorithm

I've sent you up some blind alleys already, so you need to create a systematic plan for implementing this algorithm:

1 Extend the range of your unit tests to reflect the kind of population and sample sizes your code will be faced with in practice.

2 Blindly translate the published pseudocode, warts and all, into F#, and get the tests passing. I say this because the pseudocode plainly has considerable room for refactoring. But if you start with the literal-minded implementation, you won't saddle yourself with the dual tasks of both interpreting the pseudocode and refactoring it in one pass.

3 Refactor the implementation into reasonably elegant F# code, ensuring that the tests continue to pass.

For step 1 of this plan, the following listing contains a somewhat extended set of tests that probe the response of the algorithm to some high values of *n*.

Listing 10   Test cases for some larger inputs

```
[<TestCase(1,10,0.5,0.0107421875)>]
[<TestCase(2,10,0.5,0.0546875)>]
[<TestCase(3,10,0.5,0.171875)>]
[<TestCase(4,10,0.5,0.376953125)>]
[<TestCase(5,10,0.5,0.623046875)>]

[<TestCase(5,11,0.5,0.5)>]
[<TestCase(5,12,0.5,0.38720703125)>]
[<TestCase(5,13,0.5,0.29052734375)>]
[<TestCase(5,14,0.5,0.21197509765625)>]

[<TestCase(5,20000,0.001,7.14974861864806E-05)>]      Larger inputs
[<TestCase(6,20000,0.002,2.74846740618111E-11)>]
[<TestCase(7,20000,0.003,5.11871527472253E-18)>]
                                                     From failing cases
[<TestCase(179,12798,0.012013,0.9797611704)>]
[<TestCase(12798,12798,0.012013,1.0)>]               Whole population
```

And for step 2, the next listing presents a deliberately simple-minded implementation of the pseudocode.

Listing 11   Literal implementation of the Excel pseudocode

```
let Binomial x n p =

    let f = float

    let cumulative = true              Cumulative
                                       version required
    let mutable totalUnscaledP = 0.
    let mutable unscaledResult = 0.
    let essentiallyZero = 10.E-12
```

```
let m = (f(n) * p) |> truncate |> int

totalUnscaledP <- totalUnscaledP + 1.

if m = x then unscaledResult <- unscaledResult + 1.
if cumulative && m < x then unscaledResult <- unscaledResult + 1.
let mutable previousValue = 1.
let mutable isDone = false

let mutable k = m + 1

while not isDone && k <= n do
    let currentValue = previousValue * f(n - k + 1) * p / (f(k) * (1. - p))

    totalUnscaledP <- totalUnscaledP + currentValue
    if k = x then unscaledResult <- unscaledResult + currentValue
    if cumulative && k < x then unscaledResult <- unscaledResult +
 currentValue
    if currentValue <= essentiallyZero then isDone <- true
    previousValue <- currentValue
    k <- k + 1

previousValue <- 1.
isDone <- false
k <- m - 1

while not isDone && k >= 0 do
    let currentValue = previousValue * f(k + 1) * (1. - p) / (f(n - k) * p)
    totalUnscaledP <- totalUnscaledP + currentValue
    if k = x then unscaledResult <- unscaledResult + currentValue
    if cumulative && k < x then unscaledResult <- unscaledResult +
 currentValue
    if currentValue <= essentiallyZero then isDone <- true
    previousValue <- currentValue
    k <- k - 1

unscaledResult / totalUnscaledP
```

Well-written pseudocode often translates directly into F#, and there's something to be said for leaving the code at that. But before you make any refactoring decisions, you'd better check your tests.

They don't all quite pass, but they're close:

```
Test 'ExcelAlgorithm+Given the Binomial function.the result is calculated
correctly<Double>(4,10,0.5d,0.376953125d)' failed:
  Expected: 0.376953125d
  But was:  0.37695312500000006d
    at FsUnit.TopLevelOperators.should[a,a](FSharpFunc`2 f, a x, Object y)
```

Let's address that slight floating-point accuracy error. It's common in this kind of coding to accept a degree of inaccuracy; and certainly in the actuarial domain, where so much else is approximated, an error in the 17th decimal place is acceptable. Using FsUnit and NUnit, it's easy to change the test to accept a degree of approximation, using the equalWithin function:

```
member t.``the result is calculated correctly``(x, n, p, expected) =
    let errorMargin = 10E-9
    let actual = Binomial x n p
    actual |> should (equalWithin errorMargin) expected
```

At this point, you could argue, you're done! You've got an algorithm that works, that's quick, that's based on a published and reputable source, that passes all tests, and that will integrate seamlessly into the project codebase. I'd definitely check in my code when it reached this stage!

But it's not polished yet. In the next section, you'll do some refactoring work to make your code idiomatic and eliminate such nasties as repetition.

Refactoring

Any astute reviewer of your code as it stands would want to address at least the following issues:

- You should always calculate the *cumulative* binomial distribution, so the cumulative flag and associated logic should be eliminated.
- The first and the second while loops have a suspicious amount in common. Would it be possible to eliminate this repetition?
- There are a lot of mutable values. There's nothing inherently wrong with this, especially if, as in this case, the mutation is all local. But it would at least be interesting to see what happens to the logic when these are eliminated. (Doing so can often lead to a deeper insight into the algorithm you're implementing.)
- In a similar vein, functional programmers often want to explore the replacement of loops with recursion, so you should see how that plays out.

Let's take these issues one at a time.

Eliminating the cumulative flag

The code includes the cumulative flag because it's a literal-minded implementation of the pseudocode. You don't need it, because the requirement is always for the cumulative version of the binomial calculation. Removing it is a fairly simple exercise, but it still manages to eliminate several lines.

Listing 12 Removing the `cumulative` flag

```
let Binomial x n p =

    let f = float

    let mutable totalUnscaledP = 0.
    let essentiallyZero = 10.E-12

    let m = (f (n) * p) |> truncate |> int

    totalUnscaledP <- totalUnscaledP + 1.

    let mutable unscaledResult =
        if m <= x then 1.
        else 0.

    let mutable previousValue = 1.
    let mutable isDone = false
```

```
let mutable k = m + 1

while not isDone && k <= n do
    let currentValue = previousValue * f(n - k + 1) * p / (f(k) * (1. - p))
    totalUnscaledP <- totalUnscaledP + currentValue
    if k <= x then unscaledResult <- unscaledResult + currentValue
    if currentValue <= essentiallyZero then isDone <- true
    previousValue <- currentValue
    k <- k + 1

previousValue <- 1.
isDone <- false
k <- m - 1

while not isDone && k >= 0 do
    let currentValue = previousValue * f(k + 1) * (1. - p) / (f(n - k) * p)
    totalUnscaledP <- totalUnscaledP + currentValue
    if k <= x then unscaledResult <- unscaledResult + currentValue
    if currentValue <= essentiallyZero then isDone <- true
    previousValue <- currentValue
    k <- k - 1

unscaledResult / totalUnscaledP
```

Identifying common functions between the two while loops

The two `while` loops in the code have a lot in common. Perhaps this repetition can be eliminated so the code is closer to the ideal of Don't Repeat Yourself (DRY).

To begin, four points in the two `while` loops can be pulled out into separate functions. Currently the refactoring is something of a leap of faith, because you may end up making the code longer. But by extracting these lines as functions, you pave the way for later, more concise refactoring.

Here are the four functions you can extract. This line

```
let currentValue = previousValue * f(n - k + 1) * p / (f(k) * (1. - p))
```

and this line

```
let currentValue = previousValue * f(k + 1) * (1. - p) / (f(n - k) * p)
```

become this function:

```
let CalcCurrent value k =
    if k > m then
        value * float(n - k + 1) * p / (float(k) * (1. - p))
    else
        value * float(k + 1) * (1. - p) / (float(n - k) * p)
```

This line

```
if k <= x then unscaledResult <- unscaledResult + currentValue
```

becomes this function:

```
let CalcUnscaled x k acc increment =
    if k <= x then acc + increment
    else acc
```

This line

```
if currentValue <= essentiallyZero then isDone <- true
```

becomes this function:

```
let Done current = current <= essentiallyZero
```

And finally this line

```
k <- k + 1
```

and this line

```
k <- k - 1
```

become this function:

```
let NextK k = if k > m then k + 1 else k - 1
```

This leaves the loops looking like the next listing.

Listing 13   Pulling out some common functions

```
while not isDone && k <= n do
    let currentValue = CalcCurrent previousValue k
    totalUnscaledP <- totalUnscaledP + currentValue
    unscaledResult <- CalcUnscaled x k unscaledResult currentValue
    isDone <- Done currentValue
    previousValue <- currentValue
    k <- NextK k

while not isDone && k >= 0 do
    let currentValue = CalcCurrent previousValue k
    totalUnscaledP <- totalUnscaledP + currentValue
    unscaledResult <- CalcUnscaled x k unscaledResult currentValue
    isDone <- Done currentValue
    previousValue <- currentValue
    k <- NextK k
```

It's important not to get carried away and try to unify the two loops at this point. It's better to run tests (and possibly even check in or at least shelve the changes) so that you can have confidence in the newly extracted functions before changing anything else.

Eliminating duplication, mutables, and loops

The tests still pass, so let's move on to trying to unify the loops. At this stage you can't avoid tackling three problems at once, because these are different faces of the same issue:

- The code duplication represented by the two while loops
- The use of mutable values
- The use of loops rather than recursion

It's probably worth reiterating at this point that there is nothing *inherently* wrong with the use of (local) mutable values or loops, but their presence is often an indicator that a more fundamental manifestation of the algorithm is available. Whether you listen to this cue is an interesting balance of performance, personal style, and readability. There's no general right answer.

What still differs between the two while loops? Not much: they run for different ranges of k, a couple of flags and values are reset between the first and second loops, and two values set in the first loop are updated further in the second. Let's write a function that's equivalent to both loops and worry about how to invoke for both ranges later. The following listing shows a recursive function that embodies the logic from both manifestations of the loop.

Listing 14 Calculate **function that replaces both loops**

```
let rec Calculate k totalUnscaledProbability previous unscaled =
    let current = CalcCurrent previous k
    let totalUnscaledProbability' = totalUnscaledProbability + current
    let unscaled' = CalcUnscaled x k unscaled current

    if Done current then
        unscaled', totalUnscaledProbability'
    else
        Calculate (NextK k) totalUnscaledProbability' current unscaled'
```

Listing 14 still uses the four functions you pulled out of the loops—these functions remain unchanged—and passes those values that need to change between iterations as parameters.

Unfortunately, you do need to accept that the new recursive function must be called twice. This is because the function has to be calculated for two different ranges, with the inputs of the second call derived from the outputs of the first. Here's how you can tie it together.

Listing 15 Calling Calculate **for both ranges of k**

```
let InitialUnscaled = if (m <= x) then 1. else 0.

let UnscaledResultAboveM, TotalUnscaledProbabilityAboveM =
Calculate (m+1) 1. 1. InitialUnscaled

let UnscaledResult, TotalUnscaledProbability =
Calculate (m-1) TotalUnscaledProbabilityAboveM 1. UnscaledResultAboveM

UnscaledResult / TotalUnscaledProbability
```

When you run the unit tests against this logic, they pass! At this point I'd regard the code as production ready and would check it in and move on to the next problem.

Summary

Cumulative binomial distribution is a statistical formula that at first sight seems comparatively straightforward to code. But the intermediate factorial values you need to calculate using the canonical formula make a straightforward algorithm impractical. Fortunately, F# makes it easy for you to "fail fast" in your attempt to code the algorithm in a naïve way, and it also allows you to express a more appropriate algorithm easily and concisely.

In this chapter you learned a little about creating custom operators—which should be used only with care and restraint—and about aliasing functions locally for greater conciseness. You installed FsUnit and NUnit to facilitate unit testing, and you used FsUnit's `equalWithin` function to allow a margin of approximation for your floating-point tests. You saw how unit test cases can be generated easily in Excel and pasted straight into code. If you're interested in testing, chapter 12 discusses the topic in depth.

F# is a great language for implementing calculations. But as F# exponents are fond of saying, it's not a magic bullet. You must combine exploratory coding with the greater rigor of unit testing to ensure production-ready results.

About the author

Kit Eason is a senior software developer for Adbrain, a data intelligence company. He has developed software for automotive engineering companies, universities, energy suppliers, banks, and financial services corporations. Kit has also run many educational and training courses, including evening classes, women's electronics classes, and CNC training for engineers. Kit is a regular speaker at SkillsMatter in London and at various conferences and meet-ups. He works mainly in F# and C# and speaks on F# and related matters. You can find him on Twitter @kitlovesfsharp and via his blog: www.kiteason.com.

3 Parsing text-based languages

Tomas Petricek

I've been writing a blog for a number of years now. Since the beginning, I wanted the website to use clean and simple HTML code. Initially, I wrote articles in HTML by hand, but lately I've become a big fan of *Markdown*—a simple text-based markup language that can be used to produce clean HTML. It's used by sites such as Stack Overflow and GitHub. But none of the existing Markdown implementations supported what I wanted: I needed an efficient parser that could be extended with custom features and that allowed me to process the document after parsing. That's why I decided to write my own parser in F#.[1]

In this chapter, I'll describe the key elements of the project. You won't be able to implement a parser for the *entire* Markdown format in just one chapter, but you'll learn enough to be able to complete it easily. We'll first look at the source code of a sample document and then write the document processor in five steps (see figure 1). You'll see how to represent documents and how to parse inline text spans and blocks. Then you'll write a translator that turns the document into HTML rendered in a web browser. Finally, we'll look at how to process documents.

Writing a Markdown parser might sound like an ambitious goal, but you'll see that you can implement a surprising amount of functionality in a single chapter. In terms of the business themes from chapter 1, you can quickly develop a working version (*time to market*), and the use of active patterns lets you tackle the *complexity* of parsing in an elegant and powerful way.

You might not need to implement your own text formatting engine, but you may often face similar tasks. Text processing is useful not only when working with external files (test scripts, behavior specifications, and configuration files), but also when processing user input in an application (such as commands or calculations).

---

[1] The Markdown parser I wrote is now a part of F# documentation tools available at http://tpetricek .github.io/FSharp.Formatting/.

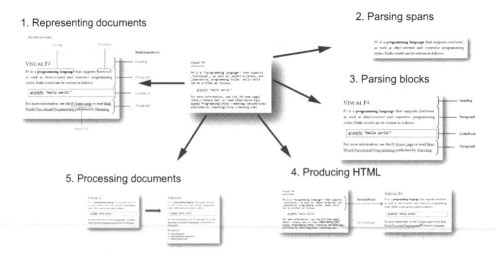

Figure 1   Steps for developing the document processor

Introducing the Markdown format

The Markdown format is a markup language that was designed to be as readable as possible in a plain-text form. It's inspired by formatting marks, such as *emphasis*, that are often used in text files, emails, and README documents. It specifies the syntax precisely so it's possible to translate Markdown documents to HTML.[2] Markdown is a popular format that has implementations in numerous languages (including a .NET implementation in C#). In this section, we'll look at one Markdown example and explain why we need yet another implementation of a Markdown processor.

Formatting text with Markdown

The formatting of Markdown documents is based on whitespace and common punctuation marks. A document consists of block elements (such as paragraphs, headings, and lists). A block element can contain emphasized text, links, and other formatting.

The following sample demonstrates some of the syntax:

```
# F# Programming language

F# is a **programming language** that supports _functional_, as
well as _object-oriented_ and _imperative_ programming styles.
Hello world can be written as follows:

    printfn "Hello world!"

For more information, see the [F# home page] (http://fsharp.net) or
read [Real-World Functional Programming](http://manning.com/petricek)
published by [Manning] (http://manning.com).
```

- **❶ First-level heading**
- **❷ Paragraph with bold and italics**
- **❸ Embedded code sample**

---

[2] For more information about Markdown, see John Gruber's Markdown page on Daring Fireball: http://daringfireball.net/projects/markdown.

This document consists of four block elements. It starts with a heading ❶. In Markdown, headings are prefixed with a certain number of # characters at the beginning of the line; for example, ## Example is a second-level heading. An alternative style (not implemented in this chapter) is to write the text on a single line, followed by another line with a horizontal line written using = (for first-level headings) or - (for second-level headings).

The second block is a paragraph ❷, followed by a code sample ❸ and one more paragraph. The text in paragraphs is formatted using ** (strong) and _ (emphasis). Both asterisks and underscores can be used for strong and emphasized text—one character means emphasis, and two characters means strong text. You can also create hyperlinks, as demonstrated by the last line.

From a programming language perspective, formats such as Markdown can be viewed as domain-specific languages (DSLs).

External domain-specific languages

The term *domain-specific languages* (DSLs) refers to programming languages that are designed to solve problems in a particular domain or field. DSLs are useful when you need to solve a large number of problems of the same class. In that case, the time spent developing the DSL will be balanced out by the time you save when using the DSL to solve particular problems.

DSLs can be categorized into two groups. *Internal DSLs* are embedded in another language (like F# or C#). Functions from the List module with the pipelining operator (|>) can be viewed as a DSL. They solve a specific problem—list processing—and solve it well without other dependencies.

External DSLs are languages that aren't constructed on top of other languages. They may be used as embedded strings (for example, regular expressions or SQL) or as standalone files (including Markdown, configuration files, Makefile, or behavior specifications using languages such as Cucumber[3]). In this chapter, we'll focus on this class of DSLs. As the examples demonstrate, the application range for external DSLs is broad.

Now that I've introduced the Markdown format and DSLs in general, let's look at a number of benefits that you can expect from a Markdown parser written in F#.

Why another Markdown parser?

Markdown is a well-established format, and a number of existing tools convert it to HTML. Most of these are written using regular expressions, and there are implementations for almost any platform, including .NET. So why do we need yet another processor? Here are a few reasons:

---

[3] For more information, see chapter 12, which discusses behavior-driven development (BDD).

- Creating a custom syntax extension for Markdown is difficult when using an implementation based on regular expressions. It's hard to find where the syntax is being processed, and changing a regular expression can lead to various unexpected interactions.
- Most of the tools transform Markdown directly to HTML. This makes it hard to add a custom processing step, such as one that processes all code samples in the document before generating HTML.
- HTML is the only supported output. What if you wanted to turn Markdown documents into another document format, such as Word or LaTeX?
- Performing a single regular-expression replacement may be efficient, but if the processor performs a huge number of them, the code can get CPU-intensive. A custom implementation may give you better performance.

As discussed in chapter 1, languages like F# often let you implement better algorithms, because they allow you to tackle more complex problems. This is exactly what we'll do in this chapter—we'll implement a new parser that's more extensible and readable. The key element of the solution is an elegant functional representation of the document structure.

Representing Markdown documents

When solving problems in functional languages, the first question you often need to answer is, "What data structures do I need, to represent the data that I work with?" In the case of a Markdown processor, the data structure represents a document; and as discussed earlier, a document consists of blocks of different kinds. Some of the blocks (like a paragraph) may contain additional inline formatting and hyperlinks (see figure 2).

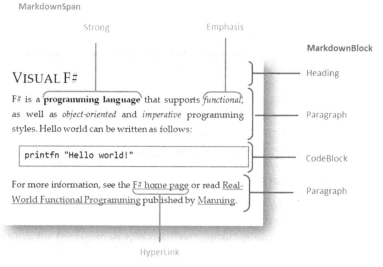

Figure 2   You can see how `MarkdownBlock` **elements and different** `MarkdownSpan` **elements are used to format the sample document. All other unmarked text is represented as** `Literal`**.**

The types that model Markdown documents are shown and explained in the following listing.

Listing 1   Representation of a Markdown document

```
type MarkdownDocument = list<MarkdownBlock>

and MarkdownBlock =
  | Heading of int * MarkdownSpans
  | Paragraph of MarkdownSpans
  | CodeBlock of list<string>

and MarkdownSpans = list<MarkdownSpan>

and MarkdownSpan =

  | Literal of string
  | InlineCode of string
  | Strong of MarkdownSpans
  | Emphasis of MarkdownSpans
  | HyperLink of MarkdownSpans * string
```

A block can be a heading, paragraph, or code snippet. The last one contains a list of code snippet lines; the first two contain text that can be further formatted.

Span elements can be either plain Literals or one of four formatting elements: InlineCode for typewriter font; Strong and Emphasis for bold and italic, respectively; and HyperLink for links.

A Markdown document is a list of block elements. It's represented by the MarkdownDocument type, which is an F# alias for a list of MarkdownBlock values.

This type represents formatted text. It's formed by a list of Markdown-Span elements and is defined as an F# type alias.

The listing defines the types as mutually recursive using the and keyword, for two reasons. First, the MakdownSpans and MarkdownSpan types are mutually recursive, and they both reference each other. Second, starting with a type that represents the entire document rather than starting from the span makes the explanation easier to follow.

Now that you have a representation of your documents, you can take the next step and start implementing the parser. We'll start with a direct solution and improve it later on.

Parsing spans using recursive functions

Despite the rise of alternative input methods, such as pen-based input and touch, the most common way to write computer documents is still to type them on a keyboard. The purpose of a parser is to turn the stream of characters into a richer structure. In this chapter, the structure is a representation of a document, but the same problem appears elsewhere—whether you're parsing configuration files, user-scenario specifications, or even binary files.

The first implementation of a Markdown parser that we'll look at will use a number of mutually recursive functions that model different states of the parser and call each other when the parser transitions between states. This style of parser is called a *recursive descent parser* because it "descends" into new states when it reaches a symbol that begins a syntactic construct you want to parse. To keep the initial version simple, let's focus on inline formatting (the MarkdownSpans type), demonstrated in figure 3.

For example, inline code in Markdown is written as `code`. To parse this syntax, the parser needs to switch to a parsingInlineBody state when it finds the opening backtick (`). In this state, it continues consuming characters until it finds the closing

> F# is a **programming language** that supports *functional,*
> as well as *object-oriented* and *imperative* programming
> styles. Hello world can be written as follows:

Figure 3   **In this and the next section, you'll write a parser that processes inline formatting commands for strong text, emphasis, and inline code. The parser generates a sequence of** `MarkdownSpan` **elements.**

backtick, and then it returns back to the main state, waiting for other formatting markup. This functionality is implemented in the following listing.

Listing 2   Parsing the inline code span

```
let rec parseInlineBody acc = function                 Reached the end
  | '`'::rest ->                                        of a command
      Some(List.rev acc, rest)        <────┘
  | c::chars  ->                                   Continues
      parseInlineBody (c::acc) chars        <────┘ consuming input
  | [] -> None
                                                  <─── Closing backtick
let parseInline = function                              is missing
  |'`'::chars ->
      parseInlineBody [] chars    <──┐
  | _ -> None              <──┐         Parses the body
                               │        of a command
                        Input isn't
                        a command
```

The `parseInline` function represents the entry point for parsing the inline code command. It employs pattern matching using `function` to accept `List` as a single input argument and tests whether it starts with a backtick. If that's the case, it continues parsing using `parseInlineBody`; otherwise it returns `None`.

The `parseInlineBody` function keeps the body characters that have been consumed so far in the `acc` parameter. When it finds the end of the command, it returns the body (in the correct order) together with the remaining unprocessed characters. Otherwise, it continues processing the input until it reaches the end.

To test the `parseInline` function, you can use F# interactively and test whether it succeeds in parsing some sample input that starts with an inline code command:

```
> "`code` and" |> List.ofSeq |> parseInline;;
val it : (char list * char list) option =            Output from the F#
  Some (['c'; 'o'; 'd'; 'e'], [' '; 'a'; 'n'; 'd'])  Interactive console
```

> **NOTE**   Italic in the code snippets is used to indicate the output from commands entered in the F# Interactive (FSI) console.

The result is an option type, because the function fails if the string doesn't start with the inline code command. If it succeeds, it returns a tuple consisting of the body and the unconsumed input.

Parsers for inline commands such as `**strong text**` could be written in the same style. To complete the parsing of inline spans, you'd need to write a main parsing function that takes an input and turns it into a sequence of Literals, inline code, and other spans. The `parseSpans` function is shown in the following listing.

Listing 3 Parsing spans using functions

Helper function that converts a list of characters to a string. This is needed when you want to return parsed characters.

Lazy sequence that yields a single Literal span with the characters that were accumulated while processing earlier input that didn't contain any special formatting command. Nothing is emitted if the character list was empty.

The main part of the function attempts to parse the input using the parseInline function and then pattern-matches on the result as well as on the original input.

```
let toString chars =
    System.String(chars |> Array.ofList)

let rec parseSpans acc chars = seq {
    let emitLiteral = seq {
        if acc <> [] then
            yield acc |> List.rev |> toString |> Literal }

    match parseInline chars, chars with
    | Some(body, chars), _ ->
        yield! emitLiteral
        yield body |> toString |> InlineCode
        yield! parseSpans [] chars
    | _, c::chars ->
        yield! parseSpans (c::acc) chars
    | _, [] ->
        yield! emitLiteral }
```

❶ The input is an inline code span.

❷ Continues processing the input

❸ Emits the last Literal

Function that parses text into span elements. It's implemented as a sequence expression that takes chars, keeps unprocessed characters in acc, and emits span elements of type MarkdownSpan.

The core functionality is implemented using pattern matching. To recognize the three different cases, you need to match on both the result of `parseInline` and on the original input. If the text starts with an inline code span ❶, you emit three groups of spans:

- A `Literal` formed by the characters immediately before the inline code span (or nothing if there were no preceding characters)
- An `InlineCode` span formed by the parsed body
- Other span elements obtained by a recursive call to `parseSpans`

If the input doesn't start with any command ❷, you add the current character to the list of unprocessed characters and continue processing recursively. Finally, when you reach the end of the input list ❸, you need to emit the last `Literal` consisting of unprocessed elements.

> **TIP** The `parseSpans` function is implemented as a recursive sequence expression. The cases where the function needs to process the rest of the input are implemented as a recursive call using the `yield!` keyword. This doesn't cause performance issues, because the recursive call is in a tail-call

location. Just as with standard tail-call recursion, the F# compiler optimizes tail-call recursion in sequence expressions so the current stack frame (and a corresponding `IEnumerator` object) will be dropped and can be garbage collected.

You started writing a parser so you could read Markdown documents stored in plain text files. The code that you started writing in this section would get you there, but it has a number of limitations. If you added functions to parse more commands (like `parseInline`), you'd have to call them all before you could pattern-match on the result. This would make the code inelegant (imagine `match` with 10 arguments!) and also inefficient (they would all be executed before you could inspect the result of the first one). One way to improve this code is to use F# active patterns.

Implementing the parser using active patterns

Parsers rely heavily on pattern matching. Listing 2 uses patterns such as `'`'::rest` and `[]` to identify the start of a command. Checking the elements of a list is a low-level technique, because it uses the representation directly and doesn't express any higher-level intention.

Active patterns are an F# language feature that provides a higher-level abstraction for pattern matching. You can use them to specify that you want input starting with a specified list; input that's delimited by the specified character or characters (on each side), input that's bracketed by given opening and closing characters, or even input that starts with an inline code span. Ideally, you'd like to write something like this:

```
match chars with
| Delimited ['`'] (body, rest) ->
    // Parsed body delimited by the backtick (e.g. `hello`)
| Delimited ['*'; '*' ] (body, rest) ->
    // Parsed body delimited by double asterisk (e.g. **hello**)
```

In this example, `Delimited` is an active pattern that recognizes text wrapped between opening and closing sequence of symbols. This goes beyond the standard patterns for lists (such as `x::xs` for separating the head and tail). Active patterns execute user-defined code. In the case of `Delimited`, it recursively traverses the list and finds the end of the delimiter. Now let's see how you can implement such an active pattern.

Parsing spans using active patterns

You could modify the code in listing 2 to define an `InlineCode` active pattern and add a number of other, similar, active patterns to recognize strong or emphasized text. That would work, but it would make the code slightly repetitive.

A better technique is to use *parameterized active patterns*. These are active patterns that take one or more input parameters, much like functions that take input parameters. The parameters define the behavior of the pattern, so a single active pattern can recognize an entire class of cases, just as the behavior of a function depends on its parameters.

As I suggested previously, most inline Markdown commands can be handled using a single parameterized active pattern. The Delimited pattern detects a string that starts with specified characters, contains some body, and then ends with the same character sequence. To detect inline code, you can use the Delimited pattern with ['`'] as an argument.

The implementation of the Delimited pattern and a few helper functions and patterns is shown in listing 4. This code implements a new version of the parseSpans function, so if you're typing the code, you can comment out the implementation from listing 3; but you'll still need the rest of the code from earlier.

Listing 4 Implementing the `Delimited` active pattern

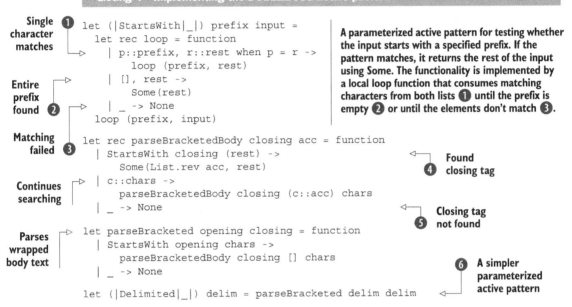

The two core functions in the listing implement the parsing of bracketed text—text that starts with a specified character list and ends with a (possibly different) character list. The parseBracketed function takes two parameters specifying the opening and closing sequences. It's implemented using function, meaning it will immediately pattern-match on its third argument. When the input starts with opening, the StartsWith pattern returns the remaining input as chars. If that's the case, the function then calls parseBracketedBody, which keeps accumulating the body (in the acc parameter) until it finds the closing character sequence ❹ or the end of the input ❺.

Finally, the Delimited active pattern ❻ is defined using *partial function application*. It calls the parseBracketed function using the same sequence of characters, as both the opening and closing sequence.

This is all you need for parsing inline code and emphasized and strong text. For other spans, you'll also need an active pattern that takes both parameters separately. Equipped with the Delimited pattern, it's now easy to update the parseSpans function from listing 3 to elegantly parse most of the formatting. You can see the new version in the following listing.

Listing 5   Parsing Markdown spans using active patterns

Detects a block of text delimited using the backtick (`) symbol. When you detect a formatting command, you first emit accumulated characters as a Literal ❶, then emit the currently recognized span ❷, and then continue parsing recursively ❸.

```
let rec parseSpans acc chars = seq {
  let emitLiteral = seq {                                    Sequence expression
    if acc <> [] then                                        that emits a Literal from
      yield acc |> List.rev |> toString |> Literal }         the accumulated input,
                                                             provided it's not empty
  match chars with
❶ | Delimited ['`'] (body, chars) ->
❷     yield! emitLiteral
      yield InlineCode(toString body)
❸     yield! parseSpans [] chars

  | Delimited ['*'; '*' ] (body, chars)
❹ | Delimited ['_'; '_' ] (body, chars) ->
      yield! emitLiteral
      yield Strong(parseSpans [] body |> List.ofSeq)
      yield! parseSpans [] chars

  | Delimited ['*' ] (body, chars)
❺ | Delimited ['_' ] (body, chars) ->
      yield! emitLiteral
      yield Emphasis(parseSpans [] body |> List.ofSeq)
      yield! parseSpans [] chars

  | c::chars ->                           Takes the current character, adds it to
      yield! parseSpans (c::acc) chars    the list of accumulated characters, and
  | [] ->                                 continues processing the rest of the input
      yield! emitLiteral }
```

The second and third patterns recognize strong ❹ and emphasized ❺ text. Both commands can be written with either an asterisk or underscore, so you use a pattern (two lines separated by a bar |) to handle both cases. The order of the patterns is important, because text delimited by a double asterisk (or underscore) could be parsed as text delimited by a single asterisk (or underscore).

This function has the same structure as the earlier version, but the pattern matching on chars is now implemented using active patterns. This means you no longer have to call individual parsing functions in advance. Instead, you just match on chars and then write a number of patterns to identify various commands.

In the pattern-matching, the syntax Delimited ['`'] invokes the active pattern with an argument that specifies the delimiter. This is followed by a (body, chars) pattern that defines two symbols to hold the delimited body and the remaining input.

When you parse the InlineCode span, you convert the parsed body to a string using the toString function. Conversely, emphasized or strong text may contain other formatting or hyperlinks. This means you call parseSpans recursively once more during the parsing to process the body of the emphasized or strong text.

This function is powerful, and this kind of abstraction is exactly what makes F# great for handling complex problems while keeping the time to market reasonable. The function handles three different formatting commands, but all of them are encoded using a single flexible active pattern.

The following F# Interactive session tests the behavior:

```
> "**important `code`** and _emphasized_"
  |> List.ofSeq |> parseSpans [] |> List.ofSeq
  ;;
val it : MarkdownSpan list =
  [ Strong [Literal "important "; InlineCode "code"]
    Literal " and ";
    Emphasis [Literal "emphasized"] ]
```

Output from the F# Interactive console

The input "**important** `code` and *emphasized*" should be parsed as a strong span containing a Literal "important" and inline code "code", followed by a Literal "and" and an emphasized span containing "emphasized". The F# Interactive output shows that the input is parsed as expected. Although you don't do this step here, you could copy the output and turn it into an assertion in a unit test for the parse-Spans function.

To practice your F# programming skills, exercises 1 and 2 suggest two extensions of parseSpans that you can implement as the next steps. Exercise 2 requires going back to the representation of Markdown documents (listing 1) and adding a new kind of MarkdownSpan.

Exercise 1

One feature of the Markdown format that I introduced earlier is the syntax for writing inline hyperlinks. The HyperLink case was also included in the MarkdownSpan type declaration, so your task here is just to add the parsing of hyperlinks to parseSpans.

The syntax for hyperlinks is as follows:

For more information, see [F# home page](http://fsharp.net).

You can read the syntax as a link body bracketed using square brackets, [and], immediately followed by a URL bracketed using parentheses, (and).

The best way to parse the syntax is to define a Bracketed parameterized active pattern that behaves like Delimited but takes two parameters (opening and closing characters). Then you can write a nested pattern (using Bracketed twice) to match the input against [link body]rest. This gives you the link body and the rest of the input. You can then match the rest of the input against (link url)rest.

If you want to make further extensions, you can look at the Markdown syntax (http://daringfireball.net/projects/markdown/syntax) and try implementing the remaining features. Note that the syntax for images is almost the same as the syntax for hyperlinks,

Exercise 2

Another useful feature of Markdown is the ability to add a hard line break (which is translated to the `<br />` element in HTML). To support this feature, you first need to go back to the definition of `MarkdownSpan` and add a new `HardLineBreak` case without any properties.

A hard line break is written as two spaces followed by both the `\n\r` characters or by either of them. Parsing the syntax in `parseSpans` should be easy: you just need to match the input list against a list starting with these three or four characters, which can be nicely done using the `StartsWith` active pattern.

After you add the extension, you should see the following behavior in F# Interactive:

```
> "hello  \n\rworld  \r!!!"
  |> List.ofSeq |> parseSpans [] |> List.ofSeq;;
val it : MarkdownSpan list =
  [ Literal "hello"; HardLineBreak;
    Literal "world"; HardLineBreak;
    Literal "!!!"]
```

As you can see, the Literals are separated by hard line breaks, and there are no remaining `\r` or `\n` characters or spaces, because they're consumed when parsing the line breaks.

so they can be parsed in a uniform way if you define an active pattern for the common part. We don't have enough space to implement all the features in this chapter, so we'll now move on to the next part of the parser.

As explained previously, in the "Representing Markdown documents" section, Markdown documents have two levels. The first level consists of blocks (such as headings and paragraphs), and the second level consists of inline formatting (such as emphasis and links). You've finished writing the parser for the second level, so all that remains to be done is to parse the first level: block elements.

Parsing blocks using active patterns

When parsing Markdown spans, you needed to process input in the form of a character list. You did that by defining active patterns that work on character lists, such as `StartsWith` and `Delimited`. In this section, you need to parse Markdown blocks, which are defined in terms of lines of text (see figure 4). For example, a paragraph is a sequence of lines followed by a blank line, a code snippet is a sequence of lines that all start with four spaces, and so on.

You can start by defining a few active patterns that operate on lists of lines. Using a combination of these new patterns and patterns for pattern-matching on individual lines, you'll then be able to express most of the parsing rules.

The following listing starts by defining patterns that find lines followed by a blank line, and lines that are all prefixed with a specified string.

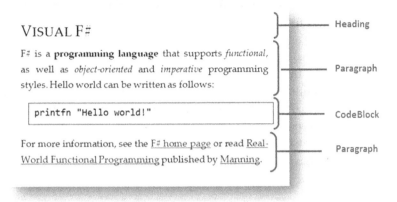

Figure 4   In this section, we're moving on from parsing inline formatting commands, such as emphasis or strong text, to parsing block elements. You'll write code that splits the input into headings, paragraphs, and code blocks.

Listing 6   Active patterns for parsing line-based syntax

This function walks over a list, taking elements that match a given predicate ❶ and returning them as the first element of the resulting tuple ❷. The remaining elements are returned as the second element (this is similar to using Seq.takeWhile and Seq.skipWhile).

This active pattern takes a list of lines and collects all lines (from the beginning of the input) that start with a given prefix ❸. Next, it removes the prefix from the found lines ❹ and returns them together with the remaining lines.

```
module List =
    let partitionWhile f =
      let rec loop acc = function
        | x::xs when f x -> loop (x::acc) xs
        | xs -> List.rev acc, xs
      loop []

let (|PrefixedLines|) prefix (lines:list<string>) =
    let prefixed, other =
      lines |> List.partitionWhile (fun line ->
        line.StartsWith(prefix))
    [ for line in prefixed ->
        line.Substring(prefix.Length) ], other

let (|LineSeparated|) lines =
    let isWhite = System.String.IsNullOrWhiteSpace
    match List.partitionWhile (isWhite >> not) lines with
    | par, _::rest
    | par, ([] as rest) -> par, rest

let (|AsCharList|) (str:string) =
    List.ofSeq str
```

This active pattern splits input lines into two lists using the first blank line as a separator. The implementation collects all lines until the first blank. To build a predicate that checks whether a line isn't blank, you use function composition ❺.

This simple (complete) active pattern views a string as a list of characters.

If the second returned list isn't empty, it starts with a blank line that you want to remove. This is done by building an or pattern that skips one element of a non-empty list (_::rest) or matches an empty list and gives it a name ([] as rest).

This listing demonstrates a key technique of functional programming: the use of higher-order functions to extract and reuse common functionality. Both `Prefixed-Lines` and `LineSeparated` split the input line list using a predicate. You capture this common functionality using a function and then use it twice in the implementation of the active patterns. To make the `partitionWhile` function easily discoverable, you define it in a `List` module so that it can be found by typing `List` followed by a dot.

The first of the two patterns, `PrefixedLines`, will be useful later for detecting code snippets. Note that the pattern is *complete*, meaning it can't fail. If there are no lines starting with a given prefix, the first returned list will be empty.

You can test the behavior of the pattern interactively:

```
> let (PrefixedLines "..." res) = ["...1"; "...2"; "3" ]
  printfn "%A" res;;
(seq ["1"; "2"], seq ["3"])
> let (PrefixedLines "..." res) = ["1"; "...2"; "...3" ]
  printfn "%A" res;;
(seq [], seq ["1"; "...2"; "...3"])
```

The `LineSeparated` active pattern will be used similarly for identifying paragraphs. You can check whether it works as expected using F# Interactive as an exercise.

Now you can easily complete the parser using a combination of the three active patterns from the previous section as well as patterns for matching on the content of an individual line. The `AsCharList` pattern is useful when you need to match on individual lines, because it turns a string into a character list that can be passed to patterns such as `StartsWith`.

Listing 7 creates a parser for Markdown blocks with just a few lines. Much like `parseSpans`, the `parseBlocks` function is written as a recursive sequence expression that emits individual `MarkdownBlock` values as it consumes the lines of input. It takes a list of unprocessed `lines` as a parameter and matches it against a number of patterns.

Listing 7   Parsing Markdown blocks using active patterns

These two patterns recognize first-level ❶ and second-level ❷ headings. A heading is a single line that starts with one or two hash characters (#) and a space. To match the first line, you use standard pattern for lists (::). A line is represented as a string, so you convert it to a list of chars using AsCharList. This allows you to use the StartsWith pattern to recognize headings.

```
let rec parseBlocks lines = seq {
  match lines with
❶ | AsCharList(StartsWith ['#'; ' '] heading)::lines ->
      yield Heading(1, parseSpans [] heading |> List.ofSeq)
      yield! parseBlocks lines
❷ | AsCharList(StartsWith ['#'; '#'; ' '] heading)::lines ->
      yield Heading(2, parseSpans [] heading |> List.ofSeq)
      yield! parseBlocks lines
  | PrefixedLines "    " (body, lines) when body <> [] ->
      yield CodeBlock(body)
      yield! parseBlocks lines
```

This pattern detects code snippets. It specifies that you want lines prefixed with four spaces. The PrefixedLines pattern always succeeds, so you use the when clause to ignore cases when the body is empty.

```
| LineSeparated (body, lines) when body <> [] ->
    let body = String.concat " " body |> List.ofSeq
    yield Paragraph(parseSpans [] body |> List.ofSeq)
    yield! parseBlocks lines

| line::lines when System.String.IsNullOrWhiteSpace(line) ->
    yield! parseBlocks lines

| _ -> () }
```

This pattern is used to skip blank lines. This is required, because the parsing of headings, paragraphs, and code snippets may leave empty lines at the beginning of the input.

To generate a Paragraph Markdown block, you concatenate lines of the paragraph and use parseSpans to handle formatting in the paragraph.

The function in listing 7 completes the Markdown parser. Writing proper tests for the function is outside of the scope of this chapter (see chapter 12 for more on testing), but you can at least test it interactively. To do that, you can use one minor but handy innovation of F# 3.0. You can write the sample document as a single string using triple quotes, which means it can freely contain quotes without escaping:

```
> let sample = """# Introducing F#
F# is a _functional-first_ language,
which looks like this:

    let msg = "world"
    printfn "hello %s!" msg

This sample prints `hello world!`
""";;
val sample : string = (...)

> let sampleDoc =
    sample.Split('\r', '\n') |> List.ofSeq
    |> parseBlocks |> List.ofSeq;;
val sampleDoc : list<MarkdownBlock> = [
  Heading (1,[Literal "Introducing F#"]);
  Paragraph
   [ Literal "F# is a "; Emphasis [Literal "functional-first"];
     Literal " language, which looks like this:"];
  CodeBlock ["let msg = "world""; "printfn "hello %s!" msg"];
  Paragraph [Literal "This sample prints "; InlineCode "hello world!"]]
```

To run the parser, you split the string into individual lines and then call parseBlocks. You can check that the result is an expected Markdown document consisting of a heading, a paragraph, a code block, and one more paragraph (with emphasis on the first line and inline code on the last one).

Although you can already write rich documents, there are a number of Markdown features that you can still add to the parser. Exercise 3 suggests one such addition: to solve the last part of the exercise, you'll need to go back to the definition of the MarkdownBlock type (listing 1) and add a new kind of block. Exercise 4 has you add support for another kind of block that's supported by Markdown: a block quote.

Exercise 3

The code for parsing headings in listing 7 is slightly repetitive. The bodies of the two clauses that recognize first-level ❶ and second-level ❷ headings are exactly the same, with the only difference being the number representing the size of the heading.

You can correct that by defining an active pattern, `Heading`, that detects and returns the heading together with its number. Using that, you should be able to rewrite the pattern matching as follows:

```
| Heading(size, heading, lines) ->
    yield Heading(size, parseSpans [] heading |> List.ofSeq)
    yield! parseBlocks lines
```

This function supports only one style of headings. It handles headings written on a single line starting with the hash (#) symbol, but it doesn't handle the alternative: a single line of text followed by a line consisting of three or more occurrences of the equals sign (=) or dash (-).

Supporting this alternative style is another interesting exercise. You'll need to define a new active pattern to add this functionality, but the key aspect—searching for a line containing equals or dashes—can be done using `List.partitionWhile`. If you design the active pattern well, you can also use it to handle horizontal rules, which can be written as a line of dashes preceded by a blank line.

Exercise 4

In a Markdown document, a quote can be written by prefixing the text with the > character followed by a space. But there are a few interesting details.

If a quotation contains a longer paragraph, you don't have to mark all the lines of the paragraph, but instead just the first line of each paragraph:

```
> This is a hand-written quotation
which consists of two paragraphs.
> The second paragraph is quite short.
```

Quotations aren't limited to paragraphs. They may contain code snippets, headings, and other block elements:

```
> This is a quotation that contains F# code:
>
>     printfn "Hello from quoted code!"
```

To implement quotations, you need to add a `BlockQuote` case to the `Markdown-Block` type. Unlike `Heading` or `Paragraph`, which contain `MarkdownSpans`, the case representing quotations needs to contain `MarkdownBlocks`, because quotations can contain not just text, but other blocks. In the parsing code, you also need to call `parseBlocks` recursively to process the body of the quoted text.

The source code for this chapter comes with a number of examples that you can use to test whether your implementation of quotes works as expected.

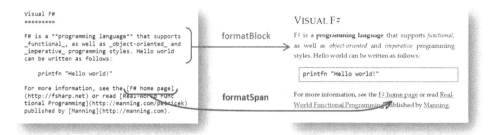

Figure 5 The functionality that turns a Markdown document into HTML is implemented using two functions. The `formatBlock` function emits tags corresponding to `MarkdownBlock` values, and `formatSpan` generates HTML for `MarkdownSpan` elements.

Most of the common implementations of Markdown take a document and turn it directly into HTML, usually using regular expressions. As discussed earlier, this approach means it's hard to generate other outputs (for example, Word documents or LaTeX), and it also means it's difficult to postprocess the document.

By writing a parser that turns Markdown documents into an F# data type, we've opened a number of interesting possibilities. Code that turns the representation into HTML (or any other format) can be written with just a few lines of F#.

Turning Markdown into HTML

The .NET framework provides a number of ways to generate HTML documents. If you were using ASP.NET, you could use the ASP.NET object model to generate HTML elements. You could use the LINQ to XML library (and `XDocument`) to generate XHTML and guarantee that the generated code is valid XML. Finally, you can also generate HTML by hand.

In this section, you'll use the last option to keep the code short and simple. As demonstrated in figure 5, you'll write two functions that format blocks and spans. You'll use imperative style, so both functions take a standard .NET `TextWriter` object, use it to generate HTML, and return `unit`. Alternatively, you could compose and return a `string`, but this is an inefficient operation in .NET.

Most of the HTML-generation code in the `formatBlock` and `formatSpan` functions will generate HTML elements of the form `<tag attr1="value">body</tag>`, with zero or more attributes. The body in the HTML element can be generated by other code.

In your first attempt to write the code, you could call the `Write` method (for the opening tag), followed by code to generate the body and another call to `Write` for the closing tag. This works fine, but you can simplify the code slightly using the following helper function:

```
open System.IO

let outputElement (output:TextWriter) tag attributes body =
  let attrString =
    [ for k, v in attributes -> k + "=\"" + v + "\"" ]          Joins the
    |> String.concat " "                                        attributes into
                                                                a single string
```

```
output.Write("<" + tag + attrString + ">")
body ()                                          ◁─┐  Runs the function that
output.Write("</" + tag + ">")                      │  generates the body
```

The first argument of the `outputElement` function is a `TextWriter` object representing the output stream. The next three arguments specify what should be written: the tag name, attributes, and a function that generates the body. It's a perfect example of the Hole in the Middle pattern:[4] the idea is that you have some repeated code (the generation of the opening and closing tags) with a variable part in the middle. In functional languages, the pattern can be abstracted using a higher-order function that takes the body as a function and calls it where the changing part is needed.

The following listing shows the remaining code needed to implement HTML generation.

Listing 8 Generating HTML from a Markdown document

```
let rec formatSpan (output:TextWriter) = function
  | Literal(str) ->                                    Writes a Literal
      output.Write(str)                             ◁─ directly to the output
  | Strong(spans) ->
      outputElement output "strong" [] (fun () ->
        spans |> List.iter (formatSpan output))    ◁─┐  Uses a partial function
  | Emphasis(spans) ->                               ❶  application to call List.iter
      outputElement output "em" [] (fun () ->
        spans |> List.iter (formatSpan output))
  | HyperLink(spans, url) ->                              Passes a single
      outputElement output "a" ["href", url] (fun () ->  ◁─ attribute to
        spans |> List.iter (formatSpan output))          outputElement
  | InlineCode(code) ->
      output.Write("<code>" + code + "</code>")    ◁─┐  The body is
                                                      │  just a string.
let rec formatBlock (output:TextWriter) = function
  | Heading(size, spans) ->
      outputElement output ("h" + size.ToString()) [] (fun () ->
        spans |> List.iter (formatSpan output))
  | Paragraph(spans) ->
      outputElement output "p" [] (fun () ->
        spans |> List.iter (formatSpan output))
  | CodeBlock(lines) ->
      outputElement output "pre" [] (fun () ->     ❷  Uses WriteLine as an
        lines |> List.iter output.WriteLine )    ◁─    argument to List.iter
```

This is possibly the least inspiring code sample in this chapter, because it's so straightforward. Both functions use the `function` keyword to pattern-match on their argument and then implement the rendering of HTML using the `outputElement` helper.

---

[4] See Brian Hurt's "The 'Hole in the middle' pattern" article on the *Enfranchised Mind* blog, July 10, 2007, http://mng.bz/Lcs8. Using a more traditional OO design patterns perspective, this can be also viewed as the Strategy pattern or the Template Method pattern.

When you need to render all child elements (for example, in `Strong` ❶ or `Code-Block` ❷), you use the `List.iter` function. In this case, I prefer the `iter` function over a `for` loop, because you can nicely use partial function application. When you use (`formatSpan output`) as an argument, you create a function that takes a `MarkdownSpan`, so you can pass it directly to `List.iter`, which calls it for all `MarkdownSpan` elements in the input list.

> ### Formatting HTML efficiently
>
> Listing 8 generates most of the HTML code by concatenating a fixed number of strings and by using the `Write` and `WriteLine` methods of `TextWriter`. Some of the code could be written more elegantly using the F# `Printf.fprintf` function, which supports standard F# format strings in a type-safe way. In my first implementation of Markdown in F#, the HTML formatting was one of the main bottlenecks. But it's worth noting that the efficiency of the `printf` function has been largely improved in F# 3.1.
>
> That said, you should always use a profiler to find out whether this is a problem for your application. In most situations, the performance of string formatting won't be an issue.

Let's now test the function in F# Interactive. To do that, you need to go back to the end of the "Parsing blocks using active patterns" section, where you created a sample document, `sampleDoc`. The following snippet shows how to render the document and store it as a string:

```
> let sb = System.Text.StringBuilder()
  let output = new StringWriter(sb)
  sampleDoc |> List.iter (formatBlock output)
  sb.ToString()
  ;;
val it : string =
  "<h1>Introducing F#</h1><p>F# is a <em>functional-first</em> language,
    which looks like this:</p><pre>let msg = "world"
printfn "hello %s!" msg
</pre><p>This sample prints <code>hello world!</code></p>"
```

To save the generated HTML as a string, you allocate a new `StringBuilder` and create a `StringWriter` that can be passed to the `formatBlock` function. Once again, you use `List.iter` and partial function application to print all blocks of the document.

The generated HTML code is correct, although not very readable because the function that generates it doesn't add any indentation or line breaks. The only line breaks are in the `<pre>` tag, where they are required. Changing the implementation to produce nice and readable HTML code is a good exercise.

Processing Markdown documents

One of my key motivations for writing a custom Markdown parser was that I wanted to be able to easily write functions that transform the document in various ways. Such

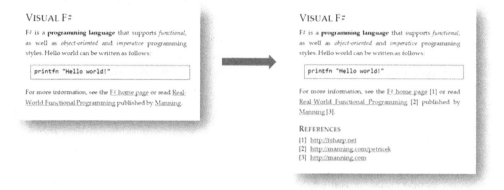

Figure 6   Document transformations that are implemented in this section. You'll create a document that's suitable for printing by numbering all the hyperlinks and adding a "References" section that shows the URLs of referenced web pages.

functions, for example, could count the number of words in the document (excluding code snippets), find all CodeBlock blocks and run a syntax highlighter on the source code, or automatically number all headings in the document. The processing you'll implement in this section is illustrated in figure 6.

The F# representation makes document-processing tasks easy. Once you parse the document, you can recursively walk through the MarkdownBlock and MarkdownSpan types and implement any transformation or processing you need.

Implementing the tree-processing patterns

If you want to implement a single transformation, you can do that directly; but if you need multiple transformations, you won't always want to repeat the same boilerplate code. For every processing function, you'd have to pattern-match on all Markdown-Block and MarkdownSpan cases, call the function recursively on all child elements, and then reconstruct the original element.

Using F#, there are several ways to hide the boilerplate. The standard functional approach is to write a number of higher-order functions like map and fold that capture some processing patterns (transform a certain node to another node; aggregate some values computed from individual elements). This works well if your processing matches a supported pattern, but complex transformations require complex higher-order functions. The code still tends to be concise, but it may become more difficult to understand.

An alternative option that you'll use here is to define active patterns that provide a more general view of the document structure. Instead of classifying elements based on their kind, you can classify elements by whether they contain children. The recursive processing then needs only a single case to handle all elements with children.

This programming idiom is used by the ExprShape module in the standard F# library. The following listing implements the same pattern for the MarkdownBlock and MarkdownSpan types.

Listing 9 Active patterns that simplify the processing of Markdown documents

The functionality is in a separate module to clarify that the active patterns are derived patterns and not part of the declaration of Markdown-Span and Markdown-Block.

This active pattern matches when a MarkdownSpan represents any span element that contains other MarkdownSpan values as children. In that case, it returns the children ❶ together with an opaque representation of the span (a boxed span).

```
module Matching =

  let (|SpanNode|_|) span =
    match span with
    | Strong spans | Emphasis spans | HyperLink(spans, _) ->
        Some(box span, spans)
    | _ -> None

  let SpanNode (span:obj, children) =
    match unbox span with
    | Strong _ -> Strong children
    | Emphasis _ -> Emphasis children
    | HyperLink(_, url) -> HyperLink(children, url)
    | _ -> invalidArg "" "Incorrect MarkdownSpan"

  let (|BlockNode|_|) block =
    match block with
    | Heading(_, spans)
    | Paragraph(spans) -> Some(box block, spans)
    | _ -> None

  let BlockNode (block:obj, spans) =
    match unbox block with
    | Heading(a, _) -> Heading(a, spans)
    | Paragraph(_) -> Paragraph(spans)
    | _ -> invalidArg "" "Incorrect MarkdownBlock."
```

❶
❷
❸
❹

The code for processing MarkdownBlock follows the same pattern: define an active pattern ❸ and a function of the same name ❹. The names don't clash, because they're different constructs. Using the same name makes the processing code more readable.

This function rebuilds a span that was decomposed using the SpanNode active pattern. It unboxes the object representing the shape ❷ and builds an element of the same kind, but using the new children specified by the caller.

This listing implements an active pattern and a function with a corresponding name for both of the types that represent a Markdown document. The idea of the idiom is that you can use the SpanNode active pattern to handle all MarkdownSpan values that contain child spans. The active pattern returns a list of children together with an opaque object that represents the shape (or the kind) of the span. In this implementation, the opaque object is just a boxed MarkdownSpan value to keep the code short, but you could define another type to make it less error-prone.

When the pattern matches, you can process the children as you wish, but you can't perform any operation on the shape. The only thing you can do is reconstruct a span of the same shape, possibly with different child spans.

For example, when processing a HyperLink, the shape captures the fact that the span is a hyperlink and stores the linked URL. The children are MarkdownSpan elements from the body of the hyperlink. When you transform the children, you process the body of the hyperlink. To reconstruct the hyperlink, you use the Matching.SpanNode function, which builds a `HyperLink` using the original URL and new children. What makes this idiom elegant is that the same code will also work on other elements with children, such as `Strong` and `Emphasis`.

If you're still slightly puzzled by the idea, don't worry. It will all become clear when we look at an example in the next section.

Generating references from hyperlinks

When generating a printable version of a document, you need to transform the entire document in order to add numbered references to all hyperlinks. This means your recursive function for processing blocks will essentially take an original `Markdown-Block` and return a new `MarkdownBlock`.

The processing of spans is trickier. You can't return a new `MarkdownSpan` as the result, because when you find a `HyperLink`, you need to return multiple spans as the result. This means you need to turn a single `MarkdownSpan` into a list of `MarkdownSpan` values and then concatenate all of them to get a list of children.

In addition, you need to keep state during the processing. In particular, you need to build a list of references that contains URLs and their associated indexes. In listing 10 you do that using the `ResizeArray` type. The same thing could be done using an immutable list, but the solution using a mutable collection is simpler. Using an immutable list, you'd have to return the new state as part of the result instead of just returning a list of spans.

Listing 10   Generating a document with references for printing

When you find a link in the document, you generate a new index for the URL, add it to the mutable list of references, and then return the original span, followed by a newly generated Literal with a bracketed reference number.

```
let rec generateSpanRefs (refs:ResizeArray<_>) = function
  | HyperLink(body, url) as span ->
      let id = sprintf "[%d]" (refs.Count + 1)
      refs.Add(id, url)
      [span; Literal(id)]
  | Matching.SpanNode(shape, children) ->
      let children = children |> List.collect (generateSpanRefs refs)
      [Matching.SpanNode(shape, children)]
  | span -> [span]
let generateBlockRefs refs = function
  | Matching.BlockNode(shape, children) ->
      let children = children |> List.collect (generateSpanRefs refs)
      Matching.BlockNode(shape, children)
  | block -> block
```

If a span doesn't contain children, you return it in a singleton list.

Using the SpanNode pattern, you can handle all spans that contain children. You recursively process all children and concatenate the generated lists using List.collect. Then you re-create a span with the same shape, but different children.

The BlockNode pattern matches all blocks with children. You recursively process the children using List.collect and re-create the block element.

This implementation consists of two functions that recursively process MarkdownSpan and MarkdownBlock types. The last two cases of pattern matching in both functions are similar. They implement a transformation that visits all nodes of the document but creates a copy that's exactly the same. Thanks to the patterns and functions from the Matching module, you don't have to explicitly handle all cases. You need just two: a case for elements with children, and a case for elements without children.

To implement a transformation that does something interesting, you need to add an additional case of the pattern matching and look for specific elements (such as HyperLink). Then you transform the element to one or more other elements, while all other elements are handled by the last two cases and copied without change.

To run the transformation on an entire document, you need to use List.map to apply generateBlockRefs on all blocks of the document:

```
let doc = [ """For more information, see the [F# home page]           Last paragraph
  (http://fsharp.net) or read [Real-World Functional Programming]      of the sample
  (http://manning.com/petricek) published by [Manning]                 document
  (http://manning.com).""" ] |> parseBlocks |> List.ofSeq

let refs = ResizeArray<_>()
let printable = doc |> List.map (generateBlockRefs refs)
```

When you run the code using F# Interactive and enter the individual values as separate commands (to make sure their value is printed), you get the following output:

```
val doc : MarkdownBlock list = (...)
val refs : System.Collections.Generic.List<string * string> =
  seq [ ("[1]", "http://fsharp.net");                                  Automatically
        ("[2]", "http://manning.com/petricek");                        generated list
        ("[3]", "http://manning.com") ]                                of references
val printable : MarkdownBlock list =
  [Paragraph                                                           Every
    [ Literal "For more information, see the ";                        hyperlink is
      HyperLink ([Literal "F# home page"],"http://fsharp.net");        now followed
      Literal "[1]"; Literal " or read ";                              by a reference
      (...) ] ]
```

Now that you've transformed the document to a version with numbered hyperlinks, you should also append a "References" heading followed by a list with the values from refs. The best way to do that would be to use ordered lists, but you don't support this Markdown feature yet (the rules for parsing lists are slightly subtle). As a simple alternative, you could add a new kind of block—say, HtmlBlock—that could contain arbitrary HTML and be written directly to the output when rendering the document. In fact, Markdown supports inline HTML, so this would be a sensible extension.

Implementing HtmlBlock, or even ordered and unordered lists, makes for an interesting exercise. Exercise 5 offers a couple of suggestions that involve the processing of documents, and it should be easy to complete. If you want to check the results, your function should report that the sample document from the start of the chapter (in the "Formatting text with Markdown" section) has 45 words.

Exercise 6 is also easy when you do it for a `MarkdownBlock` from listing 1, but it's interesting if you've completed exercise 4.

Exercise 5
The transformation that you implemented in the last example turns a document into a new document, but you can use the same programming idiom to write code that turns a document into some other value. In this exercise, your task is to implement a word counter for `MarkdownDocument`. You shouldn't count words that appear in code samples (either `InlineCode` or `CodeBlock`). This essentially means you should only count words in the `Literal` span, but keep in mind that a `Literal` may contain multiple words separated by whitespace or punctuation.

Exercise 6
In this exercise, your task is to implement a document transformation that automatically adds numbers to headings. For example, take the following document:

```
# Paradigms
## Object-oriented
## Functional
# Conclusions
```

Your algorithm should add the numbers 1 and 2 to top-level headings (resulting in "1. Paradigms" and "2. Conclusions" and numbers 1.1 and 1.2 to the two subheadings (resulting in "1.1 Object-oriented" and "1.2 Functional"). To implement the processing, you only need to walk through a list of `MarkdownBlock` values (because `MarkdownSpan` can't contain headings), but you need to find a good data structure for remembering current numbers.

If you completed exercise 4, you'll need to decide how to handle quoted headings. Are they numbered as part of the main document, or are headings in a quotation numbered separately? Or perhaps they shouldn't be numbered at all.

If you attempt to automatically number headings in quotations, you can also extend the patterns in the `Matching` module (listing 9). A `Blockquote` element is tricky. It contains child elements, but, in contrast with `Paragraph`, the child elements aren't `MarkdownSpan` values, but other `MarkdownBlock` values. This means you can't handle them using `Matching.BlockNode`. For this reason, you'll need to add another active pattern named `Matching.BlockNested` that returns an opaque shape together with children of type `MarkdownBlock`. For now, you need this pattern only for quotes, but later you'd also need it for lists and other complex blocks.

The Markdown format is rich, and there's a lot of potential for extending the code in this chapter. If you want to go beyond the standard exercises, you can contribute to the more complete F# Markdown parser that inspired this chapter.[5] That implementation

---

[5] The implementation can be found at http://tpetricek.github.io/FSharp.Formatting/.

follows exactly the same principles as the code here. Interesting projects include turning the parser into a complete blogging system and adding different backends that convert the parsed document to other formats, such as HTML5 presentations and Word documents.

Summary

You can see the Markdown format as an external DSL—that is, a language or document that has its own syntax and represents a script, document, or command. In addition to writing documents, external DSLs are useful when you face repetitive programming tasks, such as describing financial contracts or writing scripts or configurations. Creating external DSLs can be a time-consuming task, so it's typically only worth doing when they're used often or when they allow nonprogrammers to contribute to your system (such as by specifying system behavior in a simple format).

When creating DSLs in F#, the first step is always to define an F# representation of the language (in this case, `MarkdownBlock` and `MarkdownSpan`). Then you can add parsers and processing operations, such as generating a list of references. The fact that you can use the F# representation of Markdown in a number of ways is the main benefit of the solution. If you used a parser that turns Markdown directly into HTML, it would be almost impossible to add different backends or to preprocess documents.

Recalling chapter 1, you can see all the four key issues in action in this chapter. The use of active patterns makes it possible to parse *complex* formats using readable code, which makes it easier to check the *correctness* of the implementation. At the same time, you can easily compose a few primitive active patterns to cover a large part of the Markdown format, which decreases *time to market*. Finally, the F# compiler produces code that's more *efficient* than a standard C# parser based on regular expressions.

About the author

Tomas Petricek is a long-time F# enthusiast and author of the book *Real-World Functional Programming* (Manning, 2010), which explains functional programming concepts using C# 3.0 while teaching F# alongside. He is a frequent F# speaker and does F# and functional training in London, New York, and elsewhere worldwide.

Tomas has been a Microsoft MVP since 2004, writes a programming blog at http://tomasp.net, and is also a Stack Overflow addict.

He contributed to the development of F# during two internships at Microsoft Research in Cambridge. Before starting a PhD at the University of Cambridge, he studied in Prague and worked as an independent .NET consultant.

## PART 2

Developing analytical components

When talking about F# from a business perspective in chapter 1, we mostly focused on the development of analytical components. These are the components that underlie the business value of an application. Think about financial models, artificial intelligence in games, recommendation engines in retail applications, and data analysis and visualization components.

As you saw in chapter 1, choosing F# for developing analytical components will solve existing problems for your business, including taming complexity, guaranteeing correctness and performance of solutions, and making it easier and faster to turn an application from an idea and a prototype into a deployed system.

The chapters in this part of the book demonstrate many of these benefits using three interesting practical problems. In chapter 4, Chao-Jen Chen will explore the implementation of financial models in F#. Even if you're not familiar with the models discussed in the chapter, you can see that F# makes it easy to turn the mathematics behind the models into code that is correct and efficient. In chapter 5, Evelina Gabasova demonstrates how to analyze and visualize social network data. Explaining why this is important would be a waste of space—your systems can get enormous value from your understanding of social networks. It's amazing how much you can achieve in a single chapter! Finally, Keith Battocchi demonstrates a recent F# feature called *type providers*. Chapter 6 shows how you can integrate external data into F#, making it extremely easy for other developers on the team to access rich data sources.

In general, if you're interested in implementing calculations, data transformations, processing of business rules, or any functionality with important business logic, choosing F# is the right option. The chapters in this part of the book only scratch the surface of what you can do, but you can find a number of other experience reports on the F# Software Foundation website at www.fsharp.org.

Numerical computing in the financial domain

Chao-Jen Chen

The modern finance industry can't operate without numerical computing. Financial institutions, such as investment banks, hedge funds, commercial banks, and even central banks, heavily use various numerical methods for derivatives pricing, hedging, and risk management. Usually the production systems of those numerical methods are implemented in general-purpose object-oriented languages like C++, C#, and Java. But there's a steady, emerging trend in the industry: financial institutions are increasingly adopting functional languages, including F#, when implementing their new derivatives-pricing or risk-control systems. One of the reasons this is happening is that a functional language like F# is relatively expressive in turning mathematical equations into code. Moreover, F# has strong support for high-performance computing techniques, such as graphics processing unit (GPU) computing and parallelization. As such, F# enables programmers and quantitative analysts to spend less time coding and at the same time avoid compromising performance.

Among the numerical methods widely used in the finance industry, we've chosen Monte Carlo simulation and its applications to derivatives pricing as our main topic. This chapter serves as an example of how F# is a good fit for implementing analytical components like a derivatives pricing engine, as mentioned in chapter 1. In this chapter, you'll see how F#'s functional features can help you write concise code for Monte Carlo simulation and, more important, make the code generic so that you can apply the same simulation code to pricing various types of derivatives. If you were to do the same in a typical object-oriented language, you'd have to implement different types of derivatives as classes and have them inherit a common abstract class or implement the same interface. Thanks to higher-order functions and function currying in F#, you don't have to construct the cumbersome inheritance hierarchy (although you could still choose to do that in F# because F# also supports the object-oriented style of polymorphism).

Introducing financial derivatives and underlying assets

A *financial derivative* is a contract that usually involves two parties, buyer and seller, and is defined in terms of some underlying asset that already exists on the market. The payoff of a financial derivative is contingent on the market price of its underlying asset at some time point in the future, such as the agreed expiry time of a contract. Many different types of financial derivatives are traded on the market. Our discussion here is limited to a tiny slice of the derivatives world. The types of financial derivatives we'll be looking at in this chapter are all European style—that is, each derivative contract has only one payoff at the expiration date and has no early-exercise feature.

Before we describe the derivatives we'll be looking at, let's talk about underlying assets. Although there are all kinds of underlying assets, such as equities, bonds, crude oil, gold, and even live stocks, this chapter focuses only on stocks as underlying assets. More precisely, we'll look at only non-dividend-paying stocks. One famous example of non-dividend-paying stocks is Warren Buffett's Berkshire Hathaway Holding, which never pays any dividends.

Non-dividend-paying stocks

Why do we assume that underlying assets have to be non-dividend-paying? Because we need more complicated mathematical treatments in order to model dividend-paying behaviors, which is too much to cover here. But as far as derivatives pricing is concerned, the scope of non-dividend-paying stocks is perhaps broader than your imagination. As long as the underlying stock of the derivative contract you're considering doesn't pay out any dividend during the period from today to the expiry of the derivative, the stock can be viewed as a non-dividend-paying stock when you price the derivative contract. Derivatives with stocks as underlying assets are usually called *stock options* or *equity options*.

European call options

Let's assume that, for a non-dividend-paying stock S, S_t denotes its share price at time t. Then, a European call option with strike K and expiry T on stock S pays $\max(S_T - K, 0)$ to the holder of the call option at time T. In other words, the call option pays $(S_T - K)$ to the option holder if S_T (the share price at the expiry of the call option) exceeds K, and it pays nothing otherwise. For convenience, we've defined a shorthand notation for $\max(S_T - K, 0)$. Given any real number r, $(r)^+ = \max(r, 0)$, which is called a *positive part function*. So the European call payoff $\max(S_T - K, 0)$ can be shortened to $(S_T - K)^+$.

Before we jump into derivatives pricing, let's review some fundamental probability concepts that you'll need in this chapter.

Using probability functions of Math.NET

Probability theory underlies most pricing algorithms. We'll explain all the important concepts as we go. In addition to probability, we also need to explain a bit about some

F# settings you'll need throughout the chapter. We'll introduce Math.NET Numerics, an open source library, which you'll use in Monte Carlo simulation.

Configuring F# Interactive

F# Interactive (FSI) is a great tool whereby you can execute F# code interactively, like other interactive numerical computing languages such as MathWorks' MATLAB and Mathematica. If you want to test F# code, you type it in or send it to FSI and then immediately run it and get its results in FSI, which saves you from building an entire Visual Studio project just to do a small test. You'll be using only FSI in this chapter, although you can also choose to create a new Visual Studio project.

Here's another good thing about using FSI: it's easy to *profile* your code—that is, to measure how much time your F# code takes for execution—because FSI comes with a built-in timing feature, which you'll use later in this chapter. To enable FSI's timing feature, type the #time command in FSI:

```
> #time;;
--> Timing now on
```

Another useful FSI setting is Floating Point Format, which controls how many decimal places FSI should print for a float. The default is 10, which is too many for this discussion. The following FSI command configures the printing:

```
> fsi.FloatingPointFormat <- "f5";;
val it : unit = ()

> 10.0/3.0;;
val it : float = 3.33333
```

As you can see, floating-point values are now printed with only five decimal places, which is enough for our purpose.

Downloading and setting up Math.NET Numerics

The Math.NET project (www.mathdotnet.com) is a set of open source libraries for different purposes, including numerical computing, signal processing, and computer algebra. Among those libraries, you'll need only Math.NET Numerics, which you'll use to generate random numbers and compute basic statistics. You can get Math.NET from http://numerics.mathdotnet.com or via the NuGet package MathNet.Numerics; the latest version as of this writing is v2.6.2. Assuming the library is installed in the Program Files folder, you can load it in FSI as follows:

```
#r @"C:\Program Files\MathNet.Numerics-2.6.2\Net40\MathNet.Numerics.dll"
open MathNet.Numerics.Distributions
open MathNet.Numerics.Statistics
```
Namespaces required in this chapter

You'll use the Normal class defined in the namespace MathNet.Numerics.Distributions and the extension method Variance() defined in the class MathNet.Numerics.Statistics.Statistics.

Random variables, expectation, and variance

The first mathematical thing you need to know about is the concept of random variables, because stock prices in the future are random as of today. Monte Carlo simulation itself is also a random variable.

Random variables

As you may know, there are two types of random variables: discrete and continuous. A *discrete random variable* is one that has a (finitely or infinitely) countable range, like the set of all positive integers. In contrast, a *continuous random variable* has an uncountable range, like all positive reals or all the reals between 0 and 1. As far as the Monte Carlo methods and stochastic processes you'll use in this chapter are concerned, you need only continuous random variables.

A random variable X is a function that maps random events to real values. A value produced by X is called a *sample* drawn from random variable X. Due to randomness, every time you try to draw a sample from X, you get a different value. You can't know for sure what value X will produce next until you've drawn the next sample from X. Although you can't know beforehand what the next sample will be, you can study the probability for a particular range of values to be taken by X. This question can be answered by X's probability density function $f(x)$, which satisfies the following conditions:

$f(x) \geq 0$, for all x

$\int_{-\infty}^{\infty} f(x)dx = 1$ (if x could take on values ranging from $-\infty$ to ∞)

A random variable X has quite a few characteristics, which can be defined in terms of its probability density function. The Monte Carlo simulation, the most important one, is expectation $\mathbb{E}[X]$.

Expectation

$\mathbb{E}[X]$ denotes the expectation of random variable X and is defined as follows:

$\mathbb{E}[X] = \int_{-\infty}^{\infty} x \cdot f(x)dx$

As you can see, the mathematical definition involves integration. Usually there are a few ways to interpret the definition. One common, straightforward interpretation is that the expectation of a random variable is the weighted average of all possible values that the random variable can produce. Another interpretation, which is more relevant to our study of Monte Carlo simulation, is that if you could draw infinitely many samples from X, $\mathbb{E}[X]$ should equal the average of those samples. To a certain extent, Monte Carlo simulation computes the integral numerically.

In this chapter, you'll use arrays to hold random samples. Why adopt arrays rather than other immutable data structures like lists or sequences? Because arrays are a few times faster than lists or sequences with respect to the operations you need here. Let's take a quick look at computing the average of an array of samples. You'll use the `Array.average` function provided by the F# Core Library:

```
> let x = [|1.0..10000000.0|];;
Real: 00:00:01.199, CPU: 00:00:01.216, GC gen0: 2, gen1: 2, gen2: 2

// the printout of x is not included as it is long and irrelevant.

> let avg1 = x |> Array.average;;
Real: 00:00:00.119, CPU: 00:00:00.124, GC gen0: 0, gen1: 0, gen2: 0

val avg1 : float = 5000000.50000

> let avg2 = x.Mean();;
Real: 00:00:00.244, CPU: 00:00:00.234, GC gen0: 0, gen1: 0, gen2: 0

val avg2 : float = 5000000.50000
```

In addition to the `Array.average` function, the example shows the extension method `Mean()` provided by `MathNet.Numerics`, which can also produce the sample average you want but is significantly slower than F#'s built-in `Array.average` function. That's why you should use the `Array.average` function, but please note that the result of this comparison may vary from computer to computer. In other words, it's possible that you'll see the `Mean()` method run faster than the `Array.average` function.

Having described expectation, let's proceed to another important characteristic of *X*: *variance*, which plays a key role when later in this chapter we talk about how to measure and improve the accuracy of the Monte Carlo simulation.

Variance

Var(*X*) denotes the variance of random variable *X*, which is defined as follows:

$$Var(X) = \mathbb{E}[(X - \mathbb{E}[X])^2]$$

Var(*X*) is used to give you an idea of how a large number of samples from *X* are spread out: do they cluster in a small area, or do they spread across a wide range? People tend to dislike uncertainty; more often than not, you'd prefer a random variable with a lower variance. If you have to observe a random variable for whatever reason, you'll usually want to see samples that cluster around expectation. This is exactly the case when it comes to Monte Carlo simulation. The smaller its variance is, the higher the simulation accuracy will be.

As for computation of variance, you'll use the extension method `Variance()` from `MathNet.Numerics`. The following example shows how:

```
> let x = [|1.0..10000000.0|];;
Real: 00:00:01.149, CPU: 00:00:01.154, GC gen0: 0, gen1: 0, gen2: 0
```

The printout of x isn't included because it's long and irrelevant.

```
> let var1 = x.Variance();;
Real: 00:00:00.406, CPU: 00:00:00.405, GC gen0: 0, gen1: 0, gen2: 0

val var1 : float = 8333334166666.63000
```

Now that you know how to observe the expectation and variance of a set of samples, let's move on to producing those samples. You want them to follow a particular probability distribution.

Generating normal random samples

The only probability distribution you'll use in this chapter is a normal distribution. You'll generate normally distributed random samples and use those samples to simulate stock prices. Those simulated stock prices won't be normally distributed—instead, based on the stochastic process employed here, they'll be lognormally distributed. It's easy to see that it doesn't make sense to make stock prices normally distributed, because stock prices can't go negative.

Normal distribution

Let $N(u,\sigma^2)$ denote a normal distribution with mean u and variance σ^2. If we say random variable X follows $N(u,\sigma^2)$, that means X has the following probability density function:

$$f(x) = \frac{1}{\sqrt{2\pi\sigma^2}}e^{-\frac{1}{2}\left(\frac{x-\mu}{\sigma}\right)^2}$$

Perhaps you have already seen this expression because of the ubiquity of normal distributions, but we aren't going to play with it algebraically. In this chapter we care only about how to draw samples from a random variable with the probability density function. The key point is that you use normal distribution to model the logarithmic return of the underlying asset.

Various algorithms are available for generating normal random samples. Fortunately, you don't have to study and implement those algorithms yourself, because Math.NET has implemented a random number generator for normal distributions, which is sufficient for this study of Monte Carlo simulation. The following code snippet shows how to use the normal random number generator provided by Math.NET:

```
let normal = Normal.WithMeanVariance(0.0, 1.0)       ①  Instantiates an object
                                                          of the Normal class

normal.RandomSource <- new System.Random()           ②  Random source

let m = Array.init 5 (fun _ -> normal.Sample())      ③  Draws samples and
                                                          puts them in an array
```

The code instantiates an object of the `Normal` class from the `MathNet.Numerics` `.Distributions` namespace ①. The object is named `normal` and represents a normal distribution with mean 0.0 and variance 1.0: $N(0.0, 1.0)$. For this object to be able to generate normally distributed random samples, you have to give it a random source[1] ❷. The random source must be a direct or indirect instance of the `System.Random` class and is supposed to produce uniformly distributed random samples in the interval between 0.0 and 1.0. Math.NET provides a variety of alternatives for this purpose. But as far as this chapter is concerned, the `System.Random` class provided by the .NET Framework is sufficient. Having specified a random source, you invoke the `normal.Sample()` method[2] to draw five samples from $N(0.0, 1.0)$ and put them in an array named m ❸.

Geometric Brownian motion and Monte Carlo estimates

This section begins our discussion of Monte Carlo simulation. The idea is that you create a model that generates a possible price path of the stock you're interested in. For each generated price path of the stock, you can compute the payout of the derivative contract you're pricing. Then you run the model several times and average the simulated payouts to get a Monte Carlo estimate of the contract's payoff.

To model stock price movement, you'll use so-called *geometric Brownian motion (GBM)*. We'll describe and define the Monte Carlo estimate and apply it to pricing a European call, an up-and-out barrier call, and an Asian call. Along the way, we'll also explain how to analyze the accuracy of a Monte Carlo estimate. And finally, we'll introduce a widely adopted technique for improving accuracy.

Modeling stock prices using geometric Brownian motion

If you're considering a particular option—say, a three-month European call option on a stock—the first step to price it is to model the dynamics of the stock during a certain time interval, $[0, T]$, where 0 is the current time and T is the option's expiry expressed in terms of years. In the case of a three-month option, $T = 0.25$ *years* . You then divide time interval $[0, T]$ into N periods. Each of the periods has length $\Delta t := T/N$. For $n = 0, 1, 2, \ldots, N$, let $t_n := n\Delta t$ be the nth time point. As such, you can see that $t_0 = 0$ and $t_N = T$. Assuming today's share price is known and denoted by S_{t_0}, simulating a price path means that you need to somehow simulate the following prices: $S_{t_1}, S_{t_2}, S_{t_3}, \ldots, S_{t_N}$.

To generate these prices, you have to choose a stochastic process to model the price movements of the stock. Generally speaking, a *stochastic process* is a sequence of random variables indexed by time. Each of these random variables represents the state of the stochastic process at a particular point in time. In this case, the sequence of random variables is $\{S_{t_1}, S_{t_2}, S_{t_3}, \ldots, S_{t_N}\}$. A stochastic process can be specified by doing the following:

- Giving an initial start point, which is S_{t_0} in this case
- Defining the dynamics of the stock price $\Delta S_{t_n} = S_{t_{N-1}} - S_{t_n}$

---

[1] If you omit the second line, the `Normal` class will automatically use `System.Random` by default. But to make clear which uniform random number generators are being used, we chose to explicitly state it.

[2] The `Sample` method provided by Math.NET implements a popular algorithm for normal random number generation, the polar form of the Box-Muller transform.

The idea is to define how the price changes between two consecutive time points in a path. If you can somehow sample all the differentials, $\{\Delta S_{t_0}, \Delta S_{t_1}, \Delta S_{t_2}, \ldots, \Delta S_{t_{N-1}}\}$, then you can generate a full path of share prices because you can use the generated differentials to infer all the share prices in the path.

To model stock prices, researchers and practitioners use many different types of stochastic processes. GBM is probably the most fundamental stochastic process for the purpose of derivatives pricing. In a GBM process, ΔS_{t_0} is defined by the following stochastic differential equation (SDE):

$$\Delta S_{t_0} = rS_{t_n}\Delta t + \sigma S_{t_n}\Delta W_{t_n}.$$

From this expression, you can see that ΔS_{t_n} is defined as a sum of two terms—a *drift term* ($rS_{t_n}\Delta t$) and a *diffusion term* ($\sigma S_{t_n}\Delta W_{t_n}$)—where

- r is the risk-free interest rate paid by a bank account.[3]
- σ is the annualized volatility of the stock, which is usually estimated based on historical price data of the stock and may be adjusted by traders based on their view on the market. For example, if the annualized volatility of Apple stock is 25%, it means that statistically the Apple stock might go either up or down by 25% in one year's time on average. In other words, the higher the volatility, the more volatile the stock price.
- ΔW_{t_n} is the Brownian increment at time t_n. As far as our study of Monte Carlo simulation is concerned, you can view it as a sample drawn from a normal distribution with mean 0 and variance Δt. This is designed to model the uncertainty of share-price movement.

Although the definition of ΔS_{t_n} looks simple, it's an important model that almost every textbook in mathematical finance begins with, because it captures the following realistic ideas:[4]

- Changes in a stock's price ought to be proportional to its current price level. For example, a $10 move is more likely at $S_{t_n} = 100$ than at $S_{t_n} = 20$.
- A stock's price can't go negative. If you can let Δt go infinitesimal, it can be proved that the prices modeled by a GBM process never go negative, as long as the initial price S_{t_0} is positive.

---

[3] Why must the coefficient of the drift term be the interest rate r times share price? In short, because you assume that there exists one (and only one) bank account in your model, which pays interest at rate r continuously in time, and you use the bank account as *numéraire*—that is, you measure the value of assets in terms of a bank account rather than in terms of dollars. We can't explain the entire theory in detail here. If you're interested in the theoretic details, a good book to consult is *The Concepts and Practice of Mathematical Finance, 2nd edition,* by Mark S. Joshi (Cambridge University Press, 2008).

[4] But the GBM setting for ΔS_{t_n} also has drawbacks. The most criticized one is probably the assumption of volatility σ being a constant, which is strongly inconsistent with empirical results. Quite a few models address this issue. If interested, you can look up local volatility models and stochastic volatility models. Those models can be viewed as extensions of the GBM model by allowing volatility to change in time or randomly. In particular, stochastic volatility models are the primary ones being used to price stock options in the industry.

If the description of ΔS_{t_n} makes sense to you, the next thing we'd like you to consider is that usually you don't directly simulate ΔS_{t_n}. Instead, you simulate log differential $\Delta \log S_{t_n}$, which is how the logarithm of the price evolves. You do that for a few reasons. Two of them are as follows:

- When you run a simulation, you can't let Δt go infinitesimal, not only because time complexity of the simulation may be overwhelming as Δt gets smaller and smaller, but also because all the floating-point data types you typically use to represent Δt have limited precision. Therefore, if you directly implement the definition of ΔS_{t_n}, your simulation might generate one or more negative share prices, which is definitely wrong.
- Simulating by $\Delta \log S_{t_n}$ isn't as sensitive to the choice of length Δt as directly simulating by ΔS_{t_n}.

Given this GBM definition of ΔS_{t_n}, log differential $\Delta \log S_{t_n}$ can be deduced[5] as follows:

$$\Delta \log S_{t_n} = \left(r - \frac{\sigma^2}{2}\right)\Delta t + \sigma \Delta W_{t_n}$$

This is the mathematical expression you'll implement. Neither of the two terms contains S_{t_n}, which is why simulating by $\Delta \log S_{t_n}$ is more robust. Once you've sampled all the log differentials, $\{\Delta \log S_{t_0}, \Delta \log S_{t_1}, \Delta \log S_{t_2}, \ldots, \Delta \log S_{t_{N-1}}\}$, you can recover any absolute price level S_{t_n} using the following formula:

$$S_{t_n} = S_{t_0} e^{\sum_{i=0}^{n-1} \Delta \log S_{t_i}}$$

In other words, to compute S_{t_n} you sum up all the log differentials from $\Delta \log S_{t_0}$ to $\Delta \log S_{t_{n-1}}$, exponentiate the sum, and multiply the exponentiated sum by S_{t_0}. As you can see from the expression, if you simulate by $\Delta \log S_{t_0}$ rather than ΔS_{t_n}, S_{t_n} will always stay positive, regardless of how you choose Δt, because S_{t_0} is given positive and the exponential function always returns a positive value.

Now you're ready to see how to write F# code to generate a GBM path by sampling $\Delta \log S_{t_n}$. Earlier you learned how to use the statistics functionality provided by Math.NET to generate random samples from a normal distribution with a particular mean and a particular variance. Let's use that to come up with a function that can generate ΔW_{t_n}. The function get_dW, shown in the following listing, is a higher-order function. get_dW returns a generator function, which generates N random samples from a normal distribution with mean 0 and variance Δt.

---

[5] This is the result of applying the famous Ito's Rule to the logarithm function and the GBM definition of ΔS_{t_n}.

Listing 1   Generating Brownian increments

```
let get_dW rnd dt N =
    let dW = Normal.WithMeanVariance(0.0, dt)
    dW.RandomSource <- rnd
    (fun () -> Array.init N (fun _ -> dW.Sample()))
```

> **Argument dt represents Δ*t*; argument rnd is an instance of System.Random()**

To generate a GBM path, you invoke the generator function returned by get_dW so as to generate *N* samples of ΔW_{t_n}. Once you have the initial share price S_{t_0} and *N* samples of ΔW_{t_n}, you can then infer a full stock-price path using the expression of S_{t_n} in terms of $\Delta \log S_{t_1}$. If you repeat this procedure *M* times, you can then generate *M* different paths of stock prices, which is exactly what the following function does.

Listing 2   Generating GBM paths

> **S0 is for S_{t_0}, r is for *r*, sigma is for σ, T is for *T*, N is for *N*, and M is for *M*. Only N and M are integers. rnd is an instance of System.Random(), and the rest are of type float.**

Calculates Δ*t*

Pre-computes the drift term because it doesn't change over time

```
let generate_GBM_paths_by_log rnd S0 r sigma T N M =
    let dt = T / (float N)
    let drift = (r - 0.5 * (sigma**2.0)) * dt
    let generator = get_dW rnd dt N

    Array.init M (fun _ -> generator()
                |> Array.map (fun dWt -> drift + sigma * dWt)
                |> Array.scan (+) 0.0
                |> Array.map (fun x -> S0 * exp(x)) )
```

Initializes the generator function of ΔW_{t_n}

> **Generates *M* paths, each of which consists of *N* + 1 data points, including the initial share price**

Now you're ready to generate some paths. Run the following in FSI:

```
let paths = generate_GBM_paths_by_log (new System.Random()) 50.0 0.01
    0.2 0.25 200 3;;
```

The array paths contains three different simulated stock-price paths. You can plot them using any charting software or API you like. The chart in figure 1 shows a sample

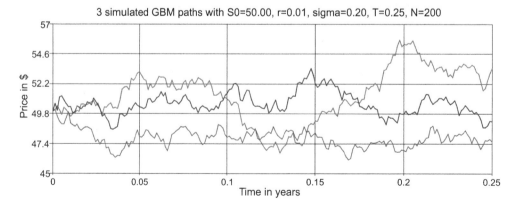

Figure 1   An example of using the generate_GBM_paths_by_log function to generate three paths of stock prices

of `paths`; we used the FSharp.Charting library to generate it, as shown in the accompanying sidebar. The chart you get will be different from this one due to randomness.

Plotting stock price paths using FSharp.Charting

FSharp.Charting, an open source charting library for F#, provides a nice interface to the data-visualization charting controls available on Windows in .NET 4.x. You can download its source from GitHub or get the binary using NuGet. The following code shows how we generated figure 1:

```
#r @"..\packages\FSharp.Charting.0.90.6\lib\net40\FSharp.Charting.dll"
#r "System.Windows.Forms.DataVisualization.dll"

open System
open System.Drawing
open FSharp.Charting

let T = 0.25
let M = 3                        Monte Carlo
let N = 200                      parameters

let S0 = 50.0                    Underlying
let sigma = 0.2                  dynamics
let r = 0.01

let plot_path (T:float) (N:int) (path:float array) color =    ← Function to generate a chart object for each price path
    let dt = T/ (float N)
    path |> Array.mapi (fun n p -> ((float n)*dt, p))
    |> Chart.Line                                             Simulates GBM paths
    |> Chart.WithStyling(Color = color, BorderWidth = 2)

let rnd = new System.Random()                                Determines the maximum and minimum for the Y-axis
let paths = generate_GBM_paths_by_log rnd S0 r sigma T N M ←

let mx, mn = paths |> Array.fold (fun (mx,mn) p ->    ←
                    (max mx (Array.max p), min mn (Array.min p)))
                    (Double.MinValue,Double.MaxValue)

let colors = [| Color.Green; Color.Red; Color.Blue |]        Assigns a color to each path chart
let path_charts = Array.map2 (plot_path T N) paths colors ←

let title = sprintf                                   ←
            "3 simulated GBM paths with S0=%.2f,       Generates the combined chart
      r=%.2f, sigma=%.2f, T=%.2f, N=%d"
            S0 r sigma T N
let chart = Chart.Combine path_charts
            |> Chart.WithStyling(Margin=(2.0, 12.0, 2.0, 2.0))
            |> Chart.WithTitle(Text=title, FontName = "Arial",
                        FontSize = 14.0, FontStyle =
                        FontStyle.Bold,
                        InsideArea = false)
            |> Chart.WithXAxis(Title="time in years", Max=T, Min=0.0,
                        TitleAlignment = StringAlignment.Center,
```

(continued)

```
|> Chart.WithYAxis(Title="price in $",
                        Max=(Math.Round(mx) + 1.0),
                        Min=(Math.Round(mn) - 1.0),
                        TitleAlignment = StringAlignment.Center,
                        TitleFontName = "Arial",
                        TitleFontSize = 14.0, TitleFontStyle =
                        FontStyle.Bold)
chart.ShowChart()
```

Now that you've learned how to simulate paths of share prices of a stock, you can use these simulated paths to price a derivative—that is, to compute the price of the derivative at time 0.

Payoff function, discounted payoff, and Monte Carlo estimates

The types of derivatives we're considering in this chapter are the ones that mature at time T, where $T > 0$, and pay only at time T a single cash flow. The amount of the cash flow at time T is contingent on how share prices evolve over the time interval $[0,T]$—that is, the actual time-T payoff of the derivative is decided by a payoff function f of x and θ, where x is a path of share prices between time 0 and T, and θ is a tuple of static parameters written in the derivative contract. Usually θ is called the *contract parameters*. The content of θ depends on the type of the derivative. If it's a European call option with strike K, then $\theta = (K)$. If it's an up-and-out barrier option with strike K and barrier H, then $\theta = (K,H)$.

Time value of money

In this chapter, we assume that there exists a bank account paying continuously compound interest at an annualized rate r, and that one dollar in the bank account today will be worth e^{rT} dollars by time T. As such, one dollar today and one dollar tomorrow aren't the same thing. Before you can compare them, you have to either discount tomorrow's one dollar back to today or compound today's one dollar to tomorrow.

When you price a derivative whose payoff occurs at time T in the future, you need to discount it back to time 0 (today) by multiplying the payoff by a discounting factor e^{-rT}. If you don't discount, you'll misprice the derivative in the sense that you admit arbitrage.

Given static parameters θ and a particular price path x, let $Y := e^{-rT} \cdot f(\theta,x)$ denote the discounted payoff for the option represented by $f(\theta,x)$. Because the entire path x is random as of time 0, Y is also a random number as of time 0. If you simulate a price path x, you can apply f to x in order to generate a sample of Y. Therefore, although you may not know exactly the probability distribution of Y, you do know how to draw a sample of it.

Let C denote the time-0 price of the derivative contract you're considering. Using the fundamental theorem of asset pricing, you know that

$$C = \mathbb{E}[Y]$$

which is the expectation[6] of Y. The problem is how to compute the expectation $\mathbb{E}[Y]$. If Y is a random variable whose distribution is known and that has a nice analytic expression for its probability density function, perhaps you can derive a closed-form solution for $\mathbb{E}[Y]$. But when either the derivative's payoff function or the dynamics of the share prices are slightly more complex or exotic, it can easily become intractable to find a closed-form solution.

Various numerical methods have been developed to tackle those scenarios where you can't easily solve for an analytic solution. Monte Carlo simulation is one of the numerical methods. The way Monte Carlo works is based on the strong law of large numbers. First, you generate M samples of Y, called Y_1, Y_2, Y_3, ..., Y_M, each of which is independently and identically distributed as Y. Then the Monte Carlo estimate of C is denoted by $\hat{C}_M$ and defined as follows:

$$\hat{C}_M := \frac{Y_1 + Y_2 + Y_3 + \dots + Y_M}{M}$$

$\hat{C}_M$ itself is also a random variable. Note that $\mathbb{E}[\hat{C}_M] = C$, so $\hat{C}_M$ is an unbiased estimator. The strong law of large number guarantees that if you use a large number of samples (M goes to ∞), the price that you calculate using the Monte Carlo method will get closer to the actual price, namely C. The more samples you draw, the better the approximation you achieve.

Before we explore the implementation of the Monte Carlo estimate, let's look at how to define the payoff function in F# for a European call option and an up-and-out barrier call option.

Listing 3 Payoff functions

```
let S_T (path:float array) = path.[path.Length - 1]

let european_call K (path:float array) =
    max ((S_T path) - K) 0.0

let up_and_out_call K H (path:float array) =
    if Array.max path.[1..] >= H then 0.0
    else european_call K path
```

Helper function to retrieve the last price of a path, S_T

Payoff function of a European call, which depends only on S_T. K is the strike of the call.

Payoff function of an up-and-out barrier call option. H is the barrier, and K is the strike. If the share price never goes beyond H by time *T* and so doesn't knock out, then the option behaves like a European call option. We'll discuss barrier options in detail later.

----

[6] To be more precise, in order to avoid arbitrage, this expectation has to be taken with respect to a risk-neutral probability measure. Although this chapter doesn't explain the concept of risk-neutral probability measures and the fundamental theorem of asset pricing, the Monte Carlo methods introduced in this chapter do price derivatives under a risk-neutral probability measure. For more details, Tomas Björk's *Arbitrage Theory in Continuous Time, 3rd Edition* (Oxford University Press, 2009) is a good source.

Note that in each of the payoff functions in listing 3, the `path` parameter appears at the rightmost position, after all contract parameters. You do this because you want the Monte Carlo simulation code to be generic, meaning you want to be able to price as many different types of payoff functions as possible. You'll use the function-currying feature of F# to apply only contract parameters to a payoff function so that you get a curried function that maps a path (represented by a float array) to a real-valued payoff (represented by a float). Then you pass in this curried function to the Monte Carlo code to draw a large number of samples of *Y*.

The next listing shows the `simulate_payoffs` function, which is responsible for generating *M* simulated payoffs—that is, *M* samples of *Y*.

Listing 4   `simulate_payoffs` function

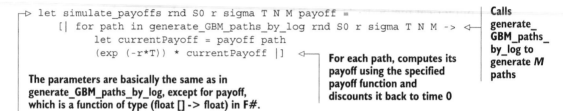

```
let simulate_payoffs rnd S0 r sigma T N M payoff =                       Calls
    [| for path in generate_GBM_paths_by_log rnd S0 r sigma T N M ->     generate_
        let currentPayoff = payoff path                                  GBM_paths_
        (exp (-r*T)) * currentPayoff |]                                  by_log to
                                                                         generate M
                                          For each path, computes its    paths
The parameters are basically the same as in   payoff using the specified
generate_GBM_paths_by_log, except for payoff, payoff function and
which is a function of type (float [] -> float) in F#.  discounts it back to time 0
```

Although the function is called `simulate_payoffs`, it returns an array of "discounted" payoffs, because you multiply each payoff by the discounting factor `exp(-r*T)`.

You may be wondering why we chose to discount each individual payoff sample rather than take their average first and then discount the average. Yes, it should run faster and give the same result if you factor out the discounting factor. The reason we chose to discount each sample before taking their average is that it's easier to measure the accuracy of the Monte Carlo simulation, as covered in more detail later in this chapter.

The `simulate_payoffs` function will generate the samples in the numerator of $\hat{C}_M$, so what's left is to take an average of those samples. And that's the purpose of the `price_option` function.

Listing 5   `price_option` function

```
                                                    Parameters are basically the
                                                    same as in simulate_payoffs
let price_option rnd S0 r sigma T N M payoff =
    simulate_payoffs rnd S0 r sigma T N M payoff
    |> Array.average                                    Calls simulate
                                                        _payoffs to generate
                            Takes the average of the    M simulated payoffs
                            M discounted payoffs
```

The output of the `price_option` function is exactly $\hat{C}_M$. Now you're ready to price some options. Let's start with a European call option on a stock with strike $K = 100.0$ and expiry $T = 0.25$ years. The dynamics of the stock follow a GBM with spot price $S_{t_0} = 100.0$, an interest rate of $r = 2\%$, and annualized volatility of $\sigma = 40\%$. For Monte Carlo simulation, you need to choose N (how many data points to sample in a path) and M (how many paths to simulate).

A European call is a typical example of non-path-dependent options, so you need to simulate only the final share prices—that is, the share prices at expiry—and therefore you can set $N = 1$. For M, let's start with $M = 10,000$. You can then run the simulation in FSI as follows:

```
let K, T = 100.0, 0.25
let S0, r, sigma = 100.0, 0.02, 0.40
let N, M = 1, 10000
let rnd = new System.Random()
let payoff = european_call K
let C = price_option rnd S0 r sigma T N M payoff
```

The c value on the last line is a draw of the random variable $\hat{C}_M$. After running the code snippet, the option price c should be around 8.11849. How precise is this pricing result? Fortunately you can use the famous Black–Scholes pricing formula[7] for this European call scenario. If you substitute in all the parameters, including K, T, S0, r, and sigma, to the formula, the theoretic, correct option price C should be $8.19755. The difference is about $0.079.

To improve the accuracy of the simulation, what should you do? In this case, because the call option you're looking at relies only on the final share price, increasing N doesn't help. But as implied by the strong law of large numbers, increasing M does help improve the accuracy of the simulation results. Let's try different Ms from 10,000 to 10,000,000 and compare the simulation results to the theoretic price C:

	$\hat{C}_M$	Absolute difference between $\hat{C}_M$ and C
$M = 10,000$	8.11849	0.07906
$M = 100,000$	8.17003	0.02753
$M = 1,000,000$	8.21121	0.01366
$M = 10,000,000$	8.19100	0.00656

The results show a clear trend that $\hat{C}_M$ does get closer to the true price C as you increase M, which is consistent with our expectation. Because an analytic formula exists for pricing a European call on a stock following GBM dynamics, and it can compute the true price in no time, you don't need to run a CPU-and-memory-bound application like a Monte Carlo simulation to price the call option. But it's good practice to start out with something whose true price you do know, so you can use it as a sanity check to see if your Monte Carlo code works as expected.

In this example, you measure the simulation accuracy by taking the absolute difference between $\hat{C}_M$ and C, because you knew the true value of C. But more often

---

[7] See "Black–Scholes model," *Wikipedia*, http://en.wikipedia.org/wiki/Black-scholes.

than not, you'll have scenarios where there's no analytic solution available, and numerical methods like Monte Carlo simulation are the only means to compute or approximate C. In such cases, you typically don't know the true value of C and can't compute the difference. How do you measure simulation accuracy in those cases? Let's discuss this topic in the next section.

Analyzing Monte Carlo estimates using variance

As mentioned, in general you can't directly measure the difference between a Monte Carlo estimate $\hat{C}_M$ and the true value C. What else can you do to measure the accuracy of $\hat{C}_M$? Recall that the Monte Carlo estimate $\hat{C}_M$ itself is a random variable, so you observe a different value of $\hat{C}_M$ every time you run a new simulation, even if all the parameters remain the same. But you want the range of the values coming out of $\hat{C}_M$ to be in some sense as narrow as possible. One of the ways to achieve that is to increase M. When M is large, you'll probably observe that the first few digits of the values drawn out of $\hat{C}_M$ are somewhat stabilized—that is, they almost don't change. How do you measure the "narrow-ness"?

The answer is the standard error of $\hat{C}_M$, which is the square root of the variance estimate of $\hat{C}_M$. Let ε_M and $\mathrm{Var}(\hat{C}_M)$ denote the standard error and variance estimate of $\hat{C}_M$, respectively. Then ε_M and $\mathrm{Var}(\hat{C}_M)$ can be computed as follows

$$\varepsilon_M = \sqrt{\mathrm{Var}(\hat{C}_M)} = \sqrt{\frac{\hat{\sigma}_M^2}{M}}$$

where

$$\hat{\sigma}_M^2 := \frac{1}{M-1} \sum_{m=1}^{M} (Y_m - \hat{C}_M)^2$$

Basically, $\hat{\sigma}_M^2$ is nothing but the sample variance of the random variable Y (the discounted payoff). Before we delve into any more theoretical discussions, let's see how to enhance the price_option function you wrote in the previous section to compute $\hat{\sigma}_M^2$ and the standard error ε_M. The following listing shows the new version of price_option.

> **Listing 6 price_option_v2 function**

All the parameters are the same as in price_option.

```
let price_option_v2 rnd S0 r sigma T N M payoff =
    let Ys = simulate_payoffs rnd S0 r sigma T N M payoff
    let C_estimate = Ys |> Array.average
    let Y_var = Ys.Variance()
    let std_error = sqrt(Y_var / (float M))
    (C_estimate, Y_var, std_error)
```

Invokes simulate_payoffs to generate M simulated payoffs

Invokes the extension method Variance() provided by MathNET to compute $\hat{\sigma}_M^2$

Computes ε_M

Computes $\hat{C}_M$

With the new `price_option_v2` function, run the test with the same parameters you used the previous section. The only difference is that this time you'll use `price_option_v2` instead of `price_option`. The following table shows the new output from the `price_option_v2` function. (We didn't fix the seed of `System.Random()`, so the results of the option prices will differ slightly from those in the previous section.)

	$\hat{C}_M$	$\hat{\sigma}_M^2$	ε_M
$M = 10,000$	8.35733	177.43527	0.13320
$M = 100,000$	8.15513	176.43275	0.04200
$M = 1,000,000$	8.20136	177.21966	0.01331
$M = 10,000,000$	8.19788	177.40473	0.00421

When M is large enough, $\hat{\sigma}_M^2$ approaches the true variance of Y, which is a constant that's usually unknown; therefore you need to estimate it by $\hat{\sigma}_M^2$. Unlike ε_M, the expectation of $\hat{\sigma}_M^2$ doesn't depend on M. As you can see from the table, the observed values of $\hat{\sigma}_M^2$ stay close to the same level across different Ms, whereas ε_M shrinks at a rate of $\sqrt{10}$ when you increase M by 10 times. The point is that if you view $\hat{\sigma}_M^2$ as a constant (in an approximate sense), then $\text{Var}(\hat{C}_M)$ is a constant divided by M. As such, when M gets larger, the standard error ε_M gets smaller. This explains why a large M can help improve the accuracy of Monte Carlo simulation.

You can see that the time cost of improving accuracy by increasing M is high. If you want to reduce the standard error by one digit, you have to run 100 more simulations by comparing $M = 10,000$ to $M = 1000,000$ and $M = 100,000$ to $M = 10,000,000$. Therefore, it's natural for researchers to come up with alternatives to reduce standard error. Instead of manipulating M, the denominator of $\text{Var}(\hat{C}_M)$, those alternatives tweak the numerator, $\hat{\sigma}_M^2$. They reformulate Y in such a way that the expectation of $\hat{C}_M$ remains the same but the theoretic variance of Y becomes smaller. As a result, both $\hat{\sigma}_M^2$ and the standard error ε_M also get smaller. Those alternatives are known as *variance-reduction techniques*. You'll see a variance-reduction technique used in a later section, but let's first try to price other types of stock options.

Pricing path-dependent options

In this section, we'll explore Asian options and barrier options. These options are all European style, meaning they make only one payment at expiry to the option holder and have no early-exercise feature. They're considered path-dependent, because, unlike European call options, their final payoffs depend on not only the final price of the underlying but also the prices observed at a set of prespecified intermediate times between now and expiry. Even if two paths end up at the same final price, any discrepancies at prespecified observation times could result in very different payoffs at expiry.

PRICING ASIAN OPTIONS

First let's discuss Asian options. The word *Asian* here means that option payoffs involve averaging observed prices. There are quite a few variants of Asian options, and we have to be very specific about what Asian option we're discussing in this section. Assume that today is the first day of the month, and you're considering a particular Asian call option on a GBM underlying *S* with expiry *T*, strike *K*, and payoff as follows:

$$\left(\frac{S_{t_1} + S_{t_2} + S_{t_3}}{3} - K\right)^+ \text{ where } t_1 = \frac{1}{3}T, \ t_2 = \frac{2}{3}T, \ t_3 = T$$

If you assume $T = 0.25$ years (3 months), the payoff at expiry averages three monthly close prices[8] and takes the positive part of the average minus fixed strike *K*. As you might expect, unlike pricing a European call, to price this particular Asian option you have to simulate not only the final price at time t_3 but the two prices at times t_1 and t_2. Based on the code you've seen so far, how do you make sure you simulate the average of prices at the three time points? The easiest way is probably to set $N = 3$ (so that $\Delta t = T/3$) and code the Asian payoff function as shown next.

Listing 7   asian_call function

```
let asian_call K (path:float array) =
    let S_avg = path.[1..] |> Array.average
    max (S_avg - K) 0.0
```

Uses the array-slicing feature to exclude S_{T0} and then takes the average of the rest

Computes the Asian call payoff

If the Asian option designates *l* equally spaced observation times, the path array should contain exactly *l* +1 elements, because the first element is S_{T0}. In the case, you're looking at *l* = 3.

You're ready for testing. Price the Asian call using the following parameters: $S_{t_0} = 100$, $r = 2\%$, $\sigma = 40\%$, $T = 0.25$, $K = 100$, $N = 3$, and $M = 10,000,000$. These parameters are much the same as the ones you've been using so far, except that now you set $N = 3$. The F# code for the Asian call test is as follows:

```
> let K, T = 100.0, 0.25
  let S0, r, sigma = 100.0, 0.02, 0.4
  let N, M = 3, 10000000
  let rnd = new System.Random()
  let payoff = asian_call K;;
(...)

> let (C,Y_var,std_error) = price_option_v2 rnd S0 r sigma T N M payoff
  ;;
Real: 00:00:22.677, CPU: 00:00:22.323, GC gen0: 984, gen1: 223, gen2: 1

val std_error : float = 0.00295
val Y_var : float = 86.75458
val C : float = 5.88672
```

---

[8] In reality, the observation times may or may not be equally spaced within the option's life. But it's not difficult to change your code to handle unevenly spaced observation times.

The simulation says that the Asian option is worth about $5.88672 as of today. How do you verify this pricing result? Unfortunately, there's currently no close-form solution available for computing true prices of arithmetic averaging Asian options. Although you can't know the true price for certain, academic research over the past two decades has provided analytic formulas for approximating the true price or inferring tight lower or upper bounds.

Another validation technique involves comparing the simulation results with the ones computed by other numerical methods, such as finite difference methods. Although we can't go into depth on the topic of analytic approximation or other numerical methods, there's still one simple sanity check you can do. If you compare the results of the Asian call to the prices of the European call you computed in the previous section, you can see that they share the same parameters. But due to the averaging nature, the price of the Asian call should be smaller than that of the European call—which is the case, as you can see from the numerical results.

PRICING BARRIER OPTIONS

Now let's move on to barrier options. There are quite a few different types of barrier options. Our example is an up-and-out barrier option with discrete observation times, meaning the option contract designates a barrier H and a finite set of times; at each time, the underlying price is observed to determine if the price has reached or gone beyond H.

If the stock price reaches or exceeds H, the option is worthless and terminates immediately, which constitutes a *knock-out event*. If the option survives all observation times, it pays a European call payoff at expiry. Assume that this example is a newly issued barrier option with expiry $T = 0.25$ *years* = 3 *months*, a monthly observation schedule of ($t_1 = \frac{1}{3}T$, $t_2 = \frac{2}{3}T$, $t_3 = T$), barrier $H = 125$, and strike $K = 100$. Therefore, the option's payoff can be expressed as follows:

The option pays nothing if $S_{t_i} \geq H$ for any t_i, otherwise it pays $(S_T - K)^+$ at time T.

As in the previous Asian option example, you need to sample at three time points in each price path. These three time points are equally spaced, so you need to set $N = 3$. Earlier, listing 3 showed a few payoffs in F#, and one of them was for the barrier option. For convenience, let's isolate the barrier option payoff in the next listing and discuss it in greater detail.

Listing 8 up_and_out_call function

```
let up_and_out_call K H (path:float array) =
    if Array.max path.[1..] >= H
    then 0.0 else european_call K path
```

If the barrier option designates *I* observation times, the path array should contain exactly *I* +1 elements.

Computes the final payoff if the option survives

Uses the array-slicing syntax to exclude S_{T0}, and checks if the option has knocked out

As with the Asian call earlier, listing 8 uses these parameters: $S_{t_0} = 100$, $r = 2\%$, $\sigma = 40\%$, $T = 0.25$, $K = 100$, $N = 3$, and $M = 10,000,000$, along with a barrier parameter, $H = 125$. The F# code for the up-and-out barrier call test is as follows:

```
> let K, T = 100.0, 0.25
  let S0, r, sigma = 100.0, 0.02, 0.4
  let N, M = 3, 10000000
  let H = 125.0
  let rnd = new System.Random()
  let payoff = up_and_out_call K H;;
(...)

> let (C,Y_var,std_error) = price_option_v2 rnd S0 r sigma T N M payoff;;

Real: 00:00:23.785, CPU: 00:00:22.557, GC gen0: 905, gen1: 263, gen2: 3

val std_error : float = 0.00194
val Y_var : float = 37.58121
val C : float = 3.30157
```

Similar to Asian options, there's currently no analytic formula for discretely monitored barrier options, so you can't compare the pricing result to a true answer. Closed-form solutions for continuously monitored barrier options do exist, which you can apply together with the BGK barrier-adjustment formula to approximate the prices of discretely monitored barrier options. Also, a barrier call option should be cheaper than a European call option with the same parameters (except the barrier). In addition, you can set an extremely high barrier relative to the spot price S_{t_0} so that it's almost impossible for the barrier option to knock out. In this case, an up-and-out barrier call behaves like a European call.

> **Up-and-in barrier call**
>
> You can modify listing 8 to implement the payoff function for up-and-in barrier calls. As its name suggests, an up-and-in barrier call pays nothing at expiry if the price of the underlying stock never exceeds the barrier *H*; otherwise, it behaves like a European call. When pricing an up-and-in barrier call, keep in mind that a portfolio of one up-and-in and one up-and-out should behave like a European call, provided that both the up-and-in and up-and-out share the same strike, barrier, and expiry.

Variance reduction using antithetic variates

So far you've used the ordinary Monte Carlo estimate to price a European call option, an Asian call option, and an up-and-out barrier call option. You also computed their standard errors—the square root of the simulation variance. As mentioned earlier, in addition to increasing the number of simulation trials, you can take advantage of variance-reduction techniques, which may reduce simulation variance without having to increase the number of trials. Let's explore the antithetic variates (AV) method, which is widely adopted in the industry.

Recall that for $m = 1,2,...,M$, in order to sample Y_m, the mth draw of discounted payoff Y, you have to sample a price path x_m, which is determined by a vector of draws from Brownian motion W. Let $Z_m = (dW^m_{t_1}, dW^m_{t_2}, ..., dW^m_{t_N})$ denote the vector. Then you can say that Y_m is ultimately a function of Z_m. Using the AV method, you follow these steps:

1. Generate M samples of Z_m. For each Z_m sample, negate each of its elements. Let $\tilde{Z}_m = (-dW^m_{t_1}, -dW^m_{t_2}, ..., -dW^m_{t_N})$ be the negated vector.
2. For each pair of Z_m and $\tilde{Z}_m$, generate two paths, x_m and $\tilde{x}_m$ respectively.
3. For each pair of x_m and $\tilde{x}_m$, compute discounted payoffs Y_m and $\tilde{Y}_m$, respectively.
4. For each pair of Y_m and $\tilde{Y}_m$, take the average of them. Let $Y^{AV}_m = (Y_m + \tilde{Y}_m)/2$.
5. As in the ordinary Monte Carlo method, take the average of all Y^{AV}_m samples, which is the AV Monte Carlo estimate for the true price. Let $\hat{C}^{AV}_M = (Y^{AV}_1 + Y^{AV}_2 + ... + Y^{AV}_M)/M$.

Next let's compare the AV method and the ordinary Monte Carlo method in terms of expectation and variance. As you can see from the previous steps, in order to compute $\hat{C}^{AV}_M$, you use $2M$ paths, although half of them are deliberately set up and thus negatively correlated to the other half. As such, it may be fairer or make more sense to compare $\hat{C}^{AV}_M$ against $\hat{C}_{2M}$ instead of $\hat{C}_M$.

Now let's look at expectation and variance of the AV estimate $\hat{C}^{AV}_M$. It can be mathematically proven that $\mathbb{E}[\hat{C}^{AV}_M] = C = \mathbb{E}[\hat{C}_{2M}]$, so the AV estimate $\hat{C}^{AV}_M$, like the ordinary estimate $\hat{C}_{2M}$, is also an unbiased estimate for the true price C. As for how the AV estimate $\hat{C}^{AV}_M$ can reach a smaller standard error or equivalently a lower variance, the reasoning is that because Z_m and $\tilde{Z}_m$ are negatively correlated, we hope[9] Y_m and $\tilde{Y}_m$ are also negatively correlated; the negative correlation between Y_m and $\tilde{Y}_m$ can make the variance of Y^{AV}_m smaller than that of Y_m, and as a result, $\mathrm{Var}(\hat{C}^{AV}_M)$ should be less than $\mathrm{Var}(\hat{C}_{2M})$, which is our ultimate goal.

To implement the AV method, you need to revise three of the functions: `generate_GBM_paths_by_log`, `simulate_payoffs`, and `price_option_v2`. The following listing shows the new version of `generate_GBM_paths_by_log`.

Listing 9 `generate_GBM_paths_by_log_AV` function

```
let generate_GBM_paths_by_log_AV rnd S0 r sigma T N M =          ⟵ Same parameters as
    let dt = T / (float N)                                          generate_GBM_paths
    let drift = (r - 0.5 * (sigma**2.0)) * dt                       _by_log
    let dW = get_dW rnd dt N
    let dWs = Array.init M (fun _ -> dW())          ⟵ Generates M samples of Zm
    let negated_dWs =
        dWs |> Array.map (fun x ->        ⟵ For each Zm, generates
            x |> Array.map (fun y -> -y))      its negated sample Z̃m
```

---

[9] Why "hope" here? Because the negative correlation between Z_m and $\tilde{Z}_m$ alone isn't sufficient to guarantee that Y_m and $\tilde{Y}_m$ are also negatively correlated. The correlation between Y_m and $\tilde{Y}_m$ is also determined by the shape of the payoff function we're considering. If the payoff function is symmetric, applying the AV method may lead to a worse result—that is, $\mathrm{Var}(\hat{C}^{AV}_M) > \mathrm{Var}(\hat{C}_{2M})$.

Generates and returns M pairs of $(Y_m, \tilde{Y}_m)$

```
let generate_path dWs =
    dWs
    |> Array.map (fun dWt -> drift + sigma * dWt)
    |> Array.scan (+) 0.0
    |> Array.map (fun x -> S0 * exp(x))
Array.map2 (fun x y -> (generate_path x, generate_path y))
    dWs negated_dWs
```

Defines a function (generate_path) that takes either Z_m or $\tilde{Z}_m$ and returns a GBM path

So the generate_GBM_paths_by_log_AV function implements steps 1 and 2 of the AV method. You can then invoke it to generate a pair of AV paths and plot them like the chart in figure 2. The green and red paths are generated based on Z_1 and $\tilde{Z}_1$ respectively; the colors aren't visible in the printed book, but the Z_1-based path is higher than the $\tilde{Z}_1$-based path for all but the first 0.25 years. The paths look negatively correlated, as expected.

The next listing shows the new versions of the other two functions, simulate_payoffs and price_option_v2.

Listing 10   simulate_payoffs_AV and price_option_v2_AV

Same parameters as simulate _payoffs

```
let simulate_payoffs_AV rnd S0 r sigma T N M payoff =
    generate_GBM_paths_by_log_AV rnd S0 r sigma T N M
    |> Array.map (fun (x,y) ->
        0.5*((payoff x)+(payoff y))*(exp (-r*T)))
```

Invokes the new generate_GBM_paths_ by_log_AV function

Computes and returns an array of Y_m^{AV}

Same parameters as price_ option_v2

```
let price_option_v2_AV rnd S0 r sigma T N M payoff =
    let Ys = simulate_payoffs_AV rnd S0 r sigma T N M payoff
    let C_estimate = Ys |> Array.average
    let Y_var = Ys.Variance()
    let std_error = sqrt(Y_var / (float M))
    (C_estimate, Y_var, std_error)
```

Invokes the new simulate_payoffs _AV function

As you can see in listing 10, there aren't many changes to the regular simulate_payoffs and price_option_v2 functions. The new versions implement steps 3, 4, and 5 of the AV method. Before you test the AV code, let's summarize the numerical results that

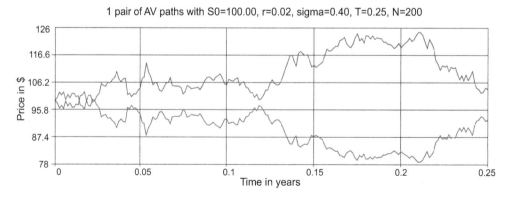

1 pair of AV paths with S0=100.00, r=0.02, sigma=0.40, T=0.25, N=200

Figure 2   An example of using the generate_GBM_paths_by_log_AV function to generate one pair of AV paths

you received in the previous sections using the regular estimate $\hat{C}_{2M}$. Let M be 5,000,000, so $2M = 10,000,000$ is exactly the number of paths you used previously:

	$\hat{C}_{2M}$	$\hat{\sigma}^2_{2M}$	ε_{2M}	Real runtime
European call	8.19788	177.40473	0.00421	19.777
Asian call	5.88672	86.75458	0.00295	22.677
Barrier call	3.30157	37.58121	0.00194	23.785

Now let's apply the new AV estimate $\hat{C}^{AV}_M$ to the same options. Here are the results:

	$\hat{C}^{AV}_M$	$\hat{\sigma}^{AV^2}_M$	ε^{AV}_M	Real runtime
European call	8.19666	54.99928	0.00332	21.713
Asian call	5.88884	26.02977	0.00228	24.466
Barrier call	3.29941	13.33717	0.00163	26.753

By comparing these two tables, you can observe the following:

- For option prices, both the regular estimate and the AV estimate produce much the same results.
- For standard error ε, ε^{AV}_M improves by 15–22% against ε_{2M}. (Take the European call as an example: $100\% - (0.00332 / 0.00421) \times 100\% = 21.14\%$.)

You may also notice that the AV estimate took about 10% more time to compute compared to the regular estimate. Therefore, you may feel that the AV estimate didn't do a good job, because you might suppose that if you chose to increase the number of paths for $\hat{C}_{2M}$ by 10%, simulation accuracy of the regular estimate in terms of standard error would probably be as good as or only slightly worse than that of the AV estimate. In other words, you might think the AV estimate could do better because it took more time.

Let's interpret the two tables in another way by answering the following question: if you want ordinary estimate $\hat{C}_{2M}$ to achieve the same level of standard error as $\hat{C}^{AV}_M$, how many paths do you have to generate? You can estimate the answer using the following formula:

$$2M = \frac{\hat{\sigma}^2_{2M}}{\varepsilon^{AV^2}_M}$$

This formula involves nothing but rearranging the definition of standard error, which we discussed earlier. Let's take the European call as an example: $2M = 177.40473 / (0.00332 \times 0.00332) = 16,094,928$, so you need 60% $((16,094,928 - 10,000,000) / 10,000,000 \cong 60\%)$ more paths, and thus roughly 60% more runtime, to match the accuracy of the AV estimate. If you do the same calculation for Asian and barrier calls, you'll see that you need 66% and 41% more paths, respectively. As a result, you'll see that the AV method does a good job in terms of reducing simulation variance.

Replacing GBM with the Heston model

In this chapter, we use GBM to model the dynamics of share prices. But GBM can't produce volatility skews and thus isn't realistic enough. In plain English, this means GBM can't explain a phenomenon in the market (or a common perception in people's mind): "The bull walks up the stairs; the bear jumps out the window." This issue can be addressed by local volatility models or stochastic volatility models.

The Heston (1993) model is one of the stochastic volatility models used in the industry. As the name suggests, it allows the volatility σ to be stochastic—that is, the volatility σ has its own dynamics. In most cases, the dynamics of σ is set to be negatively correlated with the dynamics of share price, so that when you see a large volatility, it's more likely to be used to have the share price go down rather than up. If you're interested in implementing the Heston model, a good book to consult is *Monte Carlo Methods in Financial Engineering* by Paul Glasserman (Springer, 2003). Note that you need to know how to draw correlated bivariate normals in order to simulate Heston dynamics.

Summary

This chapter explored Monte Carlo simulation. You learned how to write F# code to compute a Monte Carlo estimate, analyze its accuracy, and improve accuracy by using a variance-reduction technique. Monte Carlo simulation is widely used in science and engineering, so the concepts and techniques we discussed are applicable not only to finance but to many other areas as well.

 In this chapter, you simulated stock-price paths and derivative payoffs. You saw how higher-order functions and function currying can help you write generic code to price different types of derivatives. Furthermore, F#'s built-in support for pipelining and array processing can make your code more concise and expressive. Compared to other advanced features of F# you'll learn in this book, the functional features used in this chapter are relatively basic but can prove handy when you're writing code for numerical computations.

About the author

Chao-Jen Chen is a quantitative analyst at the fixed income trading desk of an insurance company and an instructor in the Financial Mathematics Program of the University of Chicago's Preparation Course held at its Singapore Campus. He teaches calculus, probability, linear algebra, and MATLAB with a focus in finance. He's also a senior teaching assistant in the Financial Mathematics Program, mainly responsible for running review classes for courses, including option pricing, numerical methods, and computing in F# and C++. Previously, he worked at the Structured Trade Review group of Credit Suisse AG, where he was the team lead of the Emerging Market sector and was responsible for the verification of model appropriateness and trade economics for all structured products traded in emerging markets, including structured loans, credit derivatives, fixed income derivatives, and foreign exchange derivatives.

Chao-Jen holds an undergraduate degree in mathematics (National Tsing Hua University) and postgraduate degrees in industrial engineering (National Taiwan University) and financial mathematics (University of Chicago). He has a long-term interest in computer programming, operations research, and quantitative finance. Chao-Jen writes a blog at http://programmingcradle.blogspot.com, and he can be reached via email at ccj@uchicago.edu.

5 Understanding social networks

Evelina Gabasova

Social networks play an important role in our society. When we look at the community of people who are using F#, Twitter plays an important role. People communicate and make interesting posts on Twitter. In this chapter, I'll go through a basic exploratory analysis of a part of the F# community that is active on Twitter.

Social network analysis is helpful in analyzing how groups work, the relations within groups, and how information spreads within a community of people. It can also help you identify people who are important or influential within a community.

Throughout this chapter, you'll download data from Twitter with help from the F# JSON type provider. Then we'll look at the structure of the network and compute some basic network characteristics. You'll also visualize the entire network with D3.js and use R provider for other descriptive plots. Finally, you'll implement the PageRank algorithm, which is a good measure of importance or centrality of nodes in a network. This way, you'll identify the most important people in the F# community on Twitter, according to their social connections.

Analyzing a social network can give you important information about online communities. For example, let's say you want to advertise a new product to a specific group of people. After you perform some network analysis, you can identify which people are central and most influential in the community. You can then target these specific people, and the information should spread throughout the group. You can get a good idea about the importance of people in a community purely by looking at the structure and connectivity of a network. You can also identify sub-communities in a larger social group, which may have different characteristics that can be used in advertising and marketing.

F# provides a great tool for doing all the necessary steps of exploratory data analysis. You can download and preprocess the data, compute basic characteristics of a network, look at the data in a few plots, and implement more advanced algorithms using the data. Thanks to F# type providers, you can directly work with JSON data files and call statistical and plotting functions from R. This makes F# a good

98

tool for fast exploratory data-centric analysis: you can quickly access different data sources and run analyses without having to change environment.

Social networks on Twitter

Twitter is a service that allows people to share *tweets*: short messages of up to 140 characters. To receive messages that a specific user is sharing, you can follow the user. The act of following is asymmetric; a user can follow other users without their mutual acceptance. Followers merely express shared interests; Twitter connections don't necessarily represent real-world friendships.

These factors make Twitter a good place to start with social network analysis. The nature of Twitter is open, and most of the tweets and connections are public and accessible through the API. Because people group around their shared interests, you can easily extract social networks between people.

You'll first create a network model for Twitter. A standard network is formed of nodes and links between them. The links can be either undirected or directed, with a specific orientation that's usually shown with an arrow. You're modeling a social network between users, so nodes in the network represent the users. Connections between them form the links. The direction of a link is important on Twitter because it represents the act of following. For this reason, you'll use a directed network to represent the Twitter community. On the other hand, if you wanted to represent standard connections on Facebook, you'd choose an undirected network, because those friendships are symmetric and don't have a specific orientation.

Throughout this chapter, you'll look at part of the active F# community on Twitter. You'll concentrate on the social network that exists around the account of the F# Software Foundation, @fsharporg (see figure 1). The foundation is an organization that promotes and advances the F# language and supports the F# community. This is a good starting point for an exploratory analysis of the F# community on Twitter. You can expect that people who follow this account are interested in F# and that most of them are actively involved in the F# online community. This network won't include all people interested in F# on Twitter, but it probably includes a reasonable proportion of them.

The community around @fsharporg is formed by people/accounts who follow @fsharporg or whom @fsharporg follows. You'll download a list of such accounts using the Twitter API and extract connections between them. This will form the F# social network that you'll analyze in this chapter.

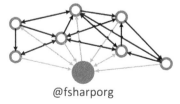

@fsharporg

Figure 1 **You'll analyze the social network around the F# Software Foundation's Twitter account, @fsharporg. Nodes in the network are user accounts that either are followers or are being followed by the @fsharporg account. Links are the connections between these users.**

Connecting to Twitter

In this section, we'll look at how to connect to Twitter from an F# application using the `FSharp.Data.Toolbox` Twitter provider. The first step in connecting to Twitter is to obtain an API key that will identify your application and authorize it to access tweets and user data. Then you'll use the Twitter provider to send requests to the Twitter API to obtain information about users connected to the F# Software Foundation.

If you want to work through this section of the chapter, you'll need to log in to your Twitter account (or open a new account). Twitter requires developers to register applications that want to connect to the Twitter API at Twitter Apps (https://apps.twitter.com/). During the registration process, you have to supply a name and purpose for the application. The application can then access your Twitter account and all other Twitter content. After registering, you receive two authorization details: an API key and an API secret. The key is used to connect to Twitter, and the secret is used to sign the request. The connection is done via the OAuth authorization framework.

Twitter offers two authentication types that give access to different sets of API requests they can send. There are also different limits on the number of possible requests per time window for each of the two methods.

The simplest method is application-only access. It requires only the application key and secret. This type of authentication can access friends and followers and search within tweets.

The second type of access requires full OAuth authentication with an explicit sign-in from a Twitter user. The application then gets full access on behalf of the user and can, for example, search for users and post tweets on behalf of the registered user.

For the purpose of this chapter, you'll use requests that require application-only access, although full access gives a higher rate of possible requests. You can find more information about both types of access in the `FSharp.Data.Toolbox` documentation and the official Twitter API documentation.

Listing 1 Connecting to Twitter

```
let key = "CoqmPIJ553Tuwe2eQgfKA"                          Authentication details
let secret = "dhaad3d7DreAFBPawEIbzesS1F232FnDsuWWwRTUg"   obtained from Twitter

let twitter = Twitter.AuthenticateAppOnly(key, secret)     Application-only
                                                           authentication

let connector = Twitter.Authenticate(key, secret)
let twitter = connector.Connect("8319329")
                                                    Full authentication: the
      After sign-in, Twitter provides a PIN        Twitter sign-in window
      that is passed to the Connect method.        appears, and you can log
                                                    in to your account.
```

After you connect to Twitter, you obtain a Twitter context in the variable `twitter`. You use the Twitter provider from `FSharp.Data.Toolbox` to send requests to Twitter and parse the response. This provider is a light wrapper around actual HTTP requests to the Twitter API. Twitter responds to requests with JSON documents containing the requested data. The F# Data Toolbox library then uses the JSON type

Figure 2   Twitter terms for different types of connections. Followers of @fsharporg are accounts that follow @fsharporg. Friends are accounts that @fsharporg itself follows.

provider to get statically typed access to the data and exposes this statically typed view of the response.

Downloading the social network around the F# Software Foundation

As I've described, you'll download the social network around the F# Software Foundation's account, @fsharporg. The Twitter documentation uses a specific terminology for social connections in its network. When an account follows @fsharporg, it's called a *follower*. On the other hand, if an account is being followed by @fsharporg, it's called a *friend*. Figure 2 illustrates these two relations.

Now that you know the terminology, you can say that nodes in the network are the followers and friends of @fsharporg. Links are the relations between these friends and followers. This way, you get a closed group of users around @fsharporg. I don't include the actual @fsharporg node in the network because it would be connected to all the nodes and wouldn't give you any additional insight.

Using the Twitter API provider and the Twitter context you opened in listing 1, you can directly download friends and followers of a specific account:

```
let friends =
    twitter.Connections.FriendsIds(screenName="@fsharporg")    ←   Gets friends of
                                                                    @fsharporg
let followers =                                                     (accounts that
    twitter.Connections.FollowerIds(screenName="@fsharporg")        @fsharporg
                                                                    follows)
let idsOfInterest = Seq.append friends.Ids followers.Ids |> set    ←
```

Gets followers of @fsharporg

Creates a set of Twitter ID numbers from friends and followers that will form nodes in the social network

The functions `twitter.Connections.FriendsIds` and `twitter.Connections.Follower-Ids` take the screen name of the F# Software Foundation and return JSON documents that contain a list of Twitter ID numbers of friends and followers. Twitter IDs are unique numbers that are assigned to users when they register. Because users can change their screen names, Twitter uses the IDs as unique identifiers of accounts.

After downloading the ID numbers, you extract them from the JSON object and collect them into an immutable set, `idsOfInterest`. Because the set doesn't allow duplicate entries, you automatically include accounts that are both friends and followers of @fsharporg only once:

```
> follows.Ids.Length;;
val it : int = 16
> followedBy.Ids.Length;;
val it : int = 1100
> idsOfInterest.Count;;
val it : int = 1109
```

At the time of writing, @fsharporg followed 16 accounts and had 1,100 followers. When combined, you have 1,109 total users in the network around @fsharporg.

Nodes in the Twitter network

The ID numbers in `idsOfInterest` now become the nodes in your social network. Although Twitter uses IDs to identify accounts, they aren't very informative. You would like to also get the user names that belong to those ID numbers. Unfortunately, Twitter doesn't give you this information directly—you have to ask for it in a separate request. The following listing shows how to download information about Twitter users using the `Lookup` function.

Listing 2   Twitter screen names from user ID numbers

```
let groupedIds =
    idsOfInterest
    |> Seq.mapi (fun i id -> i/100, id)
    |> Seq.groupBy fst

let twitterNodes =
    [| for _, group in groupedIds do
        let ids = Seq.map snd group
        let nodeInfo =
            twitter.Users.Lookup(ids)
            |> Array.map (fun node -> node.Id, node.ScreenName)
        yield! nodeInfo |]
```

Gets user ID numbers for each group **1**

One Twitter lookup request can contain up to 100 users. So, split the set of Twitter ID numbers into groups of 100.

Downloads information on nodes in the @fsharporg network from the grouped IDs

2 Lookup request to Twitter for data about the 100 users

After Twitter responds, you extract the Twitter screen name for each user. **3**

Because you can send a lookup request for up to 100 accounts at a time, you first group the IDs of interest into groups. You have 1,109 IDs, so you need 12 groups **1**. You then send a lookup request for each group separately **2**. After Twitter returns the requested data, you extract and return the screen name for each ID **3**.

There's one thing you need to keep in mind when getting information through the Twitter API: Twitter limits the number of requests allowed by a single application per 15 minutes. When you're getting screen names from user ID numbers, the number of requests is limited to 180 per time window with full authentication.[1] The limit for application-only access is only 60 requests per 15 minutes. You're sending just 12 requests, so you don't have to keep an eye on these limits yet, but they can become a limitation for downloading more data.

Links in the Twitter network

Now that you've downloaded the nodes for the social network, all you need to add to your network model are the links between them. You'll represent the links as tuples of IDs, where the first element is the source of the link and the second element is the target. Because you have a closed list of nodes in the network, you're interested only in

---

[1] Twitter, rate limits chart, https://dev.twitter.com/docs/rate-limiting/1.1/limits.

connections among this set of nodes; you'll ignore links that lead outside of the network. The next listing shows how to download a list of friends for a specific ID.

Listing 3   Twitter connections between users

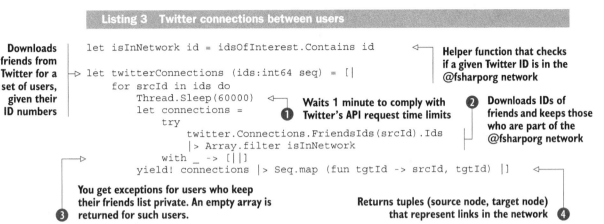

Downloads friends from Twitter for a set of users, given their ID numbers

```
let isInNetwork id = idsOfInterest.Contains id

let twitterConnections (ids:int64 seq) = [|
    for srcId in ids do
        Thread.Sleep(60000)
        let connections =
            try
                twitter.Connections.FriendsIds(srcId).Ids
                |> Array.filter isInNetwork
            with _ -> [|||]
        yield! connections |> Seq.map (fun tgtId -> srcId, tgtId) |]
```

Helper function that checks if a given Twitter ID is in the @fsharporg network

❶ Waits 1 minute to comply with Twitter's API request time limits

❷ Downloads IDs of friends and keeps those who are part of the @fsharporg network

❸ You get exceptions for users who keep their friends list private. An empty array is returned for such users.

❹ Returns tuples (source node, target node) that represent links in the network

Because you want to keep the network focused on the F# community, you first write a helper function that checks whether a given ID is a member of the network or not. You go through the set of nodes' IDs and download a list of all their friends from Twitter ❷. Again, Twitter returns ID numbers of accounts that you filter to get only those in the network. Some users on Twitter prefer to keep their connections private, in which case you can't get their friends' IDs ❸. For these accounts, you return an empty array: they will appear as isolated nodes without any connections in the final network. When you get the list of friends, you return each link as a pair of source and target nodes ❹.

Twitter again limits the number of requests your application can send per 15 minute time window. For friends and followers requests, the limits are more restrictive than for a user lookup: this time you're restricted to only 15 requests per 15 minutes, regardless of your authentication type. Because of this, the function needs to wait 1 minute between requests ❶. You have a lot of IDs of interest, so downloading lists of friends takes a long time. If you don't want to wait, the downloaded data is included in the source code for this chapter.

Network representation in the JSON format

In this section, you'll save the network downloaded from Twitter into a JSON document. I chose the JSON format because it's the input format for the visualization library D3.js that you'll use to plot the network. It's also easy to import the data back into F# with the JSON type provider.

D3.js (Data Driven Documents) is a JavaScript library for data manipulation and visualization. You'll use it to plot your F# network in SVG that you can easily incorporate into a website. You'll store the downloaded data directly in a format that D3.js can import.

First let's look at the format for storing nodes in the network. You'll use the following syntax, which lists user ID numbers and screen names as JSON values:

```
{
  "nodes":[
    {"id":12345,"name":"Alice"},
    {"id":67890,"name":"Bob"},
    ...
    {"id":11235813,"name":"Zara"}
}
```

You use the F# Data JSON extension to save data in this format. You can create JSON objects by calling the appropriate method of JsonValue. For example,

```
JsonValue.String "xyz"
```

produces a JsonValue string object that holds "xyz". The next listing shows how to export nodes into JSON objects.

Listing 4 Exporting the network's nodes into JSON

Encodes a ② Twitter ID number as a decimal value in the id attribute.

Encodes user IDs and screen names into JSON objects. The record function takes a map of names and values and creates a corresponding JSON record.

```
let jsonNode (userInfo: int64*string) =
    let id, name = userInfo
    JsonValue.Record [|
        "name", JsonValue.String name
        "id", JsonValue.Number (decimal id) |]
```

Encodes a Twitter screen name ① as a name string attribute

Exports the JSON object to a string and writes it into a file

```
let jsonNodes =
    let nodes = twitterNodes |> Array.map jsonNode
    [|"nodes", (JsonValue.Array nodes) |]
    |> JsonValue.Record
File.WriteAllText("fsharporgNodes.json", jsonNodes.ToString())
```

Converts the sequence of Twitter data about users to a JSON node record and wraps it into a JSON record called nodes

The jsonNode function transforms each user's ID number and screen name into a JSON object that holds this information ① ②. You collect the list of JSON objects into an array and wrap it in a top-level nodes object. Finally, you export the entire JSON object into a file by calling its ToString() method.

Next let's look at how to save connections between Twitter users that represent links in the social network. The JSON format used by D3.js is straightforward:

```
{
  "links":[
    {"source":0,"target":1},
    {"source":2,"target":0},
    ...
    {"source":1108,"target":267}
}
```

For each link in the network, it stores its origin (source) and its target. The nodes are represented by their indices in the list of nodes you created in the previous step.

In listing 3, you downloaded the links from Twitter; currently they're stored as pairs of node IDs, one for the origin of a link and one for its target. To save them in the desired format, you only need to change the ID number to a corresponding index into the array of nodes and save it as a sequence of JSON values.

You can create a simple dictionary to directly translate Twitter ID numbers to zero-based indices. Items in `idsOfInterest` are ordered as increasing values in the set. Let's translate it into an immutable `Dictionary`:

```
let idToIdx =
    idsOfInterest
    |> Seq.mapi (fun idx id -> (id, idx))        ◁——┤ Adds a zero-based index
    |> dict                                            to the Twitter IDs

val idToIdx : IDictionary<int64,int>
```

Now you can proceed to export the links, which is similar to converting nodes into JSON.

Listing 5   Exporting the network's links into JSON

```
let jsonConnections (srcId, tgtId) =                      ◁——  Encodes links into a JSON
    let src = idToIdx.[srcId]     Changes the Twitter ID        record. Each directed link
    let tgt = idToIdx.[tgtId]     into a zero-based index        is represented by its source
    JsonValue.Record [|                                          node and its target node.
            "source", JsonValue.Number (decimal src)            This function's inputs are
            "target", JsonValue.Number (decimal tgt) |]         original Twitter IDs.

let jsonLinks =                                  ◁——  Converts the sequence of Twitter data
    let linkArr =                                       about connections between users into
        twitterConnections idsOfInterest               JSON link records and wraps it into
        |> Array.map jsonConnections                   a JSON record called links
        |> JsonValue.Array
    JsonValue.Record [|"links", linkArr|]
                                                             Writes the JSON
File.WriteAllText("fsharporgLinks.json", jsonLinks.ToString())  ◁——  object with network
                                                                      links into a file
```

Encodes the source and target nodes in decimal source and target JSON attributes

In this section, you looked at how to save downloaded Twitter names and connections into a JSON format because it's easy to read back into F# and it's also a format that you can directly give D3.js to visualize your network. Both JSON files are included in the source code for this chapter.

Visualization with D3.js

At this moment, you have the complete Twitter network around the F# Software Foundation. An important part of every exploratory data analysis is visualization. In the context of network analysis, it gives you a good idea about what kind of network you're dealing with.

You'll use the JavaScript library D3.js for Data Driven Documents. This library can make various different visualizations that can be easily incorporated into a website. For network analysis, the library contains a so-called *force layout algorithm* for visualization. This algorithm isn't limited to D3.js; it's the basic algorithm for plotting networks, and some variant of this algorithm is present in all network analysis libraries.

This is a chapter about using F# to analyze social networks, so we won't dive too deeply into JavaScript. All you need to do to visualize the network is to download the

Force-directed layout

Force layout is an algorithm for plotting networks. The aim of all network-layout algorithms is to get a two-dimensional picture of a network where the links have approximately the same length and with as few link crosses as possible. This task is difficult for large, complex networks such as a Twitter network. Force-directed algorithms solve this problem by creating a physical simulation.

You can imagine nodes in a network as objects that repel each other. Links in a network are forces that keep connected nodes together. Force-directed layout algorithms simulate this complex physical system. In the beginning, nodes are scattered randomly. The algorithm applies the repulsive and attractive forces iteratively to update the network layout until the whole system reaches a stable state. This method usually converges to a nice visual representation of a complex network.

basic scaffolding for D3.js. At http://bl.ocks.org/mbostock/4062045, there is a code sample for visualizing a small social network of characters in *Les Miserables*.

When you look in the HTML scaffold file, the sample code reads data from a single file (miserable.json) where nodes and edges are put together. The only modification you have to make is to tell D3.js to read data from your two JSON files, one for nodes and the other for links. You can do this by changing the callback function that reads the data into two nested callback functions. The original callback function is the following:

```
d3.json("miserables.json", function (error, graph) {
...
}
```

Change this single JavaScript function into two nested callback functions, where one reads the nodes in the graph and the other reads the links:

```
    d3.json("fsharporgNodes.json", function (error, graphNodes) {
        d3.json("fsharporgLinks.json", function (error, graphLinks) {
...
        }
}
```

You also need to change the original single variable `graph` with elements `graph.nodes` and `graph.links` from the original source into two distinct variables `graphNodes` and `graphLinks`, with elements `graphNodes.nodes` and `graphLinks.links`.

Now you can finally start an HTTP server and look at your visualization. You should see a chaotic network that gradually takes a more compact and structured shape as the force layout optimizes its shape.

You'll probably notice that the visualization is far from perfect—the network gradually drifts out of the canvas as the layout adjusts itself. You'll have to make the canvas larger to fit the entire network, and you also have to tell the nodes to stay close to the center of the canvas. If you adjust a couple of parameters, the visualization should start looking better.

VISUALIZATION PARAMETERS

You'll change parameters for methods of the `force` class:

- `Gravity`—Calling this method changes the strength of the force that keeps nodes close to the center of the layout. Its default value is 0.1, which isn't enough to keep the big F# network in the canvas. If you change it to a higher value, say 1.0, the force increases and the nodes should stay in the desired area.

- `Size`—You have to increase the size of your canvas so the entire network fits in it. Try changing the size from 960×500 to 1500×800.

The relevant part of the code should now look like this:

```
var width = 1500,
    height = 800;

var force = d3.layout.force()
    .charge(-120)
    .linkDistance(30)
    .size([width, height])
    .gravity(1);
```

These changes should be enough for you to see the network form a nice compact layout (see figure 3). If you hover your mouse pointer above any node, you'll see that node's Twitter name.

The majority of the network is tightly linked together. Some nodes are isolated and not connected to the rest of the network. These nodes are either users who are

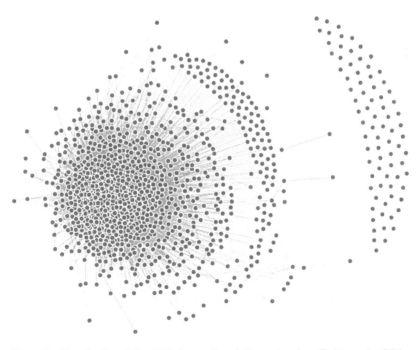

Figure 3   Visualization of the F# Software Foundation network on Twitter using D3.js

connected only to @fsharporg and not to any other node in the network, or users who keep their list of followers and friends private. The core of the network is highly connected with a surrounding circle of less-connected nodes. There are no immediately visible communities in this network. If there were any communities, the graph would appear to have more than one tightly connected center. This suggests that the F# community on Twitter is homogeneous and there are no competing sub-communities that don't talk to each other.

The visualization can be improved. Currently, many of the nodes in the middle overlap, and you can't isolate them. Play with different parameters for the `force` class methods to adjust the visualization into a nicer form.

Parameters to adjust network visualization

Some parameters you can adjust to improve the network visualization include the folowing:

- *Charge*—Adjusts the strength with which nodes repel or attract each other. Positive charge values attract nodes to each other and are better suited for other applications. In a social network, you want the layout to spread to reveal structure: therefore the nodes should repel each other, and this parameter should have a negative value. The magnitude of the charge changes how much repulsive force is applied.
- *Link distance*—Sets the ideal distance of nodes in the network, or the desired edge length between them. The layout tries to converge to this distance. By increasing the distance, the nodes in the core get more space to move around and spread.

Play with these and other parameters to get a feel how for how the layout adjusts when they change. A comprehensive description of all the methods and parameters is available in the documentation for D3.js at https://github.com/mbostock/d3/wiki/Force-Layout.

In this section, you looked at how to use your JSON documents generated in F# to easily visualize the F# Software Foundation network on Twitter. The network seems to have a tightly connected core of enthusiastic F# users; around them is a group of more casual users who aren't as deeply involved in the community. By observing a visualization of a social network, you can tell a lot about the community structure and what types of users appear there.

The next section looks in more detail at the structure of the community and individual characteristics of users. You'll see how to measure individual involvement in the network and how to find people who are worth following.

Exploring the social network

In the last section, you saw how to visualize the Twitter community around the F# Software Foundation. You've seen that the network is tightly connected, especially in the center, and that there are no communities in the network.

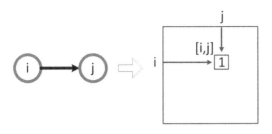

Figure 4 Encoding links as an adjacency matrix. Every link from node i to node j is a 1 in the [i,j] position in the adjacency matrix.

Questions we'll explore in this part of the chapter are about individual nodes in the network. Which users are the most connected? If you want to spread an idea through the community, whom should you contact? If a well-connected person tweets something, the message reaches many people in the group.

In the rest of the chapter, we'll look at some characteristics of the F# social network. We'll explore how much the network is connected, who is most followed, and who the most central people in the community are.

Representing a network with an adjacency matrix

We'll represent the network using a so-called *adjacency matrix* (see figure 4). This is a binary matrix that represents connections between nodes. It's a square matrix with a number of rows (and columns) equal to the number of nodes in the network. For your Twitter network, the dimension of the matrix is the number of users. If there is a link from node i to node j, the adjacency matrix has the value 1 in position [i,j]; otherwise the value is 0. The matrix isn't symmetric, because the network is directed. Note that rows of the matrix represent source nodes, and columns represent targets of each link.

Reading JSON files with type providers

In the previous part of the chapter, you downloaded users and connections from Twitter. You've saved the data in a JSON format that is easy to use as an input for force-layout visualization in D3.js. Now you'll read the network back into F# so you can analyze its properties.

In the following listing, you load both JSON files into F# with the JSON type provider. Note that you have to give a sample document to the JSON provider, and you load the actual data file afterward.

Listing 6 Loading JSON data with type providers

```
open FSharp.Data                                         ← Opens FSharp.Data to access
                                                           the JSON type provider

type Users =  JsonProvider<"fsharporgNodes.json">
let userNames = Users.Load("fsharporgNodes.json")        ← Loads the file with nodes in
                                                           the Twitter network using
                                                           the JSON type provider

type Connections = JsonProvider<"fsharporgLinks.json">
let userLinks = Connections.Load("fsharporgLinks.json")  ← Loads links in the Twitter
                                                           network from the extracted
                                                           connections with the JSON
                                                           type provider
```

The JSON type provider requires a sample file.

Now you can read the actual data from your JSON files. You first create a few helper functions that you'll use during the network analysis. For example, you might want to easily translate between Twitter ID numbers and corresponding screen names:

```
let idToName =
dict [ for node in userNames.Nodes -> node.Id, node.Name.String.Value ]
let nameToId =
dict [ for node in userNames.Nodes -> node.Name.String.Value, node.Id ]
```

In the code, you use the type `Users` that you created from the JSON file in listing 6. You look at all nodes in the JSON element `Nodes` and extract their `Id` and `Name` values. You use those to generate a list of tuples. Finally, you create an immutable dictionary from the list that you can use to translate each ID to its corresponding name and vice versa. For example, let's try @tomaspetricek, the editor of this book:

```
> nameToId.["tomaspetricek"]
val it : int64 = 18388966L
```

As the next step, you load the links from the JSON file. In listing 5, you encoded links in the network using zero-indexed source and target nodes. You'll use the zero-based index in your adjacency matrix as well. The additional helper functions in the next listing will come in handy to translate Twitter ID numbers to network indices and back.

Listing 7   Helper functions for Twitter IDs

```
let idxToId, idToIdx =                              Extracts the ID and zero-based index
    let idxList, idList =                                for each node in the network
        userNames.Nodes
        |> Seq.mapi (fun idx node -> (idx,node.Id), (node.Id, idx))    ◄───┘
        |> Seq.toList
        |> List.unzip                          Uses the IDs and indexes to create
    dict idxList, dict idList          ◄───    two immutable dictionaries that
                                                translate between each other
let idxToIdName idx =                  ◄───
    let id = idxToId.[idx]                 Returns the Twitter ID and
    id, idToName.[id]                      screen name for a specific index

let nameToIdx screenName =             ◄───    Returns an index for a
    let id = nameToId.[screenName]             specific screen name
    idToIdx.[id]
```

For convenience, you also add two functions for working with zero-based indexing. Twitter names are more user-friendly than int64 ID numbers, and the two functions can help make your code easier to interpret. The first function, `idxToIdName`, takes the zero-based index and translates it to its corresponding Twitter ID number and user name. You also want to be able to find out what Twitter name belongs to any entry in the adjacency matrix. For this, the function `nameToIdx` takes the screen name and returns the corresponding index.

You can easily find the position of any user in your network from the user's Twitter name:

```
> nameToIdx "dsyme";;
    val it : int = 313
```

It's equally straightforward to find the Twitter ID and name from an index in your network:

```
> idxToIdName 313;;
    val it : int64 * string = (25663453L, "dsyme")
```

Now you can finally create the adjacency matrix.

Listing 8 Sparse adjacency matrix

```
open MathNet.Numerics.LinearAlgebra
```
← You use Math.NET Numerics library's implementation of linear algebra functions on sparse matrices.

```
let nodeCount = userNames.Nodes.Length
```
← The number of nodes in the network is the number of rows and columns in the adjacency matrix.

```
let links =
    seq { for link in userLinks.Links -> link.Source, link.Target, 1.0 }
    |> SparseMatrix.ofSeqi nodeCount nodeCount
```
Creates a sparse adjacency matrix from a sequence of non-zero elements in the matrix. The sequence gives the coordinates and value of each non-zero element. This network has value I in coordinates [i,j] for every link i->j.

You've created a sparse matrix using data from the JSON file. Links in the JSON file are indexed from zero, so you don't have to change the values. In the JSON file, the links are stored as tuples of a source node and a target node for each directed connection. All you need to do is use the data to fill the adjacency matrix.

Because there are fewer connections than elements in the adjacency matrix, you store the data in a sparse matrix. Then you specify only non-zero elements of the matrix, and it's stored in a memory-efficient structure. (Storing the full matrix would quickly become infeasible for larger networks.) You use the sparse matrix implementation in Math.NET Numerics, a library that is part of the Fslab Nuget package.

Let's look at some information you can get about the sparse matrix in F# interactive:

```
> links;;
val it : Matrix<float> =
  SparseMatrix 1109x1109-Double 1.17 % Filled
           . . .
    {ColumnCount = 1109;
     IsSymmetric = false;
     Item = ?;
     NonZerosCount = 14412;
     RowCount = 1109;
     Storage =
     MathNet.Numerics.LinearAlgebra.Storage.SparseCompressedRowMatrixStorage`
     1[System.Double];}
```

You can see that only 1.17% of the matrix is filled. If you need to go through the matrix and work with the data, only the non-zero elements will be processed, which greatly speeds up the computation. It's also much more space efficient to store only the non-zero elements. The output also tells you that the matrix isn't symmetric. This shouldn't come as a surprise, because links in the network are directed. Undirected networks have symmetric adjacency matrices. Also note that the network has 1,109 nodes (number of rows and columns) and 14,412 edges (number of non-zero items in the matrix). It's stored as a sparse structure by row.

In this section, you've read the data stored in a JSON format into F# with type providers, and you've created a sparse adjacency matrix to represent the network. In the next section, we'll look at some simple characteristics of the network that reveal how well connected users on Twitter are.

In-degrees and out-degrees

In this section, we'll look at the degrees of nodes in the Twitter network. In general, a *degree* is the number of connections a node has. For directed networks like your social network, you can also define an *in-degree* and an *out-degree*.

The *in-degree* is the number of connections that lead into a node. Similarly, the *out-degree* is the number of links leading from a node; see figure 5. For the Twitter network, the in-degree is the number of followers each user has in the network and the out-degree is the number of friends that person follows. Nodes with a higher in-degree should be more influential because they're followed by more people. Later, we'll look at the PageRank of nodes in the network, which is a better indicator of influence.

With the adjacency matrix you created in the previous section, calculating the in- and out-degrees is straightforward. Remember that if the adjacency matrix contains 1 in position [i,j], there's a link from i to j in the network. Source nodes are in the rows of the matrix, and target nodes are in the columns.

To find the out-degree of each node in a network, all you need to do is to sum the values in each row. For a given source node, the value is 1 for every link that originates in the source node in the adjacency matrix and 0 otherwise (see figure 6). This means if you sum the values in each row, you get an array of out-degrees of all the nodes in the network. You get the in-degrees similarly by summing the values in each column, because each column has the value 1 for each link that ends in the corresponding node.

In-degree = 3   Out-degree = 4   **Figure 5   In Twitter, the in-degree is the number of followers and the out-degree is the number of friends (number of followed accounts).**

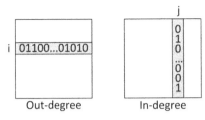

Out-degree   In-degree

Figure 6 The out-degree of a node is the sum of the elements in a row in the adjacency matrix. The in-degree is the sum of the column elements for a specific node.

Listing 9   Out-degree and in-degree

```
let outdegree (linkMatrix:float Matrix) =
    [| for outlinks in linkMatrix.EnumerateRows() -> outlinks.Sum() |]

let indegree (linkMatrix: float Matrix) =
    [| for inlinks in linkMatrix.EnumerateColumns() -> inlinks.Sum() |]

let indegrees = indegree links
let outdegrees = outdegree links
```

Enumerates rows in the sparse adjacency matrix. The sum of each row gives the out-degree of each node.

Enumerates columns in the sparse matrix. The sum of each column is the in-degree.

Using the `EnumerateRows()` and `EnumerateColumns()` methods on the sparse matrix, you can efficiently go through the matrix and sum the row and column elements. There's also a faster method to compute in- and out-degrees that uses matrix algebra, as shown in listing 10.

Faster degree computation with matrix algebra

For larger matrices, it's inefficient to explicitly go through each row/column and sum the elements. Math.NET Numerics contains an efficient implementation of sparse matrix multiplication that you can use to sum values in each row or column.

The sum of a row in a matrix is equivalent to multiplying the row by a unit column vector. A *unit vector* is a vector that contains only ones. If you multiply a matrix by a unit column vector, the result is a vector that contains a sum of every row in the matrix:

$$\text{out-degree}[s] = \Sigma^N \text{Links}[s,t] * I[t]$$

The equation says that the out-degree of a source node s is the sum of the sth row in the link matrix times a vector of ones of the same size. Because the row in the link matrix contains 0 when there's no link and 1 when there's a link, the resulting sum counts 1 for every link. The result is exactly the same as the explicit computation in listing 9. Due to efficient implementation of matrix multiplication in Math.NET, multiplying a matrix by a vector is faster than explicit row enumeration.

Similarly, you compute the in-degree by left-multiplying the link matrix by a unit vector, only this time the vector must be a row vector. This multiplication sums each column in the link matrix.

(continued)

The following figure shows a visual representation of matrix multiplication to illustrate the process.

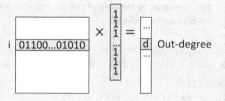

**Computing the out-degree efficiently
with matrix multiplication**

Listing 10   Calculating the in-degree and out-degree with matrix multiplication

```
let outdegreeFaster (linkMatrix: float Matrix) =
    linkMatrix * DenseMatrix.Create(linkMatrix.RowCount, 1, 1.0)

let indegreeFaster (linkMatrix: float Matrix) =
    DenseMatrix.Create(1, linkMatrix.ColumnCount, 1.0) * linkMatrix
```

**Computes the in-degree by
multiplying a unit row vector
by the adjacency matrix**

**Computes the out-degree by multiplying the link matrix by a
column vector that contains only ones. A column vector of
length L is the same as a matrix with L rows and only 1 column.**

You can compare how much faster the matrix algebra is versus explicit degree computation. Use the directive #time to turn on the timing function in F# interactive:

```
> #time;;

--> Timing now on

> outdegree links;;
Real: 00:00:00.142, CPU: 00:00:00.140, GC gen0: 0, gen1: 0, gen2: 0
> outdegreeFaster links;;
Real: 00:00:00.001, CPU: 00:00:00.015, GC gen0: 0, gen1: 0, gen2: 0
```

The increase in speed is immediately visible. It's usually significantly faster to use standard matrix algebra operations compared to element-by-element computations.

Finding the most-connected users

Now that you have in-degrees and out-degrees for every node in the F# network, you can determine the most-connected users. You can print the degree of any user using the helper functions defined in listing 7. For example, let's see how many people in the network follow Don Syme, the designer and architect of the F# language:

```
> indegrees.[nameToIdx "dsyme"];;
val it : float = 644.0
```

This result means Don Syme has 644 followers in the network. That's more than a half the nodes! Let's see who the other major accounts in the F# Foundation network are.

Listing 11 Top users from a ranking

```
let topUsers (ranking:float seq) count =
    ranking
    |> Seq.mapi (fun i x -> (i,x))
    |> Seq.sortBy (fun (i,x) -> - x)
    |> Seq.take count
    |> Seq.map (fun (i,x) ->
        let id, name = idxToIdName I
        (id, name, x))
```

Orders users based on decreasing rank

Adds indices to the rank values to keep track of which user has which ranking

Takes the specified number of top-ranking users

Finds which user belongs to the ranking, and returns their ID and name

You define a function that takes a general ranking of users in the network and returns the specified number of users with the highest ranking. Now you can get a list of people with the most followers by applying it to the in-degrees:

```
topUsers indegrees 5
|> Seq.iteri (fun i (id, name, value) ->
    printfn "%d. %s has indegree %.0f" (i+1) name value)
```

This code prints the list of top five most-followed people in the network:

```
1. dsyme has indegree 644
2. tomaspetricek has indegree 556
3. migueldeicaza has indegree 545
4. VisualFSharp has indegree 483
5. c4fsharp has indegree 457
```

You can see that Don Syme is the user with the most followers. In second place is Tomas Petricek, the editor of this book. Miguel de Icaza, founder of the Mono project (and many other open source projects), is in the third position. He is also the only person in this list who isn't directly connected to F#, which shows that people around the F# Software Foundation are interested in open source development.

How do these high-ranking nodes compare to the average number of followers in this network?

```
> Seq.average indegrees;;
val it : float = 12.99549143
```

On average, people have only 13 followers in this network. This is typical for certain types of social networks, where there are a few highly connected nodes and a large number of less-connected nodes. Let's visualize the entire degree distribution to get a bigger picture.

Using the R provider to visualize the degree distribution

Let's look at a few simple visualizations you can use to examine the degree distribution in a social network. Because F# itself doesn't have rich visualization libraries, you'll use R to produce some plots. The R language is an open source statistical programming language with rich visualization packages. Using it from F# with the R provider allows you to use all the functions that exist in R directly in the F# environment.

To be able to use the R provider, you'll need to install R on your computer from www.r-project.org. After installation, you can use R directly from F# with a help from the R type provider. Like Math.NET Numerics, the R provider is part of the FsLab package. Calling an R function is straightforward:

```
open RProvider
open RProvider.``base``
open RProvider.graphics
```
Opens R type provider namespaces to call R functions

```
R.plot(indegrees)
```

You can pass your array of in-degrees directly to the `plot` function in R, and it creates a figure with a point for every node in the network (see figure 7). The y axis in the plot represents the in-degree values of the nodes. You can see that there are a few nodes with a high in-degree and that most users are concentrated around the low in-degree values. Because most of the points blend together in the lower section of the graph, you might get a better visualization with a different type of plot.

Log degree distribution and scale-free networks

Figure 7 shows many nodes with small degrees and a couple of nodes with very high degrees. Such a highly non-symmetric distribution is usually visualized using the so-called *log-log plot*. This type of plot has a logarithmic scale on both the x and y axes. This way, it's able to show quantities with different scales in a single plot.

Let's create the log-log plot using the R `plot` function. On the x axis, you'll have unique values of in-degrees in the network. On the y axis, you'll have the number of nodes with that specific in-degree. For example, let's say you have 10 nodes with in-degree 15. There will be a dot in the plot in location [15,10]. Both axes in the plot will have a logarithmic scale.

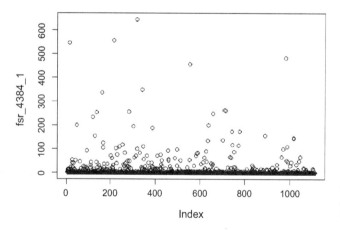

Figure 7   A simple visualization of in-degrees in the F# network with the R type provider

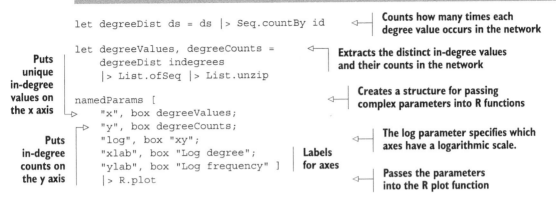

Listing 12 Degree distribution of nodes

```
let degreeDist ds = ds |> Seq.countBy id          ◁─┤  Counts how many times each
                                                        degree value occurs in the network

let degreeValues, degreeCounts =           ◁─┐  Extracts the distinct in-degree values
    degreeDist indegrees                       │  and their counts in the network
    |> List.ofSeq |> List.unzip
                                                 Creates a structure for passing
namedParams [                              ◁─┤  complex parameters into R functions
    "x", box degreeValues;
    "y", box degreeCounts;
    "log", box "xy";                         ◁─┤  The log parameter specifies which
    "xlab", box "Log degree";    ┤ Labels       axes have a logarithmic scale.
    "ylab", box "Log frequency" ]│ for axes
    |> R.plot                               ◁─┤  Passes the parameters
                                                 into the R plot function
```

Puts unique in-degree values on the x axis ↳
Puts in-degree counts on the y axis ↳

To call a function in R with the R provider, you can pass in specific named parameters that Visual Studio helpfully displays in a tooltip. Alternatively, you can use the full functionality of R and call functions with a richer set of optional parameters. Here, you want to adjust a couple of more advanced parameters in the resulting chart, such as labels and axis types.

In the R provider, any R function can take an `IDictionary<string,obj>` as its input. In this dictionary structure, you can specify values to any R parameters that the function can take. The R provider also gives you a useful function `namedParams` that creates the dictionary structure from a sequence of tuples. For any function, you can look in the R documentation to access the full list of potential parameters.

In listing 12, you compute the degree distribution, which shows how many nodes of each degree are present in the network. You include several advanced parameters for the R plot. By specifying the `log` parameter, the resulting chart in figure 8 is on a log-log scale.

When you look at the log-log plot, you can again see that there are many nodes with small degrees. As the degree increases, the number of nodes with each degree gets smaller. This degree distribution is typical for a growing social network. If the

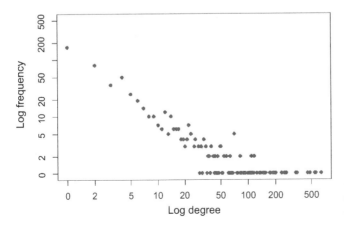

Figure 8 Log-log plot for in-degrees in the F# network. Both axes have a logarithmic scale.

in-degree distribution looks like a straight line in the log-log plot, it tells you that the network follows a power-law type of distribution.

Scale-free networks and the power law distribution

Scale-free networks are networks with a degree distribution that follows the *power law*. It can be formulated mathematically by looking at the number of nodes in the network that have an in-degree equal to *d* compared to the number of nodes in the entire network.

Let *P(d)* be the fraction of nodes of degree *d* in the network. In a scale-free network, this number is approximately

$$P(d) \sim d^{-\gamma}$$

where γ is a parameter that is specific to each network, typically around 2 or 3. The larger the degree, the smaller the number of nodes with that degree in the network. This equation is linear on the log-log scale.

Power-law networks can be modelled using the so-called *preferential attachment model*. When a network grows over time, new nodes are more likely to connect to nodes that are popular and already have many connections. This way, the older nodes have high in-degrees that keep growing. Newer nodes have less time to accumulate connections, and their in-degrees stay smaller and grow more slowly. The network has a rich-get-richer property, because the older nodes keep accumulating links due to preferential attachment. Another example of a network that follows the power-law degree distribution is the entire World Wide Web.

Some other types of social networks don't follow the power-law in-degree distribution. Networks with separate strong communities are a typical example of a different type of network.

The high-degree nodes in your network are sometimes called *hubs*. In the context of a Twitter network, hubs are users who efficiently spread information through the network. If a person with a high degree tweets something, it reaches more users in the network. Without such high-degree nodes, information spreads much more slowly.

Networks with a power-law degree distribution are also robust with respect to failure. If a node drops out of the network randomly, the hubs have a low probability of being affected. Also, if a hub disappears from the network, several other hubs still connect the network together. This is a nice property of a Twitter network: if a user closes their account, the entire community isn't significantly affected, because the other nodes in the network keep the connections in the group alive. On the other hand, if too many hubs drop out, the network splits into a set of disconnected subnetworks that don't communicate anymore.

In this section, you've learned that there are some highly connected users with many followers in the F# network. Does the high connectivity reflect the underlying importance of each node in the network? In the next section, we'll look at a better measure of node centrality.

PageRank

In-degree and out-degree aren't good measures of actual importance in the network. A node that is connected to every other node probably isn't interesting. On the other hand, an account on Twitter that is being followed only by important and well-connected nodes may be important but not widely known in the network.

In this section, we'll look at the importance of individual nodes in the network with the PageRank algorithm. The overall importance of each node doesn't depend only on its in- or out-degree, but also on who the followers of that node are.

The PageRank algorithm was originally used by Google to rank web pages based on their relative importance. When searching for a term, it's important to return not only the result that best fits a query, but also the most important page that is relevant. The importance of a web page can be estimated from the web graph using the Page-Rank algorithm. This algorithm has become very popular as a measure of the centrality of nodes in complex networks and has been used in many different areas, such as identifying cancer genes in biological networks.

PageRank and the random surfer model

PageRank is based on a probabilistic model called the *random surfer model*, developed by Google to rank web pages based on their importance. Imagine a web surfer who clicks links randomly. Each link takes the surfer to a different web page, where the surfer clicks a link again, and so on. If there's no outgoing link, the surfer jumps randomly to any other page on the web. Sometimes the surfer gets bored and jumps to any other web page randomly, so the surfer doesn't get stuck in one area of the network. This way, the surfer moves around the web indefinitely.

The PageRank value is the total proportion of time the surfer stays at each page during this infinite web-surfing session. Mathematically, it's a probability distribution over web pages; therefore the sum of all PageRank values is equal to 1.

We assume that important pages are those that have many links pointing toward them. The random surfer should visit such pages often. Also, if an important web page links to another web page, then that other web page is probably important as well. A random surfer will also visit such pages often, because important pages link to them.

Mathematical formulation of PageRank

The basic PageRank algorithm computes the importance of each node by looking at the number and importance of nodes that link to that node and at the quality of those links. The *importance* is given by each node's PageRank. The *quality* of a link is

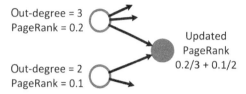

Figure 9   **Basic PageRank computation. A node's PageRank is the sum of the PageRanks of nodes that link to that node weighted by their inverse out-degree.**

measured by the out-degree of its source node. This definition of quality tells you that if an important node links to just a few other nodes, the links are significant. If an equally important node links to thousands of other nodes, the individual links don't have much weight. The fewer links lead out of a node, the more significant they are.

Let's look at a formal definition. The PageRank of a node n is computed by summing the PageRanks of all nodes that link to that node, divided by their out-degrees:

$$PageRank(n) = \sum_{links[s,\,n]} \frac{1}{\text{Out-degree}(s)} \times PageRank(s)$$

The sum in the equation goes over all links that point to a node n. For each of these links, you take the PageRank of its source node s and divide it by its out-degree. This process is illustrated in figure 9.

As you can see, this definition is recursive. Every node's value depends on the value of the nodes that link to it and also on the significance of that link. You can compute the values by iteratively cycling through all the nodes in the network until you reach a stable result.

The inverse out-degree of each node in the previous equation is equal to the transition probability. If the random surfer is in a node s and selects any outgoing link at random, the probability of choosing a link is

$$\frac{1}{\text{Out-degree}(s)}$$

You'll precompute these quantities and store them in a matrix. This matrix is called a *transition matrix* because it represents the transition probabilities. The first part of the following listing shows how to compute this transition matrix using the out-degrees you computed earlier.

Listing 13   Transition matrix

Computes the basic transition probability matrix

```
let transitionBasic =
    seq { for i, j, _ in links.EnumerateNonZeroIndexed () ->
            i, j, 1.0/outdegrees.[i] }
    |> SparseMatrix.ofSeqi nodeCount nodeCount
```

Goes through all links in the network that are represented by non-zero entries in the adjacency matrix

For every link, the sequence contains the inverse out-degree of each source node.

The resulting sequence initializes a sparse matrix.

Full transition matrix with correction for dangling nodes

```
let transitionMatrix =
    seq { for r, row in transitionBasic.EnumerateRowsIndexed() ->
            if row.Sum() = 0.0 then
                SparseVector.init nodeCount (fun i ->
                    1.0/(float nodeCount))
            else row }
    |> SparseMatrix.ofRowSeq
```

Checks if a row has a zero sum, which means the corresponding node has no outgoing links

If there are no outgoing links, replaces the row with a vector of uniform probabilities

The result is again turned into a sparse matrix.

With the basic formulation of the transition probabilities, you'll run into problems with nodes that have zero out-degree. These nodes represent users who either don't follow anyone in the community or keep their connections private. Are there any such nodes in your Twitter network?

```
outdegrees
|> Seq.countBy ((=) 1.0)

val it : seq<bool * int> = seq [(false, 969); (true, 140)]
```

There are 140 users who don't have any outgoing links in the network. Such nodes are usually called *dangling nodes*, and you have to correct for them.

In the random surfer model, if the surfer lands on a page with no outgoing links, the surfer jumps to any web page at random. You implement this by adding virtual links from dangling nodes to all nodes in the network with uniform probabilities. If the network has N nodes, the probability of randomly jumping to any of them is equal to $1/N$. The full transition matrix is implemented in the second part of listing 13.

Adding virtual links fills the sparse transition matrix with many additional entries. The effect is relatively large:

```
> transitionBasic;;
val it : Matrix<float> =
  SparseMatrix 1109x1109-Double 1.17 % Filled

> transitionMatrix;;
val it : Matrix<float> =
  SparseMatrix 1109x1109-Double 9.38 % Filled
```

The full transition matrix now has eight times more elements than the original one without the correction. This approach would quickly fill the transition matrix for networks with more dangling nodes, and you'd have to use a different approach. For this network, the transition matrix is still sparse enough that it won't affect efficiency of the code.

Now that you have all the transition probabilities, you could iterate the PageRank equation to get an estimate of importance for nodes in the network. But first you need to make an additional modification.

Calculating PageRank with a damping factor

If you implemented the basic PageRank equation and iterated over all nodes in the network, you'd run into problems with parts of the network that aren't fully connected.

Some nodes aren't accessible from other parts of the network, and other nodes have no incoming links and therefore zero PageRank values. The computation might get stuck in an isolated part and not propagate PageRanks through the entire network.

The random surfer model includes random jumps between nodes when the surfer gets bored. These jumps help avoid getting trapped in a subpart of the network. You include this behavior through an additional term in the PageRank. In the extended version of the algorithm, the random surfer follows links between nodes with probability *d*. With probability *1-d*, the surfer jumps randomly to any node in the network:

$$\text{PageRank}(n) = (1 - d) \times \frac{1}{N} + d \times \sum_{\text{links}[s,\, n]} \frac{\text{PageRank}(s)}{\text{Out-degree}(s)}$$

Probability *d* is called the *damping factor*. Generally recommended values are around 0.85. The extended equation now counts the incoming PageRank values of other nodes weighted by *d*.

Let's look at the new term in the equation. The probability of being in node *n* due to a random jump is the same for all nodes: it's equal to $1/N$, *N* being the number of nodes in the network. It's weighted by the probability of the random jump, which is $(1 - d)$.

This completes the PageRank algorithm. Let's use an iterative method to compute it for all nodes in the Twitter network. The PageRank algorithm starts by initializing all PageRank values to uniform values $1/N$. Then it iteratively computes the PageRank equation for all nodes in the network until convergence. The final PageRank value represents the overall probability of being in a node at any given time; you interpret it as the importance of the node. Figure 10 shows PageRank values for a small network of three nodes.

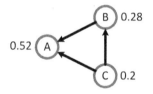

Figure 10   PageRank values for a sample network with three nodes

Here's the corresponding adjacency matrix:

	A	B	C
A	0	0	0
B	1	0	0
C	1	1	0

And here's the transition matrix:

	A	B	C
A	1/3	1/3	1/3
B	1	0	0
C	1/2	1/2	0

Using MapReduce to compute PageRank

A popular model for PageRank implementation is the MapReduce algorithm. It allows parallel distribution of computations across multiple machines and makes the PageRank algorithm applicable to large-scale problems, such as the World Wide Web. You'll use the same basic computational model on a smaller scale because it translates well into a functional paradigm.

The MapReduce algorithm has mapper and reducer stages and works with key/value pairs. For this PageRank computation, the keys will be the nodes in the network and the values will be their PageRanks.

In the first stage, the `mapper` function goes through all the key/value pairs and produces a set of key/intermediate value pairs. The `reducer` function then collects intermediate values for each key and combines them to form a new value for that key. The mapper and reducer function are implemented in the following listing.

Listing 14 Mapper and reducer functions

The mapper function's input parameters are a sparse transition matrix and current PageRank values.

Goes over all links in the network and outputs the target node with a partial PageRank contribution from the source node ❶

```
let mapper (tMatrix:Matrix<float>) (pageRank:float []) =
    seq { for (src, tgt, p) in tMatrix.EnumerateNonZeroIndexed() do
            yield (tgt, pageRank.[src]*p)
          for node in 0..transitionMatrix.RowCount-1 do
            yield (node, 0.0) }
```

Damping factor
```
let d = 0.85
```

Dummy variables keep isolated nodes from disappearing from the computation. ❷

Takes mapper's output as its input
```
let reducer nodeCount (mapperOut: (int*float) seq) =
    mapperOut
    |> Seq.groupBy fst
    |> Seq.sortBy fst
    |> Seq.map (fun (node, inRanks) ->
        let inRankSum = inRanks |> Seq.sumBy snd
        d * inRankSum + (1.0-d)/(float nodeCount))
    |> Seq.toArray
```

Groups the key/intermediate value pairs by key, and sorts them ❸

Sums intermediate PageRank values for each key ❹

Computes the new PageRank by adding the random jump weighted by the damping factor ❺

Let's look at these functions in more detail. The `mapper` function goes through all links in the network. For every link, it outputs the target node of the link as the key and as its intermediate value. The value is the partial contribution to PageRank of the target node from that particular link ❶. If you look back at the PageRank equation, these are the individual elements in the sum.

If a node has no incoming links (it's not a target for any link), it's skipped in the computation and doesn't appear as a key in any of the key/intermediate value pairs. It effectively disappears from further computations. For this reason, you add a dummy key/value pair for each node in the network with value 0 ❷. This doesn't affect the

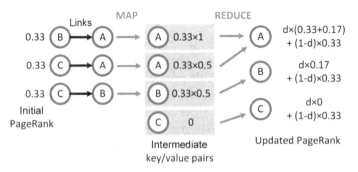

Figure 11   First iteration of the MapReduce algorithm for the PageRank computation for figure 10's simple network with three nodes

PageRank values but keeps the nodes from disappearing. The output from `mapper` is then used as an input to `reducer`.

The `reducer` function takes the intermediate values computed by `mapper` and groups them by key ❸. This way, it collects all the partial PageRank contributions that are coming to the target node through its incoming links. You sum these values for each target node, which gives you the result of the basic PageRank computation ❹. Then you add the correction for random jumps in the network via the damping factor. The results are PageRank values for all the nodes in the network ❺. The first iteration of the MapReduce algorithm for the simple network in figure 10 is shown in figure 11.

The `mapper` function can be easily parallelized or distributed among different machines because all the computations are independent of each other. `reducer` then receives data from different machines and only combines the results; again, results for different nodes are independent.

Now you can put together the full PageRank algorithm. You initialize all PageRank values to equal starting values of 1/N. Then you run `mapper` and `reducer` repeatedly until the PageRank values don't change anymore. The next listing shows a function that computes PageRank with MapReduce.

Listing 15   PageRank algorithm

To see if the algorithm converged to a solution, you set a small threshold. If the PageRank values change less than the threshold between two consecutive iterations, you can assume the algorithm reached convergence.

Initial PageRank values are the same for all nodes.

```
let startPageRank = Array.create nodeCount (1.0/(float nodeCount))
let maxIter = 100
let minDifference = 1e-6

let rec pageRank iters
        (transitionMatrix:Matrix<float>)
        (pageRankVals : float []) =
    if iters = 0 then pageRankVals
    else
        let nodeCount = transitionMatrix.RowCount
```

Maximum number of iterations for the MapReduce algorithm

Recursive function to iteratively compute PageRank values

```
let newPageRanks =
    pageRankVals
    |> mapper transitionMatrix
    |> reducer nodeCount
let difference =
    Array.map2 (fun r1 r2 -> abs (r1 - r2))
        pageRankVals newPageRanks
    |> Array.sum
if difference < minDifference then
    printfn "Converged in iteration %i" (maxIter - iters)
    newPageRanks
else pageRank (iters-1) transitionMatrix newPageRanks
let pr = pageRank maxIter transitionMatrix startPageRank
```

Runs mapper and reducer to update PageRank

If the difference is smaller than your threshold, the algorithm converged and returns the final values; otherwise it continues for another iteration.

Checks how much the values changed in this iteration

In each iteration, the function runs `mapper` and `reducer` and computes the new Page-Rank values. The new values are compared with the previous ones. If the sum of all the differences is smaller than some predefined threshold, the algorithm converged and the final results are returned.

PageRank results

When you run the MapReduce algorithm on the Twitter network, it converges after only 17 iterations. To view the results, you can reuse the function to display the top-ranking accounts in the Twitter network from listing 11:

```
topUsers pr 5
|> Seq.iteri (fun i (id, name, value) ->
    printfn "%d. %s has PageRank %f" (i+1) name value)
```

PageRank gives different result than the previous in-degree metric:

```
1. migueldeicaza has PageRank 0.033130
2. dsyme has PageRank 0.032783
3. tomaspetricek has PageRank 0.027757
4. LincolnAtkinson has PageRank 0.021993
5. VisualFSharp has PageRank 0.020233
```

Don Syme is no longer at the top; he's fallen to the second position, after Miguel de Icaza. There are differences between PageRank and in-degree in other positions, as well. For example, the account @LincolnAtkinson has a different rank in the two metrics. Based on his in-degree, he's in position 46 with in-degree 76. When you look at his PageRank, he jumps up to fourth place! This major difference is caused by the users who follow him. He's followed by users with high PageRank who pass their high rank to him as well.

You can see part of the cause when you look at the differences in average in-degree of followers for each user. You can write this function as a simple exercise. Followers of Miguel de Icaza in the Twitter network have an average of 14.6 followers. Lincoln Atkinson's followers have much a higher average number of followers: 38.7. This is one reason some accounts that don't have a high number of followers by themselves have a high PageRank.

This method gives you new insight into the Twitter network. You can even use PageRank values to suggest Twitter accounts that might be worth following. It's a more reliable measure of significance and helps to uncover important nodes in the network that aren't immediately obvious from just their number of followers. If a user with a high PageRank tweets something, it quickly reaches other important nodes in the network.

In this section, you've looked at how the PageRank algorithm works and how to implement it using the MapReduce algorithm. You've seen that this algorithm uncovers some important nodes in the network that were not apparent before. To conclude the chapter, you'll visualize the information that you got from PageRank to see where the important nodes are located in the Twitter network.

Visualizing important nodes

To see the importance of nodes, you'll use the PageRank values to modify the nodes' diameter in the network visualization. You need to go back to listing 4, where you generated a JSON document with data about nodes in the network. A simple modification of the code adds another attribute r that holds each node's PageRank value.

Listing 16 JSON file for nodes with PageRank information

```
let jsonUsersPR userIdx userPR =                      Additional JSON value that
    let id, name = idxToIdName userIdx                represents the PageRank
    JsonValue.Object                                  of each user
        (Map.ofSeq [
            "name", JsonValue.String name             For each node,
            "id", JsonValue.Number (decimal id)       creates the
            "r", JsonValue.Float userPR] )            modified JSON
                                                      object
let jsonNodes =
    let jsonPR = Array.mapi (fun idx rank -> jsonUsersPR idx rank) pr
    JsonValue.Object (Map.ofSeq ["nodes", (JsonValue.Array jsonPR)])
File.WriteAllText("pageRankNodes.json", jsonNodes.ToString())
```

Wraps the nodes in a top-level JSON object with an attribute called nodes

To update the plot you created with D3.js, you need to go back to the HTML scaffold file and add the following line:

```
node.attr("r", function (d) { return Math.sqrt(d.r) * 100 + 3; })
```

Here you read the PageRank in the r attribute. You use it to modify the radius of each node in the visualization. Additionally, you scale the value so the area of each node is proportional to its PageRank. You also need to adjust some parameters of the visualization, such as the strength of repulsive forces, gravity, and link distance, to achieve a nice plot of the entire network as shown in figure 12.

Summary

This chapter looked at part of the F# community on Twitter and gave you some new insights into this community. You determined which users are important in the network

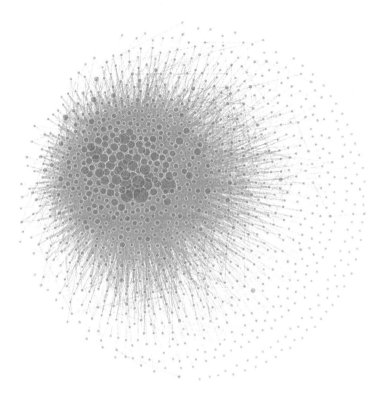

**Figure 12 Visualization of the F# Twitter network with nodes scaled
proportionally to their PageRank values**

and which users play the role of hubs. You also produced several different plots to analyze various aspects of the network's structure.

  If you want to spread information through the F# community, you know which
users you should target on Twitter. The same ideas can be used in other areas: for
example, in advertising and marketing, to create effective campaigns that use insights
from social networks.

  You downloaded data directly from Twitter, exported it for use with external
web-based visualization tools, and used the data for an advanced mathematical
analysis of the network structure. Using F# for the entire exploratory analysis
allowed you to combine all the different steps in one framework and therefore
shorten the time to market.

  The code also shows other aspects of F# that were highlighted in chapter 1.
Because the mathematical formulation of a problem is close to a functional programming style, you can easily translate PageRank equations into an *efficient* implementation. This property of functional code greatly simplifies the correct implementation of
complex mathematical problems.

About the author

Evelina Gabasova is a machine-learning and data-science enthusiast. She studied computational statistics and machine learning at University College London, and she will be finishing her PhD at Cambridge University in bioinformatics and statistical genomics in 2015.

Evelina has used many different languages in her work, such as MATLAB, R, and Python. In the end, F# is her favorite, and she uses it frequently for data manipulation and exploratory analysis. She writes a blog on F# in data science at www.evelinag.com, and you can find her on Twitter as @evelgab.

Integrating stock data into the F# language

Keith Battocchi

From its initial release, F# has always been a good language for manipulating data. The standard F# library provides a wide range of functions that help to reduce the complexity of data-processing tasks. For example, grouping, aggregation, and floating windows can be implemented in a single line of code. F#'s rich libraries, concise syntax, and support for functional programming can significantly reduce the time to market for data-driven applications. Despite these features, many data-access tasks require some amount of boilerplate code.

For example, consider the task of reading historical stock prices from the Yahoo! Finance site, which returns data as a comma-separated value (CSV) file. When pulling data, you create a simple data type representing the data stored in the rows (for example, a StockQuote type with appropriately typed properties for the date, opening price, and so on) along with a corresponding method for creating an instance of the type from the strings pulled from the columns of the file. Given the columns of the file, creating this data type is completely mechanical; but before F# 3.0, there wasn't a good way to automate this kind of metaprogramming. CSV files are just one example of a data source that has a logical schema that can be mapped to F# types—the same type of problem arises when dealing with databases, web services, XML and JSON documents, and even entire REST services.

In this chapter, you'll learn how to use a new feature in F# 3.0 called *type providers* to make accessing structured data from F# even easier. To simplify accessing stock data, you'll first build a CSV type provider, which makes it frictionless to access the data from an arbitrary CSV file.[1] Then you'll build a specialized type provider that focuses on the data exposed by Yahoo! Finance. The example demonstrates a

---

[1] The CSV type provider is a slightly simplified version of the open source CSV type provider included with the F# 3.0 Sample Pack, which can be found at http://fsharp3sample.codeplex.com.

number of business cases for F#. First, repeating boilerplate code is an error-prone approach to processing data, so removing this duplication helps you write correct code. Second, data access and parsing is a tedious task. By integrating Yahoo! Finance data directly into the language, you significantly reduce the time to market for analytical components based on this data source. In summary, type providers allow you to eliminate all the boilerplate just described and dive right in.

Introducing type providers

As you saw in the introduction, type providers are a new feature in F# 3.0, designed to make accessing external data easier. Type providers map external data sources into types that the F# compiler can understand. For example, the WorldBank type provider (see the following sidebar) provides a type WorldBank, which has an automatically generated property for each country of the world: WorldBank.``United States``, WorldBank.Ukraine, and so on. These members are generated by the type provider based on the current response from the WorldBank REST API.

F# data type providers

The standard F# distribution comes with type providers for a few data sources, including WSDL (web services) and SQL (using LINQ to Entities and LINQ to SQL). But a large number of type providers have been developed and maintained by the F# community as part of the F# Data project. The type providers include the following:

- XML, JSON, and CSV are type providers for three common file formats. They work by inferring the file schema from a sample file and generating types for accessing documents with the same structure.
- WorldBank and Freebase are specialized type providers that provide access to information provided by the World Bank (country development indicators) and Freebase (a graph-based online knowledge database).

F# Data is available on GitHub, and the package can be installed from NuGet using the package named FSharp.Data.

Before looking at the implementation of your own type provider, let's explore how type providers are used. This will help you understand the Yahoo! Finance type provider you'll implement in this chapter.

Using the CSV type provider

The CSV type provider is available in F# Data. In this section, you'll explore how it works. Providing access to CSV files will be one part of the Yahoo! Finance type provider, so you'll reimplement part of the CSV type provider later in this chapter (you could also reuse the code from F# Data, but reimplementing the CSV part will be a good example).

The files that you'll later obtain from the Yahoo! Finance service are CSV files containing stock data for a particular ticker symbol. A sample file starts with the following three lines:

```
Date,Open,High,Low,Close,Volume,Adj Close
2011-12-30,26.00,26.12,25.91,25.96,27395700,25.04
2011-12-29,25.95,26.05,25.86,26.02,22616900,25.10
```

The file starts with a header row that specifies the names of individual columns, followed by a number of lines with data that matches the scheme of the first row.

Without preprocessing the file or doing anything else, the CSV provider allows you to write a script like that in the following listing. It prints the date together with daily high and daily low prices from each row in the file that came from a day in December.

Listing 1 Using the CSV provider to print stock data from December

```
#r @"packages\FSharp.Data.2.0.0\lib\net40\FSharp.Data.dll"    References the
open FSharp.Data                                               F# Data library

type Stocks = CsvProvider<"sample.csv">              Loads data from a
let stockData = Stocks.Load("sample.csv")            (potentially different) file

let decemberEntries =
    stockData.Rows                                                Filters rows
    |> Seq.filter (fun stockRow -> stockRow.Date.Month = 12)      based on date

for entry in decemberEntries do                            Prints low and
    printfn "%A: %f - %f" entry.Date entry.Low entry.High   high prices
```

Infers the type based on a sample CSV file ❶

❷ Loads data

❸ Filters rows based on date

❹ Prints low and high prices

Listing 1 assumes that you obtained the F# Data package using NuGet, so the first line references FSharp.Data.dll from the packages directory ❶. The key part is the line that defines the Stocks type alias. The type provider looks at the specified sample file. The type provider then generates a type with a Rows property, where each row has properties corresponding to the headers in the CSV file such as Date ❸, Low, and High ❹.

Here you're running the script in F# Interactive (FSI), but you could equally compile it in a standard F# application and use the type provider to parse other CSV files by using a different filename in the call to the Load method ❷. The CSV provider gives similar benefits to using a code generator, but without the code generation! This means you can retain all of F#'s benefits as a great data-scripting language. Type providers even play nicely with the features of the integrated development environment (IDE) that make it easy to explore unfamiliar APIs from within an F# script, such as code completion.

How the CSV provider works

Perhaps the easiest way to think of a type provider is as a form of compiler plug-in. Type providers are components that match a particular interface and that are loaded from a referenced .NET assembly by the compiler at design time. At a high level, the type provider interface just specifies a set of .NET System.Type instances representing the types to provide, and these types expose provided members (such as methods, properties, and nested types). Each provided type has a corresponding .NET type that takes its place in the compiled code, and each call to a method or property has a corresponding code quotation that's inserted in its place.[2]

> **NOTE** An important part of the type-provider story is that type providers work well with editors (IDEs). When entering listing 1 into an IDE with F# support such as Visual Studio, you can type stockRow followed by a dot, and you'll get a completion list with the available columns. This means you need to consider design time (the type provider running in the editor), compile time (when the compiler is run), and runtime (when the compiled program runs).

If you look closely again at listing 1, you'll see one additional feature of type providers: the provided type (CsvProvider in this case) can be parameterized by statically known information (such as the location of the CSV file in this case, or a database connection string in the case of a type provider for connecting to SQL databases). This powerful mechanism allows the same type provider to be used to access a variety of similarly structured data sources.

The philosophy behind type providers

As listing 1 indicates, type providers fill a niche in F# that's filled by other technologies in other languages. For instance, you might use code generation to achieve something like what the type provider does in listing 1 if you were programming in another language (for example, C# developers use LINQ to Entities this way). To understand the unique benefits of type providers for F#, consider the following list of criteria:

- *Code-focused*—You want to minimize context switching. If you're using FSI, you should be able to reference a type provider and program against it interactively without having to switch to another tool first.
- *Uniform integration*—You want a single, consistent mechanism, regardless of the data source being accessed, and you want the types representing data sources to be treated just like any user-defined types. Together with the previous item, this motivates the use of .NET Type objects as the "interface" to type providers. Invoking a type provider is seamless, as opposed to some metaprogramming techniques that require explicit splicing syntax or preprocessing steps.
- *Compile-time checking*—Requiring strongly typed access means you want compile-time checking to make sure you're accessing data sources in a meaningful way. Moreover, you want to integrate with modern tooling, using code completion,

---

[2] There are two kinds of type providers: *erasing* and *generative*. In this chapter I'll only be describing the mechanics of erasing providers, because generative providers are typically used only to wrap existing .NET code generators.

tooltips, and so forth in an IDE to make you more productive. Doing so rules out techniques like metaobject protocols in dynamic languages.

- *Large-scale data sources*—You want something that scales to large data sources containing thousands or millions of logical types. For instance, exposing data in the Freebase online database (www.freebase.com) to F# programmers in a strongly typed way can't be done using naive code generation.
- *Live and evolving data sources*—You want to enable support for invalidation (for example, if the provider recognizes that the schema has changed on the server) while you're using your IDE. If you use a technique that involves a single compilation step, then there's no way to interact with a language service.

Type providers satisfy all of these criteria, whereas other techniques generally fail to satisfy some of them. For example, code generation can't scale to millions of logical types, and using dynamic languages doesn't provide the safety of a strongly typed system.

Designing and implementing the CSV type provider

Getting back to the main thread of this chapter, you want to implement a type provider that will give you type-safe, scalable access to the data available from Yahoo! Finance. The service returns data in the CSV format, so we'll start by looking at the part of the type provider that handles CSV files. As outlined in the following sidebar, the example combines two approaches to writing type providers.

General and specialized type providers

F# type providers for accessing data sources can be classified into two categories. *General-purpose* type providers provide access to data in a specific format or data store but work for any instance of the data. This includes SQL databases (where the type provider can directly use database schema) and XML, JSON, and CSV type providers (where the schema is inferred from a sample file). In all these cases, the provider can be used with any concrete database or data file.

Specialized type providers such as the WorldBank and Freebase providers are specialized to one particular kind of data. They provide type-safe access to properties from the data store (like countries, chemical elements, and so on), but they're bound directly to one data store.

The Yahoo! Finance type provider developed in this chapter is essentially an instance of the second class—it provides data access to a particular data store. But let's start with the CSV parsing part, which is an example of the first kind.

Design strategy

In my experience, the best way to design a type provider is to iterate through the following simple process:

1 Write some sample code you'd expect the user of your type provider to be able to write. In the CSV provider case, this would be the sample in listing 1.

2 Write the corresponding F# code that you'd expect the type provider to translate this to. For the CSV provider, this would use an F# runtime type that provides access to columns. For example, if the rows are represented as tuples, the translation for `stockRow.Date` would be `stockRow.Item1`.

3 Determine how to automate the translation from one to the other. At this stage, you'll sometimes discover an aspect of your proposed design that makes this hard or impossible. If that happens, back up and consider alternative designs for steps 1 and 2.

4 Implement the translation using the type provider API. The raw API (defined by the `ITypeProvider` interface) is difficult to master. I strongly recommend building on top of the ProvidedTypes API defined by the F# 3.0 Sample Pack, which exposes a much more straightforward interface.

This approach works particularly well for a few reasons. First, because type providers involve running code at design time that constructs expressions that will be invoked at runtime, it can be tricky to mentally track what's being computed at any given time. Explicitly writing down what the user will write and what the type provider should generate in response helps to keep these separate phases straight and ensures that the logic for the type provider is possible to implement.

> **TIP** The ProvidedTypes API is formed by two files that you can include in your type-provider project. The easiest way to get it is to add the `FSharp.TypeProviders.StarterPack` NuGet package to your project. The code from the package is used by F# Data and other F# community libraries (http://github.com/fsprojects), which are both good examples of how to use it.

To show how this works, consider again the code in listing 1. Listing 2 shows roughly how this code is translated by the CSV type provider.[3] If you want to see the code that a type provider generates, you can quote the code that uses the provider with the F# quotation operator (`<@ @>`) and inspect the result. Doing so can be extremely valuable for understanding how existing type providers work as well as for debugging a type provider that you're in the midst of writing.

F# type used by the provider to represent the file. Note the tuple type for the rows. ❶

Listing 2 Code emitted by the type provider

Invokes a factory method to construct the runtime representation ❷

```
let stockData =
    Runtime.CsvFile<DateTime * decimal * decimal * decimal * decimal>
        .Create(
            (fun row ->
                DateTime.Parse(row.[0]), Double.Parse(row.[1]), ...),
                (new StreamReader("sample.csv"))
```

Converts from column text values into the row tuple

---

[3] I've taken a few liberties with the translation. For example, the actual generated code contains additional information to ensure that string parsing happens in a globalization-friendly way.

```
let decemberEntries =
    stockData.Rows
    |> Seq.filter (fun stockRow -> stockRow.Item1.Month = 12)

for entry in decemberEntries do
    printfn "%A: %f - %f" entry.Item1 entry.Item4 entry.Item3
```

The Date, Low, and High properties are the tuple's first, fourth, and third items at runtime.

First, note that the provided type `CsvFile<"stocks.csv">` has been replaced by the real underlying type `Runtime.CsvFile<'T>`, which is a type that's included in the type provider's assembly. The runtime type is parameterized by the type of rows ❶. When using the type provider, this is a type with named properties, but at runtime, it's *erased* to a tuple type.

The call to the `Parse` method has been replaced by a call to `Create` ❷, which takes several arguments. These arguments specify the CSV file's location and the function used to convert the string array read out of each row into a strongly typed representation of the row. In this case, you're using a tuple type to represent the type of data in each row, with one field per column of the CSV file. Based on the contents of the file, the type provider has ensured that the conversion function converts each column's data into the right type based on the data that's in that column (that is, `DateTime` for the first column, `double` for the second column, and so on). The actual F# Data provider also takes delimiters, quotation characters, and culture information, but I omitted them here for simplicity.

Next, note that each property access on the row data (specifically the `Date`, `Low`, and `High` columns in listing 1) has been converted into a call to the tuple's corresponding item property[4] (the `Item1`, `Item4`, and `Item3` properties, respectively).

Inferring column types

The CSV type provider uses the names from the header row as the names of the properties, but it also infers the type of values in the columns. For example, in listing 1 you were able to directly access the month by writing `row.Date.Month`.

In this section, you'll implement a simple type-inference algorithm that works similarly to the one used in F# Data. You probably shouldn't expect to be able to infer the type from the first row: it's possible that you'll see a value like 5 (which you might naively take to be an integer value) even in a column containing floating-point values. This means you'll need to infer the type of a value and then the ability to combine the types—given two types, you want to *generalize* and produce a single type that can represent all values representable by the two types.

Additionally, it would be nice to infer whether or not data is required (based on whether there are any missing values in the rows you look at). This would lead to the same issue when trying to infer from only one row: just because you have a

---

[4] Although the `ItemN` properties on tuples are public, they're normally hidden from F# user code, so the literal translation isn't valid F# code.

value present in the first row doesn't mean a value is required. Although this is an important aspect of the real CSV type provider, we'll ignore this aspect to make the chapter simpler.

REPRESENTING AND INFERRING TYPES

First, you define a simple discriminated union that defines the types that your type provider supports. As mentioned earlier, this ignores missing values, and you only consider a few primitive types:

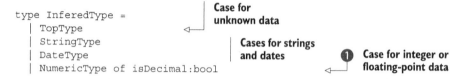

```
type InferedType =                      Case for
    | TopType                           unknown data
    | StringType                        Cases for strings
    | DateType                          and dates         ❶  Case for integer or
    | NumericType of isDecimal:bool                          floating-point data
```

Using a discriminated union means you'll be able to easily implement the generalization function later on. You have a case for strings and dates. The case for numeric types ❶ has a parameter specifying whether the numeric value can be decimal (represented as float) or integer (int).

Finally, you define a case called Top, which you'll use as a sentinel to indicate an unknown type of value to start with. Whenever you generalize among the Top type and any other type, the other type will always be chosen (so you'll end up with Top as the inferred type for a column when the data has no rows, in which case you'll default to a string).

Next, let's define the function that will infer a type from a particular string value. The actual code in the F# Data type providers is more complicated, because it needs to handle globalization using CultureInfo, but the idea is the same:

```
let inferStringType str =
    if fst (Int32.TryParse str) then NumericType(false)
    elif fst (Double.TryParse str) then NumericType(true)
    elif fst (DateTime.TryParse str) then DateType
    else StringType
```

In the inferStringType function, you repeatedly try to parse the string, starting with the most specific type (integer) and working your way toward more general types (floating-point number, and so on), stopping whenever you find a type for which you can parse the value. The code uses the fact that methods taking out arguments can be treated as methods returning a tuple of a Boolean success value and the parsed value. You get the Boolean (indicating success) using the fst function, ignoring the parsed value.

GENERALIZING TYPES

The most interesting part of the type-inference algorithm is the function that implements generalization. Given two types, you want to find a type that's suitable for representing values of both types. Compare the implementation in the following listing with the diagram showing the relationships between types in figure 1.

Listing 3 Finding the generalized type

```
let generalizeTypes = function
  | t1, t2 when t1 = t2 -> t1
  | TopType, t | t, TopType -> t
  | StringType, _
  | _, StringType -> StringType
  | DateType, _
  | _, DateType -> StringType
  | NumericType(f1), NumericType(f2) ->
      NumericType(f1 || f2)
```

❶ Checks for equal types

❷ Ignores the top types

❸ The string type is the most general.

❹ Dates don't unify with anything else.

❺ Choose the widest numeric type.

Just as you inferred the most specific applicable type when parsing individual values from strings, you likewise try to generalize two types to the most specific type that can hold both of their values. The implementation uses the following rules:

❶ If the types are the same, then you're finished—the generalized type is the same, too.

❷ If one of the types is `TopType`, then you use the other type, which must be more informative.

❸ If either of the types is `StringType`, then you use that as the result, because anything can be read as a string.

❹ If you get `DateType` on one side and some other type (which isn't a date, because that would be handled by case ❶), you return `StringType`, because there's no other common type.

❺ Finally, if you have two numerical types, then you return the "wider" type. You only support floating-point numbers and integers, so you treat floating-points as wider than integers (because an integer can be parsed as a float).

The rules respect the relationship between types demonstrated in figure 1. For any two types, you always return their common supertype—that is, a type to which there's an arrow from both of the source types.

As a concrete example of how this inference process works, assume the values in a column are 5, 6.5, and 1 million. Before reading any data, you start with `TopType` as your initial guess at the type because you have no information to go on. After reading the first value, 5, you refine your inferred type to `NumericType(false)` because that's the most specific type for which you can parse this value. Then you read the floating-point

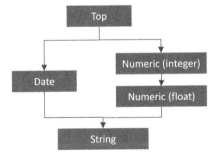

Figure 1 The subtyping relationship between inferred types. An arrow pointing from one type to another (for example, from `Date` to `String`) means a value of the first type can also be treated as a value of the other type. Any value can be treated as `String`, so you can always generalize any two types.

value and infer the type `NumericType(true)`. When you generalize the combination of `NumericType(false)` and `NumericType(true)`, you get `NumericType(true)`. Finally, you read 1 million and infer type `StringType`, because the value can't be automatically treated as numerical. You generalize `NumericType(true)` and `StringType` to get the final inferred type for the column: `StringType`.

Exercise

The type inference implemented here is basic. You can extend it in a number of interesting ways. First, try extending the hierarchy of the numerical types. When a value doesn't fit into the `Int32` type, it could be a large integer that can be represented as an `Int64` value. Also, if a value isn't an integer but is small enough, you can fit it in a more precise `Decimal` type. To do this, you'll need to change `NumericType` to carry another flag (or perhaps a number) as an argument. You can also add support for Booleans.

Your second task is more difficult: currently, a missing value will be treated as an empty string (`" "`), so all columns with missing values will become strings. Change the definition of `InferredType` to carry an optional flag (this isn't needed for strings), and update the inference and generalization functions accordingly.

Let's take a step back and look at what you've implemented so far. You wrote an inference algorithm that looks at a sequence of string values and infers the most appropriate type. Even though it's only a few lines, it's an amazing achievement! The key part of the implementation was handled by a single pattern-matching expression—this is another example of how F# lets you implement fairly complex logic in a few lines of code.

The next step toward building a type provider is implementing the runtime and writing code that generates types using the runtime types.

Implementing the runtime and type provider

The type provider implemented in this chapter works by generating provided types that are *erased* to actual runtime types. For example, the `Stocks` type declared in listing 1 was erased to runtime type `CsvFile<'T>` as shown in listing 2. In this section, you first implement the target runtime type and then look at the type-provider component that generates the erased type.

IMPLEMENTING THE CSV PROVIDER RUNTIME

At runtime, you need to have some representation for your CSV data. The CSV format supports quoting (for strings containing commas and newlines) and escaping, so writing a proper parser isn't easy. Fortunately, you can reuse the parser that's already available in F# Data to make your life easier. The functionality you'll need at runtime is simple. In particular, you'll need to do the following:

1 Read the contents of the specified file, either from a local file or from a URL.
2 Split the rows at the delimiters (ignoring delimiters that occur inside a quoted string). You use the CSV parser from F# Data for this.

3 Convert the column data to the row type. You do this by iterating over the rows and invoking a specified function on each row. The function is dynamically generated by the type provider based on the inferred type.

To encapsulate this functionality, you'll use a generic type, with the generic parameter indicating the type of the data for each row. Your type provider will always use a tuple type as the generic argument. Listing 4 contains the definition for the type used for CSV runtime support. The type uses the nongeneric `CsvFile` type from the F# Data library (which you can reference using the `FSharp.Data` package from NuGet).

Listing 4 CSV runtime support

```
open FSharp.Data                                          Generic parameter that
                                                          specifies the type of rows
type CsvFile<'T>
      (parser:(CsvRow -> 'T), file:string) =
   let data = CsvFile.Load(file)                          Takes a function for
   member x.Headers =                                   ❶ parsing single row
      data.Headers
   member x.Rows = seq {
      for row in data.Rows do                             Returns statically
         yield parser row }                             ❷ typed rows
```

The type would be more complicated if you had to reimplement CSV parsing, but it would still be simple. Why do you need to implement it? Because you now want to write code that generates a type that's erased to `CsvFile<'T>` as its runtime representation, so you need a specific structure of the type. In particular, the constructor takes the row parser and file to load ❶, and the `Rows` property returns the rows as a sequence of parsed values of the `'T` type ❷.

BUILDING CODE QUOTATIONS

The final piece of the puzzle for the type provider's implementation is to generate a type representing the specific CSV file structure (like `Stocks`) and the type representing its rows. The only difficult part is creating the conversion function, which maps the columns passed as strings into a tuple type that's used to represent the row at runtime.

The first thing you need to do is to map column types to parsing functions for individual columns. The function in listing 5 takes `InferredType` and returns its .NET representation together with a function that builds a code quotation representing the parsing of another quotation provided as an argument. This part is tricky, so look at the code first and then I'll explain what's going on.

Listing 5 Building quotations for parsing types

```
let getTypeAndParser = function
  | NumericType(false) ->                                   Numerical types
     typeof<int>, fun e -> <@@ Int32.Parse(%%e) @@>         become integers
  | NumericType(true) ->                                    or floats.
     typeof<float>, fun e -> <@@ Double.Parse(%%e) @@>
```

```
| DateType ->
    typeof<DateTime>, fun e -> <@@ DateTime.Parse(%%e) @@>
| StringType | TopType ->
    typeof<string>, fun e -> e
```

> Returns the
> string as is

> ❶ **DateType is parsed using DateTime.**

The parsing functions are returned as the second element of the tuple. They take expressions representing the string to parse and return other expressions representing the code that parses the specified parameter. You build an untyped quotation using <@@ ... @@>; this represents some F# code that can be compiled. The parameter e is another quoted expression, and you *splice* it into the entire expression using %%e. The parameter will be provided when you want to build the parsing function. For example, given row.Columns.[0], the expression for parsing dates ❶ will be Date-Time.Parse(row.Columns.[0]).

F# code quotations

F# code quotations are similar to LINQ expression trees. They represent code as a data structure that can be manipulated, processed, and compiled. In this chapter, you're using them to generate blocks of code in the type provider that are then passed to the compiler and used in the produced code.

Another important use of quotations is translation of F# code to some other runtime. For example, queries can be translated to run in SQL databases (as in LINQ to SQL). But F# code can also be translated to run as JavaScript (using FunScript or Web-Sharper) or as GPU code using Alea.cuBase.

The function that generates types based on a sample CSV file is a bit more complicated, so let's first explore its structure. It takes a CsvFile as a sample. This is the sample file that's specified as the static parameter, and its headers and rows are used to generate the type for a concrete CSV file. The structure of the function is as follows:

```
open ProviderImplementation.ProvidedTypes
open Microsoft.FSharp.Quotations

let generateTypesAndBuilder (sample:CsvFile) =
  let fieldInfos = [ ... ]

  let tupleTy = ( ... )
  let rowTy = ProvidedTypeDefinition( ... )
  (...)

  let builder = ( ... )
  rowTy, tupleTy, builder
```

> Gets the names
> and types of fields

> Gets the erased tuple
> type and generates a
> type representing Row

> Generates the code that reads
> the row as a typed tuple

Let's start with the first part of the function. The code in the next listing reads individual fields and uses the NumberOfColumns property of the CsvFile file together with the Headers property to get the names of the headers.

Listing 6   Getting the names and types of fields

```
let rows = sample.Rows |> Array.ofSeq
let fieldInfos =
  [ for i in 0 .. sample.NumberOfColumns - 1 do
        let header = sample.Headers.Value.[i]
        let typ =
            [ for row in rows ->
                  inferStringType row.Columns.[i] ]
            |> Seq.fold (fun t1 t2 ->
                  generalizeTypes(t1, t2)) TopType
        yield i, header, (getTypeAndParser typ) ]
```

Caches the
sample rows ⟵

Gets the name
of the column ⟵

❶ Infers the type from
the sample rows

❷ Generalizes from
the inferred types

For each field, you get its name (using `sample.Headers`) and then infer the type based on the rows of the sample CSV file. To infer the type, you first call `infer-StringType` to get the type of individual values ❶ and then combine the types using the `generalizeTypes` function, starting with the `TopType` ❷. Finally, you return the index, name, and type together with a parser quotation. Here you're running through the rows of data, splitting on delimiters, and using the `generalizeTypes` function to combine the inferred type for a given row with the inferred type based on all previous rows.

Next, you use F#'s reflection facilities to get the type of a tuple containing all of these fields and create a `Row` type that will erase to the tuple type, with a named property for each column.

Listing 7   Generating the provided `Row` type

```
let elementTypes = [| for (_, _, (ty, _)) in fieldInfos -> ty |]
let tupleTy = Reflection.FSharpType.MakeTupleType(elementTypes)

let rowTy = ProvidedTypeDefinition("Row", Some(tupleTy))
for i, fieldName, (fieldTy, _) in fieldInfos do
    let prop = ProvidedProperty(fieldName, fieldTy)
    prop.GetterCode <- fun [row] ->
        Quotations.Expr.TupleGet(row, i)
    rowTy.AddMember(prop)
```

❶ Builds the tuple
representing
rows at
runtime

Generates ❷
the
provided ⊳
Row type

Generates the
provided property ⟵

❸ Getter code that returns
the *i*th element of a tuple

The code starts by using F# reflection to build a tuple type that's used to represent the rows at runtime in the erased code ❶. The most interesting part is using `Provided-TypeDefinition` ❷ to build a new type called `Row`. The second parameter specifies the runtime representation of the type, which is your tuple built earlier.

The rest of the code iterates over all the known columns and generates a new `ProvidedProperty` of the type obtained from the type inference. Before adding the property to the `Row` type, you set its getter ❸. This is a function that takes a quotation representing the `this` instance and returns the code of the body. Here, the getter gets the *i*th field from the tuple.

Now you need to create a function that converts `CsvRow` to a typed tuple so that you can later pass it to the `CsvFile<'T>` runtime as the first argument. In principle, you need to generate code that looks something like this:

```
fun row ->
  (DateTime.Parse(row.Columns.[0], Double.Parse(row.Columns.[1]))
```

The parts marked in bold are those that you need to build now. The rest of the code—the parsing—is code you already have from the `getTypeAndParser` function in listing 5. The code generation is shown next.

Listing 8 Generating the parsing function

```
let rowVar = Var("row", typeof<CsvRow>)            ◁──┐  Input variable of
let rowExpr = Expr.Var(rowVar)                         ❶  the function

let convertedItems =
  [ for i, _, (ty, parser) in fieldInfos ->                ❷  Generates column
      let index = Expr.Value(i)                                access and the
      parser <@@ (%%rowExpr:CsvRow).Columns.[%%index] @@> ] ◁──  call to parser

let tupleExpr = Quotations.Expr.NewTuple(convertedItems)  ❹  Constructs the builder
let builder = Quotations.Expr.Lambda(rowVar, tupleExpr)   ◁──  lambda function
```

Expression returning the variable → (point to `let rowExpr = Expr.Var(rowVar)`)

Builds ❸ a tuple from the expressions → (point to `let tupleExpr = Quotations.Expr.NewTuple(convertedItems)`)

You start by creating a variable named `row` of type `CsvRow` ❶ that represents the input of the lambda function. Next you build a list with expressions representing the individual tuple arguments. Here, you use a quotation literal `<@@ ... @@>` with splicing using `%%` ❷ to build an expression that takes the variable you built earlier and accesses the current column. The quotation is then passed to `parser`, which generates the parsing code around it—turning `String` into the appropriate element type. Finally, you create an expression representing the body of the lambda function ❸ and the lambda function itself ❹.

Completing the CSV type provider

The last step in the implementation of the CSV type provider would be to write a new type that inherits from `TypeProviderForNamespaces`, annotate it with the `Type-Provider` attribute, and write code to generate the concrete type representing the entire file (such as `Stocks` in the earlier example).

Accomplishing this isn't that much work, and you can find the complete example on the book's website. But the main goal of this chapter is to build a type provider for Yahoo! Finance that uses the CSV provider functionality to provide access to financial data. So, let's skip the final part of building the CSV provider and instead look at how to obtain information about companies. Then you'll wrap the financial data into a type provider for Yahoo! Finance, which will rely on all the functionality you've implemented so far. The CSV data handling that you implemented in this section may be simple and doesn't handle various corner cases, but it's a great example of what needs to be done to implement the internals of a type provider.

Implementing the Yahoo! Finance type provider

General-purpose type providers, like the CSV type provider, are useful because they can be used with a wide variety of data sources. Indeed, our CSV type provider can work not only with local CSV files, but also with CSV files served via the web. And fortunately, there are providers such as Yahoo! Finance that make such data publicly available.

Unfortunately, the URLs for Yahoo! Finance's data are a bit esoteric and take stock tickers as parameters. To get data for IT companies like Microsoft and Yahoo!, you need to know that their ticker names are MSFT and YHOO. Moreover, the URL can also encode other information. For example, to get weekly stock prices for Yahoo!'s stock between January and March of 2012, you'd use a URL like

```
http://ichart.yahoo.com/table.csv?s=YHOO&a=0&b=1&c=2013
    &d=2&e=31&f=2013&g=d&ignore=.csv
```

Although it's no problem to use these complicated URLs with the CSV type provider, the need to create them adds room for error and makes it hard to explore the data.

In cases like these, it's often nice to create a type provider that makes accessing a specific data source more convenient. Toward that end, in this section you'll create a type provider that makes it easy to navigate through a directory of companies and get their stock prices. For example, you'll be able to write the following code:

```
open DeepDives

type tech = Yahoo.Technology
type goods = Yahoo.``Consumer Goods``

let companies =
  [ tech .``Technical & System Software``.``Adobe Systems Inc``
    tech.``Internet Information Providers``.``Google Inc.``
    goods.``Electronic Equipment``.``Apple Inc`` ]
```

If you haven't done so already, have a look at the complete sample on the book's website. When you use the type provider in an F# editor, you'll get autocompletion as you navigate through the different sectors and companies. This makes the type provider a fantastic tool for explorative data programming. The remainder of this section shows you how to build a specialized provider like this one.

Getting company information using YQL

To implement this type provider, you'll build on top of a Yahoo! service called the Yahoo! Query Language (YQL), which you can use to access Yahoo! Finance service endpoints for enumerating sectors and industries. YQL enables you to encode queries to those services in the form of specially formatted URLs. When you issue web requests to those URLs, you get XML responses representing the query results. As an example, to get the results of the YQL query

```
"select * from yahoo.finance.sectors"
```

you issue a request to the corresponding URL:

```
http://query.yahooapis.com/v1/public/yql?q=select%20*%20from%20
➥ yahoo.finance.sectors&env=store%3A%2F%2Fdatatables.org%2
➥ Falltableswithkeys
```

The response you get looks like this:

```
<?xml version="1.0" encoding="UTF-8"?>
<query xmlns:yahoo="http://www.yahooapis.com/v1/base.rng"
    yahoo:count="9" yahoo:created="2013-04-19T10:14:58Z">
  <results>
    <sector name="Basic Materials">
      <industry id="112" name="Agricultural Chemicals"/>
      <industry id="132" name="Aluminum"/>
      <industry id="110" name="Chemicals - Major Diversified"/>
      <!-- ... -->
    </sector>
    <sector name="Conglomerates">
      <!-- ... -->
    </sector>
  </results>
</query>
```

You could read the data using a standard .NET library for working with XML, but because your code already uses F# Data, you can use the XML type provider in the implementation of your higher-level Yahoo! Finance type provider. Before drilling into the implementation, let's write a simple script that prints the relevant information:

```
#r @"..\packages\FSharp.Data.2.0.0 \lib\net40\FSharp.Data.dll"      ❶ References the F#
open FSharp.Data                                                        Data library in a
                                                                       new script file

type Sectors = XmlProvider<                                          ❷ Gets the type for
    @"http://query.yahooapis.com/v1/public/yql?q=                       sample XML results
➥ select%20*%20from%20yahoo.finance.sectors&env=store
➥ %3A%2F%2Fdatatables.org%2Falltableswithkeys" >

for s in Sectors.GetSample().Results.Sectors do                     ◀── Lists all sectors
    printfn "Sector: %s" s.Name
    for sub in s.Industries do                                      ◀─┤ Prints each industry
        printfn "  - %s (%d)" sub.Name sub.Id                          │ name and ID
```

You're using the code in a new script file, so you need to start by referencing F# Data ❶. Then you use the XML type provider to get a type for type-safe access to the YQL query results (based on the sample query discussed earlier). Note that the sample URL ❷ is printed as multiline here, but it needs to be on a single line without spaces.

The rest of the code is simple thanks to the fact that the XML type provider generates a nice type for reading the data. You use the GetSample method to read the XML document specified as the sample ❷ and iterate over all sectors and the industries they contain, and then you print the details.

You can iterate through the industry nodes in the same way. When you do so, you extract the industry ID and issue another YQL query along the lines of "select * from `yahoo.finance.industry where id="112""` (depending on the ID of the industry you're drilling into). From there you can get the set of companies associated with that industry.

Implementing the type provider

As the chapter nears its end, let's look at the code needed to build a type provider! In this subsection, you start by writing a type provider `YahooProvider` that contains one nested type for each sector, which then contain one more deeply nested type for each industry. The following listing implements the part of the type provider that lets you easily navigate through different sectors. You'll add the companies and get the data in the next two subsections.

Listing 9   Type provider for navigating through industries

```
type Sectors = XmlProvider<"...">                         ◁─── Type for reading
                                                               sectors using YQL
module YahooRuntime =
  let yahooIndustries = Lazy.Create(fun () ->              ◁─┐ Global value
    [ for sector in Sectors.GetSample().Results.Sectors ->   │ storing the sectors
        let industries =                                     ❶ and industries
          [ for sub in sector.Industries -> sub.Id, sub.Name ]
        sector.Name, industries ] )

  [<TypeProvider>]                                          ❷ Defines a type-
  type YahooProvider(cfg:TypeProviderConfig) as this =        provider type
    inherit TypeProviderForNamespaces()

    let asm = System.Reflection.Assembly.GetExecutingAssembly()  ⎤ Hosting assembly and
    let ns = "DeepDives"                                         ⎦ generated namespace

    let generateIndustry id name =                          ❸ Generates the type
      ProvidedTypeDefinition(name, None)                       for an industry

    let generateType () =
      let yahooTyp = ProvidedTypeDefinition(asm, ns, "Yahoo", None)   ⎤ Adds the sector
      for sector, industries in YahooRuntime.yahooIndustries.Value do │ type as a child
        let sectorTyp = ProvidedTypeDefinition(sector, None)          │ of the global
        yahooTyp.AddMember(sectorTyp)                                 │ type
        for id, name in industries do                         ◁──────┘
          sectorTyp.AddMember(generateIndustry id name)      ◁─┐ Generates a child
        yahooTyp                                               ❻ for each industry

    do this.AddNamespace(ns, [ generateType() ])
```

Side annotations (left):
- **Returns the sector name with a list of industries** ▷ (points to `sector.Name, industries ]`)
- **Generates the global type with a subtype for each sector** ❹ ▷
- **Builds the type for a sector** ❺ ▷
- **Registers the main type** ▷

The code starts by wrapping the previous snippet in the `YahooRuntime` module, which contains a single lazy value ❶ that returns the list of sectors and their industries with the name and the ID. You use a lazy value to avoid downloading the list multiple times.

The type provider is implemented as a type `YahooProvider` ❷, which is marked with the `TypeProvider` attribute and inherits from `TypeProviderForNamespaces`. The type definition, followed by the code to get the current .NET assembly, is boilerplate code shared by most type-provider implementations.

**Figure 2   The Yahoo! Finance type provider in action. So far, the
type provider lets you browse different sectors (such as Technology).
When you select a sector, you can then navigate through the
industries. In Visual Studio or Xamarin Studio, you'll see the different
available sectors and industries in the autocompletion lists.**

Most of the interesting code is implemented in the generateType ④ and generate-
Industry ③ functions. The former is the main function that generates the global type
named Yahoo ④, and the latter is a simple function that builds a type representing
each specific industry. In the global type, you build a new type for each sector ⑤ and
add it as a direct child of the global type. The industry types are added as children of
the sector type ⑥, which gives you a nice nested structure that can be explored interactively by typing a dot (.) and looking at the child types.

So far, you've built a type provider for exploring the hierarchy of Yahoo! Finance
sectors and industries. You can see how it looks in figure 2. The next step is to get the
list of companies in the generateIndustry function.

Generating company names lazily

If you use the type provider, you'll notice that it takes some time before the autocompletion list appears initially. This is because the type provider first needs to run the
YQL query to get the sectors and industries. Now imagine that you also had to run
another YQL query to get the companies for each industry!

Fortunately, the F# type-provider mechanism is designed to scale to extremely large
data sources. The mechanism has the ability to expose members of provided types
lazily. Taking advantage of laziness is easy: instead of using the AddMember method on
ProvidedType, as you did in the previous example, you call the AddMembersDelayed

method. Listing 10 shows a new version of the generateIndustry function, together with one more XML type for reading YQL results (you'll need to put this into the Yahoo-Runtime module).

Listing 10   Lazily loading the industry contents

```
type Companies = XmlProvider<                                            ❶ Parses
   @"http://query.yahooapis.com/v1/public/yql?q=select                     the YQL
   ➥ %20*%20from%20yahoo.finance.industry%20where%20id%3D%22852%22         company
   ➥ &env=store%3A%2F%2Fdatatables.org%2Falltableswithkeys" >              search

let generateIndustry id name =
   let industryTyp = ProvidedTypeDefinition(name, None)              ❷ Generates
   industryTyp.AddMembersDelayed(fun () ->     ◁                       companies lazily
```
```
Gets the ❸  let companies = Companies.Load(@"http://query.yahooapis.com/v1/" +
companies in       @"public/yql?q=select%20*%20from%20yahoo.finance.industry" +
the current        @"%20where%20id%3D%22" + (string id) + @"%22&env=store" +
industry           @"%3A%2F%2Fdatatables.org%2Falltableswithkeys")            ❹ Builds a
                                                                                property
   [ for c in companies.Results.Industry.Companies ->                         for each
      let companyProp = ProvidedProperty(c.Name, typeof<string>) ◁             company
      companyProp.IsStatic <- true
      companyProp.GetterCode <- fun _ -> <@@ "TODO" @@>   ◁     Returns a dummy
      companyProp ] )                                      ❺  string for now
   industryTyp
```

Listing 10 starts by defining a type, Companies ❶, which is later used for parsing the results of an YQL query returning the list of companies in a given industry ❷. Note that the URL in the first case needs to be on a single line, but we had to split it into multiple lines here. When getting the list of companies, you build the URL dynamically ❸ and include the ID of the current industry.

The part that generates the type first creates ProvidedTypeDefinition (as before), but now you use the AddMembersDelayed function to add an industry's companies in a lazy fashion. The operation takes a lambda function as an argument and calls it when the members are needed (such as when the user looks at the members in the code editor). The function needs to return a list of members to be added. Here, you iterate over all the companies and add a static property for each company ❹.

In this listing, all properties (representing the companies) are of type string, and their getter code always returns the "TODO" string ❺. The final step is to replace this with a call to the CSV type provider runtime that you implemented earlier in this chapter.

Reusing the CSV provider

Once you get down to the individual company level, you're ready to read the data from Yahoo!'s CSV files. This gives you an opportunity to reuse your existing CSV provider in the implementation of the Yahoo! Finance provider. Fortunately, because the structure of the CSV files is fully known, it's much easier to generate the right quotation this time around. Listing 11 shows the new version of the `generateIndus-try` and `generateType` functions. The former is now a bit more complex, because it needs to generate a body for each of the properties. The latter is similar to the code shown earlier. The only difference is that it fetches sample CSV data and generates a row type that's shared by all the properties accessing specific company stock prices.

Listing 11   Using the CSV components in the Yahoo! Finance provider

```
let generateIndustry id name (rowTy:Type) (tupleTy: Type) convFunc =      ❶ Builds a
  let industryTyp = ProvidedTypeDefinition(name, None)                       specialized
  industryTyp.AddMembersDelayed(fun () ->                                    CsvFile and
                                                                             gets its
    let csvFileTy = typedefof<CsvFile<_>>.MakeGenericType(tupleTy)           constructor
    let csvCtor = csvFileTy.GetConstructors() |> Seq.head
```
```
    let companies = Companies.Load( ... )
    [ for c in companies.Results.Industry.Companies ->
        let url = "http://ichart.yahoo.com/table.csv?s=" + c.Symbol      ❷ Builds the
        let body =                                                         body of the
          Expr.PropertyGet                                                 property
            ( Expr.NewObject(csvCtor, [convFunc; Expr.Value(file)]),       getter
              csvFileTy.GetProperty("Rows") )

        let rowSeqTy = typedefof<seq<_>>.MakeGenericType(rowTy)     ◀─┐  Returns
        let companyProp = ProvidedProperty(c.Name, rowSeqTy)              the type in
        companyProp.IsStatic <- true                                      a sequence
        companyProp.GetterCode <- fun _ -> body                           of rows
        companyProp ] )
    industryTyp
```
URL with data for the company → points to the `let url = ...` line.
Sets the body of the getter → points to the `companyProp.GetterCode <- fun _ -> body` line.

```
let generateType () =                                                   ❸ Infers the
  let yahooTyp = ProvidedTypeDefinition(asm, ns, "Yahoo", None)           CSV type
  let sample = CsvFile.Load("http://ichart.yahoo.com/table.csv?s=FB")     format from
  let rowTy, tupleTy, convFunc = generateTypesAndBuilder sample          the sample
  yahooTyp.AddMember(rowTy)                                               data

  for sector, industries in YahooRuntime.yahooIndustries.Value do
    // ( ... )
    for id, name in industries do
      let industryTyp = generateIndustry id name rowTy tupleTy convFunc
      sectorTyp.AddMember(industryTyp)
```
Passes the details to generate-Industry → points to the `let industryTyp = generateIndustry ...` line.

In the `generateType` function, you call the `generateTypesAndBuilder` function ❸ from earlier in this chapter. This gives you two types: `rowTy`, which represents the generated type for rows (with named properties), and `tupleTy`, which is the underlying tuple type. You also get a quotation representing a function for converting from a `CsvRow` to the underlying tuple type. The rest of the function is the same as earlier, with the only difference being that all the information is passed to `generateIndustry`.

When generating types for an industry, you first build a type `CsvFile<'T>`, where `'T` is the underlying tuple type, and you get the constructor of the type ❶. The most interesting part is the code that builds body ❷. This is an expression that reads the CSV file and returns the rows. The expression that you want to build looks like this:

```
(new CsvFile<DateTime * float * float>(
    (fun row ->
        DateTime.Parse(row.Columns.[0]),
        Double.Parse(row.Columns.[0]),
        Double.Parse(row.Columns.[0]) ),
     "http://ichart.yahoo.com/table.csv?s=MSFT" )).Rows
```

The code to construct the quotation uses two methods from the `Expr` type. You call `Expr.NewObject` to build an expression that represents a constructor call with the function and the string value as arguments. Then you create an expression that returns the `Rows` property of the type using `Expr.PropertyGet`.

To conclude the chapter, let's have a quick look at the completed type provider.

Yahoo! Finance provider in action

The Yahoo! Finance type provider is focused on providing easy access to one specific data source. This makes it a great fit for interactive scripting. The general-purpose CSV provider might be a better fit for writing applications and libraries.

The main strength of the Yahoo! Finance provider is that it lets you explore the data available to you through the type system. This makes it easy to write scripts that work with data of specific companies. For example:

```
#r "YahooProvider.dll"
open DeepDives

type tech = Yahoo.Technology                           Accesses sectors as
type goods = Yahoo.``Consumer Goods``                  named properties

let companies =
  [ tech .``Technical & System Software``.``Adobe Systems Inc``   Navigates through
    tech.``Internet Information Providers``.``Google Inc.``       industries and
    goods.``Electronic Equipment``.``Apple Inc`` ]               companies

for c in companies do
  let latests = c |> Seq.maxBy (fun r -> r.Date)        Accesses CSV data
  printfn "%A" latests.Open                             in a typed fashion
```

In this example, you first define two type aliases for types representing Technology and Consumer Goods sectors. You then get a list of several companies from each of the sectors and find the latest opening price for each of the companies. The types help you in two ways. First, they greatly reduce the time to market for such interactive analyses. Imagine the code you'd have to write to issue the YQL queries by hand, parse the returned XML, and then read the CSV data!

Second, having the names available in the types also reduces the potential for bugs. Misspelling a stock ticker could easily give you code that returns data for a completely different company than you intended. Using a type provider, you use the full name, and the compiler makes sure the company exists.

I hope this chapter has convinced you that writing a type provider isn't black magic but rather a fun problem! Of course, in many cases you can use the existing type providers for formats like JSON, XML, and CSV, but there are certainly some good uses for writing custom providers.

Building real-world type providers

To make this chapter reasonably short, I ignored a couple of issues that you may have to face when writing real-world type providers. The first issue is *caching*. When you use our sample provider, you'll notice that it occasionally takes some time before you get the autocompletion list. To improve this, you should cache the YQL query results and use the cached values.

The second issue appears when you want to write type providers that work as portable libraries (for mobile apps). In that case, you need to separate the runtime component (which is portable) from the type-provider component (which isn't portable and runs as a compiler plug-in). Both of these issues are solved, for example, in the F# Data type providers, so the project source code might give you a good hint as to how to solve them.

Summary

In this chapter, you learned about type providers and how to use them. You saw how type providers make accessing strongly typed data simple and safe. Although writing a type provider isn't trivial, it's easier than you might think. When you repeatedly need to access a specific data source, writing a custom type provider can significantly reduce the time you spend writing the data-access code.

You implemented two kinds of type providers in this chapter. A general CSV type provider lets you access arbitrary CSV files in a strongly typed fashion, regardless of whether the files are found locally or on the internet. This is a great way to handle common file formats, and it can be used in both scripting and compiled applications.

Then you implemented a type provider specific to Yahoo! Finance, to make it easier to navigate the vast set of financial data that's available. This type provider is more suitable for scripting purposes when you're interested in getting data for a specific company. It lets you do interesting financial analyses without leaving the F# editor.

Along the way, you learned how to design type providers. You saw how to build code quotations to express the code that a type provider emits, and you also learned how to take advantage of lazy loading to ensure that large spaces of provided types can be explored in an ad hoc manner without pulling back large quantities of data over the web.

About the author

Keith Battocchi is a developer in the Conversational Understanding team in Microsoft's Applications and Services Group. Previously he spent two years working on the design and applications of type providers with the F# team at Microsoft Research.

## PART 3

Developing complete systems

In the previous part, we talked about using F# for implementing the core business logic, or *analytical components* of larger applications. As discussed in chapter 1, this is an area where the benefits of a functional-first approach are an easy sell.

But functional-first programming isn't useful *only* for analytical components. Many developers and companies use it to build complete systems. If you're an individual or have a small team that already knows F#, you can build incredible applications in F#, and you'll benefit from the expressivity and safety of the language even when building games, user interfaces, or large concurrent systems.

In this part, you'll see four examples: two focused on the front end and two on the backend side. In chapters 7 and 9, Dmitry Morozov and Johann Deneux talk about building UI-oriented applications: trading applications and games. You'll see that F# lets you nicely handle difficult problems like data binding and implementing asynchronous game logic. In chapters 8 and 10, Simon Cousins and Yan Cui look at the backend, covering the agent-based programming model for data analytics and development of a server for social games.

You'll see that the business cases discussed in chapter 1 also apply to the development of complete systems. When writing games, efficiency and the ability to get the game ready as soon as possible are crucial. Trading systems and concurrent data analyses are fundamentally complex systems, and F# lets you correctly solve problems that would be hard to tackle in other languages.

7

Developing rich user interfaces using the MVC pattern

Dmitry Morozov

With the recent advance of mobile apps and web apps based on HTML5 and JavaScript, you might think that native desktop applications are no longer relevant. This couldn't be further from the truth—the majority of business applications still run on the desktop. Many domains still require sophisticated user interfaces; they need to perform complex computations efficiently (benefiting from multiple CPUs) and display rich, interactive visualizations.

Two things are crucial for the development of rich desktop applications. First, you need a powerful framework that allows you to build the best user experience by taking full advantage of the capabilities of the underlying system. For Windows, Extensible Application Markup Language (XAML) based frameworks (Windows Presentation Foundation [WPF], Silverlight, and Windows Runtime) are the de facto choice. Second, you need a programming language that makes it easy to express the domain model and encode complex user interactions.

From a business perspective, the most important reason for adopting F# for desktop UI development is handling *complexity*. User interface development isn't easy, and you need a language that lets you build the right abstractions. At the same time, the rich type system of F# gives you many *correctness* guarantees.

The most common way to structure the code base of XAML applications is the well-known Model-View-ViewModel (MVVM) pattern (see the sidebar "State of the Art: The MVVM Pattern"). But in this chapter, you'll use a different approach that allows you to benefit from F#'s strengths. The examples build on my experience developing an F# Model-View-Controller (MVC) framework.[1] I'll show you how to build the entire application from the beginning.

---

[1] My series "F# MVC Framework for WPF" is available at http://mng.bz/ZCKC. If you feel like exploring concepts of developing a WPF GUI in F#, I encourage you read the series in full.

State of the art: the MVVM pattern

The MVVM pattern can be used with F#, but it was originally designed and optimized for C#/VB.NET and so doesn't take advantage of many unique features that F# brings to the table. In particular, it doesn't let you benefit from immutability, a powerful type system, and a functionally oriented computation model. That's why this chapter builds on the MVC pattern—another pattern that is often implemented in UI applications.

MVVM is a variation of Martin Fowler's Presentation Model pattern. It follows the classic object-oriented programming (OOP) approach where state and behavior are combined in one monolithic object (ViewModel). This makes the pattern inappropriate for function-first languages such as F# where immutable state is separated from behavior.

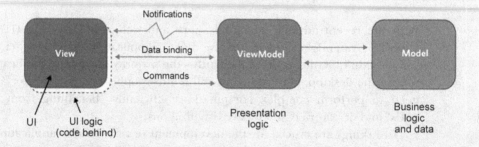

The MVVM pattern

In MVVM, the state between View and ViewModel is synchronized by data binding. Events are communicated to the ViewModel via the *command* mechanism. Commands are limited, so developers must use a direct event subscription or another extension technique called *behaviors*. This variety makes event processing non-uniform and therefore hard to compose, test, and reason about. In addition to the visual state (usually properties participating in data binding), the ViewModel usually contains an operational state like a database connection or web service proxies. This adds another level of complexity to an already far-from-simple combination of logic and mutable state.

Commands, bindings, and behaviors represent a form of coupling, but all of them bypass a type system because they're expressed in terms of object type. It makes them implicit runtime dependencies, which are the trickiest of all to track.

GUI development is a vast topic and can't be fully covered in one chapter. I'll focus on a way to organize logic around individual screens that's different from the MVVM pattern. To do so, let's go back to the roots and use a variation of the MVC pattern.[2]

---

[2] The closest pattern is probably Martin Fowler's Supervising Controller.

Setting the scene

As an example, I put together a trading application that's simple enough to be covered in one chapter and yet has a "real world" touch. This section introduces the trading application. You'll also explore the MVC pattern, which will define the structure underlying the implementation.

The trading application

After the application starts, the user enters a tradable security symbol (such as MSFT) and clicks the "i" button to retrieve security information from Yahoo. Selecting the Price Feed Simulation check box activates a feed from one year ago to the current day (Yahoo historical pricing). The button in the Position Management section shows the current price and available action: Buy or Sell. On the right, a chart displays the price history (see figure 1).

The next step a user can take is to open a position. The available action changes from Buy to Sell, and the chart is divided into two areas: profit (light green) and loss (light red). The profit and loss (P&L) value for the open position is either red (under water) or green. At this point, a user can choose to close the position manually or set up Stop Loss At and Take Profit At thresholds. Once the position is closed, no actions can be taken on it (see figure 2).

As mentioned earlier, the application design is based on the MVC pattern. Before I delve into the details of the individual components for the trading application, let's look at a simple example that demonstrates how the components look and interact in the functional setting.

Introducing the MVC pattern

The MVC pattern is a set of components for building a UI. The key idea is Model-View and View-Controller separation (see figure 3).

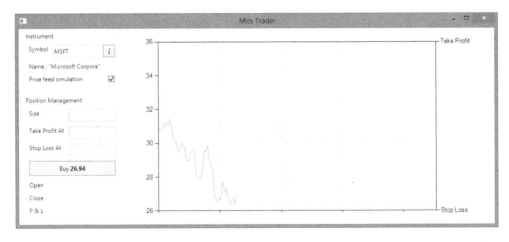

Figure 1   The sample application: the user has entered a security symbol and started the price feed.

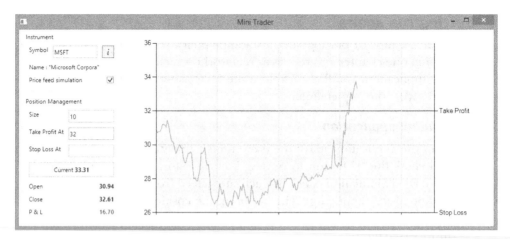

Figure 2   The position is closed.

Event processing is at the heart of any GUI application. F# embraces events as first-class values. For
example, they can be passed in or out of functions,
or they can make up collections. Event streams are
particularly useful because they can be transformed
and composed in a familiar functional style. With
this concept in mind, let's describe the hypothetical,
purely functional architecture behind a UI widget
that's a numeric up/down control, like the one shown
in figure 4, using only types:

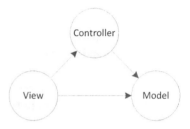

Figure 3   MVC pattern

```
type UpDownEvent = Incr | Decr
```
⟵ **Different kinds of events generated by the view
are represented as cases in a discriminated union.**

```
type View = IObservable<UpDownEvent>
```
⟵ **View, abstracted as an event stream**

```
type Model = { State : int }
```
⟵ **Sample model that holds a single field, State.
Defined as an F# record; immutable.**

```
type Controller = Model -> UpDownEvent -> Model
```
⟵ **The Controller function
takes the model and event
and returns a new model.
For simplicity, think of
Controller as an event
handler.**

```
type Mvc = Controller -> Model -> View -> Model
```
⟵

**The Mvc function applies the Controller function to
each event in the stream, threading a model
argument through the computation.**

This design is dramatically different from MVVM. It has a functional twist: the model is
immutable, the view exposes an event stream, and the events are modeled using a discriminated union. Functional gurus may spot remarkable similarity between the Mvc
type and Seq.fold. Interestingly, you can get a pretty good idea of the application
structure just by reading the type definitions. Describing design intent with types may

```
  10 ▲▼
```
Figure 4   Numeric up/down control

seem unusual to somebody accustomed to methods like UML, but it makes sense—
functional types are succinct and won't go out of date as your application evolves.

This architecture is a good starting point, but it's impractical to use. The immutable model is incompatible with data binding, which XAML relies on heavily. With some improvements, the model looks like this:

```
type UpDownEvent = Incr | Decr
type View = IObservable<UpDownEvent>
type Model = { mutable State : int }
type Controller = Model -> UpDownEvent -> unit
type Mvc = Controller -> Model -> View -> IDisposable
```

All the components are well separated: `Model` can be any type, `View` is an interface generalized by the `UpDownEvent` type, the `Controller` function applies `Event` to `Model` by mutating state, and `Mvc` is a mediator that glues all the pieces together. A type parameter for `View` has no special constraints, but it's best expressed as a discriminated union. It allows you to represent different events raised by a single view. A concrete implementation of the pattern for the up/down control looks like this:

```
open System

let subject = Event<UpDownEvent>()
let raiseEvents xs = List.iter subject.Trigger xs
let view = subject.Publish

let model : Model = { State = 6 }

let controller model event =
    match event with
    | Increment -> model.State <- model.State + 1
    | Decrement -> model.State <- model.State - 1

let mvc: Mvc = fun controller model view ->
    view.Subscribe(fun event ->
        controller model event
        printfn "Model: %A" model)

let subscription = view |> mvc controller model
raiseEvents [Increment; Decrement; Increment]
subscription.Dispose()
```

The `Event<_>` type from the F# core library plays two roles: observer, via the Trigger method, and subject (event source) because it inherits from `IObservable<_>`.

When this code snippet is executed in FSI, it outputs the following:

```
Model: {State = 7;}
Model: {State = 6;}
Model: {State = 7;}
```

Controller pattern-matches on the `UpDownEvent` to provide case-specific processing logic. If one of the cases isn't handled (try to comment out the `Increment` case, for example), the compiler warns, "Incomplete pattern matches." This compiler-checked event handling enables a clean, loosely coupled, yet cohesive architecture.

Defining the model[3]

To support data binding between the WPF UI and the model, the type representing the model needs to implement the INotifyPropertyChanged interface. This notifies the view when the values of the model change so that it can be automatically updated.

Naive implementations of INotifyPropertyChanged often suffer from tedious and error-prone invocations to raise the PropertyChanged event inside the setter of every single property. A clever way to avoid this is to use dynamic proxy interception. Proxy objects allow calls to virtual members (including property setters) of an object to be intercepted without modifying the code of the class. In the postprocess phase, the interceptor raises the PropertyChanged event.

> **TIP** Castle DynamicProxy is a component for generating lightweight .NET proxies on the fly at runtime. It's part of the bigger Castle.Core library available via NuGet (www.nuget.org/packages/Castle.Core).

To use dynamic proxy interception, you need to write the code as follows:

- A property eligible for interception must be defined as virtual (or abstract).
- The factory method Model.Create must be used to create a model instance.
- Application-specific models must inherit from the base model type and have a parameter-less constructor.

When you're dealing with dynamic invocations, some reflection-based coding is inevitable. To avoid duplication and make it more palatable, you can create some helpers.

Listing 1   Helper active patterns for implementing interception

```
open System.Reflection

let (|PropertySetter|_|) (m : MethodInfo) =          ◁─┐  Checks if the method is a
  match m.Name.Split('_') with                           property setter. If so,
  | [| "set"; propertyName |] -> Some propertyName       extracts the property name.
  | _ -> None

let (|PropertyGetter|_|) (m : MethodInfo) =          ◁─┐  Checks if the method is a
  match m.Name.Split('_') with                           property getter. If so,
  | [| "get"; propertyName |] -> Some propertyName       extracts the property name.
  | _ -> None

let (|Abstract|_|) (m : MethodInfo) =         ◁─┐  Is it an abstract
  if m.IsAbstract then Some() else None            method?
```

Now you can implement the base type for custom models with the Create factory method, which sets up interceptors.

---

[3] The term *model* here means a presentation model, not a domain model.

Listing 2 Base class for implementing models

```
[<AbstractClass>]
type Model() =
  static let proxyFactory = ProxyGenerator()
  static let notifyPropertyChanged =
    { new StandardInterceptor() with
        member this.PostProceed invocation =
          match invocation.Method, invocation.InvocationTarget with
          | PropertySetter propertyName, (:? Model as model) ->
              model.TriggerPropertyChanged propertyName
          | _ -> () }

  let propertyChangedEvent = Event<_,_>()
  interface INotifyPropertyChanged with
    [<CLIEvent>]
    member this.PropertyChanged = propertyChangedEvent.Publish

  member internal this.TriggerPropertyChanged propertyName =
    let args = PropertyChangedEventArgs propertyName
    propertyChangedEvent.Trigger(this, args)

  static member Create<'T when 'T:> Model and 'T: not struct>(): 'T =
    let interceptors : IInterceptor[] =
      [| notifyPropertyChanged; AbstractProperties() |]
    proxyFactory.CreateClassProxy interceptors

and AbstractProperties() =
  let data = Dictionary()

  interface IInterceptor with
    member this.Intercept invocation =
      match invocation.Method with
      | Abstract & PropertySetter propertyName ->
          data.[propertyName] <- invocation.Arguments.[0]

      | Abstract & PropertyGetter propertyName ->
          match data.TryGetValue propertyName with
          | true, value -> invocation.ReturnValue <- value
          | false, _ ->
              let returnType = invocation.Method.ReturnType
              if returnType.IsValueType then
                let res = Activator.CreateInstance returnType
                invocation.ReturnValue <- res
      | _ -> invocation.Proceed()
```

The interceptor responsible for raising the PropertyChanged event can be static because it's stateless.

Creates a singleton instance using F# object expression. StandardInterceptor makes it easy to intercept the postprocess step only.

Custom model instances must be created via the Create factory method, which sets up interception.

notifyPropertyChanged is a static singleton, AbstractProperties: one per model instance.

Clever use of active patterns (Abstract and PropertyGetter) makes code readable and helps avoid duplication—there is only one fallback branch.

For value types, returns the default type value; for reference types, it's null.

In comparison to a typical base model definition, this requires more code. The ability to provide backend storage for purely abstract properties adds extra complexity. But the payoff is obvious for any application of reasonable size. Defining custom models is a breeze:

```
type PositionState = Zero | Opened | Closed

[<AbstractClass>]
type MainModel() =
    inherit Model()
```

```
abstract Symbol : string with get, set
abstract InstrumentName : string with get, set
abstract Price : Nullable<decimal> with get, set
abstract PriceFeedSimulation : bool with get, set
abstract PositionState : PositionState with get, set
abstract IsPositionActionAllowed : bool with get, set
abstract PositionSize : int with get, set
abstract OpenPrice : Nullable<decimal> with get, set
abstract ClosePrice : Nullable<decimal> with get, set
abstract PnL : decimal with get, set
abstract StopLossAt : Nullable<decimal> with get, set
abstract TakeProfitAt : Nullable<decimal> with get, set
```

This type definition is as close as it gets to declarative data structures (similar to F#
records with mutable fields). With a fairly small amount of code in listing 2, you can
build the right abstractions. Once you have the abstractions in place, handling the
complexity of the model implementation is an easy task—if you decide you need to
include more properties in the model, it's just a matter of adding a single line! Now,
let's look at the view part of the MVC pattern.

Implementing the main trading view

The view plays two vital roles: the event source and the data binding target. You start
by implementing a reusable interface that represents a view. In the sample application
you create only a single concrete view, but you could easily add more screens showing
different aspects of the trade. The interface is as follows:

The first responsibility of the view is event sourcing.

```
type IView<'TEvent, 'TModel> =
    abstract Events : IObservable<'Event>
    abstract SetBindings : model : 'TModel -> unit
```

The view's second responsibility is setting up the appropriate data bindings and data context.

A concrete implementation of the view needs to provide two members: the `Set-`
`Bindings` member takes a model as an argument and is responsible for setting up data
bindings that update the view when the model changes, and the `Events` member
exposes to the controller events that happen in the UI. Although the interface is fully
generic in both event and model types, you should always use discriminated unions to
represent the type of events. This gives you a powerful way to report events that's difficult to achieve in classic OOP languages.

> **NOTE** At first it may seem that discriminated unions can be replaced
> with standard .NET enumeration types. This isn't true. First, enumeration
> types don't work smoothly with pattern matching.[4] Plus, it's often useful
> to pass additional event data to a handler. Discriminated-union cases may
> carry extra information, but enumeration cases can't.

---

[4]   For details, see Scott Wlaschin, "Enum types," *F# for Fun and Profit*, July 9, 2012, http://fsharpforfunandprofit
.com/posts/enum-types.

You can define a view implementation in many different ways, but this chapter uses a mixed F#/C# approach. C# projects are used only to host XAML definitions and generate static types for WPF windows or controls. I won't go into the details of the XAML part of the application, but let's briefly discuss the most important parts.

The implementation of the IView<'TEvent, 'TModel> interface in listing 3 is where the most interesting things happen. There is no need for the Observable.FromEvent-Pattern factory that's frequently used in C#, because the F# compiler automatically maps all .NET events to IEvent<'T>, which is inherited from IObservable<'T>.

Listing 3 IView implementation in the sample application

```
type MainEvents =
    | InstrumentInfo
    | PriceUpdate of decimal
    | BuyOrSell

type MainView(window : MainWindow) =
    ...
    interface IView<MainEvents, MainModel> with
        member this.Events =
        [ window.InstrumentInfo.Click
          |> Observable.map (fun _ -> InstrumentInfo)
          priceTicksSource
          |> Observable.map (fun value -> PriceUpdate value)
          window.Action.Click
          |> Observable.map (fun _ -> BuyOrSell) ]
          |> List.reduce Observable.merge

        member this.SetBindings(model) =
            window.DataContext <- model
            window.Symbol.SetBinding(TextBox.TextProperty, "Symbol") |> ignore
    ...
```

> View initialization omitted; it mostly deals with chart control setup.

> Typical call to set up a data binding in WPF. Other bindings are similar.

The theme of first-class events pops up again in the implementation of the Events property. Notice how easily events can form standard lists or be transformed via Observable.map or combined via Observable.merge.

There are other options for implementing the XAML-based view. In addition to adding a C# project, you could use the dynamic lookup operator (?) or the XAML type provider to get a statically typed view of elements in an embedded XAML file. Now, let's move on to the last component of MVC: the controller.

Handling interactions in the controller

The controller is the chief component of MVC because it contains most, if not all, of the presentation logic. Its essential responsibility is to execute event-specific computations while reading and updating the model state in process. The simplest variation of the controller is the event-handling function of type ('TModel -> 'TEvents -> unit), as you saw earlier.

Most screens in GUI applications aren't empty when first opened—they display information immediately. This means the view model needs to be initialized. Suppress your initial instinct, inherited from the good old OOP days, to put the model initialization logic in the model's constructor. This practice forces the model to have dependencies on external resources such as database connections and web services, and eventually testability will suffer. Placing this code in the controller's `InitModel` and employing the principle of dependency inversion helps. Ideally, the model is a purely declarative data structure and contains no logic. This is a typical separation for a functional paradigm. To encourage external initialization, a parameter-less constructor constraint exists on model implementation.

With these requirements in mind, you can define the controller interface as follows:

```
type IController<'TEvent, 'TModel> =
    abstract InitModel : 'TModel -> unit
    abstract EventHandler : 'TModel * 'TEvent -> unit
```

The concrete controller has a dependency on an external service that validates an instrument symbol and resolves it to a company name. The following default sample implementation uses Yahoo Financial Services.

Listing 4   Default `Symbology` service implementation

```
module Symbology

open System

let yahoo symbol =
  use wc = new Net.WebClient()
  let yahoo = "http://download.finance.yahoo.com/d"
  let uri = sprintf "%s/quotes.csv?s&f=nl1" yahoo symbol
  wc.DownloadString(uri)
    .Split([| "\n\r" |], StringSplitOptions.RemoveEmptyEntries)
    |> Array.map (fun line ->
        let xs = line.Split(',')
        let name, price = xs.[0], xs.[1]
        if price = "0.00" then None else Some name
    )
    |> Seq.exactlyOne
```

The implementation of the controller in the next listing contains core application logic: resolving the stock symbol, starting the price feed, entering and exiting positions, and displaying metrics.

Listing 5   `IController` implementation in the sample application

```
type MainContoller(?symbology: string -> string option) =

    let symbologyImpl = defaultArg symbology Symbology.yahoo

    let closePosition(model : MainModel) =
        model.ClosePrice <- model.Price
        model.PositionState <- PositionState.Closed
        model.IsPositionActionAllowed <- false

    interface IController<MainEvents, MainModel> with
```

The symbology callback is an example of an external dependency. It can be an interface or abstract type as well.

Unless specified (for example, for testing purposes), the default implementation is used.

```
                    member this.InitModel model =
Defaults to    ┌ ─ >   model.Symbol <- "^GSPC"
the S&P    │          this.GetInstrumentInfo model                    ← ─┐  External
500 index  │                                                              │  dependency, used
                         model.PositionSize <- 10                         │  to initialize model
                         model.PositionState <- PositionState.Zero
                         model.PositionActionAllowed <- true

                    member this.EventHandler(model, event) =
                      match event with
                      | InstrumentInfo -> this.GetInstrumentInfo(model)
                      | PriceUpdate newPrice -> this.UpdateCurrentPrice(model, newPrice)
                      | BuyOrSell -> this.MoveToNextPositionState(model)

                    member this.UpdateCurrentPrice(model: MainModel, newPrice) =   ← ─┐  Based on the
                        let prevPrice = model.Price                                    │  new price,
                        model.Price <- Nullable newPrice                              │  updates
                        if model.PositionState = PositionState.Opened                 │  metrics and
                        then                                                          │  keeps the
                            model.PnL <-                                              │  position value
                                let diff = model.Price ?-? model.OpenPrice            │  within limits
                                let pnl = decimal model.PositionSize *? diff
                                pnl.GetValueOrDefault()
                            let takeProfitLimit =
                                prevPrice ?< newPrice && newPrice >=? model.TakeProfitAt
                            let stopLossLimit =
                                prevPrice ?> newPrice && newPrice <=? model.StopLossAt
                            if takeProfitLimit || stopLossLimit
                            then closePosition model

                    member this.MoveToNextPositionState(model: MainModel) =   ← ─┐  Entrance or
                        match model.PositionState with                             │  exit position
                        | PositionState.Zero ->
                            model.OpenPrice <- model.Price
                            model.PositionState <- PositionState.Opened
                        | PositionState.Opened ->
                            closePosition model
                        | PositionState.Closed -> ()

               member this.GetInstrumentInfo(model : MainModel) =
                   model.Symbol
                       |> symbologyImpl
                       |> Option.iter (fun x -> model.InstrumentName <- x)
```

Here are the key points about this implementation:

- The model initialization includes an invocation to an external symbol-resolution service. This dependency is well controlled and isolated to one type. For example, it can be replaced with a fake during testing. Imagine this initialization logic moved to the model constructor: it would turn the model from a simple declarative data structure into a nontrivial class with imperative logic and complex dependencies. The overall architecture would become spaghetti-like.

- When a pattern matches on different event cases, the compiler warns you if you miss any. This makes it a compiler-checked map.

- Writing a unit test for a specific event is as easy as calling a method like `Get-InstrumentInfo`. External dependencies like a database connection still need to be mocked. There is little value in unit testing the `EventHandler` method because it's mostly done by type system (again!) and the compiler.

Gluing together the MVC pieces

Now that all the components are defined, you need to connect them, start the event loop, and coordinate event processing. Technically these responsibilities can be assigned to the controller. You could create a base class, put this logic there, and require all controllers to inherit from this class, but doing so would lead to fragile subclass coupling. A better solution is to define a separate component that plays the mediator/coordinator role (see figure 5).

We're about to wrap up this section, so let's look at the main module that starts the application, together with the relevant interfaces (discussed earlier) from the core framework.

Listing 6   MVC

```
type IView<'TEvent, 'TModel> =
    abstract Events : IObservable<'TEvent>
    abstract SetBindings: model : 'TModel -> unit

type IController<'TEvent, 'TModel> =
    abstract InitModel: 'TModel -> unit
    abstract EventHandler: 'TModel * 'TEvent -> unit

module Mvc =
    let start (model: #INotifyPropertyChanged,
               view: IView<_, _>,
               controller: IController<_, _>) =
        controller.InitModel model
        view.SetBindings model
        view.Events.Subscribe(fun event ->
            controller.EventHandler(model, event))
```

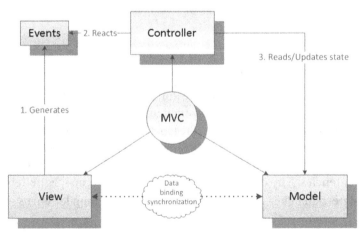

Figure 5   The F# MVC for WPF framework

I think it's impressive how much you can express in about a dozen lines of code without losing clarity. Even though developing UIs is a complex task, a simple type definition using first-class events (IObservable<'T>) and discriminated unions (when implementing the view) saves the day!

To finish the application, you just need to add a new file with the main function:

```
[<STAThread>]
[<EntryPoint>]
let main _ =
    let mainWindow = MainWindow()
    let mvc = Model.Create(), MainView mainWindow, MainContoller()
    use eventLoop = Mvc.start mvc
    Application().Run(mainWindow)
```

Table 1 sums up the roles of the individual components.

Table 1   Roles of the individual components

Component	Responsibilities	Collaboration
Model	Holds state	
	The model carries a subset of the view state projected via data binding. Data binding is the key responsible for synchronizing the model with the view, hence the INotifyPropertyChanged constraint in the Mvc.start type signature. Follow best practices of functional programming, and keep the model declarative (*dumb*, if you prefer this term). Avoid presentation logic in the model—it belongs in the controller.	
View	Event source Data-binding target	Events Model
	The view hides details of the underlying GUI framework behind a generic and simple IView<'TEvent, 'TModel> interface. This interface is an example of both parametric polymorphism (by 'TEvent type, which allows you to define a single generic implementation of the Mvc type) and subtype polymorphism (which uses different IView implementations).	
Controller	Event processor	Events Model
	The controller is dependent only on events and the model. It makes the architecture loosely coupled (and therefore more testable) yet cohesive (pattern matching ensures that all event cases are handled).	
Mvc	Mediator Coordinator	Events Model IView Controller
	The Mvc type depends on everything, but it doesn't matter because it stays fixed. There is no need to extend or change it.	

So far, you've looked at the overall architecture of an MVC application and seen how to build a simple application. I could end the chapter now, but doing so would leave out many aspects that are important in the real world.

Living in an asynchronous world

There is no need to explain the importance of asynchronous programming. These days it's everywhere, whether you want to express complex interaction logic using asynchronous programming models, or your application retrieves data from the web or calls REST-based APIs. In any case, you need asynchronous programming to avoid creating applications that block the UI and become unresponsive.

F# was one of the earliest mainstream languages to provide first-class support for asynchronous programming. *Support* in the context of the MVC framework developed in this chapter means first and foremost using asynchronous event handlers in addition to synchronous ones.

Designing software with types

There is a popular opinion that statically typed languages are all about program correctness—verification and tooling support (IntelliSense, refactoring, and so on). This isn't 100% accurate. Using static types is a great vehicle for design and exploration that lets you handle program design complexity. These capabilities are often overlooked. Exploration plays an important role when you're starting to work with an unfamiliar code base. Design comes along during the construction or refactoring phase.

First, let's walk through the same design process I used when facing the task of supporting asynchronous computations in the framework. Keep a close eye on how types guided me through the process. Here are the refactoring steps toward the final solution:

1 Redefine `EventHandler` as a curried F# function as you did earlier:

```
abstract EventHandler : ('TModel -> 'TEvent -> unit)
```

2 Change the order of the arguments, moving the model to the end:

```
abstract EventHandler : ('TEvent -> 'TModel -> unit)
```

3 When I saw the new type signature, a light bulb went off in my head. F# functions are right-associative. So, the previous signature can be replaced with this:

```
abstract EventHandler : ('TEvent -> ('TModel -> unit))
```

Now it becomes obvious that this is not only an event handler but something bigger: it's an event-handler factory. When partially applied to the first argument of type `'TEvent`, it returns a handler for a specific case.

4 Let's separate the event handler into a standalone type. Doing so will make it possible to introduce two kinds of event handlers (synchronous and asynchronous) in the next step:

```
type EventHandler<'TModel> = 'TModel -> unit
type IController<'TEvent, 'TModel> =
    abstract InitModel: 'TModel -> unit
    abstract Dispatcher : ('TEvent -> EventHandler<'TModel>)
```

5 How do I define two kinds of event handlers? With a discriminated union. Bingo!

What did I arrive at in the end? You can see the final result in the following listing.

Listing 7 `Controller` and `Mvc` with support for asynchronous programming

```
type EventHandler<'Model> =
  | Sync of ('Model -> unit)
  | Async of ('Model -> Async<unit>)

type IController<'TEvent, 'TModel> =
  abstract InitModel : 'TModel -> unit
  abstract Dispatcher : ('TEvent -> EventHandler<'TModel>)

module Mvc =
  let start ( model: #INotifyPropertyChanged,
              view: IView<_, _>,
              controller: IController<_, _> ) =
    controller.InitModel(model)
    view.SetBindings(model)
    view.Events.Subscribe(fun event ->
      match controller.Dispatcher event with
      | Sync eventHandler -> eventHandler model
      | Async eventHandler -> eventHandler model |> Async.StartImmediate)
```

Dispatcher returns the proper handler for the particular event: Sync or Async.

For Async, delegated invocation to Async.Start-Immediate

For Sync, invokes as before

The `Async.StartImmediate` method starts the asynchronous computation on the invocation thread. This is important because it allows you to capture a synchronization context that you can later use to continue the GUI thread.

In the sample application, there is an invocation to a remote service that validates the instrument symbol the user entered (the default implementation goes to the Yahoo service). It's certainly better to use asynchronous computation to keep the UI responsive, as shown in the next listing.

Listing 8 Sample controller implementation with `Async`

```
type MainContoller(?symbology: string -> Async<string option>) =
  ...
    interface IController<MainEvents, MainModel> with

      member this.InitModel model = ...

      member this.Dispatcher = function
        | InstrumentInfo -> Async this.GetInstrumentInfo
        | BuyOrSell -> Sync this.MoveToNextPositionState
        | PriceUpdate newPrice -> Sync(this.UpdateCurrentPrice newPrice)

  member this.GetInstrumentInfo(model : MainModel) = async {
    let context = SynchronizationContext.Current
    let! secInfo = symbologyImpl model.Symbol
    do! Async.SwitchToContext context
    secInfo |> Option.iter (fun x -> model.InstrumentName <- x)
  }
    ...
```

The symbology service is expected to respond asynchronously.

The local binding and InitModel didn't change.

Dispatches the event to the proper handler

Async prefix for asynchronous handlers

Sync prefix for synchronous handlers

Sync prefix with a curried method that returns event handler

Async event handler

Recovers the saved synchronization context

The other methods didn't change.

Here are the key points about listing 8:

- The .NET method `EventHandler` is replaced by the `Dispatcher` property of type `function`. The new name reflects the nature of this function best: it dispatches the event to the proper event handler.
- The new implementation of `Dispatcher` in `MainController` takes advantage of all changes. It's now a high-order pattern-matching function. I can't imagine a more expressive implementation.
- For multiparameter event-handler implementations (like `UpdateCurrentPrice`), partial function application is simpler when the model is the last parameter.
- Don't forget to include an invocation to `Async.SwitchToContext` to make sure the UI is updated in the proper thread.

The need to validate security symbols asynchronously may not be convincing enough for you. But remember, this is a sample application with limited scope. Imagine trading many securities at once. If the GUI is blocked while pulling information about one security when a user needs to sell another, money can be lost. If it's still not appealing to you, then think of environments like Silverlight where a network call is always asynchronous, or Windows Runtime, where any timely (more than 50 ms) invocation is asynchronous.

We wouldn't be able to arrive at such a simple and elegant solution without types. Look at C#, which has a weaker type system and computational model. Version 5.0 introduced support for asynchronous computation that surfaces in the form of the `async` and `await` keywords. At first glance it seems identical to F#, but when you dig deeper, the difference between the type system–based and compiler "black magic" approaches becomes obvious. It's relevant to GUI programming. The return type `async void` exists only to support asynchronous event handlers. This creates a famous issue of `async void` versus `async Task` return-type semantics; Tomas Petricek has a detailed blog post on the subject.[5] For skeptics, I suggest the following: try implementing something similar to what I've shown you in this chapter in C#.

Exercise 1

The current implementation lacks exception handling. This is especially confusing for asynchronous event handlers because exceptions are ignored. Your task is to extend `Mvc.start` to save exceptions into an event log or file. Try to preserve an accurate stack trace.

---

[5] Tomas Petricek, "Async in C# and F#: Asynchronous gotchas in C#," *Tomas Petricek's Blog*, April 15, 2013, http://tomasp.net/blog/csharp-async-gotchas.aspx.

Exercise 2

Sometimes GUI applications have a heavy model initialization because they load a lot of data or perform intense computations. Users get annoyed when they have to wait a long time for the screen to appear initially. Your task is to address this issue by splitting `Controller.InitModel` into two parts: synchronous and asynchronous. The type signature of `Controller.InitModel` must be preserved.

Exercise 3

Introduce support for canceling long-running asynchronous invocations.

Making data binding safer

Data binding is a mechanism that ensures that any change made to the data in a UI control is automatically carried over to the view model (and vice versa). Traditionally, the property names of source objects are passed as strings. This can be done either in XAML

```
<TextBox Name="PositionSize" Text="{Binding PositionSize}"
```

or in code:

```
window.Symbol.SetBinding(TextBox.TextProperty, "Symbol") |> ignore
```

Are magic strings the only choice?

Let's have another look at the `IView` interface:

```
type IView<'TEvent, 'TModel> =
    abstract Events : IObservable<'TEvent>
    abstract SetBindings : model : 'TModel -> unit
```

In the previous section, you didn't use the fact that the interface is also generic in the type of the model (called `'TModel`). You just passed the model as a value for `Data-Context`, which accepts any object. But when you perform data binding that way, the type goes unnoticed by the type system. Therefore, helpful things like compiler verification and tooling support (IntelliSense, refactoring, and so on) are missing.

Here's a simple example that illustrates the problem. Let's say that during refactoring you rename the `Price` property of the model to `CurrentPrice`. You fix obvious compilation errors and then compile and run the program. A strange thing happens: there is no exception, but the current price doesn't show a value. A careful search through hundreds of lines in the debug output window in Visual Studio reveals the following message:

```
System.Windows.Data Error: 40:
BindingExpression path error: 'Price' property not found on 'object'
```

I'm sure many WPF, WinRT, and Silverlight developers have gone through this painful experience. This happens whether bindings are set programmatically or in XAML. In my opinion, defining bindings in XAML is a worse option because it erases all the benefits of the separation between declarative XAML and application logic.

Are magic strings the only choice? Of course not. Let's see how you can handle data binding in a statically typed way using the F# quotation mechanism.

Introducing statically typed data binding

Begin by mapping the quoted F# assignment statement

```
<@ symbol.Text <- model.Symbol @>
```

to the data binding setup call:

```
symbol.SetBinding(TextBox.TextProperty, "Symbol")
```

The following listing shows a fairly simple implementation.

Listing 9 Mapping the assignment statement to the data-binding expression

```
module Binding

open System.Reflection
open System.Windows
open Microsoft.FSharp.Quotations.Patterns

let ofExpression = function
    | PropertySet
        (
            Some( FieldGet( Some( Value( window, _)), control)),
            targetProperty,
            [],
            PropertyGet( Some( Value _), sourceProperty, [])
        ) ->
            let target : FrameworkElement =
                window |> control.GetValue |> unbox
            let dpPropertyName = targetProperty.Name + "Property"
            let dp =
                targetProperty
                    .DeclaringType
                    .GetField(dpPropertyName)
                    .GetValue(null)
                    |> unbox<DependencyProperty>

            target.SetBinding(dp, path = sourceProperty.Name) |> ignore
    | expr -> failwithf "Invalid binding quotation:\n%O" expr
```

Annotations:
- Control (binding target) from the left side of the assignment
- Property from the left side of the assignment
- The right side has a reference to the model (binding source) and property (binding path)
- Single case active pattern. Fails at runtime if it can't be matched.
- Following WPF convention, the dependency property name is formed by adding the suffix "Property" to the .NET property.

Here is the actual invocation in the `MainView` type:

```
Binding.ofExpression <@ symbol.Text <- model.Symbol @>
```

Neat. Next let's try binding for the `PriceFeedSimulation.IsChecked` property as a target.

```
Binding.fromExpression <@ priceFeedSimulation.IsChecked <- model.PriceFeedSimulation @>
```

> This expression was expected to have type
> Nullable<bool>
> but here has type
> bool

Figure 6   Mismatch between source and target property types

Handling nullable values in data binding

Unfortunately, the compiler gives an error (see figure 6) because the left side is of type `Nullable<bool>` but the right is `bool`. There are two ways to fix this issue. The first is to change the `PriceFeedSimulation` property type on the model to `Nullable<bool>`. This is slightly inconvenient because you know the property can't be null. The second option is to insert a fake call to the `Nullable<bool>` constructor inside the quotation, discard it at runtime, and let the WPF data-binding engine handle the conversion.

Let's try the second approach:

```
Binding.ofExpression
    <@
        priceFeedSimulation.IsChecked <- Nullable model.PriceFeedSimulation
    @>
```

Unfortunately, this approach fails because the quotation-parsing logic isn't prepared to handle it. To refactor it to a working solution (see listing 10), you need to make the following changes:

- Extract logic that finds a companion dependency property for the regular .NET property.
- Support quotations containing more than one assignment statement.
- Delegate parsing the parts of the assignment statement quotations to helpers. Figure 7 shows the correspondence between the key components of binding, parts of a single assignment statement, and items available after decomposition using the `PropertySet` active pattern.

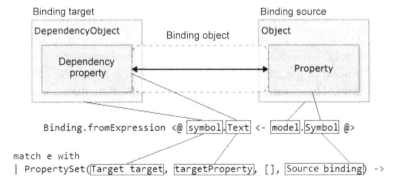

Figure 7   Assignment statement deconstructed

Listing 10   Refactored typed data binding

```
type PropertyInfo with
    member this.DependencyProperty =                    ◁──  The extension property returns a
        this.DeclaringType                                    companion dependency property
            .GetField(dpPropertyName)                         following convention.
            .GetValue(null)
            |> unbox<DependencyProperty>               The (|Target|_|) partial active pattern
                                                       extracts the data-binding target from the
let (|Target|_|) = function                     ◁──    left side of the assignment statement
    | Some( FieldGet( Some( Value( window, _)), control)) ->
        window |> control.GetValue |> unbox<DependencyObject> |> Some
    | _ -> None
                                                              (|Source|_|) parses
let rec (|Source|_|) = function                    ◁──       the right side of
    | PropertyGet( Some( Value _), sourceProperty, []) ->     the assignment
        Some( Binding(path = sourceProperty.Name))           statement and
    | NewObject( ctor, [ Source binding ] )                   returns an instance
        when                                                  of the Binding type.
            let declType = ctor.DeclaringType
            declType.GetGenericTypeDefinition() = typedefof<_ Nullable> ->
        Some binding
    | _ -> None                                        Split function
                                                       decomposes into
let rec split = function                        ◁──    individual expressions
    | Sequential(head, tail) -> head :: split tail
    | tail -> [ tail ]
                                                   Iterates over the list of assignment
let ofExpression expr =                            statements, mapping each into a
    for e in split expr do                   ◁──   call to the data-binding setup
        match e with
        | PropertySet(Target target, targetProperty, [], Source binding)
            ->
            BindingOperations.SetBinding(
                target, targetProperty.DependencyProperty, binding)
            |> ignore
        | expr -> failwithf "Invalid binding quotation:\n%O" expr
```

Some WPF UI elements (actionText and price in the sample application) aren't
descendants of FrameworkElement. That's why (|Target|_|) yields a result of
type DependencyObject and BindingOperations is used to set up binding.

Listing 10 refactors the quotation-processing logic into small functions that are easy
to understand. The issue of mapping the model property of type `bool` to control the
property of type `Nullable<bool>` is handled by the second case in (|Source|_|). It
matches the invocation to the `Nullable` constructor, discards it, and recursively invokes
(|Source|_|) again. The compiler is happy and runtime semantics are managed by
WPF data binding. This can be confusing, because the actual runtime behavior can differ from what you'd expect when you look at the code. It's certainly a deviation from the
full fidelity type system, but it's significantly better than magic strings.

Note that the implementation would be verbose and error-prone without the
entire set of F# language features: pattern matching, active patterns, recursive definitions, extension properties, and of course type inference.

Handling conversions

You now have several `TextBox` controls that represent numerical values. For example, let's try `PositionSize`:

```
Binding.ofExpression <@ positionSize.Text <- model.PositionSize @>
```

The attempt to bind fails, and you see the error message "This expression was expected to have a type `string` but here has type `int`." This is similar to the earlier problem of the `bool` and `Nullable<bool>` mismatch. But this issue has a different angle:XAML controls have most of their properties defined in terms of generic `obj` or `string` types. It makes them widely applicable but typeless. As in the previous case, there two ways to solve the problem: you can define the model property of the matching type or insert a type conversion "shim" to satisfy the compiler. Both approaches have pros and cons, but the second requires less manual coding because WPF does many conversions behind the scenes. To make it work, the following listing introduces a pseudo-function called `Binding.coerce` and makes a small change in (`|Binding-Instance|_|`).

Listing 11 Mapping typed properties of the model to strings

```
module Binding =
    ...
let coerce _ = raise <| NotImplementedException()   <───   A meta or flag function. It is
                                                            never invoked. It only closes
let rec (|Source|_|) = function                             the F# type system and
    ...                                                     signals that the default WPF
    | SpecificCall <@ coerce @> (None, _, [ Source binding ]) ->   conversion should be used.
        Some binding
    ...
    Binding.ofExpression
        <@
            positionSize.Text <- Binding.coerce model.PositionSize     Usage
            ``open``.Text <- Binding.coerce model.Open                 inside
            close.Text <- Binding.coerce model.Close                   MainView
          pnl.Text <- Binding.coerce model.PnL
        @>
```

This solution diminishes the value of the F# type system because an instance of any type can pass through the `coerce` function. But whatever is left is still valuable and makes trying the approach worthwhile. Plus, this extreme method doesn't have to be used often. I expand on the topic of conversions later in the chapter.

The WPF `Binding` type allows formatted output via a property called `String-Format`. It's used to show the security name retrieved from Yahoo's symbology service:

```
let binding = Binding(path = "InstrumentName", StringFormat = "Name : {0}")
instrumentName.SetBinding(TextBlock.TextProperty, binding) |> ignore
```

Converted to the new notation, it looks like the following:

```
Binding.ofExpression
<@
    instrumentName.Text <- String.Format("Name : {0}", model.InstrumentName)
@>
```

You can include a small change in the quotation-parsing logic to handle the new case:

```
let rec (|Source|_|) = function
    ...
    | SpecificCall
        <@ String.Format: string * obj -> string @>
        (
            None,
            [],
            [ Value(:? string as format, _);
            Coerce( Source binding, _) ]
        ) ->
        binding.StringFormat <- format
        Some binding
    ...
```

Note how a single line of pattern matching replaces dozens of lines of the `Visitor` pattern commonly used to traverse expression trees in mainstream OOP languages. A savvy F# developer might ask, "Why not use the F# native `sprintf` function inside the quotation rather than the .NET BCL `String.Format`?" Unlike `sprintf`, `String.Format` has a straightforward mapping to the `StringFormat` property of the `Binding` type. Later, in the "Heavy Lifting: Derived Properties" sidebar, I'll show you how to apply `sprintf` to build formatted output.

Adding transformations

Setting up bindings in XAML has a drawback: it's impossible to add transformation logic. An example from the sample application is the position state (zero, opened, or closed) on the model mapped to the label on the action button. Table 2 shows the button labels and the corresponding position states they represent.

Table 2   Button labels and states

Button label	Value of PositionState model's property
Buy 529.69	Zero (Empty)
Sell 520.17	Opened
Current 549.03	Closed

Luckily, you set up data binding programmatically. The workaround is to use a converter, as shown next.

Listing 12 Typeless data binding with transformation done via a converter

```
actionText.SetBinding(
    Run.TextProperty,
    Binding("PositionState", Converter = {
        new IValueConverter with
            member this.Convert(value, _, _, _) =
                match value with
                | :? PositionState as x ->
                    match x with
                    | Zero -> "Buy"
                    | Opened -> "Sell"
                    | Closed -> "Current"
                    |> box
                | _ -> DependencyProperty.UnsetValue
            member this.ConvertBack(_, _, _, _) =
                DependencyProperty.UnsetValue
    })
) |> ignore
```

Although the converter implementation is fairly succinct thanks to F# object expressions, this code still doesn't look pretty. With a new code-oriented approach, there must be a better way to express it. The next listing shows a minor change in (|Source|_|):

Listing 13 Parsing the source value transformation function

```
let rec (|Source|_|) = function
...
    | Call(None, method', [ Source binding ]) ->
        binding.Mode <- BindingMode.OneWay
        binding.Converter <- {
            new IValueConverter with
                member this.Convert(value, _, _, _) =
                    try method'.Invoke(null, [| value |])
                    with _ -> DependencyProperty.UnsetValue
                member this.ConvertBack(_, _, _, _) =
                    DependencyProperty.UnsetValue
        }
        Some binding
```

Equipped with the new logic, you can write a mapping function and apply it in the binding expression:

```
let positionStateToAction = function
    | Zero -> "Buy"
    | Opened -> "Sell"
    | Closed -> "Current"
...
Binding.ofExpression
    <@
        actionText.Text <- positionStateToAction model.PositionState
    @>
```

The mapping function can also be static or an extension method as long as it follows the type signature 'a -> 'b, where 'a is a type of model property and 'b is a type of control property. As another example, the next two listings show how you can use this function to map the model profit and loss (PNL) value to the pnl TextBlock's font color.

Listing 14 Mapping the PNL value to font color via a traditional binding converter

```
pnl.SetBinding(
    TextBlock.ForegroundProperty,
    Binding("PnL", Converter = {
        new IValueConverter with
            member this.Convert(value, _, _, _) =
                match value with
                | :? decimal as x ->
                    if x < 0M then box "Red"
                    elif x > 0M then box "Green"
                    else box "Black"
                | _ -> DependencyProperty.UnsetValue
            member this.ConvertBack(_, _, _, _) =
                DependencyProperty.UnsetValue
    })
) |> ignore
```

Listing 15 Mapping the PNL value to font color in the binding expression

```
type MainView ...

    static member GetColorForPNL x =
        let color =
            if x < 0M then "Red"
            elif x > 0M then "Green"
            else "Black"
        BrushConverter().ConvertFromString color |> unbox<Brush>

    ...
    Binding.ofExpression
        <@
            pnl.Foreground <- MainView.GetColorForPNL model.PnL
        @>
```

Another popular approach is to define a separate property on the model and update it in the controller (ViewModel in MVVM) along with the property it depends on. In the example application, the IsPositionActionAllowed property by default is true but switches to false once the position is closed (as shown earlier in listing 5). The Buy / Sell / Current button's IsEnabled property is bound to the IsPositionAction-Allowed value. The next listing simplifies the logic by using an extension property[6] as a converter.

---

[6] It could also be an extension method.

Listing 16 Replacing the model property and controller logic with a converter

```
type MainModel() =
    ...
    abstract IsPositionActionAllowed : bool with get, set
    ...
type MainContoller ...

    let closePosition(model : MainModel) =
        model.ClosePrice <- model.Price
        model.PositionState <- PositionState.Closed
        model.IsPositionActionAllowed <- false

    interface IController<MainEvents, MainModel> with

        member this.InitModel model =
            ...
            model.IsPositionActionAllowed <- true

[<AutoOpen>]
module MainModel =
    ...
    type PositionState with
        member this.ActionAllowed = this <> Closed
    ...
type MainView ...
    ...
    Binding.ofExpression
        <@
            action.IsEnabled <- model.PositionState.ActionAllowed
        @>
```

The closePosition helper is invoked when the position is closed manually or the threshold is hit.

All of the above is replaced with an extension property and a statically typed binding with a converter.

The mapping functions in listing 16 are clearly separated and can therefore be easily unit-tested. It's tempting to return the color as a string[7] instead of an instance of type Brush from the PnlToColor method and to have Binding.coerce(MainView.Pnl-ToColor model.PnL) on the right side of the binding expression. This works, but why cheat on the type system? As mentioned earlier, this nasty trick with the Binding.coerce function isn't required often.

Implicit conversion (done by WPF behind the scenes) works well only for one-way bindings. For two-way bindings, I strongly recommend avoiding implicit or explicit converters (converters that implement both the Convert and ConvertBack methods). Here's an example that shows why. Suppose a user follows this workflow to open a position:

1 The user enters a symbol (GOOG) and starts the price feed.
2 The user enters 12 as the position size.
3 The user enters 770 as the Stop Loss At limit.
4 The user switches back to position size, intending to change it, but accidentally clears it.
5 The user clicks the Buy button.

---

[7] WPF uses the default conversion logic.

6 The position was opened with size 12, and the error message "could not be converted" and a red border around the Size field clearly indicate a user input error (see figure 8).

What happened here? The explanation is simple: the built-in WPF text-to-number converter threw an exception, conveying this information to the view but not to the model. Therefore, the controller was completely unaware of any user input errors. The key takeaway? Two-way converters are dangerous.

To wrap up, the following listing shows all the typed data bindings for the example application. For simplicity, I skipped some corner cases and minor details that are necessary for a production-quality typed data-binding library.

Listing 17 All the typed data bindings for the example application

```
Binding.ofExpression
    <@
        symbol.Text <- model.Symbol
        instrumentName.Text <-
            String.Format("Name : {0}", model.InstrumentName)
        priceFeedSimulation.IsChecked <- Nullable model.PriceFeedSimulation

        positionSize.Text <- Binding.coerce model.PositionSize

        action.IsEnabled <- model.PositionState.ActionAllowed
        actionText.Text <- positionStateToAction model.PositionState
        price.Text <- Binding.coerce model.Price

        ``open``.Text <- Binding.coerce model.Open
        close.Text <- Binding.coerce model.Close
        pnl.Text <- Binding.coerce model.PnL
        pnl.Foreground <- MainView.GetColorForPNL model.PnL
    @>
```

I think you'll agree that this is a significant improvement over the earlier attempts in terms of readability and safety.

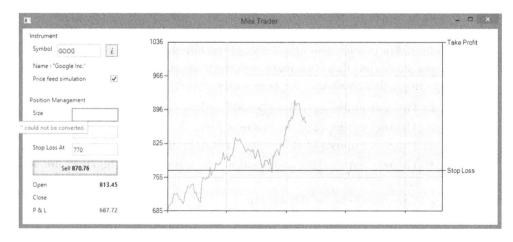

Figure 8 Problem with two-way converters

Heavy lifting: derived properties[8]

The data-binding transformations introduced earlier are a handy feature. They allow you to run mapping computations every time the property changes. But this can be limiting. What if you need to execute a computation in response to a change in a set of properties? So far, you've had to keep those inside the controller. A specific example is the PNL calculation. Somewhere in the controller is the following code:

```
model.PnL <-
    let x = decimal model.PositionSize *? ( model.Price ?-? model.Open)
    x.GetValueOrDefault()
```

The PNL calculation depends on three other properties of the model: position size, current price, and open price. If any of these values change, PNL has to be recalculated. Because these changes can be caused by different events, the calculation needs to be handled in more than one place in the controller's code. This quickly becomes a daunting task and can lead to duplication and errors.

An elegant solution to this problem is a feature called *derived properties*. You define a regular property on the model and mark it with `DerivedPropertyAttribute`, which is defined as a type alias of `ReflectedDefinitionAttribute`:

```
[<DerivedProperty>]
member this.Pnl =
    let x = decimal this.PositionSize *? ( this.Price ?-? this.Open)
    x.GetValueOrDefault()
```

There is a limitation: the derived property type must exactly match the target property type. A converter can't be applied to it. You could make `model.Pnl` of type `string`, but you'll see in a moment why doing so isn't a good idea. How do you bind it to the `TextBlock.Text` property of type `string`? The easiest solution is to use `String-Format`. Now you have a normal property that fires the `PropertyChanged` event and is recalculated every time any dependencies change. It's a normal-looking .NET property that can be unit-tested for complex calculations. This is different from other approaches that use Microsoft intermediate language (MSIL) rewriting.

Properties that have transitive dependencies on other derived properties must be marked as derived too. Remember, you had a binding mapper that calculated color based on the PNL numeric value to emphasize profit (green), loss (red), or neutral (black). The only option you have is to create another derived property, because the converter can't be applied to the `PnL` property anymore. The derived property `Pnl2Color` has a transitive dependency on the other derived property `PnL`. That's why you keep the `PnL` property of the decimal value as opposed to the string:

```
open System.Windows.Media

type MainModel with
  [<DerivedProperty>]
  member this.Pnl2Color =
```

---

[8] Due to space constraints, I'll skip the implementation details and focus on usage. Curious readers are welcome to check this chapter's source code.

(continued)

```
    let color =
        if this.PnL < 0M then "Red"
        elif this.PnL > 0M then "Green"
        else "Black"
    BrushConverter().ConvertFromString color |> unbox<Brush>

Binding.ofExpression
<@
    actionText.Text <- model.PositionState.ToAction()
    pnl.Text <- String.Format("{0}", model.PnL)
    pnl.Foreground <- model.Pnl2Color
@>
```

F# type-safe string formatting can be used inside *derived properties* instead of the .NET BCL `String.Format`. For example, another way to bind the PNL value to the control property of type `string` is to define another derived property that converts decimals to strings:

```
type MainModel with
    ...
    [<Binding.DerivedProperty>]
    member this.PnlAsString = sprintf "%M" this.PnL

Binding.ofExpression
<@
    ...
    pnl.Text <- model. PnlAsString
    ...
@>
```

**Binding inside
MainView.SetBindings**

Using derived properties is a natural fit for complex formatting because more than one property can be referenced without losing support for the automatic `Property-Changed` notification.

Although they come with minor restrictions, derived properties are a powerful feature and save you from writing a lot of boilerplate code. Declarative in nature, derived properties don't contradict the idea of a controller as a central repository for presentation logic.

Exercise 4

Extend type-safe data binding to accept expressions on the right side. For example:

```
Binding.ofExpression
    <@ action.IsEnabled <- model.PositionState <> Closed @>
```

Allow only a single model property to be used in computation. Multiproperty expressions should be handled using derived properties.

Summary

I believe GUI programming is inherently hard. The essential complexity in GUI applications is caused by the fact that interactions between a human and a computer are far more informal and subtle than between two computers. Unfortunately, in the software industry, responding to complexity often results in even more of it. The original rise in popularity of OOP was due to its ability to create and manage deep hierarchies of classes with hundreds of mutable properties that tune the behavior of specific UI gadgets. As a modern language, F# provides innovative tools to tame such complexity. It combines these tools with fundamental concepts like functional programming and a powerful type system. One of the key strengths of F# is its smooth integration with the underlying .NET platform. New systems can be built using the function-first style, at the same time using existing libraries that have many years of development behind them.

F# has a well-deserved reputation as a great tool used to express complex algorithms, crunch numbers, and process all kinds of data. But as a general-purpose language, it also excels at everyday tasks like developing WPF GUI applications. It works best in code-oriented solutions with a thin functional adaptive layer over the traditional OOP API.

The most important message of this chapter is, "The type system is a developer's best friend." A types-first approach helps you design and write code that is intention-revealing (readable) and maintainable, and that has fewer defects. Understandably, many developers were disappointed by the type system in languages like C++, Java, and C#. So they turned to dynamically typed languages or convention-based approaches in statically typed languages. But the F# type system is a different game. Although it's not ideal, it strikes a good balance between simplicity and power.

F# code that solves complex problems often looks deceptively simple because it's standing on the shoulders of two giants: the type system and functional programming.

About the author

Dmitry Morozov is an experienced software developer, an F# enthusiast, and an active contributor to several F# OSS projects. He has been successfully using F# to build production applications since 2009. Currently Dmitry is a member of the engineering team at Tachyus, a company that creates technology to optimize energy production for the oil and gas industry.

8 Asynchronous and agent-based programming

Colin Bull

The real world consists of independent entities interacting through asynchronous exchanges of information. Programming languages that provide abstractions for asynchronous computations and agents are ideally suited for modeling real-world problems. This chapter introduces asynchronous workflows and agent-based concurrency in F#.

All about asynchronous workflows

Programming in the functional style promotes a compositional approach to problem solving. The solution to a complex problem can be composed from the solution to simpler subproblems. Pure functions and immutable data structures are the fundamental building blocks used to implement solutions using this approach. Code written in this style is clear, concise, and easy to reason about.

Unfortunately, for any program to be useful, it also has to interact via side effects with the real world. Interactions with the real world involve coming to grips with functional programming's so-called "awkward squad," including I/O and concurrency. A challenge for any functional-first programming language is how to express computations that interact with the real world without compromising the benefits of the compositional approach to problem solving.

The F# programming language provides abstractions for elegantly expressing asynchronous computations that can be used for I/O and concurrency without losing the benefits of composition. This chapter will show how you can use the asynchronous workflows and agents provided by F# to solve the real-world problems you'll encounter in your work as an enterprise software developer without losing any of the clarity, conciseness, or correctness of the code that you're used to when programming in a functional style.

What are asynchronous workflows?

Using asynchronous operations in your code can lead to increased performance, especially when dealing with databases, web services, or I/O. But writing asynchronous code often involves significant amounts of not entirely trivial boilerplate, and if it's not done properly it can lead to degraded performance and bugs that can be subtle. Asynchronous workflows aim to simplify the asynchronous programming model by removing a lot of the boilerplate:

```
> open System.IO
> open System.Net
> let doWebRequest (url:string) methd transformer =
    async {
        let request = WebRequest.Create(url, Method = methd)
        use! response = request.AsyncGetResponse()
        return! transformer (response.GetResponseStream())
    };;
val doWebRequest :
  url:string -> methd:string -> transformer:(Stream -> Async<'a>) ->
    Async<'a>
```

❶ Creates the web request

❷ Asynchronously gets the requests response object

❸ Reads from the response stream and passes to the transformer function

This code creates an asynchronous computation that creates a web request ❶ and asynchronously gets the response ❷. The code then opens a stream and passes it to a handler ❸. The type of the `transformer` parameter is `Stream -> Async<'a>`, meaning it should have one parameter that takes a `Stream` and it must return an `Async<'a>`.

This code asynchronously reads the entire incoming stream as a string:

```
> let readStreamAsString (stream:Stream) =
    async {
        use streamReader = new StreamReader(stream)
        return! streamReader.ReadToEndAsync() |> Async.AwaitTask
    }
val readStreamAsString : stream:Stream -> Async<string>
```

You can now combine these two functions to download a web page, as shown in the following listing.

> **Listing 1 Composing asynchronous workflows (F# interactive)**

```
> let result =
    doWebRequest "http://www.google.com" "GET" readStreamAsString
    |> Async.RunSynchronously

val result : string =
  "<!doctype html><html itemscope="" itemtype="http://schema.org"+[43426 chars]
```

This is a nice example of how asynchronous workflows can be composed to build more complex behaviors.

Meet the agents

The goal of the agent/actor programming model is to simplify writing concurrent applications. The programming model was first introduced by Hewitt, Bishop, and

Steiger's paper in 1973.[1] In the actor model, *everything* is an actor, in the same way everything is an object in object-oriented programming (OOP). In the formal definition, actors can do the following:

- Send messages to each other
- Change the actor's message-handling behavior for the next message
- Create new actors
- Process messages in any order

In F#, the MailboxProcessor<'a> type represents the fundamental element of this computational model. MailboxProcessor<'a> is backed by a queue. Messages can be posted to the queue asynchronously and then processed in the actor loop, as shown in the next listing.[2]

Listing 2   Creating an agent (F# Interactive)

```
open System.IO
open System.Net
open Microsoft.FSharp.Control

type Agent<'a> = MailboxProcessor<'a>

type Request =
    | Get of string * AsyncReplyChannel<string>

let downloadAgent =
    Agent<_>.Start(fun inbox ->
        let rec loop (cache : Map<string, string>) =
            async {
                let! msg = inbox.Receive()          ⟵ Asynchronously waits for a message
                match msg with
                | Get(url, reply) ->
                    match cache.TryFind(url) with
                    | Some(result) ->
                        reply.Reply(result)         ⟵ ① Replies with the result
                        return! loop cache
                    | None ->
                        let! result = doWebRequest url "GET" readStreamAsString
                        reply.Reply(result)
                        return! loop (Map.add url result cache)  ⟵ Tail recursive loop with the newly cached values
            }
        loop Map.empty
    )
```

This code creates an agent that on receipt of a message downloads a string from the specified URL, stores it in a cache, and returns the result ①.

---

[1] Carl Hewitt, Peter Bishop, and Richard Steiger, "A Universal Modular ACTOR Formalism for Artificial Intelligence," *Proceedings of the 3rd International Joint Conference on Artificial intelligence*, 1973.

[2] For more information about F# agents and the MailboxProcessor type, see "Server-Side Programming with F# Agents," MSDN, http://mng.bz/44zg; or Tomas Petricek, "An Introduction to F# Agents," Developer Fusion, http://mng.bz/59L2.

You can call this agent and get a result by posting a message of type `Request` to the agent:

```
> let agentResult=
    downloadAgent.PostAndReply(fun reply -> Get("http://www.google.com",
    reply))
val agentResult : string =
  "<!doctype html><html itemscope="" itemtype="http://schema.org"+[43426 chars]
```

Repeating this call to the same URL won't result in another network call being made; instead, the value will be served directly from the cache.

The previous example directly uses the `MailboxProcessor<'a>` defined as part of the F# core library. Although it's a good, robust implementation of an actor, using the `MailboxProcessor<'a>` directly in a large actor system can cause some problems.

One such problem comes from directly referencing instances of actors. This approach quickly becomes unmanageable and hard to reason about, much like directly constructing types in a large object-oriented system. Typically, in a large object-oriented solution, you'd use some sort of container to manage the references for you, and then ask the container for the types when you need them. The same is true in a large actor system; in fact, you can broadly think of actors as being equivalent to classes. Another problem worth mentioning is the fact that `MailboxProcessor<'a>` is built on an unbounded queue; this can cause memory issues when a system gets busy. Queues can quickly build when processing individual messages takes a long time. Toward this end, you may not want to use `MailboxProcessor<'a>` as your agent implementation. To solve this, the following listing introduces some abstractions over an agent.

Listing 3   Abstracting an agent

```
type IAsyncReplyChannel<'a> =
    abstract Reply : 'a -> unit

[<AbstractClass>]
type AgentRef(id:string) =
    member val Id = id with get, set
    abstract Start : unit -> unit

[<AbstractClass>]
type AgentRef<'a>(id:string) =
    inherit AgentRef(id)
    abstract Receive : unit -> Async<'a>     ⟵  Asynchronously
    abstract Post : 'a -> unit                   waits for a message
    abstract PostAndTryAsyncReply : (IAsyncReplyChannel<'b> -> 'a) ->    to be received from
⟹  Async<'b option>                              the agent's internal
                                                 queue

type MailboxReplyChannel<'a>(asyncReplyChannel:AsyncReplyChannel<'a>) =
      interface IAsyncReplyChannel<'a> with
          member x.Reply(msg) = asyncReplyChannel.Reply(msg)
```

> Asynchronously waits for a message to be received from the agent's internal queue

> Asynchronously posts a message to an agent

> **Asynchronously posts to an agent and waits for a reply. The reply is optional because the agent may not return a reply, due to a timeout, for example.**

Listing 3 creates a simple abstract class, `AgentRef<'a>`, that encapsulates the basics of an agent. It also defines an interface, `IAsyncReplyChannel<'a>`, and `MailboxReply-Channel<'a>`. This supports the `PostAndTryAsyncReply` functionality, which is necessary because the `AsyncReplyChannel<'a>` type defined in `Microsoft.FSharp.Control`, used to support the post and reply functionality, is currently sealed. Providing this interface (see the next listing) lets you create different channels that agents can reply on.

Listing 4 Defining an agent

```
type Agent<'a>(id:string, comp, ?token) =
    inherit AgentRef<'a>(id)
    let mutable agent = None

    override x.Receive() = agent.Value.Receive()
    override x.Post(msg:'a) = agent.Value.Post(msg)
    override x.PostAndTryAsyncReply(builder) =
        agent.Value.PostAndTryAsyncReply(fun rc ->
            builder(new MailboxReplyChannel<_>(rc)))

    override x.Start() =
        let mbox = MailboxProcessor.Start((fun inbox ->
            comp (x :> AgentRef<_>)), ?cancellationToken = token)
        agent <- Some mbox
```

This code creates a type, `Agent<'a>`. This type wraps and exposes some of the functionality provided by `MailboxProcessor<'a>`. The type delegates calls to the underlying agent, which is created when the agent is started. For `PostAndTryAsyncReply`, you can't delegate the call directly to the agent. This is because the type definition for `PostAndTryAsyncReply` requires the builder function to accept an `IAsyncReplyChannel <'a>`. The `AsyncReplyChannel<'a>` instance passed by `MailboxProcessor` doesn't implement this interface; therefore you use the `MailboxReplyChannel<'a>` type to wrap this instance in a type that does support that interface.

ADDRESSING AGENTS

Using the new abstraction, you can now create a local agent.

Listing 5 Creating an agent (F# Interactive)

```
> open FSharpDeepDives
> let console =
    let agent =
        Agent("console-writer", (fun (agent:AgentRef<string>) ->
                let rec loop() =
                    async {
                        let! msg = agent.Receive()
                        printfn "%s" msg
                        return! loop()
                    }
                loop()
        ))
    agent.Start()
    agent
val console : FSharpDeepDives.DomainTypes.Agent<string>
```

You can then post to the agent by directly referencing the agent and calling the `Post` method with the message:

```
> console.Post("Writing through an agent")
```

As mentioned previously, in smaller systems, directly referencing the agents can be acceptable. But as a system grows, it becomes necessary to provide an abstraction that allows you to indirectly reference an agent. To do so, you can introduce an addressing scheme for agents.

Listing 6   A simple agent registry

```
module Registry =

    let mutable private agents = Map.empty<string, AgentRef list>

    let register (ref:AgentRef<'a>) =
        match Map.tryFind ref.Id agents with
        | Some(refs) ->
            agents <- Map.add ref.Id ((ref :> AgentRef) :: refs) agents
        | None ->
            agents <- Map.add ref.Id [ref :> AgentRef] agents
        ref

    let resolve id =
        Map.find id agents
```

This is a minimal implementation of an agent registry. The registry is a `Map<string, AgentRef list>` that's used to store and retrieve agents. The `Registry` module allows many agents to be assigned to a single ID; this provides primitive broadcast semantics. To use the `Registry`, be sure that whenever an agent is created, it's registered, as shown next.

Listing 7   Registering an agent

```
> open FSharpDeepDives
> let console =
    let agent =
        Agent("console-writer", (fun (agent:AgentRef<string>) ->
                let rec loop() =
                    async {
                        let! msg = agent.Receive()
                        printfn "%s" msg
                        return! loop()
                    }
                loop()
        ))
    agent |> Registry.register
    agent.Start()

val console : FSharpDeepDives.DomainTypes.Agent<string>
```

Once an agent is registered, you can resolve to the agent by name.

Listing 8   Resolving and posting to an agent (F# interactive)

```
> Registry.resolve "console-writer"
➥  |> List.iter (fun a -> (a :?>AgentRef<string>).Post("Hello"))
```

Although resolving agents in this manner has the additional cost of the lookup (which will impact performance if done in tight loops), the flexibility it provides outweighs this.

TIDYING UP THE IMPLEMENTATION

Currently, listings 7 and 8 are functional but ugly. It would be nice if you could tidy up the implementation and make things like registration and posting more fluent. Fortunately, you can create a module that contains some helper functions for tidying up the interface with your agents, as you can see in the next listing.

Listing 9   Providing some helper functions

```
module Agent =

    let start (ref:AgentRef) =
        ref.Start()
        ref

    let spawn ref =
        Registry.register ref
        |> start

    let post (refs:#seq<AgentRef>) (msg:'a) =
        refs |> Seq.iter (fun r -> (r :?> AgentRef<'a>).Post(msg))

    let postAndTryAsyncReply (refs:#seq<AgentRef>) msg =
        refs
        |> Seq.map (fun r -> (r :?>
➥ AgentRef<'a>).PostAndTryAsyncReply(msg))
        |> Async.Parallel

    let postAndAsyncReply (refs:#seq<AgentRef>) msg =
        async {
            let! responses = postAndTryAsyncReply refs msg
            return responses |> Seq.choose id
        }

    let postAndReply (refs:#seq<AgentRef>) msg =
        postAndAsyncReply refs msg |> Async.RunSynchronously

    let resolve id = Registry.resolve id
```

In addition to hiding some implementation details (how agents are registered), providing a module like this allows you to build a mini domain-specific language (DSL) for your agent type, as shown in listing 10. Doing so allows you to use a more fluent API when speaking the language of agents.

Listing 10   Creating an agent with a mini-DSL (F# interactive)

```
> open FSharpDeepDives
> open FSharpDeepDives.Agent
```

```
> let console =
      Agent("console-writer", fun (agent:AgentRef<string>) ->
                      let rec loop() =
                          async {
                              let! msg = agent.Receive()
                              printfn "%s" msg
                              return! loop()
                          }
                      loop()
              )
      |> spawn
```

```
val console : FSharpDeepDives.DomainTypes.Local<string>
```

Listing 10 creates an agent identical to that in listing 7, but the DSL removes some of the boilerplate and automatically registers each agent so it can be resolved by name. But this hasn't reduced the code much when compared to listing 7. The real benefit is realized when you consider resolving and posting to an agent. Listing 8 now becomes

```
> resolve "console-writer" |> post <| "Hello, world"
val it : unit = ()
```

This code feels far more natural, but confusion might arise from the use of the affectionately termed *tie-fighter syntax*. Only a small set of terms can be treated as infix operators in F#. This syntax overcomes that by exploiting the curried nature of the post function. It's exactly equivalent to the following:

```
> post (resolve "console-writer") "Hello, world"
```

It's a question of personal preference as to which style you use. Usually we just pick the form that reads the best for the given situation.

REQUEST-RESPONSE FROM AGENTS

So far in this section we've only shown how to post to agents. Posting to agents is a one-way activity; it's somewhat analogous to calling a method with void as a return type in C#. But in C# you can define methods that return any type you want. So how do you do this with agents? Well, when you defined an interface for an Agent<'a> in addition to the post method, you defined a method called PostAndTryAsyncReply. When you post a message to an agent, it's asynchronously placed onto a queue to wait to be processed. The asynchronous nature of posting a message to the agents now causes a problem because you have to wait an unknown amount of time for the agent to get to your message and reply. To return the reply to the original caller, you need to create a channel that the agent can post to with a response. Your calling code can then asynchronously wait on that channel for a response. F# provides AsyncReplyChannel<'a>, which offers the exact behavior required. Unfortunately, this type is sealed and has an internal constructor that makes it difficult to reuse. But this has already been abstracted in listing 8 with the IAsyncReplyChannel<'a> interface and the MailboxReplyChannel<'a> type. You'll see further uses of this abstraction later in this chapter.

When we first introduced agents, we showed you an example of downloading and caching the response from a URL. This example used PostAndReply, which does exactly as described earlier. But rather than asynchronously waiting for the response, `PostAndReply` blocks until a response is received. To achieve the same thing with the new DSL, the internal loop code is almost identical; the only change is the function you use to post to the agent, as you can see in the following listing.

Listing 11   URL cache with the agent DSL

```
let urlReader =
    Agent("url-reader", fun (agent:AgentRef<Request>) ->
            let rec loop (cache : Map<string, string>) = async {
                    let! msg = agent.Receive()
                    match msg with
                    | Get(url, reply) ->
                        match cache.TryFind(url) with
                        | Some(result) ->
                            reply.Reply(result)
                            return! loop cache
                        | None ->
                            let! downloaded =
                                doWebRequest url "GET" readStreamAsString
                                reply.Reply(downloaded)
                                return! loop (Map.add url downloaded cache)
                }
            loop Map.empty)
        |> spawn
let agentResult =
    resolve "url-reader" |> postAndReply <|
    (fun rc -> Get("http://www.google.com", rc))
        |> Seq.iter (printfn "%A")

val agentResult : string =
"<!doctype html><html itemscope="" itemtype="http://schema.org"+[43426 chars]
```

Exercise 1

In listing 11, you add an entry to the cache every time a new URL is passed to the agent. But the contents of URLs changes, and it's memory consuming to keep every URL requested available forever. Your task is to implement expiry for the agent.

So far you've explored agents and the abstractions you need so that they can be used in a large-scale system. You created a DSL that uses these abstractions and allows a consumer to resolve and post to an agent's name. Having these abstractions will go a long way in helping you to build a large system based on agents.

Extracting data from the world

The world is full of data in many different forms. In enterprises, almost all systems extract data from a source, transform it into a domain model, and then either perform analysis on the data or save the results for later reporting. Often, downstream systems pick up this data, and the cycle continues. This process is trivial when you control both the source of the data and the sink; but frequently this isn't the case. Data often comes from a source external to the company.

Data comes in many shapes and formats. CSV, TSV, and XML are some common formats, and JSON is becoming increasingly popular. This list is not exhaustive, and other formats can be somewhat more interesting to extract data from—PDFs or images, for example. How can you exploit your knowledge of agents and asynchronous workflows in F# to get this data into your system? We can break down almost all data-collection problems into three steps: extract, transform, and load (ETL). In the next section, you'll see how to use agents to build an ETL pipeline.

The extract, transform, and load (ETL) model

The ETL model can be easily defined in F#, as the following listing shows.

Listing 12 Simple ETL function

```
let etl extractf transformf loadf =
    extractf()
    |> transformf
    |> loadf
```

This is about as simple as you can get—and it works. You can, for example, write a simple set of functions to parse a CSV file into a string[][] type and then write the contents out as JSON to another file.

Listing 13 Using the ETL function

```
let readFile path =
    (fun () -> File.ReadAllText(path))

let writeJson path input =
    (path, JsonConvert.SerializeObject(input))
    |> File.WriteAllText

let split (char:string) (input:string) =
    input.Split([|char|], StringSplitOptions.RemoveEmptyEntries)

let parseCsv (input:string) =
    split Environment.NewLine input |> Array.map (split ",")

let result =
   etl
        (readFile "c:\data.csv")
        parseCsv
        (writeJson "c:\data.json")
```

As functional as this is, you're only dealing with the simplest case. For example, in this scenario you'd have to wrap the entire function in a try..with block. But this isn't ideal, because it gives you little information about which stage failed. In listing 13, an IOException could occur at either the extract (readFile) or load (writeJson) stages, and you'd need a debugger to get to the bottom of this exception. In the real world, you often have little control over the source system; so, as shown in listing 14, your system should always be designed to be robust and catch errors in a way that helps the support team diagnose what has gone wrong.

> **Listing 14   Protected running of each stage**

```
let etl extractf transformf loadf =
    let stage name success input =
        match input with
        | Choice1Of2(output) ->
            try Choice1Of2 <| success output with e -> Choice2Of2 (name,e)
        | Choice2Of2(err) -> Choice2Of2 err

    stage "extract" extractf (Choice1Of2 ())
    |> stage "transform" transformf
    |> stage "load" loadf
```

Here you're using the `Choice<'a, 'b>` type to protect the execution of each stage. If you get an error during the transform stage, the last stage, `load`, will forward this error on. When an error occurs, the error is wrapped in a `Choice` and has the name of the stage attached to it to aid diagnostics. At this point you could add any amount of metadata to the error. If you try to run this when the source file doesn't exist, you'll get a result like the following:

```
val result : Choice<unit,(string * exn)> =
  Choice2Of2
    ("extract",System.IO.FileNotFoundException: Could not find file
    'data_!.csv'...)
```

You can now capture errors that may occur at each stage and enrich them as you see fit.

MAKING THINGS ASYNCHRONOUS

In general, the extract and load stages of an ETL system involve some sort of I/O, whether it's reading from a file as in the previous example or writing the transformed results to a database. You should make these stages asynchronous to prevent your ETL solution from blocking the entire process while it executes. This means you can have more than one ETL pipeline executing at any one time, allowing you to parallelize this work. To make your ETL function asynchronous, you'll use F#'s existing `Async<'a>` computation expression. To make use of it, you need to change your definition of the stage function.

> **Listing 15   Asynchronous stage function**

```
let etl (extractf : Async<'a>) (transformf : 'a -> Async<'b>)
    (loadf: 'b -> Async<'c>) =
    let returnResult input = async { return Choice1Of2 input }     Wraps the
    let stage name f rest =                                         result of the
            async {                                                 final stage
                    let! f = f |> Async.Catch          Safe asynchronous
                    match f with                       execution of a function
```

```
                        | Choice1Of2 r ->
                            let! result = rest r
                            return result
                        | Choice2Of2 e -> return Choice2Of2 (name,e)
              }

    stage "extract" extractf
        (fun extracted ->
            stage "transform" (transformf extracted)
                (fun transformed ->
                    stage "load" (loadf transformed)
                        (fun result -> returnResult result))
        )
```

1 A higher-order function implementing an ETL process

The stage function in listing 15 is fairly similar to the function implemented earlier. The major difference is that you now have a somewhat nasty representation **1** for tying together the stages. F# comes with a built-in solution to this problem: as shown in listing 16, you can create a computation expression builder that does this sugaring for you and leaves you with a more imperative syntax to work with.

Listing 16   ETL computation expression

```
module Etl =

    let stage name f rest =
        async {
                let! f = f |> Async.Catch
                match f with
                | Choice1Of2 r ->
                    let! result = rest r
                    return result
                | Choice2Of2 e -> return Choice2Of2 (name,e)
        }

    let ret f = async { return Choice1Of2 f }
    let fail f = async { return Choice2Of2 f }

    type EtlBuilder() =
        member x.Bind((name,f), rest) = stage name f rest
        member x.Return(f) = ret f
        member x.ReturnFrom(f) : Async<Choice<_,_>> =  f

    let toAsync successF compensation comp =
        async {
            let! result = comp
            match result with
            | Choice1Of2 r -> return successF r
            | Choice2Of2 (name,err) -> return compensation name err
        }

let etl = Etl.EtlBuilder()
```

Listing 17 defines a computation builder that allows you to compose various ETL functions without having to worry about the awkward wiring introduced when you made your stages asynchronous.

Listing 17   Using the ETL computation builder

Listing 17   Using the ETL computation builder

```
let etl extractf transformf loadf =
    etl {
        let! extracted = "extract",extractf
        let! transformed = "transform",transformf extracted
        let! result = "load",loadf transformed
        return result
    }
```

This is far simpler and much cleaner than the previous implementation, because all the nasty boilerplate has been removed. As an added bonus, because you can arbitrarily compose functions, you no longer need the enclosing function; listing 18 shows an asynchronous version of listing 13.

Listing 18   Asynchronous file converter

```
let readFileAsync path =
    async {
        use fs = File.OpenRead(path)
        use sr = new StreamReader(fs)
        return! sr.ReadToEndAsync() |> Async.AwaitTask
    }

let parseCsvAsync (input:string) =
    async {
            return split Environment.NewLine input |> Array.map (split ",")
    }

let writeJsonAsync path input =
    async {
        let! serialized =
            JsonConvert.SerializeObjectAsync(input)
            ⇒ |> Async.AwaitTask
        use fs = File.Open(path, FileMode.Create,
                        ⇒ FileAccess.Write, FileShare.None)
        use sw = new StreamWriter(fs)
        return! sw.WriteAsync(serialized) |> Async.AwaitIAsyncResult
    }

let parseCSVAndSaveAsJson sourcePath sinkPath =
    etl {
        let! extracted = "extractCsv", (readFileAsync sourcePath)
        let! parsedCsv = "parseCSV", (parseCsvAsync extracted)
        do! ("savingJson",
            ⇒ (writeJsonAsync sinkPath parsedCsv |> Async.Ignore))
    }
    |> Etl.toAsync id (printfn "Error Stage: %s - %A")

parseCSVAndSaveAsJson "data.csv" "data.json" |> Async.RunSynchronously
```

Now that you can create ETL computation expressions that can compose asynchronous functions together into a workflow, you need a way to run or schedule the run of these computations. In the next section, we look at how to use cron expressions and system events to run these computations.

Exercise 2

In listing 18, you naively extract the entire file upon reading the file. Now suppose the file was gigabytes or terabytes in size: what would have to change in listing 18 to make this work for files that are too large to fit in memory? Your task is to refactor the functions to handle large files.

Scheduling ETL work

In the section "The extract, transform, and load (ETL) model," you created an ETL workflow. With this workflow, you can create delayed asynchronous expressions that can represent any given ETL task. You now need a way to run these tasks. There are two types of data sources: pull and push. Examples of pull data sources include reading from a file, running a query against a database, and extracting a page from a website. Push data sources include a subscription to a message bus topic, responding to data received on a network channel, and even UI events.

Earlier we talked about building on event streams and the advantages of that approach, so let's try to capitalize on that in our ETL work. The only problem is that push data sources are rare in the real world. This begs the question, how can you turn a pull data source into a push data source? The answer is simple: you schedule a file extraction to be run at given intervals, and then, as each interval passes, you raise an event to trigger some work. Okay, so it isn't a push data source in the true sense, but it's close enough for you to be able to exploit some of the nice properties of an event-driven architecture.

Version 4 of the .NET Framework introduced the `IObservable<'a>` and `IObserver<'a>` interfaces. These interfaces provide the basis for push-based notifications based on the Observer pattern. `IObservable<'a>` provides a single method, `Subscribe`, which allows an observer to observe the data source. Upon subscribing, the `Subscribe` method returns an instance of `IDisposable`, which can be used later to stop that instance of the observer from receiving notifications. The `IObserver<'a>` interface provides the means to send notifications. This interface can raise three types of notifications:

- *Data*—Notifies the observer of the next event (`IObserver<'a>.OnNext`)
- *Error*—Notifies the observer that an error occurred (`IObserver<'a>.OnError`)
- *Completed*—Notifies the observer that the stream has completed (`IObserver<'a>.OnCompleted`)

Because the framework already provides these interfaces, it makes sense to use them, but you still need a way to indicate when you want to raise these events. You could use a `TimeSpan` object, but doing so isn't flexible because you can't exclude certain days, dates, months, or years. Another option is to use a precomputed list of date-time structures, but this approach isn't scalable or robust. A better option is to use cron expressions, as you'll see next.

CRON EXPRESSIONS

Cron is a scheduling utility built into *nix-based operating systems. A *cron expression* is the specification that defines when something should happen. Cron expressions are a powerful way of representing schedules. You can use a cron expression to define almost any schedule, such as

```
0 0 1 14,18 JAN,MAR,SEP ? 2014
```

which yields the following dates:

- Tuesday, January 14, 2014 1:00 AM
- Saturday, January 18, 2014 1:00 AM
- Friday, March 14, 2014 1:00 AM
- Tuesday, March 18, 2014 1:00 AM
- Sunday, September 14, 2014 1:00 AM
- Thursday, September 18, 2014 1:00 AM

Parsing cron expressions is out of the scope of this chapter. But assuming you can parse a cron expression to a seq<DateTime>, you can then asynchronously evaluate this sequence and raise events on an observer.

Listing 19   Turning a sequence of date-times into an observable

```
module Schedule =
  (*..Other functions omitted..*)

  let toObservable (cron : string) =              ① List of available
      let observers = ref []                          observers
      let cts = new Threading.CancellationTokenSource()

      let notifyObservers f =                     ← Function that
          !observers                                asynchronously
          |> Seq.map (fun (observer:IObserver<_>) ->  ② notifies observers
                async { return f observer})
          |> Async.Parallel
          |> Async.RunSynchronously
          |> ignore

      let next value =
       notifyObservers (fun observer -> observer.OnNext value)

      let error error =
        notifyObservers (fun observer -> observer.OnError error)
        observers := []

      let completed()=
        notifyObservers (fun observer -> observer.OnCompleted())
        observers := []
                                                  ③ An asynchronous
      let worker =                                  task waiting for the
          Async.Start(async {                       next event to occur
            let enum = (toSeq cron).GetEnumerator()
```

```
        while enum.MoveNext() && not <| cts.IsCancellationRequested do
            let diff = enum.Current.Subtract(DateTime.Now)
            if diff.TotalMilliseconds >= 0. then
                do! Async.Sleep(diff.TotalMilliseconds |> int)
                do next enum.Current
        }, cts.Token)

    { new IObservable<DateTime> with
        member o.Subscribe(observer) =
            observers := observer :: !observers
            {new IDisposable with
                member this.Dispose() =
                    observers := !observers |> List.filter ((<>) observer)
            }
    }
```

Now you can schedule your convert CSV task from the previous section, as shown in the following listing.

Listing 20 Scheduling a task

```
Schedule.toObservable "0 0/1 * 1/1 * ? *"         Cron expression that
|> Observable.add (fun dt ->                       runs a computation
        printfn "Running CSV converter %A" (dt.ToString())   every minute forever
        parseCSVAndSaveAsJson "data.csv" "data.json"
        |> Async.RunSynchronously)
```

So far you've seen how to schedule a task using cron expressions and how to chain together different stages of an ETL task in a composable way. In the trivial examples you've seen so far, directly chaining together the stages has been acceptable, because they all take approximately the same amount of time to complete. But if you're in a situation where a stage may take a long time to complete, then you have a problem, because you'll end up getting a backlog of work that could keep growing until the process runs out of memory. Pipelining stages will help solve this problem, and in the next section you'll see how pipelines work.

Implementing ETL pipeline workers

Pipelines are useful if you want to process a large number of inputs in parallel and that processing consists of a set of steps that must be executed. Figure 1 shows a processing pipeline.

In a pipeline, each step is separated by a queue of fixed length. When the queue fills up, it blocks any more work from being placed in the queue. This avoids a potential runaway memory problem that can occur if there's a large differential in the execution time between the current stage and the next.

To implement a pipelined version of your ETL workflow, you can introduce an agent that has a bounded queue that blocks when the queue is full, thus preventing any more messages from being passed to it until it has a free slot.

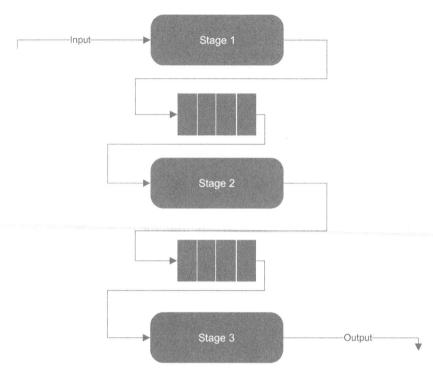

Figure 1   Simple processing pipeline

Listing 21   An agent with a bounded queue

```
type ReplyChannel<'a>() =
    let tcs = new TaskCompletionSource<'a>()

    member x.WaitResult =
       async {
           return! tcs.Task |> Async.AwaitTask
       }

    interface IAsyncReplyChannel<'a> with
       member x.Reply(msg) =
          tcs.SetResult(msg)

type BoundedAgent<'a>(id:String, limit:int, comp, ?token) =
    inherit AgentRef<'a>(id)
    let cts = defaultArg token Async.DefaultCancellationToken

    let bc = new BlockingCollection<'a>(limit - 1)

    override x.Post(msg) = bc.Add(msg)

    override x.PostAndTryAsyncReply(builder) =
        async {
            let rc = new ReplyChannel<_>()
            do bc.Add(builder(rc))
            let! result = rc.WaitResult
```

⟵ **Implementation of
IAsyncReplyChannel<'a>
❶ to support a blocking agent**

```
            return Some result
    }
  override x.Receive() = async { return bc.Take(cts) }
  override x.Start() =
      Async.Start(comp (x :> AgentRef<_>), cts)
```

Exercise 3

In listing 21, you created an agent with a different behavior to support a specific requirement. There's a myriad of other agents you can create. Your task is to create an agent that allows users from any thread to update the UI.

In listing 21, you created two types: `ReplyChannel<'a>` ❶, and `BoundedAgent<'a>`. `ReplyChannel<'a>` provides functionality identical to that of `AsyncReplyChannel<'a>` defined in the FSharp.Core library. But as previously mentioned, the constructor for this type is sealed so you can't reuse it. Fortunately the `System.Threading.Tasks` namespace provides the `TaskCompletionSource<'a>` type, which allows you to wait on a result from an asynchronous task. All you do in listing 21 is provide a wrapper around this type. With this in hand, you can then implement the `BoundedAgent<'a>` type. At the heart of the bounded agent is `BlockingCollection<'a>`, which lets you wrap other collections (that provide an implementation of the `IProducerConsumer-Collection<'a>` interface) to add blocking behavior. That way, you can add first-in, first-out (FIFO) semantics, for example, by wrapping a concurrent queue. But because agents can process messages in any order, the simple blocking collection suffices in this case.

Now that you've defined your agent, you can begin to integrate it into your ETL functions. But you have a problem: instead of passing the result of one asynchronous computation to the input of the other, you have to take the reply message from one agent and post the message to the next agent. To fix this, you can introduce a function (see listing 22) that takes an agent and the previous part of the computation and converts it into `string * Async<'a>`, which is what the `stage` function defined in listing 16 expects.

Listing 22 Tying together agents

```
type Replyable<'request, 'reply> =
    | Reply of 'request * IAsyncReplyChannel<'reply>

let pipelined (agent:AgentRef<_>) previous =
    agent.Id, async {
        let! result =
    agent.PostAndTryAsyncReply(fun rc -> Reply(previous,rc))
        match result with
        | Some(result) ->
            match result with
            | Choice1Of2(result) -> return result
```

```
                    | Choice2Of2(err) -> return raise(err)
                | None -> return failwithf "Stage timed out %s: failed" agent.Id
        }
```

Listing 22 takes a reference to an agent and creates an asynchronous computation that
wraps the call to `PostAndTryAsyncReply`. To support this, you need to define a message
type for your agents, because you need a common way of responding using the reply
channel you built earlier. To enable this, you create the `Replyable<'request,'reply>`
type. This unfortunately has the side effect of restricting your agents to accept this message, but this isn't as bad as it might seem. The type `Replyable<'request,'reply>`
doesn't impose any constraints on the request or reply payloads. Implementing an
agent that can accept this message is simple, as shown in the following listing.

Listing 23   Implementing a pipeline-able agent

```
let bounded name limit comp =
    BoundedAgent<_>(name, limit, fun (ref:AgentRef<_>) ->
        let rec loop (ref:AgentRef<_>) =
            async {
                let! Reply(msg, reply) = ref.Receive()
                let! result = comp msg |> Async.Catch
                do reply.Reply(result)
                return! loop ref
            }
        loop ref) |> Agent.spawn
```

Listing 23 creates a bounded agent that accepts the `Replyable<'request, 'reply>`
message type. When a message is received, it's unpacked, and the payload is passed to
the computation for processing. Once you have the result of the computation, it's
passed to the reply channel. The actor is then looped to await the new message.

     With all this in place, you can implement a pipelined version.

Listing 24   Pipelined file converter

```
let writeOutput (path,input) = async {
    let! serialised =
        JsonConvert.SerializeObjectAsync(input)
        |> Async.AwaitTask
    use fs = File.Open
                ( path, FileMode.Create,
                  FileAccess.Write, FileShare.None)
    use sw = new StreamWriter(fs)
    return!
        sw.WriteAsync(serialised)
        |> Async.AwaitIAsyncResult
        |> Async.Ignore }

let fileExtractor =
    Agent.bounded "extractCsv" 5 readFileAsync
let parser =
    Agent.bounded "parseCsv" 5 parseCsvAsync
```

```
let saveFile =
    Agent.bounded "saveFile" 5 writeOutput
let agentWorker sourcePath sinkPath =
    etl {
        let! extracted = Agent.pipelined fileExtractor sourcePath
        let! parsedCsv = Agent.pipelined parser extracted
        do! Agent.pipelined saveFile (sinkPath,parsedCsv) }
    |> Etl.toAsync id (printfn "Error Stage: %s - %A")
```

Fundamentally you haven't changed your ETL pipeline; you wrapped the existing functions into an agent and prefixed each of those agents with the `pipelined` function. This approach allows you to reuse all the functionality you already had.

Putting a system together

Earlier we focused on individual aspects of asynchronous and agent-based programming. This is all well and good, but you could focus so much on understanding these primitives that you lose sight of how they relate to real-world systems. In this section, you'll build a scalable information system that extracts forecast and observational power data from a UK power system operator and combines it into various views.

Introducing scalable systems

Scalability refers to an improvement of a system's overall performance by adding more resources. This improvement can be achieved by adding resources to a single piece of hardware (vertical scaling) or adding more pieces of commodity hardware (horizontal scaling). Each scaling strategy has its pros and cons. Vertical scaling is bounded by Moore's law, and horizontal scaling can make "true" consistency difficult to achieve due to nonzero latency between nodes. How you should scale your application depends on properties that are desirable for your system so that it can meet your business requirements. This section outlines several techniques that are generally applicable and that let you build a scalable system using F#.

Building on event streams

Event streams provide a continuous set of events. Given an initial application state, you can sequentially apply the events from the stream to change the state of the application to a new state. Representing the changes to application state as a sequence of events is known as *event sourcing*. Event sourcing allows a system to have its state reconstructed to any point by replaying the relevant events. But what's an event? An *event* is an immutable, one-way record of something that has happened. It should represent something of business significance to the application (see listing 25). For example, "Fuel generation data was extracted" could be an event in your ETL system.

Listing 25   Representing an event

```
type Event<'evntType, 'payload> = {
    Id : Guid
    EventType : 'evntType
    Payload : 'payload
    Timestamp : DateTimeOffset
    MetaData : IDictionary<string, obj>
}
```

What's the point of storing all intermediate events when you can just store the final state? Well, a few interesting features come out of storing the individual events:

- *Storage*—It's trivial to store events. Because events should be immutable, all you need to do is serialize them and then append them to a file. If you need to query, consider a fully fledged event store or a relational database management system (RDBMS). If you choose an RDBMS, the data model is often far simpler than the conventional fully normalized data model.
- *Error recovery*—If a worker node goes down in your cluster, you replay all the events back through the node when it comes back up, to restore the state.
- *Fault tolerance*—Because events can be multiplexed, scaling is made a lot simpler; you distribute the workers on multiple machines connected to a message bus and broadcast events to all the workers.
- *Trivial precomputation*—Because an individual event completely encapsulates the potential change to the state, it's easy to precompute a read model by applying the event and then projecting the state to the read model.

The last bullet mentions a *read model*. This is a term that arises from the Command Query Responsibility Separation (CQRS) pattern. CQRS and event sourcing are often mentioned together, but in no way does one imply the other. The idea behind CQRS is that reads and writes to a data store are separated (figure 2). As a simple example, a UI might create an event or a command, which is written to the event store. The event store then publishes the stored event. The read side subscribes to the stored event and applies the event to some application state (which may or may not cause a change). If the event does cause a change, the read model is updated and persisted in the read store. The read model is often some sort of denormalized store, where the model is optimized so that reads of the application can respond to queries as quickly as possible.

Designing for scalability

When developing applications that need to scale, the closer you get to the hardware, the harder you have to work to get performance gains. This means for an application to scale successfully, it must be designed to do so from the beginning. For an application to have a chance at being scalable, it must do the following:

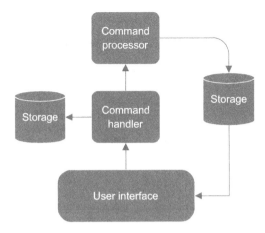

Figure 2   CQRS interfaces

- *Minimize wait times*—Use asynchronous programming to avoid blocking execution paths and allow other parts of the application to continue running.
- *Commute*—Actions can be applied in any order and still produce the same result.
- *Minimize resource contention*—Processes shouldn't fight to update a single file.
- *Keep computations pure*—Actions with side effects (such as persisting data) should occur only on the interfaces of the application.
- *Minimize dependencies*—Dependencies make applications more complex and can create bottlenecks when one side of the dependency takes significantly longer than the other to complete its task.

Combining the tenets of event sourcing and CQRS, along with implementing agents, goes a long way toward satisfying all of these properties. But a large portion of systems in the world aren't event driven. In the next section, you'll see how to extract data from the world and enable this event-driven approach to use asynchronous systems.

Implementing the system

The example system will be based on UK power generation. You'll take half-hourly fuel generation data published by ELEXON (the company that manages the UK's power-trading exchange), transform it into a type, and then compute some statistics (totals and averages) over this data. Although this isn't a complex problem, it highlights how you can build and compose asynchronous workflows and agents to create a scalable solution to problems.

To start, in the following listing you define some primitive types that you'll need to represent the application domain.

Listing 26   Representing your domain

```
[<Measure>]type MW                                      ◁── Measures in the domain;
                                                             in this case MW is the
type Trigger =          ◁── Type that represents how the    only measure
   | Cron                   entire process is triggered
   | File of string
```

```
type EventType =
    | ExtractedData of Trigger * string
    | TransformedData of Trigger * string
    | TotalStatisticUpdated
    | AverageStatisticUpdated

type SettlementPeriod = DateTime * int

type FuelSettlementPeriod  = {
    Period : SettlementPeriod
    CCGT : int<MW>
    OCGT : int<MW>
    Coal : int<MW>
    Oil : int<MW>
    Wind : int<MW>
    Nuclear : int<MW>
}

type Message =
        | Data of seq<FuelSettlementPeriod>

type FuelTypeStats = {
    CCGT : float<MW>
    OCGT : float<MW>
    Coal : float<MW>
    Oil : float<MW>
    Wind : float<MW>
    Nuclear : float<MW>
}
with
    static member Create(fsp : FuelSettlementPeriod) =
        {
            CCGT = (float fsp.CCGT |> LanguagePrimitives.FloatWithMeasure);
            (* other members omitted *)
        }
    static member Zero =
        { CCGT = 0.<MW>; (* other members omitted *) }
    static member DivideByInt(fsp: FuelTypeStats, count:int) =
        { fsp with
            CCGT = fsp.CCGT / (float count)
            (* other members omitted *) }
        }
    static member (+) (ft1, ft2) =
        {
            CCGT = ft1.CCGT + ft2.CCGT
            (* other members omitted *)
        }
```

Type that represents the context around the type of event you store

Type that represents the settlement period

Type that represents the current fuel type by settlement period

Type that represents the input message to models

1 Type that represents computed statistics

In this extremely simple domain, notice that the type FuelTypeStats **1** has some interesting members on it, including Zero and (+). The existence of these members points to the fact that the type may be monoidal[3] as long as it satisfies the three monoid laws of associativity, closure, and identity. Because this type contains only other monoidal types, your type is monoidal too. This subject is out of the scope of

---

[3] Scott Wlaschin, "The 'Understanding Monoids' Series," *F# for Fun and Profit,* http://mng.bz/n7JZ.

this chapter, but suffice to say that the fact that this type is monoidal will make it easy to compute many things over this data without having to think too hard about it.

Now that you've defined your domain, you can define how you're going to transform the data.

Listing 27 Extracting and transforming the data

```
type private YTDFuelByHalfHour =
    FSharp.Data.CsvProvider<"fuelhh_2013.txt">

let transformYtdFuelByHalfHour (input:string) =
    async {
        let rows = YTDFuelByHalfHour.Parse(input).Data
        return
          rows
          |> Seq.toArray
          |> Array.map (fun row ->
             {
                 Period = (row.``#Settlement Date``,
    row.``SettlementPeriod``)
                 CCGT = row.CCGT |> LanguagePrimitives.Int32WithMeasure
                 (* other properties omitted *)
             })
    }

let extractYtdFuelByHalfHour = function
    | Cron -> DataAccess.getHttp yearGenByFuelTypeUrl ["key", apiKey]
    | File(path) -> DataAccess.getFile path

let run (dispatcher:_ -> Async<unit>) (source:Trigger) =
    etl {
        let! extractedData =
             Agent.pipelined (
                 Agent.bounded "extract YTD Fuel" 5
    extractYtdFuelByHalfHour) source
        do! "storing extracted data", DataAccess.storeEvent
          (ExtractedData(source, "Elexon YTD Fuel")) extractedData
        let! transformedData =
             Agent.pipelined (
    Agent.bounded "parse YTD Fuel" 5
      transformYtdFuelByHalfHour) extractedData
        do! ("storing transformed data",
    DataAccess.storeEvent (TransformedData(source, "Elexon YTD Fuel"))
    transformedData)
        return (dispatcher transformedData |> Async.StartImmediate)
    }
```

① Type provider to parse CSV data, with a sample to generate the types from

Transforms the input string into your domain type

② Decides which location to extract raw data from depending on the trigger received

ETL pipeline

Storing an intermediate event

③ Executes the dispatcher function with transformed data

Listing 27 creates an ETL pipeline that stores the result from each of the stages in an event store. To extract the data **②**, you decide where to source the data based on the trigger type passed into the pipeline (more on this later). Once the raw data is extracted, you pass this data to the transform stage, which then uses a CSV type provider **①** to parse and convert the data into your domain type. You again store this transformed data in the event store. The final stage is passing the transformed data to a function, which can dispatch to your waiting models **③**.

Now that you have some data, the next thing to do is implement some models.

Listing 28   Implementing the models

```
module Models =

    open System
    open FSharpDeepDives

    let stats name eventType token (op : (seq<_> -> FuelTypeStats)) =
        Agent(name, (fun ref ->
            let rec loop (state:FuelTypeStats) (ref:AgentRef<Message>) =
                async {
                    let! (Data(fsp)) = ref.Receive()
                    let result = op fsp
                    do! DataAccess.storeEvent eventType result
                    return! loop result ref
                }
            loop FuelTypeStats.Zero ref), ?token = token)

    let total token =
        stats "total" TotalStatisticUpdated token (
            Seq.map FuelTypeStats.Create >> Seq.sum)

    let average token =
        stats "average" AverageStatisticUpdated token (
            Seq.map FuelTypeStats.Create >> Seq.average)
```

A higher-order function that ❶
wraps the computation and
event persistence of statistics

In this application, the model computations live within agents. You can abstract most of the implementation of an agent away into a single function ❶. This function takes a name, an event type, a cancellation token, and a computation. In terms of business relevance for this application, it's this computation that's important. As explained earlier, because your type implements certain members, you can use built-in F# functions (Seq.sum and Seq.average) to handle the computation. Because FuelStatsType is in fact a monoid, the statistics functions used in listing 28 would be almost trivial to define if they didn't exist in the F# core library (see listing 29).

Listing 29   Sum and average without Seq.sum and Seq.average

```
data |> Seq.reduce (+)            ◁— Sum

FuelTypeStats.DivideByInt(data |> Seq.fold (fun (last, count) curr ->
    (curr + last, count + 1) (FuelTypeStats.Zero, 0))
```
Average

Notice when computing the average that there is no divisor. Instead you use the DivideByInt member on FuelStatsType and a fold to count and sum the individual instances of FuelStatsType, giving the equivalent of Seq.average.

Next you need a way to extract and transform the raw data to a representation and a way to model the data. The next listing shows how to create triggers to kick off this process.

Listing 30 **Triggering your workflow**

```
module Triggers =

    open System
    open System.IO
    open FSharpDeepDives
    open FSharpDeepDives.ExampleApp

    let private ensurePath path =
        let di = new DirectoryInfo(path)
        di.Create(); di.FullName

    let file path =
        let watcher = new FileSystemWatcher(ensurePath path)
        watcher.EnableRaisingEvents <- true
        watcher.Created
        |> Observable.map (fun x -> Trigger.File(x.FullPath))

    let cron cronExp =
        Schedule.toObservable cronExp
        |> Observable.map (fun _ -> Trigger.Cron)
```

Listing 30 creates two triggers: a file trigger that watches a folder for any changes, and a cron-based trigger that fires at intervals that match the cron expression. When each trigger is fired, you map the event arguments in the `Trigger` type defined in listing 26.

The only thing left to do is to tie all this together, as shown in the next listing. This will be the entry point to your application.

Listing 31 **Bringing it all together**

```
module Program =

    let tokenSource = new CancellationTokenSource()          ❶ List of model
                                                                 definitions
    let models = [
                    Models.total (Some tokenSource.Token)
                    Models.average (Some tokenSource.Token)
                 ] |> List.map (Agent.spawn >> Agent.ref)

    let triggers = [                                         ❷ List of triggers that
        Triggers.file "C:\FileDrop\HalfHourFuel"                can run computations
        Triggers.cron "0 0/15 * 1/1 * ? *"
    ]

    let modelDispatcher data =
        async {
            do models |> post <| Data(data)
        }

    let run comp =
        Async.StartImmediate(comp, tokenSource.Token)

    [<EntryPoint>]
    let main(args) =
        triggers
        |> List.reduce Observable.merge
        |> Observable.add (fun trigger ->
```

```
                    Elexon.run modelDispatcher trigger
                    |> Etl.toAsync id Logger.logStageError
                    |> run)

        printfn "System Running: Press Enter to Exit"
        System.Console.ReadLine() |> ignore
        tokenSource.Cancel()

        printfn "System Exiting"
        0
```

Notice the extensibility you've achieved here. For example, if you want another statistic computed, you can write the function, wrap it in an agent, and add it to the list of model definitions ❶. Or if you want another trigger, you can add it to the list ❷. It shouldn't be hard to see how you could take this application even further and make it almost entirely data driven, by lifting the lists defined in ❶ and ❷ into configuration files.

Going beyond simple agents

Everything you've seen so far has been in terms of agents and asynchronous programming in a single process. This needn't be the case; the message passing–based nature of agents makes them almost trivial to extend into message bus–oriented architecture. For example, you could create an agent where the receive method is listening to an exchange on a message bus and the post places messages onto another exchange to which other agent instances subscribe. This opens up a world of possibilities in terms of load balancing, clustering, and resilience.

Summary

At the start of this chapter, we introduced F# asynchronous workflows and showed you how to compose these workflows together into larger, more complex workflows with ease. You then learned about agents and built a framework that helps you manage agents in large systems. From there you moved on to building extract-transform and load pipelines; you started with a simple example and built it up in stages until you had a fully fledged pipeline that allows you to balance the amount of throughput to get the best trade-off in terms of memory usage and performance. You also saw how to schedule pipelines to run using cron expressions. Finally, you built an application that extracts UK fuel-generation data and loads the results into a set of models that compute statistics over that data and store each action and computation result as an event.

About the author

Colin Bull holds a master's degree in physics from the University of Birmingham and is currently working as a consultant software developer/technical architect in the UK commodity trading sector, where he has implemented several commercial solutions in F#.

In his spare time, Colin enjoys learning about new technologies, especially ones related to functional programming, and contributes to several F# community open source projects. Colin also maintains a blog at http://colinbul.wordpress.com.

Creating games using XNA

Johann Deneux

One of the main difficulties of implementing user interfaces in games is the gap between *event-based* user interfaces—nowadays the prevalent type—and *frame-based simulation* frameworks used for games. User interfaces are typically designed to react to user input and remain asleep between user actions. Frame-based simulation divides time into small, discrete quantities and repeatedly updates the state of the simulation.

User interaction often requires a number of steps to be spread out over longer periods, up to several seconds or minutes. Long interactions have to be broken into smaller units of work, which are chained and executed in each frame. Keeping track of the current unit of work and its data commonly leads to condition-heavy code with lots of partially initialized variables. F# offers a number of elegant solutions in the form of discriminated unions and asynchronous computations. Table 1 compares explicit state using mutable variables and enum in C# to implicit state using async computations in F#, which are shorter.

Time to market, efficiency, correctness, and complexity are concepts important to every business. The same is true of games, regardless of budget. Being the first to publish a game in its genre is important because you'll benefit from additional exposure. But this is only true if your game is stable. If, like me, you're a hobbyist game developer, your main concern isn't financial success but managing to complete your project and publish it. My personal experience is that most projects are exciting initially; then they become fun to develop. But implementing all the features you want requires discipline and focus. Final polishing is annoying; passing certification is stressful. Dealing with bugs and angry players after release can drive you to insanity. Working on a title loses its fun, the more time you spend on it. For this reason, any tool that can help you reach completion early and lets you move on to the next project can make the difference between the frustration of an abandoned project and the satisfaction of a published title.

Table 1   Comparison of state management in C# and F#

Explicit state with variables in C#	Implicit state with async in F#

<pre>enum State {
  WaitingForButtonPress,
  StartSelectingStorage,
  SelectingStorage,
  Loading
}
class InitialScreen {
  State Current;
  PlayerIndex ControllingPlayer;
  IAsyncResult AsyncRes;
  StorageDevice Storage;
  Data data;
 	
  public void Update() {
    switch (Current) {
    case WaitingForButtonPress:
      if (/* Button pressed ...*/) {
        ControllingPlayer = ...;
        Current =
          StartSelectingStorage;
      }
      break;
    case StartSelectingStorage:
      AsyncRes =
        BeginShowSelector(...);
      Current =
        SelectingStorage;
      break;
    case SelectingStorage:
      if (AsyncRes.IsCompleted) {
        Storage =
      EndShowSelector(AsyncRes);
        Current = Loading;
      }
      break;
    case Loading:
      try {
        data =
          LoadFrom(Storage);
      }
      catch (SomeException e) {
        data = null;
      }
    }
  }
}</pre>
	<pre>let initialScreen =
	  async {
	    let! controllingPlayer =
	      waitForButtonPress
	    let! storageDevice =
	      showStorageDeviceSelector
	        controllingPlayer
	    let data =
	      try
	        loadFrom storageDevice
	        |> Some
	      with
	      | :? SomeException -> None
	      return data
	  }</pre>

This chapter demonstrates techniques in F# for solving a number of commonly occurring problems in game development. Many of these issues are present in regular desktop and mobile applications, and the solutions presented here apply to these sectors as well. For instance, mobile phone applications offer attractive, smooth interfaces with multiple animation effects while dealing with slow connections to remote data servers. The gap between the continuously running graphical effects and delayed data retrieval leads to the same kind of issues. You'll also see how data structures other than classes can be used to model data in a simple yet effective manner. Here again, this topic isn't specific to games—all applications need to model the data they process. Finally, you'll learn how to glue together functional code and objects provided by Microsoft's XNA framework.

Using the XNA framework

The XNA framework directly targets three platforms: PCs with Microsoft Windows, Xbox 360, and Windows Phone 7 mobile devices. Other platforms such as iOS mobile devices, PCs with Mac OS X, and Linux are available through Mono and MonoGame.

XNA Game Studio is the development environment that Microsoft makes available for free to develop XNA games. It's available as a standalone application using Microsoft Visual Studio 2010 C# Express Edition, which allows developers to write games in C# only and as an extension for other editions of Visual Studio 2010. To use F# to develop XNA games, developers must use Visual Studio 2010 Shell with the F# plug-in together with XNA Game Studio or XNA Game Studio with Visual Studio 2010 Professional Edition or higher.

It's also possible to install XNA Game Studio as an extension for Visual Studio 2013. The extension is compatible with the Express edition for the desktop and is available at http://msxna.codeplex.com.

For further information on toolkits and frameworks for game development in F#, visit http://fsharp.org/apps-and-games.

Now that you understand the problem and the technology we'll use in this chapter, let's dig into the structure of a typical game developed using the XNA framework.

Getting started

Before diving into programming techniques, I'll introduce a simple game used throughout this chapter. I'll then explore the basics of XNA games, most of which are directly applicable to MonoGame as well.

Defending Europe against incoming missiles

The game is composed of three screens, as you can see in figure 1. The initial screen prompts the player to press a key or a button. After the user complies, the next screen consists of the main game. The game presents the player with a map of Western Europe. Submarines surfacing from the depths of the Atlantic Ocean and the Mediterranean Sea launch missiles aimed at large cities; the player has to intercept missiles by firing a laser from a satellite. This isn't a game that can be won, because the pace at

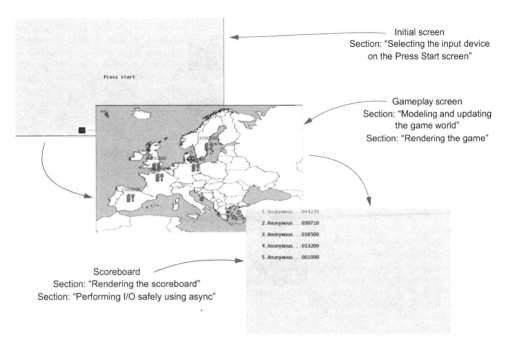

Initial screen
Section: "Selecting the input device
on the Press Start screen"

Gameplay screen
Section: "Modeling and updating
the game world"
Section: "Rendering the game"

Scoreboard
Section: "Rendering the scoreboard"
Section: "Performing I/O safely using async"

Figure 1   Screens in the sample game

which missiles are fired increases with time. When the last city is destroyed, the final score is computed based on the amount of time the player managed to resist. The next screen is the scoreboard, which shows the position of the newly achieved score with respect to the 10 earlier best scores.

Understanding the execution flow of an XNA game

Similar to most frameworks, XNA distinguishes between updating the state of the game and rendering it to the screen and the audio system. These two operations are repeatedly performed in a sequence (see figure 2).

Each operation is implemented by a method of a class that inherits from `DrawableGameComponent`. The base class provides a `Run` method that executes the operation depicted in figure 2.

The `Run` method calls three virtual methods described in table 2. First, the `Initialize` method is called, which loads the art assets and performs other initialization of the graphical system, such as running the game in full-screen or windowed mode and setting the resolution. This method also sets the game into a state where it's ready to run. This typically includes setting the position of the player in the game's world, level data, and enemy positions.

Once this is done, the `Update` and `Draw` methods are called one after another repeatedly until the game exits. `Update` reads inputs from devices such as the mouse, keyboard, gamepads, and joysticks. It then updates the state of the game.

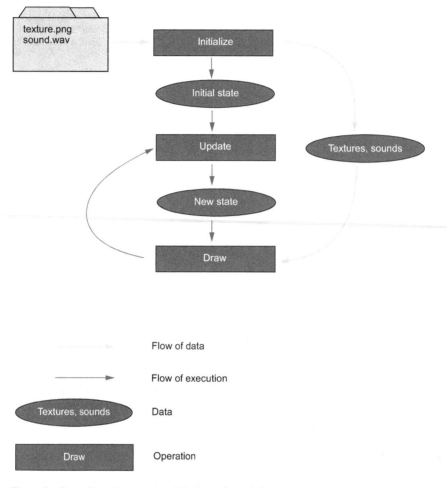

Figure 2   Execution of a game, and its flow of asset data

After it returns, the `Draw` method renders the state of the world to the screen and to the audio system.

Table 2   Methods in `DrawableGameComponent`

Method	Description
`Initialize : unit -> unit`	Called when the component is initialized. Responsible for loading game assets such as textures, music, and sounds.
`Update : GameTime -> unit`	Called every frame. Updates the state of the game.
`Draw : GameTime -> unit`	Called every frame. Draws the current state of the game.

Although this setting is suitable for simulations, it's impractical for user interfaces. Indeed, most applications that aren't game oriented are typically implemented using event-driven frameworks. Distributing a computation or a sequence of actions interacting with the user over the cycles imposed by the XNA framework can be done in a number of ways:

- Move the computation to a background thread.
- Break the computation into multiple functions taking callbacks, where each function is passed as the callback to the previous one.
- Turn the computation into a state machine implemented using discriminated unions.
- Implement the computation as an `async` computation expression.

In the background-thread approach, the computation is executed synchronously. This approach can lead to an unnecessarily large numbers of threads being created. It also doesn't explicitly support pausing, and communication across threads requires locking in order to avoid race conditions.

The second approach consists of breaking the computation into a number of non-interruptible subcomputations. Each part is responsible for enlisting the remainder of the computation as a so-called *callback* into a scheduling system that executes the callback at the appropriate time. This approach forces programmers to use continuation-passing style, which affects code readability negatively.

The third approach is viable for simple computations that can be expressed as small state machines. In video games, there are domains where state machines are traditionally popular, such as AI-controlled entities. They also have their use in other applications, typically whenever a specification uses a state machine. The last approach is similar to the callback-based solution, but it's made significantly easier to use by using dedicated syntax and special support by the compiler.

This chapter demonstrates state machines implemented using discriminated unions, an application of async computation expressions for I/O on potentially slow persistent storage, and the use of pure functions and data structures for the main game.

Structure of an XNA game in Visual Studio

Some of the build and packaging tools in XNA Game Studio don't support F# applications out of the box. For this reason, the typical solution is composed of a thin top-level C# project used as an entry point (see figure 3). This top-level C# project refers to F# libraries that contain most of the code. Each solution also contains a content project hosting the graphical and audio resources of the game, such as textures, shaders, sprite sheets, fonts, music loops, and sound effects.

Each targeted platform requires its own set of projects. For instance, if you're planning to release for the PC and Xbox 360, you'll need a PC top-level C# project, a PC F# library, and copies of these projects for the Xbox 360. The content projects can be shared between platforms.

Now that we've cleared up how to get started, let's go through each screen of the example game.

Figure 3   An F# XNA game in Visual Studio is organized as a top level in C#, a content project, and the main code in an F# library.

Content project

When developing games, the term *content* or *asset* is often used where *resource* is used in other domains. The amount of processing required to transform source assets into final data consumable by the game can be complex compared to serious applications. XNA makes it possible for developers to customize and extend asset processing. The part of the software that processes assets is called the *content pipeline*. The pipeline and how to customize it are described in the MSDN online library at http://mng.bz/XNc8.

Selecting the input device on the Press Start screen

The task of the first screen, which I'll call the Press Start screen, is to identify the player who is playing the game and which input device they will be using. On the PC, the only alternative is to use the mouse and keyboard, but on consoles such as the Xbox 360 the situation is a bit more complex. Consoles are typically connected to multiple gamepads, and you don't want to force the player to use a specific one. Instead, you let them press the Start button on the gamepad of their choice, and your game then uses that gamepad for the rest of the game as the primary input.

Implementing the process of detecting button or key presses, waiting for the button or the key to be released, and notifying the main game is a task that is nontrivial to implement on top of the game-update loop. The code in the following listing is used by two screens in the game: the Press Start screen and in the main game for pausing and resuming.

Listing 1   Input state machines and a constructor for press-then-release sequences

```
type InputStateMachine<'InputState, 'Result> =
    | Active of ('InputState -> InputStateMachine<'InputState, 'Result>)    ❶
    | Done of 'Result

let waitReleased pressed released func =                                     ❷
    let rec waitPressed() =                                                  ❸
        fun (inputState) ->
            if pressed(inputState) then
                let result = func inputState
                waitReleased result
            else
                waitPressed()
        |> Active

    and waitReleased result =                                                ❹
        fun (inputState) ->
            if released(inputState) then
                Done result
            else
                waitReleased result
        |> Active
    waitPressed()
```

❶ Discriminated union of the two states of an input state machine

❷ Creates input state machines

❸ Creates the state where you wait for a key press

❹ Creates the state where you wait for the key release

The discriminated union ❶ captures the two kinds of states in which a state machine can be. The data associated with the Active discriminant consists of a function that analyzes the state of the input devices and returns the next state. This kind of function is sometimes called a *continuation*. The Done discriminant is associated with the final result returned by the machine when it halts.

The waitReleased function ❷ simplifies the creation of state machines. It takes three other functions. The pressed function has the signature 'InputState -> bool and is responsible for detecting button or key presses. It has a counterpart called released, which has the same signature and is responsible for detecting that all buttons or keys have been released. The last function, named `func`, extracts the result from the state of the input device. It has the signature `'InputState -> 'Result`.

In `waitReleased`, there are two functions, which represent each state of the state machine. Initially, the state machine is active in a state where it waits for `pressed` to return true. To update an active state machine, you must call the continuation with the current state of the input. In the initial state, function `waitPressed` ❸ passes the state of the input to `pressed`. If it returns true, `waitPressed` returns the next state, `waitReleased` ❹. The caller can then move the state machine to the next state. You'll do that by changing the value of a mutable field in a class.

Note that `waitReleased`, unlike `waitPressed`, must be provided a parameter. It expects the final result, computed earlier in `waitPressed`, in order to return it after `released` eventually returns true.

Other uses of state machines

The example in this section focuses on state machines to interact with users, but their use extends to other areas as well. In games, state machines are also often used for AI-controlled characters interacting with their virtual environment in the game. Other applications include interaction with a remote server or client in a distributed environment, or any other situations when a process interacts with an external environment.

Figure 4 illustrates the kind of state machine this function creates. The need for distinct pressed and released functions arises from the fact that you want to detect whether a button is pressed on *some* gamepad and then wait until all buttons on *all* gamepads are released. Proceeding as soon as the button detected as pressed is released

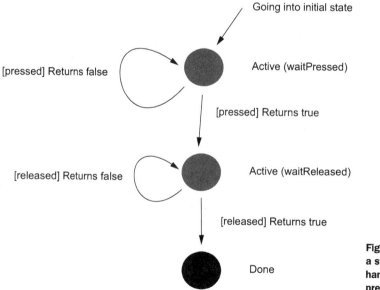

Figure 4   Skeleton of a state machine to handle keys being pressed and released

could trigger the next action too early if the user pressed multiple buttons at the same time by mistake.

Introducing generic data structures and higher-order functions to handle such a seemingly simple task as waiting for a button press may seem excessive, but it helps encapsulate internal state and avoid code duplication. In the game, `InputState-Machine` is used to handle inputs from gamepads on the one hand and from the keyboard on the other hand. It's also used to identify the player and the device used to control the game, and to detect when to pause and resume the game. This amounts to four situations, which I consider a point at which avoiding code duplication is worth the effort, regardless of the seemingly simple approach with specific code inlined directly in a class. Avoiding code duplication is a way to save time when fixing bugs, which helps reduce the time for your game and its updates to reach the market.

In this chapter, each screen is implemented as an XNA game component. The game component is registered to the XNA framework, which calls its `LoadContent`, `Update`, and `Draw` methods when appropriate. Game components are implemented as classes inheriting from `DrawableGameComponent`.

This game component has a number of mutable fields that are used to keep track of the state machine detecting button and key presses. Mutability is often frowned on by functional programmers, for good reasons. When integrating with object-oriented frameworks such as XNA, I find it appropriate to use the framework (including mutable classes) in the way it was meant to be used. Purity is used at a lower level, where its benefits help avoid bugs stemming from complex interaction between mutable types. Consider the input state machine used to detect when the Start button is pressed and who pressed it. The state machine is implemented using `InputStateMachine` and `waitReleased`, which are by themselves free of side effects (see the following listing).

Listing 2 Detecting button presses on multiple gamepads with an input state machine

```
type PressStart(game, content : Content.ContentManager) =
    inherit DrawableGameComponent(game)
    let players =
        [| 0 .. 3 |]
        |> Array.map(fun i -> enum<PlayerIndex> i)
    let getControllingPlayerFromGamePad =
        let buttons = [| Buttons.A; Buttons.Start |]
        let hasSomeButtonPressed (gamepad : GamePadState) =
            buttons
            |> Array.exists (fun btn -> gamepad.IsButtonDown(btn))
        let someButtonPressed (gamepads : GamePadState[]) =
            gamepads
            |> Array.exists hasSomeButtonPressed
        let getControllingPlayer (gamepads : GamePadState[]) =
            let idx =
                gamepads
                |> Array.findIndex hasSomeButtonPressed
            players.[idx]
```

Array of all possible players: players 0 to 3 on Xbox 360

Buttons you'll monitor. A is included for traditional reasons.

Helper function that checks if a given gamepad has button A or Start pressed

Checks if button A or Start is pressed on some gamepad

Retrieves the first index of the gamepad that has A or Start pressed

```
let allButtonsReleased (gamepads : GamePadState[]) =        Checks if
    gamepads                                                 buttons A
    |> Array.forall (fun gamepad ->                          and Start are
        buttons                                              released on all
        |> Array.forall (fun btn -> gamepad.IsButtonUp(btn))  gamepads
    )
waitReleased                     ◁┐  Calls a function that   Creates a ref cell to the
    someButtonPressed                creates an input        input machine. The machine
    allButtonsReleased               state machine           is immutable; progress is
    getControllingPlayer                                     achieved by pointing the cell
|> ref                                               ◁┘      to a new machine.
```

> **Type inference**
>
> Can you identify the type of `getControllingPlayerFromGamePad`? Informally speaking, it's an input state machine, but the concrete type can be hard for a tired programmer to determine and write down. Fortunately, the F# compiler doesn't require you to write the complete type. Even better, IntelliSense in Visual Studio will tell you if you hover the mouse over the identifier, letting you check that the type is what you expected.

Figure 5 illustrates the concrete input state machine used on the Press Start screen. The game component adopts the object-oriented idioms of the XNA framework, namely mutable class fields and events. The next listing shows how you update the input state machine and then notify listeners using an event.

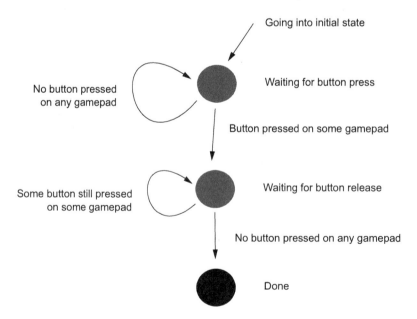

Figure 5   Concrete state machine used to detect the primary gamepad

Listing 3 Updating the input state machine and sending out a result

Notifies the environment which player has pressed the Start button →

```
let startPressed = new Event<PlayerIndex>()
member this.StartPressed = startPressed.Publish
override this.Update(gt) =
    let result =
        match !getControllingPlayerFromGamePad with
        | Active update ->
            let nextState =
                players
                |> Array.map (fun pi -> GamePad.GetState(pi))
                |> update
            getControllingPlayerFromGamePad := nextState
            None
        | Done result ->
            Some result
    match result with
    | None ->
        ()
    | Some result ->
        startPressed.Trigger(result)
```

Exposes an event as a property

Updates the input state machine

❶ **The state machine is active.**

Computes the next state ❷

❸ **Updates the mutable reference to new state**

❹ **The input state machine has completed.**

❺ **Notifies environment that Start was pressed**

The Update method is responsible for updating getControllingPlayerFromGamepad, a mutable reference pointing at the current input state. It checks the current state, and in case ❶, where the machine is still active, it computes the next state ❷. The state of the game component is finally mutated in ❸. In case ❹, the machine has already completed, meaning the user has pressed Start, and ❺ raises the event notifying listeners which gamepad is to be used to control the game.

Another mutable field is used to store the graphical resources used to render the screen. An immutable record, Resources, holds the only two resources you'll use: a font to render "Press Start" and a sprite batch, an XNA object used to render 2D graphics.

Note that one mutable field optionally holding a record whose members are immutable and non-null is preferable to two mutable fields holding potentially null values. The second approach can hypothetically represent the situation where only one of the resources has been acquired, which in reality can't happen. The following listing shows how game assets are loaded and released.

Listing 4 Loading game assets and releasing their resources

```
type Resources =
    { Font : SpriteFont
      Batch : SpriteBatch }
type PressStart(game, content : Content.ContentManager) =
    inherit DrawableGameComponent(game)
    let mutable resources = None
    override this.LoadContent() =
        let font = content.Load("font")
        let batch = new SpriteBatch(this.GraphicsDevice)
        resources <- Some { Font = font; Batch = batch }
```

Resources needed to render the screen

None until LoadContent is executed

Initializes resources; executed once by the XNA framework

```
override this.Dispose(disposeManaged) =
    base.Dispose(disposeManaged)
    if disposeManaged then
        match resources with
        | Some { Batch = batch } -> batch.Dispose()
        | None -> ()
```
Releases resources when the game component is unregistered

The Draw method checks if resources have been acquired, and if so renders a blinking Press Start at the center of the screen:

```
override this.Draw(gt) =
    match resources with
    | Some rsc ->
        let isVisible = gt.TotalGameTime.Milliseconds % 1000 < 700
        if isVisible then
            let text = "Press start"
            let pos =
                let size = rsc.Font.MeasureString(text)
                let safe = this.GraphicsDevice.Viewport.TitleSafeArea
                let posx = safe.Left + (safe.Width - int size.X) / 2
                let posy = safe.Top + (safe.Height - int size.Y) / 2
                Vector2(float32 posx, float32 posy)
            try
                rsc.Batch.Begin()
                rsc.Batch.DrawString(rsc.Font, text, pos, Color.White)
            finally
                rsc.Batch.End()
    | None ->
        ()
```

Note that the let bindings size, safe, posx, and posy used to compute the central position of the blinking label are nested in the definition of the position itself. Although it's not obviously beneficial in such a small method, in longer code blocks, limiting the scope of such variables helps the reader skim over implementation details.

You've seen how to use discriminated unions and generic higher-order functions to process input. The code can be customized for different tasks—for instance, to detect which player will control the game, and to detect when to pause the game. It can also be customized to detect inputs from the gamepads or from the keyboard:

Waits until the user presses Enter or the spacebar (PC only)

```
let getControllingPlayerFromKeyboard =
    let keys = [| Keys.Enter; Keys.Space |]
    let isKeyPressed (state : KeyboardState) =
        keys
        |> Array.exists(fun k -> state.IsKeyDown(k))
    let getControllingPlayer _ = PlayerIndex.One
    let areKeysReleased (state : KeyboardState) =
        keys
        |> Array.forall(fun k -> state.IsKeyUp(k))
    waitReleased isKeyPressed areKeysReleased getControllingPlayer
    |> ref
```
Keys to monitor. Checks if one of the monitored keys is pressed. The player controlling the keyboard is always the first one. Checks if all monitored keys aren't pressed

The input-detection mechanism presented here can be used for other tasks beyond detecting when a specific button is pressed.

> ### Exercise 1: Detecting sequences and combinations of button presses
>
> A popular football game on Xbox uses combinations of button presses to perform advanced actions. For instance, performing a shot is done by pressing button B, but doing a precise shot requires the user to press button B and the right bumper at the same time.
>
> Timing and order are also relevant. A ground cross requires quickly tapping button X three times. An early ground cross requires quickly tapping button X three times while holding the left bumper. As a last example, pressing button B and then pressing button A and moving the left joystick at the same time performs a fake shot.
>
> The exercise consists of implementing detection of a complex sequence. You should start by designing a state machine that recognizes these sequences and combinations of inputs. There should be two final states indicating whether 1) the sequence was performed correctly and the character in the game should perform the action, or 2) the sequence wasn't completed. A sequence isn't completed if the wrong button is pressed or too much time passes between presses.
>
> Once you've drawn the state machine, implement it using the `InputStateMachine` from listing 1.

You've also seen how to use pure functional programing to implement an application's logic with immutable records and higher-order functions free of side effects, and how to use mutable state in classes in an object-oriented framework to keep track of state at the application's top level.

In a complete game, the Press Start screen is typically followed by the main menu and its submenus. Although they're more complex than the Press Start screen, their implementation follows the same pattern: to monitor button presses and raise events. The example here omits menus. Let's now look at updating the main part of the game, consisting of the game logic, and rendering graphical and audio effects.

Modeling and updating the game world

The game is played on a map where cities must be protected from attacks by nuclear missiles launched from submarines. The player controls a pointer with the mouse or the gamepad that can be used to trigger explosions to detonate incoming missiles before they reach cities.

Many ways are available to build data structures and functions that implement the game just described. I like to separate updating the state of the game from its rendering. This approach makes it possible to test the update logic without setting up the user interface.

I keep the description of the level, which is static, separate from the current state of the game, which changes with each frame. Most numeric types use units of measure, which helps avoid bugs in the physics code and in rendering. Typical physics bugs include forgetting to include the frame time, which leads to games that are tied to the rate of refresh. When running the game on faster hardware, the game also plays faster, which increases the level of difficulty. Similarly, rendering code can easily be involuntarily tied to a specific screen resolution, which causes bugs when attempting to run the game on display sizes that weren't available at the time of writing.

Declaring units of measure is simple:

```
[<Measure>]
type s           ⟵┘  Seconds
[<Measure>]
type h                   Humans: number of
                    ⟵│  survivors in cities
[<Measure>]
type m           ⟵─  Meters
[<Measure>]
type pix         ⟵─  Pixels
```

Numeric types such as `int` and `float32` can be used with units of measure. Vector types, though, aren't aware of units of measures, and you must write wrappers. The following code shows a wrapper around XNA's two-dimensional vector:

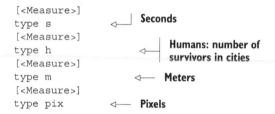

```
type TypedVector2<[<Measure>] 'M> =    ⟵│  Type parameter 'M must      │  Inner vector, which
    struct                                │  be a unit of measure.       │  isn't aware of units
        val v : Vector2                                              ⟵   │  of measure
        new(x : float32<'M>, y : float32<'M>) =
            { v = Vector2(float32 x, float32 y) }       │  Constructor from a
        new(V) = { v = V }                          ⟵   │  unit-less vector
        member this.X : float32<'M> =
            LanguagePrimitives.Float32WithMeasure this.v.X      │  Builds a float32 with
        member this.Y : float32<'M> =                           │  a measure from a
            LanguagePrimitives.Float32WithMeasure this.v.Y      │  unit-less float32
    end
```

Constructor taking two 32-bit floats of unit 'M

Note the use of `Float32WithMeasure<'M>`. This generic function converts a unit-less number to a number with unit of measure `'M`. In nongeneric code, adding units of measure can also be done by multiplying by a constant with the right type:

Retrieves the area of the screen, which is guaranteed to be visible on all TV sets and monitors. It lacks units of measure.

```
let titleSafeArea = this.GraphicsDevice.Viewport.TitleSafeArea    ⟵┐
let width = 1.0f<pix> * titleSafeArea.Width                    ⟵┐
```

Multiplies the unit-less number by constant 1.0f with unit pix to create a number representing the width in pixels

Useful functions working on typed vectors introduced in the previous code are provided in a module:

```
[<RequireQualifiedAccessAttribute>]   ⟵┤  Functions in this module must be accessed using the
module TypedVector =                     │  module name, such as TypedVector.add2. This is similar
                                         │  to standard modules such as List, Array, and Map.
```

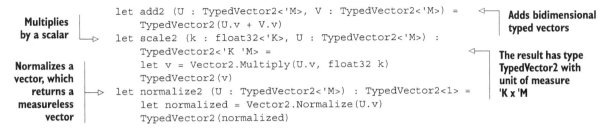

Multiplies by a scalar

Normalizes a vector, which returns a measureless vector

```
let add2 (U : TypedVector2<'M>, V : TypedVector2<'M>) =
    TypedVector2(U.v + V.v)
let scale2 (k : float32<'K>, U : TypedVector2<'M>) :
    TypedVector2<'K 'M> =
    let v = Vector2.Multiply(U.v, float32 k)
    TypedVector2(v)
let normalize2 (U : TypedVector2<'M>) : TypedVector2<1> =
    let normalized = Vector2.Normalize(U.v)
    TypedVector2(normalized)
```

Adds bidimensional typed vectors

The result has type TypedVector2 with unit of measure 'K x 'M

TypedVector2 is extended to provide convenient operators and constants:

```
type TypedVector2<[<Measure>] 'M>
with
    static member public (*) (k, U) = TypedVector.scale2 (k, U)
    static member public (+) (U, V) = TypedVector.add2 (U, V)
    static member public Zero = TypedVector2<'M>()
```

At this point, you can define types to describe the world using units of measure, as shown in the following listing.

Listing 5 Data representing a level in the game

```
type City =
    { Name : string
      Population : int<h>
      Position : TypedVector2<m>
    }
type Submarine =
    { Position : TypedVector2<m>
      Period : float32<s>
    }
    static member SurfaceTime = 0.5f<s>
type World =
    { Cities : City[]
      Submarines : Submarine[]
      TopLeft : TypedVector2<m>
      BottomRight : TypedVector2<m>
    }
```

Initial population of the city, before it's hit by a missile

Position of the city on the map

Position of the submarine on the map

Initial amount of time between missile launches

Initial delay between becoming visible and launching (in seconds)

Coordinates of a rectangle of the playable world map

In this modeling, submarines don't move. Making them movable would make the game a bit more interesting, because the player wouldn't know the exact positions where submarines might surface.

Exercise 2

Replace Submarine.Position with a data structure representing a closed path defining the travel of the submarine.

A *path* is a sequence of waypoints. A *waypoint* is a geographic location and a time. Once a submarine reaches the last waypoint, it travels back to the initial waypoint.

The level of difficulty is controlled by varying the amount of time between missile launches. The longer the cities survive, the shorter the time between missile launches, resulting in a larger number of missiles present on screen (see the next listing).

Listing 6 Data representing the current state of a game

```
type Missile =
    { Position : TypedVector2<m>
      Velocity : TypedVector2<m/s>
      Target : TypedVector2<m>
    }
    static member Speed = 3000.0f * 340.0f<m/s>
type Explosion =
    { Position : TypedVector2<m>
      Time : float32<s>
    }
    static member MaxTime = 0.5f<s>
    static member Radius = 100000.0f<m>
    static member ShieldRadius = 100000.0f<m>
type WorldState =
    { Survivors : float32<h>[]
      Submarines : float32<s>[]
      Missiles : Missile list
      Explosions : Explosion list
      Shields : Explosion list
      Difficulty : float32
      DifficultyTimeLeft : float32<s>
      Score : float32
      DefenseCoolDown : float32<s>
      ReticlePosition : TypedVector2<pix>
    }
    static member DefenseMaxCoolDown = 1.0f<s>
    static member DifficultyIncreasePeriod = 30.0f<s>
```

Annotations:
- Speed of a missile, in meters per second. Set to 3,000 times the speed of sound.
- Time passed since the explosion started
- Time the explosion lasts, in seconds
- Radius of the explosion, in meters
- Radius of the anti-missile shield
- Population left in each city
- Time since the last missile launch by each submarine
- Amount of time before the player can shoot at a missile again
- 1.0 means normal; increases with time
- Time left before the next difficulty increase
- ❶ Position of the reticle controlled by the player, onscreen
- Time between difficulty increases, in seconds
- Minimum amount of time between defensive shots, in seconds

The declaration of `ReticlePosition` ❶ shows the value of units of measure. There are two equally valid options for the unit of measure: meters and pixels. The unit of measure helps you avoid mixing the two options, which would otherwise be indistinguishable from the compiler's point of view.

In the case of traveling submarines, the state of the world should account for the location of each submarine.

Exercise 3

Replace the field `WorldState.Submarines` with an array of submarine states. The state of a submarine must account for the amount of time since the submarine last launched a missile and for its current position.

The state of the game is updated by a function that takes a state as input and returns the new state. This function also takes in actions by the players and returns audio events to be played by the rendering system.

Representing the world state in an immutable data structure has a number of advantages. When debugging, it's easy to compare the state before and after the update, because both states remain available in memory. Another positive point is that it's possible to execute the update and the render functions in parallel with minimal locking at the state of each frame.

As shown here, the update thread creates a new state at the same time the render thread draws the previous state:

Update thread	Render thread
Initialize state 0	
Create state 1 from state 0	Render state 0
Create state 2 from state 1	Render state 1
...	...

Figure 6 shows the flow of data through the update and render functions. Listing 7 shows the signature of the update function and the definition of the order and event types.

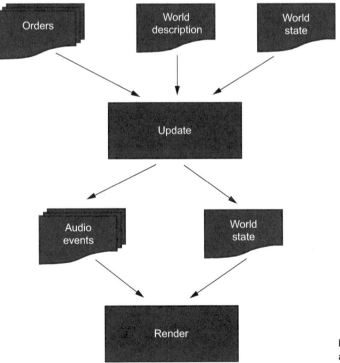

Figure 6 **The update and render functions**

Efficiency of immutable data structures in games

I've developed an asteroid-shooting game in 3D that requires handling collisions and rendering thousands of asteroids. Both tasks take more than 8 ms each, meaning the game can't run at 60 frames per second if the update and render functions are run sequentially. Using immutable data structures for the game state made it easy to parallelize the two operations by avoiding data races. The negative aspect is that using immutable data requires producing large amounts of short-lived new copies, which triggers garbage collection frequently. Because rendering and updating each took at most 13 ms, it left a little over 3 ms for the sole purpose of garbage collection, which in this case was sufficient.

Listing 7   The update function

Types of orders from players →

```
type Order =
    | DeployShield of TypedVector2<m>
    | MoveReticle of TypedVector2<pix>
type Event =
    | PlayExplosion
    | PlayShield
let update
    (random : System.Random)
    (world : World)
    (dt : float32<s>)
    (orders : Order list)
    (state : WorldState) : WorldState * Event list =
```

Player requests to trigger a defensive explosion at the specified world coordinates

Player has moved the aiming reticle of the defensive shield to specified screen coordinates

Types of audio events triggered by update

The update function (which takes a world state and a list of orders and returns a new world state and a list of audio events) is pretty long, yet simple. Most of it is implemented using standard functions from the List module (see listing 8). For instance, explosions are updated using List.map, and old explosions are removed using List.filter. List.fold updates the position of the aiming reticle for the defensive shield and produces the audio event of a defensive explosion.

Listing 8   Updating world state using the List module

```
let decr v = v - dt
let incr v = v + dt
let state, playShieldEvent =
    orders
    |> List.fold (fun (state, ev) order ->
        match order with
        | DeployShield pos ->
            if state.DefenseCoolDown > 0.0f<s> then
                state, ev
            else
                { state with
                    Shields =
                        { Position = pos
                          Time = 0.0f<s> } :: state.Shields
```

Decrease and increase time values by dt

Hold new state and audio events after executing DeployShield orders

Checks if the minimum delay since the last shield deployment hasn't yet passed →

Deploys the shield and adds a corresponding audio event

```
                              DefenseCoolDown = WorldState.DefenseMaxCoolDown
                          },
                          PlayShield :: ev
              | MoveReticle pos ->
                { state with ReticlePosition = pos }, ev
            ) (state, [])
    let explosions =
        state.Explosions
        |> List.map (fun ex -> { ex with Time = incr ex.Time })
    let explosions =
        explosions
        |> List.filter (fun ex -> ex.Time < Explosion.MaxTime)
```

Updates the position of the aiming reticle

Starts with the old state and empties the list of audio events

Lets explosions age

Filters out explosions, which burn off

The next listing shows the final steps of the update function.

Listing 9   Building the new world state and the list of audio events

```
let update
    (random : System.Random)
    (world : World)
    (dt : float32<s>)
    (orders : Order list)
    (state : WorldState) : WorldState * Event list =
...
    let playExplosionEvent =
        if List.isEmpty newExplosions then
            []
        else
            [PlayExplosion]
    let events = playShieldEvent @ playExplosionEvent
    let state =
        { Survivors = survivors
          Submarines = subs
          Missiles = missiles
          Explosions = List.append explosions newExplosions
          Shields = shields
          Difficulty = difficulty
          DifficultyTimeLeft = diffTimeLeft
          Score = state.Score + points
          DefenseCoolDown = defCoolDown
          ReticlePosition = state.ReticlePosition
        }
    state, events
```

① newExplosions is the list of newly triggered explosions (its definition is omitted from the listing).

② Creates an audio event for the explosions

③ Concatenates the lists of audio events for the shields and the missile explosions

④ Updated state of the game world

⑤ The result of the function is the game state and the audio events.

Identifier newExplosions **①** is bound to a list of explosions caused by missiles hitting cities and missiles destroyed by shields. Its definition is in the omitted part of listing 9. At the end of the function, you generate a single explosion audio event **②** if at least one new explosion was triggered. The result of the function is a pair **⑤** composed of the new world state **④** and all audio events **③** generated during this update round.

You've seen how to model the game's data using records and lists, and how to update the state using standard higher-order functions manipulating lists. This approach is an alternative to the class-oriented approach common in the software industry.

Instead of relying entirely on the single concept of the class for the purposes of data modeling and modularity, functional programming uses simple data types for data modeling and the concept of modules for modularity. All classes of applications, regardless of domain, can benefit from this simpler approach. You've also seen how units of measure can be used to increase code readability and avoid errors in arithmetic expressions. You'll now see how to render the graphics and audio of the game in each frame.

Rendering the game and the scoreboard

Unlike game-state update logic, rendering doesn't produce any data. All the work is performed through side effects. Seen from a high level, rendering is a task that takes a state and issues drawing orders. We'll look at two different kinds of states commonly encountered in games. The active part of the game often looks like a simulation. The action can be decomposed in tiny slices of time, and the player can influence the action continuously. Each state can be computed from the previous state and the user's input. We'll also look into rendering the scoreboard using animations. Unlike the previous phase, this isn't an interactive session. Each state depends on how much time has passed since the animation started.

Rendering the game

In this section, you'll see how to render submarines and their animations. What makes this case interesting is that it uses a number of animations showing submarines going to the surface of the water, staying at the surface for a while and firing a missile, and then diving back under the water. Figure 7 shows a surfaced submarine in the upper-left corner firing a missile, apparently aimed at London or Paris.

The way I have modeled the game state, information about the state of the animation isn't directly available. But it can be deduced from the initial firing period of the submarine, `Submarine.Period`, the current difficulty level, `WorldState.Difficulty`, and the time since the last launch, `WorldState.Submarines`.

> ### Adapting data
>
> The kind of problem where the data available isn't readily usable by a consumer is a common occurrence in software development. The Adapter design pattern is one of the techniques employed in this situation when dealing with objects, and active patterns can be seen as filling a similar role when dealing with immutable data encountered in functional programing.

From the point of view of the rendering code, it would be convenient if the submarine's state was modeled using a discriminated union, where each alternative represents the type of animation to play. To bridge the two different views, you use an active pattern.

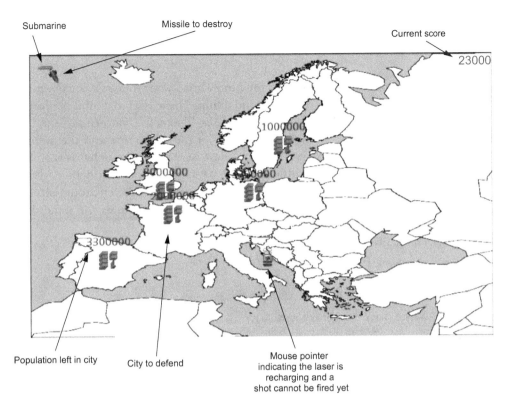

Figure 7 Screen capture from the game

```
let render
    (soundInstances : SoundEffectInstances)
    (gd : GraphicsDevice)
    (rsc : Resources)
    (world : World)
    (oldState : WorldState, state : WorldState) events =
    let (|Diving|UnderWater|Surfacing|OnSurface|)
        (timeBetweenLaunches : float32<s>, timeSinceLaunch :
    float32<s>) =
        let timeBetweenLaunches = timeBetweenLaunches / state.Difficulty
        let t = timeSinceLaunch / timeBetweenLaunches
        let divingTime = 0.2f
        let underWaterTime = 0.5f
        let surfacingTime = 0.2f
        let surfaceTime = 0.1f
        if t < divingTime then
            Diving (t / divingTime)
        elif t < divingTime + underWaterTime then
            UnderWater
        elif t < divingTime + underWaterTime + surfacingTime then
            Surfacing ((t - divingTime - underWaterTime) / surfacingTime)
```

Annotations on figure:
- Submarine
- Missile to destroy
- Current score
- Population left in city
- City to defend
- Mouse pointer indicating the laser is recharging and a shot cannot be fired yet

Annotations on listing:
- ① Animation types
- ② Submarine timing data
- ③ Accounts for difficulty level
- 0%–20%: Submarine is diving
- 20%–70%: Submarine is underwater
- 70%–90%: Submarine is surfacing
- 90%–100%: Submarine is surfaced and firing

```
        else
            OnSurface
                ((t - divingTime - underWaterTime - surfacingTime) /
                surfaceTime)
```

The active pattern ❶ is a special function whose name follows a convention specifying each case in the desired discriminated union. There is a fixed limit of seven cases, and it's therefore suitable only for simple cases. The active pattern takes a pair of numbers ❷ denoting the initial firing period of the submarine and the amount of time that has passed since the last launch. The time between launches is corrected to take into account the current difficulty level ❸. Like any other function, active patterns can be defined as nested closures that capture parts of the environment. In this case, the current state is captured, making it unnecessary to pass the same data in each invocation in the render function.

The active pattern can now be used to provide convenient access to the game's logic state for rendering animations.

Listing 11 Using the active pattern to animate submarines

```
for submarine, timeSinceLaunch in
        Array.zip world.Submarines state.Submarines do          ◁──┐  Launch timing data
    match (submarine.Period, timeSinceLaunch) with  ◁──            ❶  for each submarine
    | OnSurface t ->
        getFrameRectangle rsc.Submarine t  ◁──                       Matches launch
        |> drawRectangleCentered                                     timing data using
            rsc.SpriteBatch                                       ❸  the active pattern
            rsc.Submarine
            (transform submarine.Position)          ❹  Draws the submarine
                                                        on the surface
    | Diving t ->
        getFrameRectangle rsc.Surfacing (1.0f - t)  ◁──┐  The diving
        |> drawRectangleCentered                           animation is the
            rsc.SpriteBatch                                surfacing animation
            rsc.Surfacing                             ❺  in reverse.
            (transform submarine.Position)
    | Surfacing t ->
        getFrameRectangle rsc.Surfacing t  ◁──          Draws the frame from
        |> drawRectangleCentered                     ❻  the diving animation
            rsc.SpriteBatch
            rsc.Surfacing                             ❼  Does nothing; underwater
            (transform submarine.Position)               submarines aren't drawn.
    | UnderWater -> ()          ◁──
```

Single array for all submarines built from two arrays ❷

A single array ❷ of pairs denoting the launch timing data for each submarine is built from two arrays. The first originates from the world's definition and indicates how much time separates two missile launches at difficulty level 1.0. The second comes from the current state of the game and represents the amount of time spent since the last launch by each submarine. You match ❸ each pair ❶ with animation states and draw the corresponding animation frame. In the case of the submarine being on the surface ❹, you render the frame from the sprite sheet of the submarine on the surface. For a diving submarine ❺, you render the frame from the sprite sheet for the diving submarine. Note that the time frame, which varies between 0 and 1, is subtracted from 1. The effect is that the diving animation is played backward. A surfacing submarine is drawn using the surfacing animation played forward ❻. A submarine under water ❼ isn't drawn.

You've seen how active patterns can provide convenient views of data, and you've seen them applied to animating sprites. The next section also explores the topic of animation, specifically vector-based effects in the scoreboard.

Rendering the scoreboard

To make the scoreboard exciting to watch after playing, the final score isn't shown instantaneously at its correct rank as the board is displayed. Instead, a new entry is added at the bottom, showing the name of the player and a number ticking toward the final score value. The entry rises in the board as the number ticks up, eventually settling at the correct rank, as shown in figure 8.

At each frame, the render function is called to render the current step in the animation sequence. To correctly place onscreen each entry in the scoreboard, the render function must know the current position of the rising entry on the scoreboard. Depending on the value of the new score, the current frame of the animation is one of three cases:

1 The new score was too low to be featured among the 10 best scores. In that case, it's shown in red below the scoreboard as the last entry.

2 The animation has completed, in which case the new score is rendered in green at its rank in the scoreboard.

Figure 8 Scoreboard animation

3 The animation is going on, and the displayed value is counting toward the score value. The entry is located at the rank of the counter.

The update function is responsible for producing the new current position from the previous position and the amount of time that has passed since the last call.

A record represents a scoreboard and the new score that the player just achieved. The rendering state is modeled as a discriminated union, one discriminant for each case enumerated:

```
type ScoreBoard =
    { Scores : (string * int) []
      NewScore : string * int }
```

The names and scores, ordered by decreasing score

The new score to insert in the table if it's among the 10 highest

The new score is too low and is rendered at the bottom.

```
type RenderingState =
  | DoneAtBottom
  | DoneInserted of int
  | Busy of int * float32
```

The new score has reached its position on the board.

The new score is rising to its position on the board.

The initialize function produces the initial state, depending on the existing scores and the new score to add:

```
let initialize board =
    let (_, newScore) = board.NewScore
    match board.Scores,
          Array.tryFindIndex
              (fun (_, s) -> s <= newScore)
              board.Scores with
    | [||], _ ->
        DoneInserted 0
    | _, None ->
        DoneAtBottom
    | _, Some idx ->
        let startingRank = board.Scores.Length
        let startingScore = 0.0f
        Busy(startingRank, startingScore)
```

The score array is empty. ❷

❶ **Matches on the content of the score array and position to insert a new score**

❸ **The new score is lower than any score on the board.**

❹ **Starts the animation by displaying the score at bottom of the board with value 0**

The match expression ❶ matches two expressions. The first is the array of scores; the second is the rank at which the new score should be inserted in the table, knowing that it's sorted in descending order. The pattern [||] in ❷ matches an empty array, and the underscore matches anything. It catches the special case where the table is empty, which occurs when the game is run for the first time. In that case, the animation should jump directly to its final state, where the score is shown at the first position.

The second part of the match expression, consisting of a call to Array.tryFind-Index, tries to find the first score that's lower than the new score. Knowing that scores are sorted in descending order, if such an entry is found, you've found the rank at which the new score should be inserted. Case ❹ initiates the animation in the Busy state, which has two parameters consisting of the current rank of the score and the value currently shown, ticking up toward the value of the new score. If no such entry is found, it means the new score is worse than any score currently present in the table, and ❸ initiates the animation in a state where the score should be shown with its final value below the table.

The update function computes the new state, given the old one. When the score has reached its rank in the table and its value, the animation stops and remains in the same state. Otherwise, the ticking value of the score is increased by an amount that depends on the time passed since the last update, and the new rank is computed:

```
let update board scoreIncrement dt state =
    match state with
    | DoneInserted _
    | DoneAtBottom -> state
    | Busy(idx, score) ->
        let (_, target) = board.NewScore
```

DoneInserted and DoneAtBottom are final states.

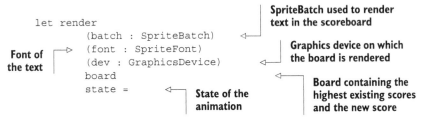

The render function renders the current frame of the animation:

```
let render
        (batch : SpriteBatch)
        (font : SpriteFont)
        (dev : GraphicsDevice)
        board
        state =
```

SpriteBatch used to render text in the scoreboard

Font of the text →

Graphics device on which the board is rendered

State of the animation ←

Board containing the highest existing scores and the new score

Before doing any rendering, you declare a few helper functions to render strings aligned to the left:

Vertical position of the first line (highest score)

Maximum number of lines in the scoreboard: the 10 best scores and the new one

The part of the screen visible to the user (TV sets typically have sides covered by plastic)

Vertical space between each line in board

```
let maxNumLines = 11
let safe = dev.Viewport.TitleSafeArea
let spacing = safe.Height / maxNumLines
let y0 = safe.Top
let x = safe.Left + 50
```

Horizontal position of each line

Builds a string from a rank, a player name, and a score value

```
let format idx name score = sprintf "%2d.%8s...%06d" idx name score

let drawString (s : string, y : int, color : Color) =
    batch.DrawString(font, s, Vector2(float32 x, float32 y), color)
let renderSlice (y, idx, first, last) =
    let mutable y = y
    let mutable idx = idx
    for name, score in board.Scores.[first .. last] do
        let s = format idx name score
        drawString(s, y, Color.White)
        y <- y + spacing
        idx <- idx + 1
    (y, idx)
```

Renders a string at a given vertical position and color

Renders a portion of the scoreboard and returns the vertical position of the next line and its rank

Rendering the board is a matter of rendering the part above the current position of the new score (if any), followed by the score, followed by the rest (if any). If the new score was too low to make it to the 10 highest scores, it's rendered in red; otherwise it's rendered in green:

```
try
    batch.Begin()
```

❶ Each rendering operation using a SpriteBatch must be preceded by a call to SpriteBatch.Begin.

Renders the new score at the bottom in red →

```
match state with
| DoneAtBottom ->
    let y, idx = renderSlice(y0, 1, 0, board.Scores.Length - 1)
    let name, score = board.NewScore
    let s = format idx name score
    drawString(s, y, Color.Red)
| DoneInserted pos ->
    let y, idx = renderSlice(y0, 1, 0, pos - 1)
    let name, score = board.NewScore
    let s = format idx name score
    drawString(s, y, Color.Green)
    renderSlice(y + spacing, idx + 1, pos, board.Scores.Length - 1)
    |> ignore
| Busy(pos, score) ->
    let y, idx = renderSlice(y0, 1, 0, pos - 1)
    let name, _ = board.NewScore
    let score = int score
    let s = format idx name score
    drawString(s, y, Color.Green)
    renderSlice(y + spacing, idx + 1, pos, board.Scores.Length - 1)
    |> ignore
finally
    batch.End()
```

← **Renders the new score inserted at its final position**

← **Renders the new score at a position matching the animated score value**

② **Each call to SpriteBatch.Begin must be followed by SpriteBatch.End.**

The `try...finally` block ensures that the call to `SpriteBatch.Begin` **①** is followed by a call to `SpriteBatch.End` **②** even if exceptions are thrown. In the case where the score is too low to enter the high-scores table, the animation is pretty disappointing, because it results in displaying the score table without any effects.

> ### Exercise 4
> When the player fails to produce a score high enough to be featured in the table, do the following: show a consolation message, wait for a button press, let the message fade away, and finally show the table with the low score below it.

If you intend to distribute your XNA game on platforms other than the PC, you should write the top level of the application in C# using the template from XNA Game Studio, and have most of your code in one or multiple F# libraries. F# types and modules are accessible as .NET constructs from other languages, but they aren't convenient to use. I recommend that you avoid using F#-specific types and functions in interfaces of F# libraries meant to be callable from other languages. The F# code should therefore be wrapped in constructs that are easily accessible from such languages, such as classes and methods. `DrawableGameComponent` is well suited for this purpose, as shown next.

Listing 12   Wrapping the scoreboard functions and data in a game component

```
type Resources =
    { Font : SpriteFont
      Batch : SpriteBatch
    }
```

← **Font and sprite batch used to render the scoreboard**

```
type ScoreComponent(game, content : Content.ContentManager, board) =
    inherit DrawableGameComponent(game)
    let mutable resources = None
    let mutable state = initialize board
    let scoreIncrement =
        let animationLength = 5.0f
        float32 (snd board.NewScore) / animationLength

    override this.LoadContent() =                        Called at start
        let font = content.Load("font")                 during initialization
        resources <-
            Some {
                Font = font                                 Updates the
                Batch = new SpriteBatch(this.GraphicsDevice) state machine
            }                                               only if the
    override this.Update(gt) =                              component is
        if this.Enabled then                               enabled
            let dt = float32 gt.ElapsedGameTime.TotalSeconds
            state <- update board scoreIncrement dt state
        base.Update(gt)
                                                         Draws the current frame
    override this.Draw(gt) =                             of animation, if the
        match resources with                            resources were created
        | Some rsc ->
            render rsc.Batch rsc.Font this.GraphicsDevice board state
        | None ->
            ()
        base.Draw(gt)
    override this.Dispose(disposeManaged) =
        base.Dispose(disposeManaged)
        match resources with
        | Some { Batch = batch } ->
            batch.Dispose()
        | None ->
            ()
```

You've seen how state machines implemented with discriminated unions can be used to implement animations. Asynchronous methods in XNA present the same kind of challenge as animations: computations that spread over multiple frames are difficult to fit into the update-draw cycle. Unlike animations, interactions with users and storage devices require complex execution flows that are too complex for the technique presented in this section. The next section shows how async computations help deal with these issues.

Performing I/O safely using async

The XNA framework offers an API to perform I/O on a range of platforms, including the Xbox 360, whose access to persistent storage differs a bit from the way the PC platform does it. In particular, it's worth mentioning that all access to storage requires the interaction of the user when multiple devices are available. Typical Xbox 360 setups include an internal hard disk and external storage in the form of a memory card or a USB stick. Unlike typical PC software, which can assume that reading and

Why not do it with classes in the first place?

To illustrate the qualities of this technique, I'll show you an alternative approach that uses a record instead of a discriminated union to represent the state of animation. Records are similar to classes, which are the primary construction block in a number of popular object-oriented languages that lack discriminated unions and pattern matching. This approach is representative of the typical implementation of small state machines in these languages:

Using discriminated unions	Using records
| ```
type RenderingState =
  | DoneAtBottom
  | DoneInserted of int
  | Busy of int * float32

let update
      board
      scoreIncrement
      dt
      state =
  match state with
  | DoneInserted _
  | DoneAtBottom ->
      state
  | Busy(idx, score) ->
      ...
``` | ```
type GameBoardState =
  { IsAtBottom : bool       ❶ Current state of
    IsCompleted : bool          the machine;
    IsBusy : bool               exactly one is true
    Pos : int
    Score : float32 }      ❷ Data associated
                              with some states
let update
      scoreIncrement
      dt
      state =

  match state with
  | { IsCompleted = true }
  | { IsAtBottom = true } ->
      state                ❸ Catch-all to
  | { IsBusy = true } ->      silence the
      ...                     warning
  | _ ->                      about
      failwith                incomplete
        "Unexpected state"  ◀ matches
``` |

At first, it may seem this code is just as compact and readable as the first approach, and we have pattern-matching to thank for that. ❸ is an indication that something might be wrong. The record is capable of representing more states than intended, which is in my experience a breeding ground for bugs. In particular, combinations of the Booleans in ❶ where all are false, or more than one is true, are combinations that the record can represent but that I don't want to handle. Another issue is that the relationship between state data ❷ and the state is unclear. Is score meaningful when isAtBottom is true?

writing small amounts of data is immediate, console games must account for the fact that the user may be shown a dialog box asking which device should be used. For this reason, the XNA API for accessing persistent storage in StorageDevice is exclusively asynchronous.

Games typically don't use this API to load levels, textures, or sounds. They use it for personal preferences and persistent high scores. To access a file, a game must first select a storage device. This is done by requiring one asynchronously using `Begin-ShowSelector` and `EndShowSelector`. This operation returns a `StorageDevice` or null (for example, if the user canceled the dialog displaying all available storage devices).

After this, the game requests a `StorageContainer` from the `StorageDevice`, which is the area where the game can store data. Each game has its own private area, and access to data from other games isn't possible. Requesting and obtaining a storage device is once again done asynchronously using `BeginOpenContainer` and `EndOpenContainer`.

At this point, files can be created, opened, or deleted from the container. I/O is performed on .NET streams as usual.

> **TIP** In my experience, most newcomers who attempt to publish a game for the first time fail because of storage-related crashes. The API has failure points that must be handled properly for a game to pass certification and make it to the Xbox Live Independent Games Marketplace. For instance, if the player yanks the memory card used for storage between calls to `Begin-OpenContainer` and `EndOpenContainer`, an exception is thrown by the latter call. Moreover, each storage device may have at most one storage container opened at any time. It's therefore important to dispose of instances of `StorageContainer` as soon as they're not needed anymore.

The requirements for proper handling of failure aren't very demanding. That the game should remain responsive is all that's required. Because the API uses exceptions to report failures, it's enough to catch these exceptions and handle them in some way, such as reporting them to the user and returning to the main menu or continuing with default data. Nevertheless, properly handling exceptions in state machines can significantly increase the length of the source code and introduce much repetition. The async functionality in F# offers a convenient way to help implement state machines that includes exception handling.

Safe asynchronous programming

Although using exceptions to report errors is often frowned on in guidelines, it's a common practice. Their use is viable in the case of synchronous programming, but dealing with exceptions in asynchronous scenarios without support from the language is a difficult task. All situations involving asynchronous programing benefit from the async functionality found in F#. Examples involve any kind of application working with a remote server, such as mobile apps, media set top boxes, and distributed systems.

On the Xbox 360, before you can read or write a file, you need to ask for a storage container, which is a two-step operation. First you show the user a storage-device selector, which the user can choose to forcibly close, thus denying you access to a storage device. If the user picks a device, you can proceed to open the area on the device reserved for your application, a so-called *storage container.*

```
let showSelector =
    Async.FromBeginEnd(
        StorageDevice.BeginShowSelector, StorageDevice.EndShowSelector)
let forceShowSelector =
    let rec work() =
        async {
            while GamerServices.Guide.IsVisible do
                do! Async.Sleep(500)
            try
                let! dev = showSelector
                return
                    match dev with
                    | null -> None
                    | _ -> Some dev
            with
            | :? GamerServices.GuideAlreadyVisibleException ->
                return! work()
        }
    work()
```

Waits until the guide is available, and then shows the storage-device selector

Idiomatic F# code: uses Option instead of null for an optional value

❶ You can't show the selector if the guide is already open.

Sleeps, making the thread available for other operations

Protects against GuideAlready-VisibleException ❷

❸ Tries again

The guide is part of the operating system of the Xbox 360, and it's always accessible by pressing the big button at the center of the gamepad. It's used to perform basic administration of the console and the user account. It's also used to prompt the user which device should be used. ❶ checks that the guide is available before attempting to use it. Attempting to access the guide while it's already in use results in an exception, which is handled by ❷. In that case, ❸ goes back to the beginning through a recursive call in tail position. Note that ❶ isn't enough to safely start using the guide, because the guide may be opened again between ❶ and ❷. You could in principle rely solely on ❷, but I've observed that repeatedly requesting access to the guide when it's not available causes the console to become unresponsive.

You've seen how async can be used to decouple user interaction from the update-draw cycle. You've also seen that it simplifies exception handling. You'll now learn how to assemble all the parts.

Putting it all together

At this point, you've seen how to implement each screen, but you have yet to bind them together into a complete game. Top levels of games typically extend the Game class from the XNA framework:

```
type Game() as this =
    inherit Microsoft.Xna.Framework.Game()
    let graphics = new GraphicsDeviceManager(this)
    do this.Content.RootDirectory <- "Content"
```

All the work of chaining and switching between game screens is defined and started from the Initialize override:

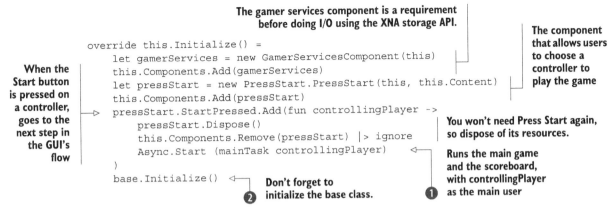

The `mainTask` function takes a `PlayerIndex` and produces an F# async, which is started at ❶. The method then calls the default implementation of `Initialize` in the base class. It's easy to forget this call ❷, in which case graphics and audio assets aren't properly loaded.

The `mainTask` function is as follows:

```
let mainTask (controllingPlayer : PlayerIndex) =          Asks users which
    async {                                                storage device
        let! maybeDevice = AsyncStorage.forceShowSelector  they want to use
        match maybeDevice with
        | None ->
            do! doWhenGuideNoLongerVisible                 User canceled the dialog;
                <| showAlert                               continue without loading
                    "Alert"                                or saving scores
                    "No storage device chosen, scores will not be loaded."
        | Some _ ->
            ()
        let gameplay =                                     Awaits the end
            new GameplayComponent.Component(this, controllingPlayer)  of the gameplay
        this.Components.Add(gameplay)                      session,
        let! score = Async.AwaitEvent(gameplay.GameOver)   retrieving its
        gameplay.Dispose()                                 score
        this.Components.Remove(gameplay) |> ignore
        match maybeDevice with                             If the user
        | None -> ()                                       chose a storage
        | Some device ->                                   device, shows
            return! afterGamePlay controllingPlayer device score  the score table
                                                           and saves it
```

Creates and registers the gameplay component

The `afterGameplay` function provides an async computation that saves the new score table and displays it:

```
let afterGamePlay
    (controllingPlayer : PlayerIndex)
    (device : Storage.StorageDevice)                       Loads the
    score =                                                scores
    async {                                                asynchronously;
        let! scores =                                      it's a slow
            AsyncStorage.loadScores device "SampleGame" "scores"  operation
```

```
      match scores with
      | AsyncStorage.IOResult.Successful scores ->
          let name =
              let ggs = GamerServices.Gamer.SignedInGamers
              match ggs.[controllingPlayer] with
              | null -> "Anonymous"
              | player -> player.DisplayName
          let board : ScoreComponent2.ScoreBoard =
              { NewScore = (name, score)
                Scores = scores.GetAsPairs()
              }

          let scoresComponent =
              new ScoreComponent2.ScoreComponent(
                  this,
                  this.Content,
                  board)
          this.Components.Add(scoresComponent)
          scores.InsertScore(
              AsyncStorage.NamedScore(Name = name, Score = score))
          scores.Truncate(10);
          let! succeeded =
              AsyncStorage.saveScores device "SampleGame" "scores" scores
          if not succeeded then
              do! doWhenGuideNoLongerVisible <|
                  showError "Failed to save scores"
      | AsyncStorage.IOResult.BadData ->
          do! doWhenGuideNoLongerVisible <|
              showError "Score data is corrupted"
      | AsyncStorage.IOResult.DeviceDisconnected ->
          do! doWhenGuideNoLongerVisible <|
              showAlert "Alert" "Storage device was disconnected"
      }
```

Retrieves the name of the player

Watch out for null values XNA may give you.

Updates the scoreboard with the new score

Creates the score component

Saves scores asynchronously; it's a slow operation

Shows error messages in case of an error; should seldom happen in practice

User removed a memory card, which they're not supposed to do; complain about it.

This example demonstrates how multiple asynchronous computations can be combined in a way similar to how functions can call other functions. The simplicity of combining functions is an important building block of large applications. Asynchronous computations add the possibility to control the execution of a computation and spread it over the entire lifetime of a process.

Summary

State machines play a central role in game programming. They're found in animation techniques and other computations that spread over multiple frames. The examples in this chapter focus on simple graphical user interface components, but the concepts are also applicable to artificial intelligence and animating characters in games.

Discriminated unions and `async` each contribute to facilitate implementing state machines. Exception handling in `async` helps you write robust code.

These techniques are also applicable to domains other than games. Most user-facing applications have a user interface that remains reactive, including when waiting for a slow storage device or while communicating over the internet. Many non-game-related mobile apps want to provide similar levels of eye candy, and animations are one way to improve the looks of a user interface. Server-side programs are facing the same challenges for different reasons. They must share execution time with large numbers of other processes on the same machine, while interacting with a slow environment, which requires asynchronous programming.

You've seen how to use units of measure to improve code readability and avoid bugs in complex mathematical expressions. Units of measure can be applied to primitive types such as `int` and `float`, and to complex types such as vectors. They're useful in computation engines found in games, simulators, and financial applications. User interfaces and CAD applications also benefit from the ability to distinguish between unscaled numerical data and screen coordinates.

About the author

Johann Deneux has a PhD from the Department of IT at Sweden's Uppsala University in formal verification of software. He currently works at Prover Technology AB, a company that specializes in the development and verification of safety-critical signaling systems for railways. His background in formal verification and his recent interest in functional programming are put to good use there, where he's developing software to model, simulate, test, and verify railway signaling systems.

His interests outside of work include developing small games for PC and Xbox 360 using the XNA framework together with F#. He's the author of Asteroid Sharpshooter, the first F# game published on the Xbox Live Indie Game channel. His experiences with the game led him to build a utility library named XNAUtils for the developing games, available on Bitbucket (https://bitbucket.org/johdex/xnautils). His continued work with yet-unpublished games provided the material for this chapter.

10 Building social web applications

Yan Cui

Social media has seen a meteoric rise in the last couple of years and has drastically changed the way we use the web and how we communicate with one another. Riding this tide of change in the technology landscape is a whole new genre of gaming—social gaming—which has managed to break down the age and gender barriers that existed with traditional PC and console-based games. Many a social game counts its user base in the hundreds of millions; and such games are monetized at such a level that the traditional giants in the game industry have no choice but to sit up and take notice.[1]

A primer on social gaming

Zynga's FarmVille reached 1 million users in its first week, much to the surprise of its developers, and at its peak FarmVille had over 50 million daily unique users (daily active users [DAUs], a common way to measure the popularity of social games). There have been many similar success stories in this space, and as of this writing the top 10 games according to AppData (www.appdata.com) all have at least 20 million DAUs. Of course, not every game succeeds—some are even scrapped soon after going live—but let's focus on the positives!

Scalability challenges go hand in hand with operating a successful social game. Having many players playing your game means there are many concurrent requests to deal with. Each action the player takes in the game is likely to alter their game state in one way or another, so there's probably a 1:1 read-to-write ratio for game-state data. It's not uncommon for a game to perform tens or hundreds of thousands of read and write operations against the database per second.

---

[1] As evident by the expensive acquisitions of Playfish and PopCap by Electronic Arts.

(continued)

To gain insights into what the players are doing in the game and drive features and promotions to better retain existing players and attract new ones, you need to be able to record a vast amount of data related to players' activities in the game, and analyze that data in as close to real time as possible. Zynga, for instance, generates tens of terabytes of analytical data every day!

For reasons such as these, cloud computing and NoSQL databases are particularly popular among social game operators. Later in this chapter, you'll learn how they can help you create a highly distributed and scalable solution for your game.

In this chapter, you'll design and implement a simple farming game in F#, called SharpVille. Although the solution will be far from complete, it will serve to outline the basic structure of a simple client-server setup that you can easily extend to add more features or adapt to create your own game (see figure 1).

Designing a social game

Let's start by defining the scope of the game, mocking up the UI, and defining the interaction between the client application and the server.

Features

Here's a list of the basic features for the game:

- You (the player) have a farm to tend to.
- You have a set number of plots to plant seeds in. You can harvest for a profit after a set amount of time.
- Different seeds cost different amounts to buy and yield different profits.
- Different seeds take a different amount of time to yield profit.

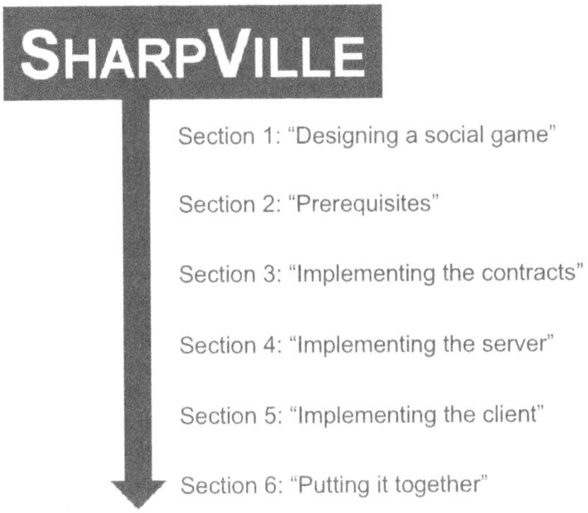

SHARPVILLE

Section 1: "Designing a social game"

Section 2: "Prerequisites"

Section 3: "Implementing the contracts"

Section 4: "Implementing the server"

Section 5: "Implementing the client"

Section 6: "Putting it together"

Figure 1 The plan for the chapter. You first decide what features you'd like in the game and design a basic, functional UI (figure 2, in the next section). You'll explore the client-server interaction required for the game and implement the contracts, server, and client components in turn. Finally, you'll put together the various components for a working demo.

- You can visit friends' farms and help them.
- As you plant seeds and harvest, you also gain experience points (EXP).
- You level up as a farmer as you collect EXP.
- As you level up, you unlock more types of seeds you can plant.
- To drive healthy competition, there will be a leaderboard with you and your friends, sorted by EXP.

Based on this feature list, it's easy to derive the data you need to track the player's game state: EXP, level, gold balance, as well as what the player has planted and where.

The UI

The UI should display the gameplay elements just described. Something simple but functional like figure 2 will do for the purpose of the demo.

Client-server interaction

In order for the game to work, the client needs to be able to communicate with the server to accomplish the following:

- Identify and authenticate the player
- Retrieve information related to the player's current game state from the server at startup, and retrieve updates to stay in sync thereafter
- Inform the server that the player wishes to perform an action, so the server is able to
  - Validate the action
  - Update the player's state if the action is valid
  - Return incremental updates to the player state after each action

Table 1 shows the operations you need to support on the server, along with the information that needs to change hands.

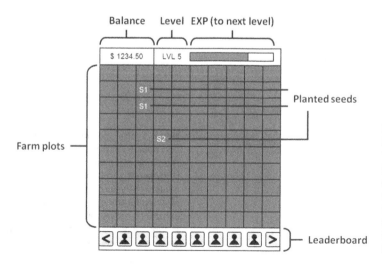

Figure 2   A rough idea of how the UI should look. The farm plot area is a 10 × 10 grid where each cell represents a plot in which the player is able to plant seeds. S1 and S2 are the IDs of the seeds that have been planted in those cells.

Table 1 The operations the server should support, and the data that should be passed in via the request and returned via the response

Operation	Input	Output
Handshake	Player ID and hash	Current EXP, level, gold balance, positions where seeds were planted, and the session ID to be used from here on
GetLeaderboard	Session ID and player IDs of the player's friends	Leaderboard profiles
Plant	Session ID, grid position, and seed ID	New EXP, level, gold balance, and positions where seeds were planted
Harvest	Session ID and grid position	New EXP, level, gold balance, and positions where seeds were planted
Visit	Session ID and friend's player ID	Grid positions where seeds were planted and the number of fertilizers left
Fertilize	Session ID, friend's player ID, and grid position of where to fertilize	The number of fertilizers left

With these things in mind, you can now establish the contract between the server and client.

Thick server and thin server

The approach we're taking here means the server is doing most of the heavy lifting, such as enforcing the rules of the game, applying the game logic with each request, and updating the game state accordingly. This isn't to say that you shouldn't do any validation on the client and allow invalid requests to make their way to the server and fail there (for example, a request to harvest a crop that's not yet ready). Instead, you should enforce some of the game rules on the client and not allow invalid requests to be made against the server based on the knowledge you have of the player's current game state on the client.

If the game state on the client is out of date (for instance, if the player is playing on multiple devices), then the server's validation will serve as the last line of defense against invalid requests. For example, if players have spent all their gold planting seeds while playing on their iPad, the server validation will stop them from being able to plant additional seeds by switching to the web version where their local state on the client is out of date and still carries enough of a balance to plant additional seeds.

This approach has the benefit of making the game difficult to cheat. Because the rules are enforced by the server—which you control, at the cost of more work performed on the server—more servers are required to deal with a given number of concurrent players. Depending on how much code you're able to share between client platforms, or how intensive the rendering task is on the client, sometimes it can

(continued)

also be advantageous to implement the bulk of the game logic on the server[2] for those reasons.

THIN SERVER

Alternatively, you can do the heavy lifting on the client and let the server act as little more than custodian for the player's game state. The client is responsible for making sure game rules aren't broken and for manipulating and managing the game state, which must be updated on the server at some point by doing either of the following:

- Replacing the player's current state with the latest snapshot on the client as a whole
- Aggregating all incremental changes on the client and applying the same changes on the latest state the server knows about

With this approach, the load on the server is minimal, but there's also a huge opportunity for savvier players to cheat the game by capturing and modifying requests to the server using HTTP proxy tools (hence bypassing any client-side validation you have in place) or creating simple programs to mimic the real client application and submitting invalid changes to the game state.

More care is also required to deal with the case when the player is playing the game on multiple devices simultaneously and the resulting version conflicts that can occur as far as game state changes are concerned.

THICK VS. THIN SERVER

Given these two approaches, you might think it's an obvious choice to go with the thick server approach (or something close to it), but it's easy to underestimate the cost and performance implications of such decisions when you've successfully amassed a sizable user base in the tens of millions! It's for these reasons that some of the biggest games on Facebook are doing much of the work on the client and have a thin server layer.

Ultimately it's a decision you'll likely make on a game-by-game basis depending on the particular needs of that game. Also, you're not limited to these two approaches—there's plenty of middle ground, and you have the opportunity for mix-and-matching depending on the actions you're performing in the game.

Prerequisites

Before you start writing code, let's make sure you have everything required to get this demo application up and running. Here's a short list of the things you'll need:

- Visual Studio 2012 or above
- F# XAML item templates (http://mng.bz/sR00)

---

[2] For instance, the Xbox One hit Titanfall uses a Microsoft Azure-hosted server solution to run all the battle simulation and enemy artificial intelligence, leaving the client to focus on rendering the intense combat scenes. As another example, the creator of EVE Online has used Amazon AppStream to stream the character creator from the server in order to get players through the door and invested in the game quickly without having to wait for a sizable download before they can even see the game.

Great! Now you're ready to start implementing the awesome game, SharpVille!

Implementing the contracts

First, let's create a new F# Library project for the contracts the client and server will share, including various types to represent the player's state as well as the request/response types. Let's call this project SharpVille.Contracts. This is a convenient time to create the solution too; name it SharpVille.

The model

Once you've created the project, delete the Library1.fs and Script.fsx files that are created by default. Then, right-click the project in the Solution Explorer to add a new F# source file called Model.fs (shown in the following listing).

> **Listing 1 Representing the model objects**

```
namespace SharpVille.Model

open System

type X          = int
type Y          = int
type SeedId     = string            Type aliases to make the
type PlayerId   = string            contract types' members
type SessionId  = Guid              more self-explanatory
type Coordinate = X * Y

[<Measure>]
type exp
                                    These units-of-measure types are
[<Measure>]                         used to provide extra safety when
type lvl                            you're doing calculations on EXP,
                                    level, and balance to make sure
[<Measure>]                         values of matching units are used.
type gold

[<Measure>]
type fertilizer
                                    Represents a
type Session =                      unique session
    {                               for a player
        Id        : SessionId
        PlayerId  : PlayerId
    }
                                    Represents a plot that has been planted
                                    with a seed. It contains the ID of the
type Plant =                        seed and when the seed was planted so
    {                               you can decide when to harvest.
        Seed        : SeedId
        DatePlanted : DateTime
                                    Represents the player's game state. It
    }                               contains the player's current EXP, level,
                                    and balance, as well as the size of the
type State =                        player's farm and what seeds the player
    {                               has planted where.
        PlayerId    : PlayerId
        Exp         : int64<exp>
        Level       : int<lvl>
```

```
        Balance            : int64<gold>
        FarmDimension      : Coordinate
        Plants             : Map<Coordinate, Plant>
    }
type Seed =
    {
        Id                 : SeedId
        RequiredLevel      : int<lvl>
        Cost               : int64<gold>
        GrowthTime         : TimeSpan
        Yield              : int64<gold>
        Exp                : int64<exp>
    }
type GameSpecification =
    {
        Seeds              : Map<SeedId, Seed>
        Levels             : Map<int<lvl>, int64<exp>>
        DefaultState       : State
    }
```

> Represents the definition of a seed. It encapsulates all the information about a seed.

> Represents the specification for the game. It contains all the seeds and levels defined in the game as well as the default state a player starts with.

The `SharpVille.Model` namespace contains the domain objects for the game, including all the data you need in order to track a player's progress in the game. Notice that all the types defined in this namespace contain data only and no behavior or logic. Any client- or server-specific logic will be implemented in the respective projects to prevent them from leaking through the abstraction layers via a shared assembly.

The `GameSpecification` type encapsulates the aspects of the game that are configurable, such as the seeds and levels. It allows the game to be data-driven and gives you the ability to tweak the game-play experience without making any code changes (which usually require more significant testing time) and the potential to run A/B testing[3] at a later date.

Requests and response objects

For this demo application, you'll follow the request-response pattern. For each of the server operations you're going to support (shown earlier in table 1), you'll create a matching pair of request and response types. Begin by adding a new F# source file, Requests.fs (shown in the next listing) just below Model.fs.

Listing 2   Request objects

```
namespace SharpVille.Model.Requests

open System
open SharpVille.Model

type HandshakeRequest =
    {
        PlayerID           : PlayerId
        Hash               : string
    }
```

> These types encapsulate the input data for the corresponding service operation.

---

[3] See "A/B Testing," *Wikipedia*, http://en.wikipedia.org/wiki/A/B_testing.

```fsharp
type GetLeaderboardRequest =
    {
        SessionID       : SessionId
        Friends         : PlayerId[]
    }

type PlantRequest =
    {
        SessionID       : SessionId
        Position        : Coordinate
        Seed            : SeedId
    }

type HarvestRequest =
    {
        SessionID       : SessionId
        Position        : Coordinate
    }

type VisitRequest =
    {
        SessionID       : SessionId
        Friend          : PlayerId
    }

type FertilizeRequest =
    {
        SessionID       : SessionId
        Friend          : PlayerId
        Position        : Coordinate
    }
```

⊲ **These types encapsulate the input data for the corresponding service operation.**

⊲ **These types encapsulate the input data for the corresponding service operation.**

The code in listing 2 is pretty straightforward. You take the input information for each of the operations in table 1 and create a request type to encapsulate it.

Let's do the same thing again and create the matching response types. Add a new F# source file, Responses.fs, just below Requests.fs.

Listing 3   Response objects

```fsharp
namespace SharpVille.Model.Responses

open SharpVille.Model

type StateResponse (exp        : int64<exp>,
                    level      : int<lvl>,
                    balance    : int64<gold>,
                    plants     : Map<Coordinate, Plant>) =
    member this.Exp     = exp
    member this.Level   = level
    member this.Balance = balance
    member this.Plants  = plants

type HandshakeResponse (exp, level, balance, plants,
                        farmDimension : Coordinate,
                        sessionId     : SessionId,
                        gameSpec      : GameSpecification) =
    inherit StateResponse(exp, level, balance, plants)
    member this.SessionId        = sessionId
```

⊲ **Base response type for any response that needs to return a new snapshot of the player state**

⊲ **These types encapsulate the output data for the corresponding service operation.**

```
    member this.FarmDimension     = farmDimension
    member this.GameSpecification = gameSpec
type PlantResponse (exp, level, balance, plants) =
    inherit StateResponse(exp, level, balance, plants)

type HarvestResponse(exp, level, balance, plants) =
    inherit StateResponse(exp, level, balance, plants)

type LeaderboardFriend =
    {
        Name             : string
        PlayerID         : PlayerId
        EXP              : int64<exp>
    }

type GetLeaderboardResponse =
    {
        Friends          : LeaderboardFriend[]
    }

type VisitResponse =
    {
        Plants           : Map<Coordinate, Plant>
        Fertilizers      : int<fertilizer>
    }

type FertilizeResponse =
    {
        Fertilizers      : int<fertilizer>
    }
```

◁—| **These types encapsulate the output data for the corresponding service operation.**

◁—| **Encapsulates the data for an entry in a player's leaderboard**

◁—| **These types encapsulate the output data for the corresponding service operation.**

One of the things you may notice in listing 3 is that some of the response types are defined as record types, whereas others are defined as class types (although immutable). This is because HandshakeResponse, PlantResponse, and HarvestResponse are all identical (at least for now), so having them all inherit from the same base class means

- You don't have to keep repeating yourself (DRY!).
- You can consolidate the response-handling code on the client to work directly against the base class.

You may wonder why you wouldn't just return the same response type from the three different service methods, instead. The answer is *future extensibility*. If you choose to return the same response type from the three methods, it restricts your ability to modify the response (add a new property, perhaps) from each of the methods in isolation without introducing breaking API changes.

Being able to keep a consistent, backward-compatible API is important because it means you're more likely to be able to release incremental changes to the server code without having to do a synchronized update to the client code. This type of synchronized updates usually means downtime, and downtime is extremely expensive, especially in this highly competitive business—players you lose during downtime might never come back.

Also, when your service starts to support both web and mobile clients, the ability to do incremental updates becomes increasingly important. You'll soon discover that updating mobile clients can be a tricky business (as anyone who has had to deal with the Apple App Store would no doubt tell you!).

The request-response pattern

The request-response pattern is all over the web, and for good reasons. As time goes by, and your application evolves, the lists of parameters to your service methods are likely to grow, and you may even need to introduce overloads to provide more variety and support optional parameters. These types of API changes have a significant blast radius in terms of the number of code files you need to touch, and they also impact the backward compatibility of your service.

By wrapping the input and output values into request and response objects, you can do the following:

- Add input/output values incrementally
- Maintain a consistent, backward-compatible public API
- Solve the problem of growing parameters
- Have an easy way to provide multiple results

Implementing the server

We're rather spoiled for choice when it comes to what technology to use to implement the server. For the purpose of demonstrating the versatility of F#, I'll show you a simple HTTP server using F#'s asynchronous workflows.[4] You'll use JSON as the wire format for the request and response objects because it's human readable, which is helpful when it comes to debugging.

Embracing the cloud

More and more companies are moving their infrastructures to the cloud each day, and the trend is likely to continue for the foreseeable future. An in-depth discussion of the merits of cloud computing is beyond the scope of this chapter, but I'd like to outline some common reasons why so many companies have decided to make the move.

TRADING CAPITAL EXPENSE FOR VARIABLE EXPENSE

Although there are many eye-catching success stories in our industry, many games fall by the wayside.[5] In general, the industry is a highly competitive place where success

---

[4] See "Asynchronous Workflows," Microsoft Developer Network, http://mng.bz/y66m.
[5] Such as Tiny Speck's experimental social game, Glitch, which despite being well executed and having a highly engaged player base, closed down only two months after its official launch; see "Glitch (Video Game)", *Wikipedia*, http://en.wikipedia.org/wiki/Glitch_(video_game).

(continued)

has as much to do with luck as quality, and even the most successful titles can't guarantee a sustained long-term future.[6]

In such a competitive market, being able to experiment and take risks is a massive business advantage and differentiator. The pay-as-you-go pricing model offered by cloud providers such as Amazon Web Services (AWS) allows you to take more risks and innovate as the cost of failure falls dramatically.

ELASTIC SCALABILITY

The amount of server capacity required for a game is as unpredictable as its chance of becoming a success, and even the best attempts to guess actual demand are likely to result in either wastage through overprovision or a bad user experience through underprovision. Unless your user base is well balanced geographically, you might even end up with a mixture of the two in a single day if your user base is highly concentrated around one time zone.

With AWS and most other cloud providers, you can scale elastically based on actual demand. This removes the need for guesswork and gives you an easy way to provision only what you need, when you need it.

INCREASED SPEED AND AGILITY

In the traditional self-hosted environment, acquiring and setting up a large number of servers to meet growing demands is a time-consuming process, not to mention the expertise and resources required to maintain a growing fleet of hardware on an ongoing basis.

In a cloud-hosted environment, you can go from having 1 to 1,000 servers in seconds with a few button clicks. Maintaining the infrastructure is the responsibility of the cloud provider and is not a distraction and expense for you. When you no longer require those capacities, it's just as easy to scale down your infrastructure and stop paying for servers.

Because your developers don't have to worry about the provisioning of the underlying infrastructure, they can better focus on the things that are important to you and your business. In return, you'll reap the rewards of improved developer efficiency.

RELIABILITY

Because operating large data centers is a core part of the business for cloud providers, you can be sure they're able and willing to hire the best engineers money can buy. Consequently, they're likely able to provide a more reliable and efficient infrastructure for you than you can provide yourself.

There have been several high-profile outages by AWS, which generated much public criticism and doubt about the public cloud in general. One aspect of these outages that many overlooked was the speed of recovery and the extremely low frequency at

---

[6] Zynga's Empires & Allies, once the most popular social game on Facebook with over 100 million monthly active users, closed down less than 2 years after its initial launch, in June 2013. See "Empires & Allies," *Wikipedia*, http://en.wikipedia.org/wiki/Empires_&_Allies.

(continued)

which outages of such scale occur. They're high-impact, infrequent events that don't truly reflect the level of service and reliability provided by the likes of AWS.

FOCUSING ON WHAT'S IMPORTANT

It's a huge advantage not to have to worry about managing the heavy lifting required to run a data center: buying and installing new hardware, setting up networks, negotiating with bandwidth providers, and so forth. These tasks aren't difficult to do on their own, but doing them at scale, and doing them well, is challenging.

We all know that good software engineers are hard to come by, so you shouldn't waste your scarce engineering resources on infrastructure, which is by all means important but hardly ever differentiates your business in any meaningful way. By leaving the infrastructure to cloud providers that specialize in it, you allow your engineers to focus on things that truly differentiate your business.

GOING GLOBAL INSTANTLY

It wasn't long ago when the cost of deploying applications to a global audience was prohibitive to all but established enterprises. Nowadays, even small startups can use the cloud to deploy their applications to a global audience. AWS, for instance, lets you deploy infrastructure in data centers around the globe and provides edge locations that let you quickly and efficiently deliver content to your customers in all corners of the world via its content-delivery network.

Common utility functions

Before you start implementing the server-side logic, you'll add a new F# Library project to your solution and call it SharpVille.Common. You'll put any shared utility functions and modules in this project. Once again, delete the default files and add a new F# source file called Utils.fs (see the following listing), where you'll create two helper functions for reading and writing JSON data.

Listing 4   Helper functions for reading and writing JSON

```
namespace SharpVille.Common

open System.Text

[<AutoOpen>]
module Utils =
    open System.IO
    open System.Runtime.Serialization.Json

    let readJson<'a> (stream : Stream) =
        let serializer = new DataContractJsonSerializer(typedefof<'a>)
        serializer.ReadObject(stream) :?> 'a

    let writeJson (obj : 'a) (stream : Stream) =
        let serializer = new DataContractJsonSerializer(typedefof<'a>)
        serializer.WriteObject(stream, obj) |> ignore
```

In listing 4 you're using the BCL's built-in `DataContractJsonSerializer` (http://mng.bz/7nc8) because it works well[7] with F#'s types, so you don't need to have third-party dependencies for the demo. Also available are a number of open source JSON serializers, including `Json.Net` (http://json.net) and `ServiceStack.Text` (https://github.com/ServiceStack/ServiceStack.Text), both of which offer a richer set of features and better performance for working with JSON from .NET.

When you're done, add another F# Library project and call it SharpVille.Server. This is where you'll implement the server-side logic for the game.

Beware of serialization costs

For high-concurrency web applications, the cost of serialization and deserialization can be nontrivial and consume a significant portion of your CPU cycles as well as bandwidth, which ultimately translates to higher operational cost. For these reasons, the folks at Google created a fast and compact wire format called *protocol buffers* (https://developers.google.com/protocol-buffers) which, based on my benchmark[8] on a simple Plain Old CLR Object (POCO), is several times more efficient than the BCL's `BinaryFormatter`.

In the specific context of building a backend for a social game, if you go down the stateless server route, it means for each call you also need to retrieve the player's current game state from a database, update it, and save the change back to the database. This pair of read-write activities also requires serialization and deserialization and can be even more expensive, depending on the size of the game state.

From experience, I've found in some of my games that the cost of serialization and deserialization accounts for up to 90% of CPU cycles used. Moving to a more efficient serializer such as protocol buffers reduced the number of servers required by up to half.

Do your own benchmarks

Although there are many publicly available benchmarks on the relative performance of various serializers and serialization formats, none will be as representative of your payload as one that runs against the real data you'll be working with. As a rule of thumb, run your own benchmarks against the actual data you'll be working with whenever possible.

The data access layer

You must take many considerations into account when deciding what persistence technology to use for the various types of data you need to store for the game. With the

---

[7] See Yan Cui, "F# – Serializing F# Record and Discriminated Union Types," theburningmonk.com, http://mng.bz/Oz10.

[8] Yan Cui, "Benchmarks," http://theburningmonk.com/benchmarks.

ever-increasing popularity and maturity of NoSQL solutions, you have plenty of options available.

For the purpose of this demo, you won't tie the implementation to any specific database. You'll instead use a simple in-memory dictionary to store the player state and session data. Implementing the `IStateRepository` and `ISessionStore` interfaces with a key-value store such as Memcached or Redis is a trivial exercise.

For now, add a new F# source file in the SharpVille.Server project and call it DAL.fs (see listing 5). You'll define the interfaces to abstract over your data access layers here and add two simple implementations using in-memory dictionaries.

Listing 5   Implementing the data access layer

```
module SharpVille.Server.DAL

open System
open System.Collections.Generic
open SharpVille.Model

type IStateRepository =
    abstract member Get      : PlayerId  -> State option
    abstract member Put      : State      -> unit

type ISessionStore =
    abstract member Get      : SessionId -> Session option
    abstract member Put      : Session    -> unit

type InMemoryStateRepo () =
    let states = new Dictionary<PlayerId, State>()

    interface IStateRepository with
        member this.Get(playerId) =
            match states.TryGetValue playerId with
            | true, x -> Some x
            | _       -> None
        member this.Put(state)  = states.[state.PlayerId] <- state

type InMemorySessionStore () =
    let sessions = new Dictionary<SessionId, Session>()

    interface ISessionStore with
        member this.Get(sessionId) =
            match sessions.TryGetValue sessionId with
            | true, x -> Some x
            | _       -> None
        member this.Put(session)  = sessions.[session.Id] <- session
```

Exercise 1

A key-value store such as Memcached, Redis, Couchbase, or MongoDB would be a great fit for the simple get/put operations required for the `IStateRepository` and `ISessionStore` interfaces. Try implementing these two interfaces using the API of a key-value store of your choice.

NoSQL in social games

By now I assume you've heard the hype about NoSQL databases. Rather than a single technology, Not Only SQL (NoSQL) is better described as a movement away from the traditional relational model and the one-size-fits-all approach that's often applied with relational databases.

What many came to realize was that although the relational approach to modeling data is capable of solving most problems, some data, such as the social graphs used by the likes of Facebook and Twitter, doesn't translate naturally to the relational model. Moreover, for these types of data, the relational model doesn't allow for an efficient way to answer the kind of typical questions that you'd want to ask, such as what common interests you share with your friends. This is one area where the graph database, a category of NoSQL databases, really shines;[9] you'll learn more about this later in this chapter.

The ACID[10] (Atomicity, Consistency, Isolation, Durability) guarantees provided by modern relational databases are powerful, but you don't often need all those guarantees, which come at a cost of performance and scalability. Many NoSQL databases allow you to trade the ACID guarantees for horizontal scalability and speed.

KEY-VALUE STORES

For many social games, such as SharpVille, the majority of the database interactions involve a key lookup into a hash to fetch a player's game state, which is by far the most important use case. Even a modestly successful social game has to deal with a sizable number of concurrent players, often performing hundreds of thousands of database operations per second with a likely 1:1 read-to-write ratio. The most important criteria for the database are the following:

- The ability to handle a large number of concurrent transactions
- The ability to scale horizontally to maintain a linear relationship between cost and scale
- Low-latency access to data

Key-value stores such as Couchbase (www.couchbase.com), Riak (http://basho.com/riak), and Amazon DynamoDB (http://aws.amazon.com/dynamodb) are great matches for these criteria. They essentially store your data in a huge distributed hash table while providing mechanisms to seamlessly replicate the data behind the scenes, to provide greater availability and fault tolerance against network partitions and hardware failures.

Many of these databases (such as Couchbase and Redis [http://redis.io]) use a memory-first storage model to provide ultra-low-latency access to data (usually in the 2–4 ms range) while giving you the option to persist data to disk for durability as

---

[9] For a more in-depth look at how graph databases can help you work efficiently with highly connected data, see Ian Robinson's talk "Tackling Complex Data with Neo4j," *InfoQ,* http://mng.bz/BHSx.

[10] See "ACID," *Wikipedia,* http://en.wikipedia.org/wiki/ACID.

(continued)

well. Document stores such as MongoDB (www.mongodb.org) and RavenDB (http://
ravendb.net) that store data in self-contained documents are also popular choices for
player states.

COLUMN DATABASES

Column databases are also referred to as *Bigtable clones* because they're inspired
by Google's 2006 paper on Bigtable,[11] a proprietary technology that's today powering
many of the data-storage services provided by Google's cloud offerings. Databases
in this category, such as popular open source solutions Cassandra (http://cassandra
.apache.org) and HBase (http://hbase.apache.org), store data in columns rather than
rows, typically scale well with size, and are most used in data warehousing and analytics applications.

As far as commercial solutions go, Vertica (www.vertica.com) has been the preferred
solution among the big social game operators[12] to provide a platform for analyzing
their large amounts of in-game events so they can understand the performance of
their games and drive features and changes forward. Zynga, for instance, operates
one of the largest data warehouses in the world and generates over 15 TB of new
data every day from its estimated 60 million daily active users.

GRAPH DATABASE

Graph databases are unique in the sense that they're based on graph theory and
store data using nodes and edges instead of rows and columns. The nodes represent
the entities stored in the database, and the edges the relationship between the
nodes. Both nodes and edges can be associated with an arbitrary set of properties,
and edges can be one way or bidirectional.

Graph databases allow you to query data by traversing the graph. They're great for
building social features. My employer, Gamesys (www.gamesyscorporate.com), for instance, uses Neo4j (www.neo4j.org), a popular open source graph database (which
is also fully ACID compliant), to power high-value social features in our cash gaming
business. In our MMORPG title Here Be Monsters, we're also using Neo4j to help us
automate the process of balancing the in-game economy.[13]

POLYGLOT PERSISTENCE

A complex application often has to deal with many types of data and may have different requirements for that data. Different databases are designed to solve different
problems, which is especially true in the case of NoSQL databases. Using the same
database for all your data needs usually leads to nonperformant solutions.

---

[11] Fay Chang, Jeffrey Dean, et al. (Google, Inc.), "Bigtable: A Distributed Storage System for Structured Data,"
Seventh Symposium on Operating System Design and Implementation, November, 2006, http://bit.ly/
1hGHDX9.

[12] Vertica Social Gaming Panel, San Francisco, CA, April 26, 2011 (video), http://mng.bz/1K81.

[13] Yan Cui, "Modelling a Large Scale Social Game with Neo4j," *Skills Matter*, April 30, 2014 (video), http://
mng.bz/9OLl.

(continued)

Increasingly, companies are realizing this and have opted for a polyglot approach by using multiple database systems that are chosen based on how the data is being used. For instance, using polyglot persistence you might end up

- Using an in-memory key-value store for session and other transient data
- Using a key-value or document store for player state
- Using a column database for analytics data and business intelligence (BI) applications
- Using a graph database to store data for social features
- Using an RDBMS to store financial and other data that requires transactional support

You face a number of challenges with polyglot persistence, including the following:

- You need to decide which database system to use for each type of data and application.
- Many NoSQL databases are still young and have rough edges.
- You may lack experience with and knowledge of operating NoSQL databases.
- You need to deal with consistency with some NoSQL databases.
- You have to work with many different APIs.

The game engine

Now that we've got some of the plumbing out of the way, let's move on to the server-side game engine. This is where you'll put all the game logic as well as validation to enforce the game rules.

In the SharpVille.Server project, add another F# source file called GameEngine.fs below DAL.fs (see listing 6). For the purpose of the demo, you'll only implement the Handshake, Plant, and Harvest calls, to demonstrate how these features would work end to end; but by the time you finish this chapter, you should be able to easily extend the existing implementation to support additional features.

Listing 6   Defining the game engine interface

```
module SharpVille.Server.GameEngine

open System

open SharpVille.Model
open SharpVille.Model.Requests
open SharpVille.Model.Responses
open SharpVille.Server.DAL

type IGameEngine =
    abstract member Handshake    : HandshakeRequest -> HandshakeResponse
    abstract member Plant        : PlantRequest     -> PlantResponse
    abstract member Harvest      : HarvestRequest    -> HarvestResponse
```

This listing uses matching request/response types for each operation. If you need to modify the input/output parameters for one of the operations in the future, you should be able to modify just the corresponding request or response type without impacting others.

Now, in the same GameEngine.fs file, you can begin implementing the IGame-Engine interface one step at a time, starting with a skeleton (see listing 7). The game engine will need to return the game specification in the HandshakeResponse, so for simplicity's sake you'll pass the current game specification into the game engine as a constructor parameter. In practice, though, you'll want to be able to update the game specification (or the entire game engine if possible!) on the fly without requiring a restart, to reduce downtime.

Listing 7   implementing the `IGameEngine` interface

```
type GameEngine (stateRepo        : IStateRepository,
                 sessionStore     : ISessionStore,
                 gameSpec         : GameSpecification) =
    let getState sessionId =
        match sessionStore.Get sessionId with
        | Some x -> match stateRepo.Get x.PlayerId with
                    | Some x -> x
                    | _      -> failwith "State not found"
        | _      -> failwith "Invalid session"

    let awardExp ({ Exp = currExp; Level = currLvl } as state) exp =
        let newExp = currExp + exp
        let newLvl = gameSpec.Levels
                     |> Seq.fold (fun acc elem ->
                            if elem.Key > acc && newExp >= elem.Value
                            then elem.Key
                            else acc) currLvl
        (newExp, newLvl)
```

Returns the current state associated with the specified session ID. Also performs simple validation against the session ID and the associated player ID.

Returns the player's new level based on their new EXP value, and handles the (unlikely) case when the player levels up multiple levels at once.

So far, you've added only two helper functions that will be required by pretty much every operation you support. The awardExp function takes the player's current state (which is fetched by calling the getState function with a valid sessionId) and returns the player's new EXP and level so you can update their state at the end of the operation.

In the following listing, you'll implement the handler for the Handshake operation, which is responsible for creating a new session and initializing default states for new players.

Listing 8   The `Handshake` handler

```
interface IGameEngine with
    member this.Handshake (req : HandshakeRequest) =
        let session = { Id = Guid.NewGuid(); PlayerId = req.PlayerID }
        sessionStore.Put(session)

        let state =
            match stateRepo.Get req.PlayerID with
            | None ->
                let state = { gameSpec.DefaultState with
                                PlayerId = req.PlayerID }
```

The handshake call is responsible for creating the session the player uses for all subsequent calls, as well as initiating a new player's state using the configured default state.

```
                    stateRepo.Put(state)
                    state
            | Some x -> x

        HandshakeResponse(state.Exp, state.Level, state.Balance,
                          state.Plants,
                          state.FarmDimension,
                          session.Id,
                          gameSpec)
```

Although the logic in the other handlers varies, they share a similar flow:

1 Fetch the current state (which also validates the request's session ID).

2 Confirm that the request is valid given the player's state.

3 Create a new player state.

4 Save the new state.

5 Return a response with the new state.

With this in mind, in the next listing you'll add a method to handle the Plant operation right below the Handshake method.

Listing 9   The Plant handler

```
member this.Plant (req : PlantRequest) =
    let state = getState req.SessionID

    let seed =
        match gameSpec.Seeds.TryFind req.Seed with
        | Some seed -> seed
        | _ -> failwithf "Invalid SeedId : %s" req.Seed
    if state.Level < seed.RequiredLevel then
        failwith "Insufficient level"
    elif state.Balance < seed.Cost then
        failwith "Insufficient balance"
    elif state.Plants.ContainsKey req.Position then
        failwith "Farmplot not empty"

    let newPlant = {
                    Seed = seed.Id
                    DatePlanted = DateTime.UtcNow
                   }
    let newExp, newLvl = awardExp state seed.Exp
    let newState =
        { state with
            Balance = state.Balance - seed.Cost
            Plants  = state.Plants.Add(req.Position, newPlant)
            Exp     = newExp
            Level   = newLvl }
    stateRepo.Put(newState)

    PlantResponse(newState.Exp, newState.Level, newState.Balance,
                  newState.Plants)
```

Step 1: Validate the session and fetch the current state.

Step 2: Validate the request given the current state.

Step 3: Apply changes to create the new state.

Step 4: Save the new state.

Step 5: Return a response with the new state.

In the case of planting a seed, you need to ensure the following:

- The player has a valid session.
- The seed specified in the request is valid.
- The player is at the required level to use this seed.
- The player can afford the seed.
- The player is not trying to plant on a farm plot that's already occupied.

If all the validations pass, you can proceed to charge the player for the seed and plant it in the requested farm plot. Note that you need to remember when the seed is planted, so that you can do the following:

- When the player resumes play (for example, after restarting the game), show them how much time is left before they can harvest the seed.
- When the player attempts to harvest the seed, validate that the required amount of time has passed since the seed was planted.

The player is rewarded with a small amount of EXP based on the seed they've planted and can potentially level up as a result. Fortunately, the aforementioned `awardExp` function takes care of all the heavy lifting here, so you just need to use the returned values to create an updated state for the player.

Similarly, the following listing adds another method to handle the `Harvest` operation right below the `Plant` method.

Listing 10   The `Harvest` handler

```
member this.Harvest (req : HarvestRequest) =
    let state = getState req.SessionID          ← Step 1: Validate the
                                                   session and fetch
                                                   the current state.
    let plant =
        match state.Plants.TryFind req.Position with
        | Some plant -> plant
        | _          -> failwith "No plants found"

    let seed = gameSpec.Seeds.[plant.Seed]
    if DateTime.UtcNow - plant.DatePlanted < seed.GrowthTime then
        failwith "Plant not harvestable"

    let newExp, newLvl = awardExp state seed.Exp          ← Step 3: Apply
    let newState =                                           changes to
        { state with                                         create new state.
            Balance = state.Balance + seed.Yield
            Plants  = state.Plants.Remove(req.Position)
            Exp     = newExp                                 Step 4: Save
            Level   = newLvl }                               the new state.
    stateRepo.Put(newState)                          ←

    HarvestResponse(newState.Exp, newState.Level, newState.Balance,
                    newState.Plants)
```

Step 2: Validate the request given the current state.

Step 5: Return a response with the new state.

To harvest a previously planted seed, you need to validate the following:

- The player has a valid session.
- The farm plot that the player is trying to harvest isn't empty.
- The seed is fully grown and ready to be harvested.

Note that you don't validate the seed ID in this case. This is because in order for the seed ID to be in the player state, you must have validated against it when the player tried to plant the seed initially, so there's no need to do the same work twice.

Exercise 2

You probably noticed that although the validation rules are different for the `Plant` and `Harvest` methods, there's a fair amount of duplicated code in these two methods. As an exercise, try refactoring the common code out into a higher-order function that does the following in two functions:

- Performs the validation
- Creates a new player state based on the current state

Then rewrite the `Plant` and `Harvest` methods to make use of these new functions.

Stateless vs. stateful server

The approach you're taking with SharpVille is a stateless approach where the game servers don't hold any player states. That way, upon each request, the server needs to retrieve the player's state from the database, modify it, and save the changes back to the database.

On the other hand, with a stateful approach, the game servers hold onto the player's state for some period of time, commonly the duration of one game session.

The stateless approach has the advantage of allowing your cluster of game servers to be easily scaled up and down using AWS's Auto Scaling service (http://aws.amazon.com/autoscaling), for instance, because they don't hold any states. This approach has several drawbacks:

- A heavy load is placed against the database, because every request requires two database operations.
- Serialization and deserialization of the user state are heavy on the CPU.
- High latency results from the database operations.
- Bandwidth usage is high.
- You have to run more game servers and database nodes, which means higher operational costs.

By comparison, the stateful approach addresses these inefficiencies but in turn creates a number of complexities of its own. You must do the following:

- Ensure that the player always talks to the same server that holds their state.
- Avoid hot spots by balancing the load; you can no longer rely on the load-balancer alone.

(continued)

- Avoid players hogging a server, so the server can be terminated when scaling down the cluster of game servers.
- Ensure that all state changes are persisted before the server can be terminated.

Which approach should you choose? That again is a decision you need to make on a game-by-game basis. Generally I find the simplicity offered by the stateless model most attractive; but for certain games, such as our MMORPG title Here Be Monsters (https://apps.facebook.com/herebemonsters), the player state is big and will continue to grow as more contents are introduced into the game. Thus the cost of the stateless approach becomes infeasible.

For Here Be Monsters, when we moved to the stateful server approach, we observed a 500% improvement in efficiency (that is, the same server can handle five times the number of concurrent requests) as well as a 60% reduction in average latency. With fewer game servers and database nodes to manage, it also eases day-to-day monitoring and maintenance of our production environment.

The HTTP server

To tie everything together for the server implementation, add another F# source file called HttpServer.fs just below GameEngine.fs.

Listing 11   HttpServer.fs

```
module SharpVille.Server.Http

open System
open System.IO
open System.Net

open SharpVille.Common.Utils
open SharpVille.Model
open SharpVille.Server.DAL
open SharpVille.Server.GameEngine

let inline handleReq (f : 'req -> 'resp) =
    (fun (req : HttpListenerRequest) (resp : HttpListenerResponse) ->
        async {
            let inputStream = req.InputStream
            let request = inputStream |> readJson<'req>
            try
                let response = f request
                writeJson response resp.OutputStream
                resp.OutputStream.Close()
            with
            | _ -> resp.StatusCode <- 500
                   resp.Close()
        })
```

Listing 11 contains a helper function, handleReq, that encapsulates the common plumbing code required for handling a web request:

1 Read the input stream as JSON.
2 Dispatch the request object to the specified handler function.
3 Write the response object as JSON to the output stream.
4 Handle exceptions.

For the JSON serialization, it uses the readJson and writeJson functions created earlier in listing 4. It uses an async workflow to perform these operations asynchronously.

Next, let's create a simple HttpListener (http://mng.bz/Y9a6) for each service endpoint to listen for incoming HTTP requests, handle the plumbing, and route the request to the corresponding method on the game engine. Just below the handleReq function, add the following HttpListener extension method and the startServer function.

Listing 12 Implementing the `HttpListener`

```
type HttpListener with                                   Extension method that starts a new instance
    static member Run (url:string, handler) =  ◄─┤  of HttpListener that continuously listens for
        let listener = new HttpListener()             incoming HTTP requests and starts a new
        listener.Prefixes.Add url                     F# async workflow to handle each request
        listener.Start()                              by invoking the supplied handler function

        let getContext = Async.FromBeginEnd(listener.BeginGetContext,
                                            listener.EndGetContext)
        async {
            while true do
                let! context = getContext
                Async.Start (handler context.Request context.Response)
        } |> Async.Start
        listener
let startServer (gameEngine : IGameEngine) =              ◄─┐  Helper function that
    HttpListener.Run("http://*:80/SharpVille/Handshake/",      creates the routing
                    handleReq gameEngine.Handshake)           from a specified HTTP
    |> ignore                                                 endpoint address to a
                                                              specified method on
    HttpListener.Run("http://*:80/SharpVille/Plant/",         the game engine
                    handleReq gameEngine.Plant)
    |> ignore

    HttpListener.Run("http://*:80/SharpVille/Harvest/",
                    handleReq gameEngine.Harvest)
    |> ignore
```

The startServer function configures the routing for all the service endpoints, using an implementation of the IGameEngine interface. If you need to add new service endpoints to support new features in the future, you can amend this function to add the new routing.

Implementing the client

Next, you'll add a project for the WPF client, using the project type F# Empty Windows Application (WPF). You should have access to this if you've followed along and installed the F# XAML Item Templates extension. Call this new project SharpVille .Client.WPF.

Exercise 3

One feature of SharpVille is the ability to visit a friend's farm. Now that the basic structure of the server implementation is in place, your task is to extend the game engine and the HTTP server to add support for this feature by adding a new `Visit` method to the game engine, which handles all calls to the HTTP endpoint http://*:80/SharpVille/Visit/.

The XAML

The newly created project will have the basic skeleton for your simple WPF client. Open and modify the MainWindow.xaml file as shown next.

Listing 13   Implementing the UI in XAML

```xaml
<Window xmlns="http://schemas.microsoft.com/winfx/2006/xaml/presentation"
        xmlns:x="http://schemas.microsoft.com/winfx/2006/xaml"
        Title="SharpVille" Height="650" Width="510" Margin="0">

    <Grid Margin="0" Name="MainContainer">                          ⟵⌐ The main
        <Grid.RowDefinitions>                                            container for
            <RowDefinition Height="50"></RowDefinition>                  the entire UI
            <RowDefinition Height="500"></RowDefinition>
            <RowDefinition Height="100"></RowDefinition>
        </Grid.RowDefinitions>

        <Grid Name="StateContainer" Background="DarkSlateGray">  ⟵⌐ The container
            <Grid.ColumnDefinitions>                                    for the game
                <ColumnDefinition Width="170"></ColumnDefinition>       state data
                <ColumnDefinition Width="130"></ColumnDefinition>
                <ColumnDefinition Width="200"></ColumnDefinition>
            </Grid.ColumnDefinitions>

            <StackPanel Orientation="Horizontal">               ⟵⌐ The container
                <Label Content="$ "                                     for the player's
                        Foreground="White" FontSize="30"               balance
                        FontWeight="Bold"></Label>
                <Label Content="{Binding Balance}"
                        Foreground="White" FontSize="30"
                        FontWeight="Bold"></Label>
            </StackPanel>                                             ⟵⌐ The container
                                                                         for the
            <StackPanel Orientation="Horizontal" Grid.Column="1">  ⟵    player's level
                <Label Content="LVL "
                        Foreground="White" FontSize="30"
                        FontWeight="Bold"></Label>
                <Label Content="{Binding Level}"
                        Foreground="White" FontSize="30"
                        FontWeight="Bold"></Label>
            </StackPanel>

            <Rectangle Name="NextLevel"
                Grid.Column="2" Fill="White" Margin="10"
                        HorizontalAlignment="Left" Width="200"></Rectangle>
```

Represent the player's progress (EXP) to the next level ⟶

```
                    <Rectangle Name="Exp"
                        Grid.Column="2" Fill="DodgerBlue" Margin="10"
                            HorizontalAlignment="Left" Width="0"></Rectangle>
                  </Grid>

                  <Grid Name="FarmPlotContainer" Grid.Row="1"
                            Height="500" Width="500" Margin="0"
                            VerticalAlignment="Top" HorizontalAlignment="Left">
                  </Grid>

                  <StackPanel Name="LeaderboardContainer" Grid.Row="2"
                            Height="100" Margin="0"
                            Background="White">
                  </StackPanel>
              </Grid>
          </Window>
```

The container for all the tiles where you can add plots to plant seeds (points to `<Grid Name="FarmPlotContainer"`)

The container for the leaderboard (points to `<StackPanel Name="LeaderboardContainer"`)

Represent the player's progress (EXP) to the next level (points to `<Rectangle Name="Exp"`)

Listing 13 creates a simple UI in XAML, based on the original mockup (shown earlier in figure 2). There are two things to note from this XAML.

First, you bind the Content of some labels to the Balance and Level properties of a yet-to-be-defined data type, which you'll use as the DataContext for this piece of the UI. This way, whenever the local player state is updated by the response from the server, the UI will automatically be updated to show the player's latest balance and level.

Second, you have two Rectangle objects—NextLevel and Exp—where the Exp rectangle is placed on top of the NextLevel rectangle but is invisible initially because its Width is set to 0. As you adjust the Width of the Exp rectangle based on the player's EXP and its relative distance to the next level, you can create a progress bar.

The UI generated by the XAML code should resemble figure 3.

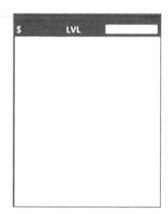

Figure 3 This is how the UI should look once you've finished updating MainWindow.xaml.

Representing the game state

Now that the basic UI is in place, you'll create a type to use as its DataContext. As mentioned earlier, the player state defined in the model doesn't define any behavior, and any server- or client-specific behavior will be implemented in the relevant projects.

For the client application, you want the player state to support data binding to make it easy for you to update the UI when the server responds with an updated state. In addition, other data is associated with the current state of the game but isn't part of the player state, such as the current session and game specification, which the client application requires to function and communicate with the server.

So, add an F# source file called GameState.fs (listing 14) to the top of the project. This file will contain all the data you need to represent the current state of the game from the client's perspective, including all the data you require to represent the player's state.

Listing 14 Representing the game state for the client

```
module GameState

open System.ComponentModel

open SharpVille.Model

type GameState (playerId : PlayerId) =
    let mutable sessionId : SessionId option          = None
    let mutable gameSpec  : GameSpecification option  = None
    let mutable dimension : Coordinate option         = None
    let mutable exp        : int64<exp>  = 0L<exp>
    let mutable level      : int<lvl>    = 0<lvl>
    let mutable balance    : int64<gold> = 0L<gold>
    let mutable plants                   = Map.empty<Coordinate, Plant>

    let event = Event<_, _>()

    member this.PlayerId                    = playerId
    member this.SessionId with get ()       = sessionId
                          and  set value    = sessionId <- value
    member this.GameSpec  with get ()       = gameSpec
                          and  set value    = gameSpec <- value
    member this.Dimension with get ()       = dimension
                          and  set value    = dimension <- value
    member this.Plants    with get ()       = plants
                          and  set value    = plants <- value

    member this.Exp                                              ◁──┐
        with get ()      = exp                                      │
        and set value =                                            │
          exp <- value                                            │
          event.Trigger(this, PropertyChangedEventArgs("Exp"))     │  These properties are
    member this.Level                                           ◁──┤  bound to the XAML
        with get ()      = level                                   │  and trigger the
        and set value =                                            │  PropertyChanged
          level <- value                                          │  event when they're
          event.Trigger(this, PropertyChangedEventArgs("Level"))   │  updated.
    member this.Balance                                         ◁──┘
        with get ()      = balance
        and set value =
          balance <- value
          event.Trigger(this, PropertyChangedEventArgs("Balance"))
    interface INotifyPropertyChanged with
        [<CLIEvent>]
        member this.PropertyChanged = event.Publish
```

In order to use this `GameState` type as the `DataContext` for the XAML UI and enable two-way binding on the `Balance` and `Level` properties, you need to implement the `INotifyPropertyChanged` interface (http://mng.bz/x07t). Unfortunately, this also means you can't implement the `GameState` type as an F# record, and you'll end up with something fairly verbose.

In practice, you can resort to using a library like Castle DynamicProxy, as demonstrated in chapter 7, to do the heavy lifting for you. Another alternative is to use C# here and use a weaver such as PostSharp (http://mng.bz/WbxL). But given that this is the only place where you've had to write verbose OO code so far, that hardly seems necessary.

Utility functions

Given the client-server nature of the game, it's reasonable to assume that you'll be making regular server calls from the client and, based on the response, updating the UI accordingly. To prevent your UI code from being convoluted due to server calls, you'll create a couple of helper functions for making these calls asynchronously. Add the following new F# source file called Utils.fs right below GameState.fs.

Listing 15   Utility.fs

```
module Utils

open System
open System.IO
open System.Net.Http
open System.Windows.Media

open SharpVille.Common
open SharpVille.Model
open SharpVille.Model.Requests
open SharpVille.Model.Responses

open GameState
let makeWebRequest<'req, 'res> action (req : 'req) =
    async {
        let url = sprintf "http://localhost:80/SharpVille/%s" action
        use clt = new HttpClient()

        use requestStream = new MemoryStream()
        writeJson req requestStream |> ignore
        requestStream.Position <- 0L

        let! response =
            clt.PostAsync(url, new StreamContent(requestStream))
            |> Async.AwaitTask
        response.EnsureSuccessStatusCode() |> ignore

        let! responseStream = response.Content.ReadAsStreamAsync()
                              |> Async.AwaitTask
        return readJson<'res> responseStream
    }
```

The makeWebRequest helper function is responsible for making the HTTP request to the server and deserializing the response into the desired type. To serialize and deserialize data to and from JSON, you're using the readJson and writeJson utility functions you created earlier in the chapter (listing 4).

From here, you can reuse the makeWebRequest function to build operation-specific helpers to make Handshake (listing 16), Plant (listing 17), and Harvest (listing 18) requests against the server.

Listing 16 Handshake helper

```
let doHandshake playerId onSuccess =
    async {
        let req = { PlayerID = playerId; Hash = "" }
        let! response = makeWebRequest<HandshakeRequest, HandshakeResponse>
                            "Handshake" req
        do! onSuccess response
    }
```

For the doHandshake helper function, you may have noticed that you deliberately set the Hash field in HandshakeRequest to an empty string. This is because you haven't yet implemented any authentication logic on the server to validate against the provided Hash value.

Listing 17 Plant helper

```
let doPlant x y sessionId seedId onSuccess =
    async {
        let req = {
                    SessionID = sessionId
                    Position = (x, y)
                    Seed = seedId
                }
        let! response = makeWebRequest<PlantRequest, PlantResponse>
                            "Plant" req
        do! onSuccess response
    }
```

Listing 18 Harvest helper

```
let doHarvest x y sessionId onSuccess =
    async {
        let req : HarvestRequest = {
                        SessionID = sessionId
                        Position = (x, y)
                    }
        let! response = makeWebRequest<HarvestRequest, HarvestResponse>
                            "Harvest" req
        do! onSuccess response

    }
```

Exercise 4: Adding support for failures

The example shown here handles only the success case, but in the real world things can go wrong at any moment—database operations can fail, the server could be terminated unexpectedly, or you could make an invalid request that fails server validation.

To ensure a smooth experience for the player, you must handle the errors gracefully. Your task is to modify the makeWebRequest function to handle error-response codes and display a message box with a user-friendly message.

The app

Finally, you'll create the client application that will hook up all the various pieces you've created thus far. In the SharpVille.Client.WPF project, modify the App.fs F# source file that was created as part of the template, as follows.

Listing 19   App.fs

```
module MainApp

open System
open System.IO
open System.Net.Http
open System.Threading
open System.Windows
open System.Windows.Controls
open System.Windows.Media
open System.Windows.Shapes
open System.Windows.Threading

open FSharpx

open SharpVille.Common
open SharpVille.Model
open SharpVille.Model.Requests
open SharpVille.Model.Responses

open GameState
open Utils

type MainWindow = XAML<"MainWindow.xaml">

let player = "test_player"

let emptyPlotBrush   = Brushes.ForestGreen
let plantedPlotBrush = Brushes.DarkGreen

let window = new MainWindow()
let root   = window.Root

let gameState = GameState(player)
root.DataContext <- gameStat
```

The project template uses the XAML type provider[14] to give you access to the elements defined in the MainWindow.xaml file.

For the purpose of the demo, use a hardcoded player ID.

Creates a new instance of the GameState type using the hardcoded player ID. By using it as the DataContext for the window, you allow the GameState.Balance and GameState.Level properties to be bound to the corresponding Label objects in the UI.

Most of the interesting operations you'll perform from here on will involve updating the current game state based on the response from the server. Remember the State-Response base type you created earlier in the chapter (listing 3)? We decided early on that any operation that will update the player state (Plant and Harvest so far) will return a response object that derives from the StateResponse. This means you can centralize the client-side handling of state updates in one place, and whenever you receive a StateResponse you should do the following:

- Mutate the existing GameState, which will automatically update the balance and level in the UI thanks to the two-way bindings you have in place.
- Recalculate the percentage progress toward the next level, and update the EXP progress bar accordingly.

---

[14] https://github.com/fsprojects/FsXaml.

With this in mind, add the following `updateState` function to App.fs.

Listing 20   `updateState` helper

```
let updateState syncContext (response : StateResponse) =
    async {
        gameState.Balance <- response.Balance
        gameState.Exp     <- response.Exp
        gameState.Level   <- response.Level
        gameState.Plants  <- response.Plants

        let expProgress =
            match gameState.GameSpec with
            | Some { Levels = lvls } ->
                let currLvlExp = lvls.[gameState.Level]
                match lvls.TryFind (gameState.Level + 1<lvl>) with
                | Some nxtLvlExp ->
                    let prog = float (gameState.Exp - currLvlExp)
                    let toNextLvl = float (nxtLvlExp - currLvlExp)
                    prog / toNextLvl
                | _ -> 0.0
            | _ -> 0.0

        do! Async.SwitchToContext syncContext
        let fullExpBarWidth = (window.NextLevel :?> Rectangle).Width
        let expBarWidth = fullExpBarWidth * expProgress
        (window.Exp :?> Rectangle).Width <- expBarWidth
    }
```

The EXP progress bar shows the percentage of EXP the player has gained toward the next level. For example, reaching levels 2 and 3 requires 10 and 24 EXP, respectively; if the player currently has 17 EXP, they're at level 2 and halfway to level 3.

This async workflow is most likely to be executed on a background thread, so you need to switch back to the UI thread to update the width of the Rectangle UI elements. You do so by calling the Async.SwtichToContext method with the SynchronizationContext object you'll capture when the application starts.

One important thing to understand about the `updateState` function is that it returns an async workflow that will be executed asynchronously.

Because WPF's UI elements can be updated only from the UI thread, you need to capture the `SynchronizationContext`[15] when the application starts and use it to switch back to the UI thread whenever you have to execute code to update any of the UI elements. The `updateState` function shown in listing 20 accepts the captured UI `SynchronizationContext` as input. It will perform its calculations on a background thread and only when ready use the `Async.SwitchToContext` (http://mng.bz/Jr0E) method to switch back to the UI thread to update the length of the EXP progress bar.

In the next listing, you'll add a couple of functions to perform the handshake, plant, and harvest operations. Because their response objects all inherit from `State-Response` (listing 3), your new `updateState` helper function will come in handy here.

---

[15] See Stephen Cleary, "It's All About the SynchronizationContext," *MSDN Magazine*, February 2011, http://mng.bz/5cDw.

Listing 21   Function that performs the handshake, plant, and harvest operations

```
let handshake syncContext = doHandshake player (fun resp ->
    gameState.Dimension <- Some resp.FarmDimension
    gameState.SessionId <- Some resp.SessionId
    gameState.GameSpec  <- Some resp.GameSpecification

    updateState syncContext resp)

let plant x y syncContext    =
    doPlant x y gameState.SessionId.Value "S1" <| updateState syncContext
let harvest x y syncContext =
    doHarvest x y gameState.SessionId.Value   <| updateState syncContext
```

Updates the UI to show the player's latest state

Uses Handshake-Response to update the current game state

For now, hardcoded to use seed S1

Remember the helper functions you added to Utils.fs in listing 16? They're doing most of the heavy lifting for you, and all you need to do here is give them continuations to call when a response has come back from the server.

Once the game has been initialized after a successful handshake, the player should be able to click anywhere on the grid to click farm plots to plant or harvest. If a farm plot is empty and the player has sufficient funds, then clicking the farm plot should create a server request to plant a seed there. Clicking a planted farm plot should create a server request to harvest the produce, if and only if the required growth time for that seed has passed.

Next you'll add an onClick function to handle what happens when the player clicks a farm plot (each represented as a Border UI element; see figure 4).

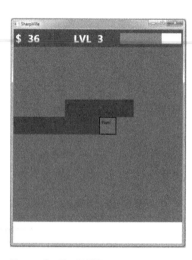

Figure 4   The WPF application running against the server code running locally

Listing 22   onClick handler

```
let (|Plant|_|) coordinate (gameState : GameState) =
    gameState.Plants.TryFind coordinate

let getPlotText x y =
    match gameState with
    | Plant (x, y) plant
        -> let dueDate = plant.DatePlanted.AddSeconds 30.0
           let now = DateTime.UtcNow
           if now >= dueDate then "Harvest"
           else sprintf "%ds" (dueDate - now).Seconds
    | _ -> "Plant"

let onClick x y syncContext (plot : Border) =
    async {
        match gameState with
        | Plant (x, y) plant
```

Returns the text you want to display over a farm plot depending on its current state

For now, hardcoded with a growth time of 30 seconds

Creates the async workflow that will be executed when a Border UI element representing a farm plot is clicked. Depending on the current state of the plot, it will make a server request to either harvest a planted plot or plant it with a seed.

```
                           -> let dueDate = plant.DatePlanted.AddSeconds 30.0
                              let now = DateTime.UtcNow
                              if now >= dueDate
                              then do! harvest x y syncContext
                                   do! Async.SwitchToContext syncContext
                                   plot.Background <- emptyPlotBrush
                                   do! Async.SwitchToThreadPool()
            | _ -> do! plant x y syncContext
                   do! Async.SwitchToContext syncContext
                   plot.Background <- plantedPlotBrush
                   do! Async.SwitchToThreadPool()
      }
```

For now, hardcoded with a growth time of 30 seconds

Finally, in the following listing, you add the finishing touches and initialize your WPF client.

Listing 23 Initializing the WPF application

```
let setUpFarmPlots syncContext (container : Grid) =
    async {
        let (Some (rows, cols)) = gameState.Dimension

        do! Async.SwitchToContext syncContext

        let plotWidth  = container.Width / float rows
        let plotHeight = container.Height / float cols

        { 0..rows-1 } |> Seq.iter (fun _ ->
            new RowDefinition(Height = new GridLength(plotHeight))
            |> container.RowDefinitions.Add)
        { 0..cols-1 } |> Seq.iter (fun _ ->
            new ColumnDefinition() |> container.ColumnDefinitions.Add)

        for rowNum = 0 to rows - 1 do
            for colNum = 0 to cols - 1 do
                let plot = new Border()
                plot.Width  <- plotWidth
                plot.Height <- plotHeight
                plot.Background        <-
                    match gameState with
                    | Plant (rowNum, colNum) _ -> plantedPlotBrush
                    | _ -> emptyPlotBrush
                plot.BorderBrush       <- Brushes.Black
                plot.BorderThickness <- new Thickness(0.0)

                plot.MouseEnter.Add(fun evt ->
                    plot.BorderThickness <- new Thickness(2.0))
                plot.MouseEnter.Add(fun evt ->
                    let label = new Label()
                    label.Content <- getPlotText rowNum colNum
                    plot.Child <- label)

                plot.MouseDown.Add(fun evt ->
                    onClick rowNum colNum syncContext plot |> Async.Start)

                plot.MouseLeave.Add(fun evt ->
                    plot.BorderThickness <- new Thickness(0.0))
                plot.MouseLeave.Add(fun evt -> plot.Child <- null)
```

Sets up the farm plots according to the current player state. The number of plots is based on the dimension of the player's farm. Each plot is represented by a simple Border element.

Uses a Border element to represent each farm plot

Hooks up the onClick function (from listing 22) whenever the MouseDown event is fired on a Border element

```
                Grid.SetRow(plot, rowNum)
                Grid.SetColumn(plot, colNum)

                container.Children.Add plot |> ignore          Captures the
    }                                                            SynchronizationContext
                                                                 for the UI thread so that
let loadWindow() =                                               you can use it later
    let syncContext =
        new DispatcherSynchronizationContext(Application.Current.Dispatcher)
        Threading.SynchronizationContext.SetSynchronizationContext(syncContext)

        async {
            do! handshake syncContext
            do! setUpFarmPlots syncContext window.FarmPlotContainer
        } |> Async.Start

        window.Root

[<STAThread>]
(new Application()).Run(loadWindow()) |> ignore
```

Exercise 5

In the onClick function in listing 22, you hardcoded 30 seconds as the time it takes a planted seed to become harvestable. But the amount of time required for a seed to grow is dependent on the type of seed planted, and that information is available in the game specification.

Your task is to modify the onClick function so that it uses the seed ID associated with the Plant instance to determine the growth time for the seed by looking into the current game state's GameSpec property. The GameSpecification type contains a Map of Seed objects keyed to their respective seed ID.

Exercise 6

In the plant function in listing 22, you hardcoded the seed ID to be S1 rather than letting players decide which seed to plant. Your task is to show a pop-up window that allows players to choose a seed from all the seeds their current level allows.

You can find all the available seeds in the current game specification. Each seed also specifies a RequiredLevel property that tells you what level players need to reach before they can use the seed.

If you're feeling courageous, try taking it a step further and remember the player's choice for all subsequent plant actions (so you don't interpret the playing experience with unnecessary pop-up windows) until the sequence is broken by a different action, such as harvesting.

Putting it together

At long last, you have a working prototype for both the server and the client! To get the server component up and running, you'll add a new F# application to the solution.

Call the project SharpVille.Server.Console. You'll use it to host your game server. Replace the default content of Program.fs so that it resembles the following listing.

Listing 24 Program.fs

```fsharp
open System

open SharpVille.Model
open SharpVille.Server.DAL
open SharpVille.Server.GameEngine
open SharpVille.Server.Http

[<EntryPoint>]
let main argv =
    let stateRepo    = InMemoryStateRepo()
    let sessionStore = InMemorySessionStore()

    let gameSpec =
        {
            Seeds =
                [|
                    ("S1", { Id = "S1"
                             RequiredLevel = 1<lvl>
                             Cost = 10L<gold>
                             GrowthTime = TimeSpan.FromSeconds 30.0
                             Yield = 12L<gold>
                             Exp = 1L<exp> })
                    ("S2", { Id = "S2"
                             RequiredLevel = 2<lvl>
                             Cost = 13L<gold>
                             GrowthTime = TimeSpan.FromSeconds 45.0
                             Yield = 16L<gold>
                             Exp = 2L<exp> })
                |] |> Map.ofSeq
            Levels      = [|
                            (1<lvl>,   0L<exp>)
                            (2<lvl>,  10L<exp>)
                            (3<lvl>,  24L<exp>)
                            (4<lvl>,  42L<exp>)
                            (5<lvl>,  64L<exp>)
                          |] |> Map.ofSeq
            DefaultState =
                {
                    PlayerId       = ""
                    Exp            = 0L<exp>
                    Level          = 1<lvl>
                    Balance        = 100L<gold>
                    FarmDimension  = 10, 10
                    Plants         = Map.empty
                }
        }

    let gameEngine = GameEngine(stateRepo, sessionStore, gameSpec)
                     :> IGameEngine
```

Specifies two seeds, S1 and S2, with different costs, growth times, and yields

Specifies five game levels

By default, a player has a 10 x 10 grid, which is a total of 100 farm plots.

```
startServer gameEngine

Console.ReadKey() |> ignore          Returns an
                                     integer exit code
0
```

Starting the console application starts the game server, which listens for requests on http://localhost:80/SharpVille/*. You can now start an instance of the WPF client to begin playing your very own SharpVille!

Summary

In this chapter, you designed and implemented a simple but nontrivial farming game that involves both client and server components. You designed the client-server interactions to enable the game features you desire, and you followed the request-response pattern for its extensibility.

This chapter focused on some of the implications of architectural decisions such as whether to store player states on the game servers or to shift the bulk of the processing onto the client. Along the way, you also explored current technology trends in the social gaming space, including the use of NoSQL databases and cloud computing and how they change the way you build large, web-scale applications.

Finally, you implemented a functional prototype of the farming game with a WPF client talking to a self-hosted game server over HTTP. Although the solution isn't feature complete, it has the basic structures in place, and you can easily extend it to incorporate additional features.

About the author

Yan Cui is a senior server-side developer at the social gaming division of Gamesys, where he focuses on building the infrastructure as well as server-side logic for the company's social games, which are played by nearly a million active players each day.

In his spare time, Yan enjoys researching and learning other technologies, and he's a big fan of functional programming, cloud computing, and NoSQL databases. Yan writes a programming blog at http://theburningmonk.com. He's also a PostSharp MVP and has been actively promoting the use of functional programming and aspect-oriented programming to developers in the United Kingdom.

## PART 4

F# in the larger context

When selecting the chapters for this book, I was lucky enough to get content from people who are successfully using F# to build a really interesting set of applications and systems. So, I have no doubt that you can now see the benefits of F# for your work and that you can think of projects or components where F# would be a great fit. Unfortunately, the world isn't that simple, and many other factors contribute to the choice of technology, especially in large companies.

In this last part of the book, we look at topics that can help you introduce F# into large and more complex ecosystems. In chapter 11, Chris Ballard talks about F# in the enterprise. You'll see how to use F# in an enterprise-friendly way; the key takeaway is that your F# projects need to smoothly interoperate, even if that means you occasionally have to resort to using mutable types or do additional work to make the interoperability hassle-free.

In chapter 12, Phil Trelford looks at software quality. The chapter starts from a bigger picture: "What is software quality about?" After answering that question, it covers a wide range of libraries and techniques that you can use to create tests in F#. Tests are often treated as second-class citizens in the codebase, so writing them in F# is a risk-free way of introducing F# into larger organizations. And as you'll see in Phil's chapter, testing can be fun!

11 F# in the enterprise

Chris Ballard

Let's be blunt: adoption of F# in the enterprise has two significant problems as things currently stand. First, existing enterprise developers typically don't know much about functional development; second, there aren't many people on the job market with demonstrable skills in functional development. Few companies can afford to send their entire development staff off to an intensive course in F# and functional programming, or to introduce this training as a general overhead for new joiners.

Organizations need to be smart and ensure that the way they develop code matches the experience levels of their development staff. Because F# is a CLR-based language, fully integrated into Visual Studio, it's easy to design software that uses F# for the "sweet spots" and C# for the rest (or even Visual Basic, if that floats your boat). Don't forget, also, that more and more functional concepts are being absorbed into the C# language, so the skills gap between imperative and functional development is definitely becoming narrower, at least in the .NET world.

In this chapter, I'll show you how F# can be used as one part of an overall enterprise project. Depending on the experience of the team, F# could play either a small or a large role. You'll use a sample project to explore building a small to medium-sized application using a mix of C# and F# (but I'm biased, so in this case it will be mostly F#!).

Sample project

To learn some of the practices needed to develop in F# as part of an enterprise development project, you'll develop an example application that mixes a number of technologies and is thus typical of a project in a corporate/commercial environment. I decided that a sensible, real-world application would be a desktop-based chat client, which allows multiple users to communicate with one another by joining a "room" and contributing to ongoing discussion threads within that room. You'll build the rough outline of this application next.

> **NOTE**   The completed application is available on GitHub here: https://
> github.com/ChrisBallard/ThePeopleWhoChat. I recommend download-
> ing it so that you can see the big picture as you work through the build-
> ing blocks in the following pages.

Obviously this is an F# book, so I'll try to keep as much of the coding in F# as possible.
You'll create a WPF application using Prism[1] for the UI and RavenDB[2] for storage.
You'll mix in some Representational State Transfer (REST) service calls and a bit of
security coding, and you'll have a good approximation of an enterprise application.
Some C# may be needed for the UI shell itself, and there will also be occasions where
perhaps something could be implemented in F#, but it's less effort and more maintainable to implement in C#. Let's see how this goes!

We'll start with some data

You'll use RavenDB for the database, because it's a modern, document-based database
designed from the ground up for the .NET platform. Also, its schema-less nature
aligns itself well to the fluidity of development in a functional language.

     As all well-behaved F# developers should, you'll start off in the F# Interactive (FSI)
window (for this chapter I'm using Microsoft Visual Studio 2012, Premium edition). First
you must install RavenDB and the .NET driver into a new Visual Studio solution using
NuGet.[3] Load the relevant assemblies into the FSI session (I've shortened the paths):

```
> #r @"...\Raven.Client.Lightweight.dll";;
--> Referenced ...\Raven.Client.Lightweight.dll'
```

This code loads the assemblies, so now you can reference the namespaces and create
some database connections. For all these demonstrations, you should have Raven
.Server.exe running locally to provide the simplest database connection logic. As you
can see here, you don't even need a connection string. All you need is to point the client to the server using the localhost URL and a default port number:

```
> open Raven;;
> open Raven.Client;;
> open Raven.Client.Document;;

> let ds = new DocumentStore();;
val ds : DocumentStore

> ds.Url <- "http://localhost:8080/";;
val it : unit = ()

> ds.Initialize();;
val it : IDocumentStore =
  Raven.Client.Document.DocumentStore
    {ApiKey = null;
     ...
     WasDisposed = false;}
```

---

[1]   Prism is a composite UI framework by Microsoft Patterns & Practices: compositewpf.codeplex.com.
[2]   RavenDB is a second-generation document database: http://ravendb.net.
[3]   NuGet is a package manager for third-party libraries—an extension for Visual Studio: http://nuget.org.

NOTE Although F# doesn't require the new keyword (used here to create the `DocumentStore`), I recommend still using it, to avoid confusing any C# developers who find themselves in the F# code. I'll mention how important it is to avoid confusing C# developers coming to F# several times in this chapter, because I think it's a key to success of any application that mixes C# and F# code.

RavenDB deals in collections and documents, which roughly translate to tables and rows in traditional relational database parlance. In addition, by default RavenDB will attempt to infer collection names based on the name of the type that you save, and there's no need for create commands—the first time a document is saved, the database will create the collection for you. So you can go straight into this code:

```
> let session = ds.OpenSession();;
val session : IDocumentSession

> type User = { mutable Id:string; name:string; password:string };;
type User =
  { mutable Id: string;
    name: string;
    password: string;}

> let bob = { Id = null; name = "bob"; password = "password123" };;
val bob : User = {Id = null;
                  name = "bob";
                  password = "password123";}

> session.Store(bob);;
val it : unit = ()

> bob.Id;;
val it : string = "users/1"

> session.SaveChanges();;
val it : unit = ()

> session.Query<User>() |> Array.ofSeq;;
val it : User [] = [|{Id = "users/1";
                      name = "bob";
                      password = "password123";}|]
```

Defines the record User and creates a user value

Stores the user Bob in RavenDB and checks the assigned ID

Commits changes to the data store

Retrieves all users from the database

Notice that at no point did you have to tell RavenDB to create a collection for users or even define what the schema for users is. You're able to create a new user and store it in the database just like that.

The pragmatic F# developer knows when to compromise

Although RavenDB can automatically serialize and deserialize documents that are F# record types, you have to make the `Id` field mutable in order for the automated identity generation to be able to work. Here you've encountered a typical compromise in F# development: you have to sacrifice the purity of an immutable type in order to gain from the flexibility of interoperating with an object-oriented third-party framework. The pragmatic enterprise F# developer will recognize and embrace these situations!

At this point, you've done enough experimentation to be able to understand how to create a central type for the chat room service, within which you can encapsulate the database connection details alongside all data operations. Next, you'll create a new F# Library project, add a package reference to the RavenDB client assemblies using NuGet, and finally add a new a new F# source file containing the following code.

Listing 1   ChatDataConnection.fs, a function within a module

```
module Data
open Raven.Client.Document

let ChatDataConnection(dbPath:string) =
    let docStore = new DocumentStore(Url = dbPath)
    docStore.Initialize()
```

This code demonstrates a typical way to write an F# module: you aren't specifically defining any .NET types here, and although this is a reasonable (or possibly even the definitive) way to construct code in an F#-only application, it violates the *principle of least surprise* for a project shared with C# code (and therefore C# developers). See figure 1 for a look at ILSpy[4] that shows what sort of Intermediate Language (IL) code (decompiled into C#) is generated by listing 1.

You can see that the module Data is translated into a static class, and the function ChatDataConnection becomes a static method of that class. This class exists within the default namespace.

Note that this code is perfectly interoperable with C#—you can refer to the static method as Data.ChatDataConnection()—but in an enterprise scenario, I recommend ensuring that any public types are created within namespaces, and as types that "play nicely" with C# code—for example, object types or records—wherever possible.

```
using Microsoft.FSharp.Core;
using Raven.Client;
using Raven.Client.Document;
using System;
[CompilationMapping(SourceConstructFlags.Module)]
public static class Data
{
    public static IDocumentStore ChatDataConnection(string dbPath)
    {
        DocumentStore docStore = new DocumentStore
        {
            Url = dbPath
        };
        return docStore.Initialize();
    }
}
```

Figure 1   Decompiled IL code generated for inline F# within a module

---

[4]   ILSpy is an open source .NET assembly browser and decompiler: http://ilspy.net.

```
using Microsoft.FSharp.Core;
using Raven.Client;
using Raven.Client.Document;
using System;
namespace ThePeopleWhoChat.Data
{
    [CompilationMapping(SourceConstructFlags.ObjectType)]
    [Serializable]
    public class ChatDataConnection
    {
        internal DocumentStore docStore;
        public ChatDataConnection(string dbPath) : this()
        {
            this.docStore = new DocumentStore
            {
                Url = dbPath
            };
            IDocumentStore documentStore = this.docStore.Initialize();
        }
        public IDocumentSession GetSession()
        {
            return this.docStore.OpenSession();
        }
    }
}
```

Figure 2 Decompiled IL code generated for an F# type defined within a namespace

The database connection may need to be called from C# code, so let's clean things up and refactor the previous snippet into an object type, declared within a namespace (see the following listing).

Listing 2   ChatDataConnection.fs as an F# type within a namespace

```
namespace ThePeopleWhoChat.Data
open Raven.Client.Document

type ChatDataConnection(dbPath:string) =
    let docStore = new DocumentStore(Url = dbPath)
    do docStore.Initialize() |> ignore

    member this.GetSession() =
        docStore.OpenSession()
```

Listing 2 produces code that's much more aligned to object-oriented development (see figure 2) and that therefore will result in fewer headaches and less confusion for your C# developers!

Now that you have the encapsulated connection code, you can check it out by choosing Execute in Interactive (or pressing Alt-Enter) to use this new type in the FSI window:

```
type ChatDataConnection =
  class
    new : dbPath:string -> ChatDataConnection
    member GetSession : unit -> IDocumentSession
  end
```

```
> let con = ChatDataConnection("http://localhost:8080");;
val con : ChatDataConnection

> let session = con.GetSession();;
val session : IDocumentSession

> session.Query<User>() |> Array.ofSeq;;
val it : User [] = [|{Id = "users/1";
                      name = "bob";
                      password = "password123";}|]
```

Next you'll create a connection to the database. You've reached the point where you'd like to store the rest of the data. With F# record types, you have a lightweight way to define a hierarchy of data access objects, as shown next.

Listing 3   Defining some types for your data objects

```
type User =
  { mutable Id: string;
    name: string;
    passwordHash: string;
    fullName: string;
    isAdmin: bool }

type Room =
  { mutable Id: string;
    name: string;
    description: string }

type Message =
  { mutable Id: string;
    roomId: string;
    timestamp: DateTime;
    userName: string;
    rawMessage: string;
    html: string }
```

> **TIP**   Because of the conciseness of F# type definitions, I recommend ignoring the "one class per file" mandate of C# development. Try to group these definitions into one appropriately named F# source file per logical group—for example, DataTypes.fs for listing 3.

At this point, you have a database connection helper and some serializable data types. To conclude this section, let's bring this all together and look at what it takes to store and retrieve this data from the local RavenDB database.

Listing 4   Putting it all together

```
namespace ThePeopleWhoChat.Data

open Raven.Client
open Raven.Client.Document

type ChatDataConnection(dbPath:string) =
    let docStore = new DocumentStore(Url = dbPath)
    do docStore.Initialize() |> ignore
```

```
member private this.sessionWrapper<'a>
        saveAfter (f:IDocumentSession -> 'a) =
    use session = docStore.OpenSession()
    let result = f(session)
    if saveAfter then session.SaveChanges()
    result

member this.AddUser(user:User) =
    this.sessionWrapper true (fun sess -> sess.Store(user))

member this.DeleteUser(user:User) =
    this.sessionWrapper true (fun sess -> sess.Delete(user))

member this.ListUsers() =
    this.sessionWrapper false (fun sess ->
        sess.Query<User>() |> Array.ofSeq)
// (...)
```

Methods for working with rooms and messages omitted

In listing 4, the connection type is expanded to include methods for each of the key data operations that you want to encapsulate. Note also that session management is moved into a higher-order function, `sessionWrapper`, which provides a convenient way for each implementation method to manage its session, including an option to automatically save changes on completion.

The database you've created is rudimentary at the moment; you haven't thought much about schema or requirements for indexing, for example. But RavenDB allows you to work this way. You have enough in place to move on to the REST-based service, which you'll learn about in the next section.

Creating the basic service implementation

You could allow the client to connect to RavenDB directly via its own REST interface, but you need to provide a further abstraction in order to manage session state and security. The next step, therefore, is to implement a Windows Communication Foundation (WCF) REST service as a middle tier for the application.

Following best practices, you'll put the service implementation in a separate project, say `ThePeopleWhoChat.Service`, which references the projects with core data types and data access layer implemented in the previous section. Once the project is created, begin by defining the operations to be used by the service. The following listing shows the F# type signatures of the functions you'll implement.

Listing 5 Service operations

```
Login: string * string -> string
Logout: string -> unit

AddUser: string * User -> string
RemoveUser: string * string -> unit
ListUsers: string -> User array
```

Listing 5 starts with a few functions that manage the session state: `Login`, which takes a username and password and returns a session token; and `Logout`, which takes the session token and returns nothing. All other functions require a valid session token as the first parameter—a robust but not particularly scalable security implementation. This implementation will suffice for this application, because you'll be supporting only a few hundred concurrent user connections.

Let's look at how you implement the main service type with one of the more trivial member functions: ListUsers. This function doesn't alter state and returns a list of users; in REST terms, this aligns with the HTTP GET verb, which is implemented in WCF as shown next.

Listing 6 Implementing an operation with HTTP GET

Specifies service hosting properties ①
Creates an instance of the data access layer ②
Obtains the token returned by the Login operation ④

```
[<ServiceContract>]
[<ServiceBehaviorAttribute
  ( ConcurrencyMode=ConcurrencyMode.Single,
    InstanceContextMode=InstanceContextMode.Single )>]
[<AspNetCompatibilityRequirements
  ( RequirementsMode = AspNetCompatibilityRequirementsMode.Allowed )>]
type ChatService() =

    let dbUrl = ConfigurationManager.AppSettings.[Consts.DbUrlSettingKey]
    let data = ChatDataConnection(dbUrl) :> IChatServiceClient

    [<WebGet( UriTemplate="users",ResponseFormat=WebMessageFormat.Json,
              BodyStyle=WebMessageBodyStyle.Bare )>]
    [<OperationContract>]
    member this.ListUsers() =
        try
            let request = WebOperationContext.Current.IncomingRequest
            let token = request.Headers.["Session-Token"]
            data.ListUsers(token)
        with Failure(e) ->
            let response = WebOperationContext.Current.OutgoingResponse
            response.StatusCode <- HttpStatusCode.BadRequest
            Array.empty
```

Specifies properties of the exposed HTTP GET method ③

This listing defines a type ChatService with a single method ListUsers. It uses ASP.NET and WCF to host the service, so the class and the method are annotated with attributes that specify how to host the service ① and how the method should be exposed as an HTTP GET operation ③.

You assume the caller will add an HTTP header to the incoming request containing the session token ④, which it obtains via a call to the Login operation you'll add in listing 7. You defer all the session management to the DB connection type, a single instance of which is maintained by the service implementation ②.

Notice, though, that you need a lot of boilerplate code to handle the token and to marshal service failures into an HTTP-friendly status code result. You can make things easier here by adding a function to wrap all the boilerplate code. Listing 7 shows a number of reusable helper functions and a nicer implementation of ListUsers. Note that it doesn't repeat the class declaration ① and initialization of the connection ②, because those stay the same.

```
let getToken() =
    let request = WebOperationContext.Current.IncomingRequest
    request.Headers.["Session-Token"]
```
Returns the token from the current request

```
let setFault status err =
    let response = WebOperationContext.Current.OutgoingResponse
    response.StatusCode <- status
    response.Headers.Add("Error-Message",err)
```
Sets the error code with an error message

```
let badrequest = setFault HttpStatusCode.BadRequest
```
Uses partial function application to report a "bad request"

```
let implementationWrapper empty f =
    try getToken() |> f
    with Failure(e) ->
        e |> badrequest
        empty
```
Wrapper calls the specified function ❶ with the token

```
[<WebGet(UriTemplate="users",ResponseFormat=WebMessageFormat.Json,
    BodyStyle=WebMessageBodyStyle.Bare)>]
[<OperationContract>]
member this.ListUsers() =
    implementationWrapper Array.empty (fun token ->
        data.ListUsers(token) )
```
Implementation becomes just two lines!

With the addition of a few helper functions and the implementation wrapper ❶, you now have a more succinct means of defining service operations. The wrapper manages the token and handles service failures. You should probably expand it to specifically handle missing or invalid tokens and return `NotAuthorized`, but we won't go into that now.

Note that the implementation wrapper function takes as arguments both of the following:

- A function that's used to determine the correct result value
- A value, of the same type as that function's return type, to represent an empty result should the function call result in an exception

With the `implementationWrapper` function in place, adding new operations becomes easy. The following operation adds a new user to the database.

```
[<WebInvoke(Method = "PUT", UriTemplate="users",
            RequestFormat = WebMessageFormat.Json,
            ResponseFormat = WebMessageFormat.Json,
            BodyStyle = WebMessageBodyStyle.Bare)>]
[<OperationContract>]
member this.AddUser(user:User) =
    implementationWrapper "" (fun token ->
        data.AddUser(token,user) )
```
Specifies the request and response format

This function takes a data structure as input. In order for this to work, you tell .NET to send it over the wire formatted as a JSON string ❶. Note how the framework automatically handles the input parameters and function result for you, so all you have to do is call the same implementation wrapper you defined earlier. Finally, let's look at a method that takes input parameters as part of the URL in true REST style.

Listing 9   Implementing an operation with HTTP DELETE

```
[<WebInvoke(Method = "DELETE", UriTemplate="users/{userIdNumPart}")>]     ◁─┐
[<OperationContract>]
member this.RemoveUser(userIdNumPart:string) =              Specifies a URI
    implementationWrapper () (fun token ->                  parameter format
        data.RemoveUser(token,"users/"+userIdNumPart) )     for the method  ①
```

This listing shows all the wiring you need to carry on and complete the service implementation. You'll have groups of functions for management of users and passwords, management of rooms, and posting and listing of messages from users in the rooms.

Creating a client wrapper for the service

In the previous section, you defined and implemented your REST-based web service. Next you'll create a new type that wraps service calls into simple member functions in order to allow the service to be easily called through your UI code.

You can either place the code for the client into a new project or add it to the project that defines the core data types for the application (ThePeopleWhoChat.Core). After you add a new file, you start by creating a class ServiceClient. Next, you'll put together the basic code needed in order to call a method with the HTTP GET verb and deserialize a JSON formatted result. The following listing shows the first version of the implementation (without the enclosing class).

Listing 10   Making an HTTP GET service call

```
member this.ListUsers(token:string) =
    let url = "http://localhost:53691/Chat.svc"
    let fullPath = String.Format("{0}/{1}",url,"users")
    let req = WebRequest.Create(new Uri(fullPath)) :?> HttpWebRequest
    req.Method <- "GET"
    req.Headers.Add("Session-Token",token)
    let res = req.GetResponse() :?> HttpWebResponse
    use resSt = res.GetResponseStream()
    let ser = DataContractJsonSerializer(typeof<User array>)
    ser.ReadObject(resSt) :?> User array
```

Once again there's a lot of boilerplate code here. Pretty much any of the REST service calls you make will follow a standard pattern: you provide a URL and optionally serialize some data in JSON format in the outgoing request, you make the request, and finally, also optionally, you deserialize JSON data from the response stream into a result (as you did earlier). Using this pattern, you can easily define a few functions that encapsulate all possible REST calls for you.

Listing 11 shows the helper functions that let you reduce the code duplication. Once you read the helper functions, you'll find a couple of methods that use them in listing 12.

Listing 11 Encapsulating REST service calls

```fsharp
type Consts =
    static member TokenHeaderName = "Session-Token"
    static member ErrorHeaderName = "Error-Message"

let jsonSerialize (data:'T) =
    use ms = new MemoryStream()
    let ser = new DataContractJsonSerializer(typeof<'T>)
    ser.WriteObject(ms, data)
    ms.Seek(0L,SeekOrigin.Begin) |> ignore
    use sr = new StreamReader(ms)
    sr.ReadToEnd()

let makeRequest verb (data:'T) (token,urlPath:string) =
    let fullPath = String.Format("{0}/{1}",url,urlPath)
    let req = WebRequest.Create(new Uri(fullPath)) :?> HttpWebRequest
    req.Method <- verb
    req.Headers.Add(Consts.TokenHeaderName,token)
    if not (typeof<'T> = typeof<unit>) then
        let json = jsonSerialize(data)
        let buffer = Encoding.UTF8.GetBytes(json)
        req.ContentType <- "application/json"
        req.ContentLength <- buffer.LongLength
        use reqSt = req.GetRequestStream()
        reqSt.Write(buffer,0,buffer.Length)
    req

let webRequestWrapper (f:unit->'U) =
    try f()
    with :? WebException as e ->
        let resp = e.Response :?> HttpWebResponse
        let err = resp.Headers.[Consts.ErrorHeaderName]
        let msg =
            match box err with
            | null -> "Service failure"
            | _ -> err
        failwith (sprintf "%s: status = %d (%s)" msg
            (int32 resp.StatusCode) (resp.StatusCode.ToString()))

let getResponse (req:HttpWebRequest):'U =
    webRequestWrapper (fun () ->
        let res = req.GetResponse() :?> HttpWebResponse
        use resSt = res.GetResponseStream()
        let ser = DataContractJsonSerializer(typeof<'U>)
        ser.ReadObject(resSt) :?> 'U )

let getResponseUnit (req:HttpWebRequest):unit =
    webRequestWrapper(fun () ->
        req.GetResponse() |> ignore )

let getData (token,urlPath):'U =
    makeRequest "GET" () (token,urlPath) |> getResponse
let putDataUnit (token,urlPath,data:'T) =
    makeRequest "PUT" data (token,urlPath) |> getResponseUnit
let putData (token,urlPath,data:'T):'U =
    makeRequest "PUT" data (token,urlPath) |> getResponse
```

Helper that serializes data and returns JSON as a string

Creates a web request for the URL sub-path

If the data isn't of type unit, serialize it into the request as JSON

Runs the specified function and handles exceptions

Makes a web request and serializes the JSON response data

Makes a web request and ignores the returned response

Operations that capture different HTTP verbs (PUT, POST, and GET)

```
let postData (token,urlPath,data:'T):'U =
    makeRequest "POST" data (token,urlPath) |> getResponse
let deleteData (token,urlPath) =
    makeRequest "DELETE" () (token,urlPath) |> getResponseUnit
```

> **Operations that capture different HTTP verbs (PUT, POST, and GET)**

We won't go through listing 11 line by line, but you can see that you're able to use the pattern defined in the previous section to give you the makeRequest method for creating the outgoing request, with or without data, and two versions of getResponse: one for making the call and getting result data, and the other for just making a "fire and forget" call. Additionally, you've created some utility functions to wrap based on the HTTP verb; these functions will allow your wrapper implementation methods to be simple.

Listing 1.2   Simplified service wrapper implementation

```
member this.AddUser(token:string, user:User) =
    putData (token,"users",user)

member this.RemoveUser(token:string, userId:string) =
    if userId.StartsWith("users/") then deleteData (token,userId)
    else failwith (sprintf "invalid userId: %s" userId)

member this.ListUsers(token:string):User array =
    getData (token,"users")
```

Giving your application a user interface

The subject of UI development is a thorny one in the world of functional languages. This style of development is, by its very nature, littered with parallel paths of execution and rife with side effects. In this section you'll see that by using a mixture of imperative object-oriented code and pragmatic functional code, you can reach a reasonable compromise.

The UI you'll develop won't be much more than a skeleton (the topic would warrant a book in its own right) but will hopefully demonstrate how an enterprise-scale client could be developed, with mixed language development. You'll use the Prism framework to develop a UI based on a shell written in C#, with a plug-in module developed in F#.

> **NOTE** I'll assume that you're familiar with Prism; if not, plenty of resources are available to help get you started. When writing this chapter, I re-familiarized myself using "Modularity QuickStarts Using the Prism Library 5.0 for WPF" at http://mng.bz/Zv8f.

Creating the basic Prism shell

To get started, you need a shell for your UI. The shell serves as the point for initializing all the wiring within Prism (showing it how to locate all the services and UI components) and provides the main window inside which all other UI components will reside.

NOTE For the purposes of demonstration, you'll start with a desktop C# WPF application: ThePeopleWhoChat.App.CS. The project could be implemented as an F# application too, but it makes a good demonstration to try to build the shell as a C# application and the plug-in UI modules as F# assemblies.

Using NuGet, search for the online package `Prism.UnityExtensions` and install it (in turn, it installs Prism itself, because this is a package dependency). This installs Prism with the Unity IoC container. Out of the box, Prism also supports MEF, so feel free to use that (by installing `Prism.MEFExtensions`), if that's your preference. The examples in this chapter use Unity.

Take a look at the source code for this application, or the Stock Trader demo application on the Prism CodePlex download, for more in-depth details. The shell boils down to the following components:

- *App.xaml.cs*—Used to override the default WPF application initialization.
- *Bootstrapper.cs*—A Prism artifact used to initialize the application and to facilitate module discovery and loading.
- *Mainwindow.xaml*—The outer view of the shell. Can contain normal WPF elements and also container elements into which the modular UI is hosted.
- *Modules.xaml*—The runtime configuration for resolving the location of plug-in modules.

For an initial demonstration, you'll define two F# libraries to contain your UI modules and dynamically load them via the module catalog in Modules.xaml.

Listing 13   Loading the F# modules with a module catalog

```xml
<Modularity:ModuleCatalog
    xmlns="http://schemas.microsoft.com/winfx/2006/xaml/presentation"
    xmlns:x="http://schemas.microsoft.com/winfx/2006/xaml"
    xmlns:sys="clr-namespace:System;assembly=mscorlib"
    xmlns:Modularity="clr-namespace:Microsoft.Practices.Prism.Modularity;
        assembly=Microsoft.Practices.Prism">
    <Modularity:ModuleInfo ModuleName="RoomsList"
        Ref="file://ThePeopleWhoChat.App.RoomsList.dll"
        ModuleType="ThePeopleWhoChat.App.RoomsList.ModuleDef,
            ThePeopleWhoChat.App.RoomsList, Version=1.0.0.0,
            Culture=neutral, PublicKeyToken=null">
    </Modularity:ModuleInfo>
    <Modularity:ModuleInfo ModuleName="MessagesList"
        Ref="file://ThePeopleWhoChat.App.MessagesList.dll"
        ModuleType="ThePeopleWhoChat.App.MessagesList.ModuleDef,
            ThePeopleWhoChat.App.MessagesList, Version=1.0.0.0,
            Culture=neutral, PublicKeyToken=null">
    </Modularity:ModuleInfo>
</Modularity:ModuleCatalog>
```

We'll explore the implementation of these modules in F# shortly, but to finish the shell, you need to ensure that MainWindow.xaml has placeholders into which Prism will wire your dynamically loaded views. You can do so with the `ContentControl` type, as shown in the following listing.

Listing 14   Hosting dynamic UI content with `ContentControl`

```
<Window x:Class="ThePeopleWhoChat.App.CS.MainWindow"
        xmlns:Regions="http://www.codeplex.com/prism"
        ... >
        <ContentControl
            Regions:RegionManager.RegionName="RoomsList" />
        <ContentControl
            Regions:RegionManager.RegionName="MessagesList" />
        ...
</Window>
```

Creating a Prism WPF plug-in module in F#

To complete this demonstration application, let's now look at how you go about writing the Prism plug-ins for WPF completely in F#. As with a standalone desktop application, you get some disadvantages in terms of Visual Studio integration. Unfortunately, at the moment you can't automatically wire a WPF (XAML) window to code-behind in F#. You'll need to do some manual wiring to connect the declarative XAML file to the code-behind type.

Even more unfortunately, a technique[5] I used previously for Silverlight doesn't translate to WPF; this is because the `Application.LoadComponent` method when called in a WPF application expects the resource stream to be BAML (the binary XAML format) and not plain XAML, which is what you get when you set the compile action to Resource.

To circumvent this limitation, I've discovered a technique to dynamically load the XAML file from an embedded resource and to use this definition to override the visual content in the code-behind file. The next listing shows this technique.

Listing 15   Dynamically loading XAML from an embedded resource

```
namespace ThePeopleWhoChat.App.RoomsList

open System.Reflection
open System.Windows.Controls
open System.Windows.Markup

type RoomsListView() as this =
    inherit UserControl()

    do
        let asm = Assembly.GetExecutingAssembly()
        let sr = asm.GetManifestResourceStream("RoomsListView.xaml")
        this.Content <- XamlReader.Load(sr) :?> UserControl
```

---

[5] See my blog (roundthecampfire.net) post "Creating Composable UI with F# and Prism" at http://mng.bz/ SF9d.

Put the contents of listing 15 in a new file, RoomsListView.fs. This represents the code-behind for the control. Next, create the corresponding file, RoomsListView.xaml, containing the XAML from listing 16. Before you compile the project, set the build action of the XAML file to Embedded Resource.

Listing 16   RoomsListView.xaml

```
<UserControl
    xmlns="http://schemas.microsoft.com/winfx/2006/xaml/presentation"
    xmlns:x="http://schemas.microsoft.com/winfx/2006/xaml" >

    <Grid x:Name="LayoutRoot" Background="Green">
        <TextBlock FontSize="36">Hello, Modular UI</TextBlock>
    </Grid>
</UserControl>
```

Later you can create a `ViewModel` type and wire it in as a data context for the `Layout-Root` Grid control, but for the time being you need to create the `ModuleDef` type (defined earlier in `modules.xaml`) and use it to allow Prism to discover the `Rooms-ListView` (see the following listing).

Listing 17   ModuleDef.fs

```
namespace ThePeopleWhoChat.App.RoomsList

open Microsoft.Practices.Prism.Modularity
open Microsoft.Practices.Prism.Regions
open Microsoft.Practices.Unity

type ModuleDef(rm: IRegionManager) =
    interface IModule with
        member this.Initialize() =
            rm.RegisterViewWithRegion("RoomsList", typeof<RoomsListView>)
            |> ignore
```

Note that this type will be initialized by Unity, which will pass in the requested `IRegion-Manager` to the constructor. You use `IRegionManager` to register the view type for the `RoomsList` region name, which corresponds to the region name in the main window `ContentControl`. It's simpler than it sounds once you get used to it!

You now have all the wiring you need (in the full source code for the project, I provide a similar implementation for the `MessagesList` module in a separate F# assembly). So if you run this application now, the main window is shown, and it includes content from the two F# plug-in assemblies, as shown in figure 3.

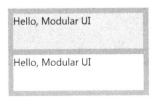

Figure 3   Output showing the main window contents, including visual elements from the two F# modules

Making your service available throughout the application

The visual wiring is complete. You can host the module UI implemented in F# in your C#-based shell. It's not much use unless you can connect to your backend data and ensure that each module can present an appropriate UI representation of that data.

To kick off this process, you'll need to set up a connection to your service layer in the application shell. So in `Bootstrapper.cs`, you'll override `ConfigureContainer`.

Listing 18   Registering the service client wrapper instance with `ConfigureContainer`

```
protected override void ConfigureContainer()
{
    base.ConfigureContainer();

    string url = "http://localhost:53691/Chat.svc";
    IChatService svc = new ServiceClient(url);
    svc.Login("root", "password1");

    Container.RegisterInstance(typeof(IChatService), null, svc,
        new ContainerControlledLifetimeManager());
}
```

For the time being, you'll hardcode the service URL and forgo a login dialog box in favor of automatically logging in as root—clearly not much use for a multiuser chat application, but at least I can demonstrate getting real data through the service to the UI.

Once you register this service with Unity, it's automatically available in any other types configured by Unity. So, to make it available to your plug-in modules, add a constructor parameter of type `IChatService` to the relevant view type—for example, the `RoomsListView`:

```
type RoomsListView(model:IChatService) as this =
    ...
```

With this knowledge, you can now create a view model class, allowing a bridge between the view and any data you need to extract from the model. In this case, you'll populate a collection of rooms by calling `ListRooms` on the service.

Listing 19   Creating RoomsListViewModel.fs

```
type RoomsListViewModel(model:IChatService) =
    let rooms = new ObservableCollection<Room>(model.ListRooms())
    member this.Rooms = rooms
```

Next, update `RoomsListView` to create an instance of the view model and attach it as `DataContext` for the top-level component.

Listing 20   Binding to the view model in the revised RoomsListView.fs

```
type RoomsListView(model:IChatService) as this =
    inherit UserControl()
```

```
do
    let asm = Assembly.GetExecutingAssembly()
    let sr = asm.GetManifestResourceStream("RoomsListView.xaml")
    let root = XamlReader.Load(sr) :?> UserControl
    root.DataContext <- new RoomsListViewModel(model) :> obj;
    this.Content <- root
```

And finally, you can update RoomsListView.xaml to add a `DataGrid` control and a binding from that to the view model's `Rooms` property.

Listing 21   Adding a bound `DataGrid` to RoomsListView.xaml

```
<UserControl
    xmlns="http://schemas.microsoft.com/winfx/2006/xaml/presentation"
    xmlns:x="http://schemas.microsoft.com/winfx/2006/xaml">
    <Grid x:Name="LayoutRoot" Background="LightGray">
        <DataGrid ItemsSource="{Binding Rooms}" />
    </Grid>
</UserControl>
```

That's your application, wired end to end. If you run this application, you can see that the service gets called from the rooms-list plug-in and that part of the UI shell is populated with real data, as shown in figure 4.

This is as far as you'll take the UI development. It's not pretty yet, but you can see how easy it is to develop an application composed of separate UI modules written in different languages.

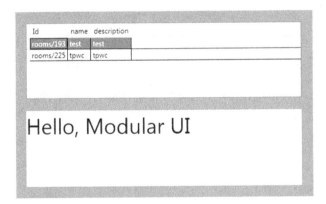

Figure 4   Output showing the main window with the rooms list populated from the service call

Summary

Obviously it isn't possible to cover the development of a major application in just a few pages. This chapter has touched on the thought process involved at the major decision points in the development of a modestly sized application, and you learned how to make pragmatic decisions about the use of F#.

In developing the database access layer, you saw how the use of F# record types provides simplifications over a similar C# implementation. You also saw how it's good practice to carefully encapsulate F# code within an object-oriented type, whose external signature will be more or less identical to an equivalent C# implementation and whose implementation will at least be understandable by anyone unfamiliar with F#.

In the service layer, you learned how to implement a REST-based service and a client wrapper entirely in F#. In addition, you saw how you can distill the implementation of the service methods and client wrapper methods down to a bare minimum through the use of higher-order functions in F#.

Finally in the UI layer, you bowed to pragmatism a little by implementing the shell itself in C#, but you saw how a technology like Prism can mean that even the UI can consist of a mixture of F# and C# components.

About the author

Chris Ballard is a senior developer and architect currently working in the financial services industry. Over the years Chris has worked on defense systems, test equipment, transportation systems, police databases, and robotic life science systems. He mostly develops in C# by day (although F# is creeping in slowly but surely), and he's a strong advocate of F# by night. You can reach Chris here: @_ChrisBallard on Twitter.

Software quality

Phil Trelford

Software quality means different things to different groups of people. In this chapter, I'll look at software quality through the perspective of my personal experience—which includes creating video games, writing a line of business applications, and, most recently, developing financial systems.

In video games and front office trading systems, performance is often the key quality issue. Arcade games typically run at 60 frames per second so they feel responsive to the player. Trading screens must also respond to user input in milliseconds, particularly during periods of high market activity, so users can take positions and (often more important) exit those positions if the market turns against them. As discussed in chapter 1, F# is compiled and efficient. We'll look at techniques for monitoring performance to make sure your F# code satisfies the performance requirements of your project.

For many line of business (LOB) applications, performance is less of an issue, and the focus is on building out functionality. Getting precise requirements isn't always easy to achieve, because often customers don't know at the start exactly what they want. To rapidly respond to changing business requirements, code should be either extensible or modular so that parts can be replaced in isolation. In video games, the game logic is often written in a scripting language like Lua, for rapid prototyping and easy change. In F#, you can achieve similar flexibility using domain-specific languages (DSLs) like the one discussed in chapter 3. Together with the interactive style of development, these are two important reasons F# has a faster time-to-market cycle.

> **F# for testing**
>
> I think F# has one of the best testing stories of any language. It uses all the testing frameworks of .NET and adds its own powerful set. The F# community takes software quality seriously, which can be seen in a plethora of libraries from FsUnit for fluent assertions to FsCheck for fuzz testing.

(continued)

Add to this a wealth of language-feature enablers that make testing easier. For example, the backtick notation lets you use whitespace in function names and write

```
``1 + 1 should equal 2``
```

rather than writing `OnePlus1ShouldEqual2`.

In my experience, testing is a great and risk-free way to introduce F# into the workflow of your company. Tests written in F# are easier to write and end up being more readable. By using F# for testing and exploration, you can also learn to write idiomatic F# code without rewriting your main system from scratch, which is never a good idea.

In this chapter, we'll explore all the features that make F# a great language for testing, and we'll look at many of the .NET and F# tools for testing, giving you a comprehensive reference in one place. You'll learn about the following:

- *Software quality being more than just unit tests*—We'll look at the F# development cycle, which often starts with exploratory programming, relies heavily on static types, and adds unit testing as a later step.
- *Unit testing*—We'll discuss simple unit testing, as well as fluent DSLs (to make F# tests more readable) and parameterized unit tests.
- *Advanced testing techniques*—We'll cover tools for *fuzz testing* that let you search for defects using random input generation and *test doubles* (that is, different ways to decouple the tests from concrete implementations).
- *Automated acceptance testing*—We'll look beyond developer-generated tests and explore user stories to see how behavior-driven development (BDD) encourages developers to work with users to capture requirements.

Throughout the chapter, you'll see plenty of F# examples using libraries, including NUnit, xUnit, FsUnit, Unquote, FsCheck, Moq, Foq, and TickSpec. If some of these names are new to you, don't worry. That's why you're reading this chapter! Similar levels of automation are possible in languages other than F#, but it has been my experience that a high-level language like F# makes writing tests simpler and faster to achieve. Before diving into the code, let's focus on the bigger picture, because software quality isn't just about code.

What software quality really means

As mentioned in the introduction, software quality means different things to different groups:

- Developers talk about readability and maintainability of the code.
- Testers often look at acceptance tests and defect counts.
- Users think of polished visuals, responsiveness, workflow, and functionality.

This chapter looks at software quality based on practical experience from all three perspectives. As developers, we'll look at interactive development style and unit tests. As testers, we'll explore tools for black-box testing based on functional properties. Finally, as users, we'll look at acceptance testing and ways of capturing the workflow and functionality.

Software quality covers both functional requirements like business rules and non-functional requirements like responsiveness that can require significantly different approaches. This means you must first understand the requirements before choosing and using any testing tools. Otherwise, you may be wasting your time testing a property that doesn't matter for the problem at hand.

Understanding requirements

In the context of software systems, functional requirements capture "what the system should do," and nonfunctional requirements capture "how the system should do it." In other words, functional requirements capture the functionality, and nonfunctional requirements capture all the other important technical aspects such as scalability, performance, and fault tolerance, and also cost and time-to-market.

NONFUNCTIONAL REQUIREMENTS

From my experience in the development of video games and trading systems, performance is the most striking example of a nonfunctional requirement. Such properties need to be tracked continuously during the entire development cycle. If you "finish" writing a game but end up with code that doesn't perform well enough, revisiting the entire codebase will be extremely difficult.

For example, trading backends must respond to high volumes of requests from thousands of clients with low latency. To ensure that a system achieves the required high performance, you can use two techniques. The first is to add key performance indicators (KPIs) at the start of the project so that you can keep track of performance throughout development. The other technique is to use exploratory testing and analyze performance as you're writing the code. We'll look at this in the context of F# Interactive (FSI) later in this chapter.

> **NOTE** In the 1980s and 90s, video games used the border area of the CRT screen to visually indicate how much of a frame flyback was being used by the game loop. Nowadays frameworks like Silverlight, Windows Presentation Foundation (WPF), and XNA show numerical statistics like frame rate overlaid over the application.

For a trading system, KPIs can be exposed via system performance counters or even a web-based console. I've found that for high-performance systems, a rapid prototyping approach based on exploratory testing works well so that you can quickly discount implementations that don't fit the performance and focus on finding the right algorithms. F# provides a read-evaluate-print-loop (REPL) with high-precision timing via the `#time` directive, which makes exploratory testing particularly easy.

FUNCTIONAL REQUIREMENTS

For many LOB applications, performance is less of an issue, and the focus is on building out functionality. Getting precise functional requirements isn't always easy to achieve, because often customers don't know at the start exactly what they want. As software developers, you and I might complain about this, but that's not going to make the problem go away. You need to understand that this is the case and find good ways to understand your users.

I've found that a collaborative approach works well, in which developers talk directly with users about requirements. Often those requirements are captured as user stories with acceptance tests. Stories and acceptance tests can be made less ambiguous by specifying functionality by example, with expected inputs and outputs.

> **NOTE** F# has access to a wide range of mature libraries for F# and the .NET Framework that aid the automation of acceptance tests. In some of them, including SpecFlow and TickSpec, scenarios are specified as plain text, making them more readable. In others, such as NaturalSpec, the scenarios are written as code, which makes them easier to run and test.

Not only are functional requirements difficult to identify initially, but they also frequently change during the development of software systems.

CHANGING REQUIREMENTS

Hardly anyone would argue that software requirements don't change. Moreover, this isn't something you should fight against. Instead, you need to write software in a way that makes it easy to adapt to changing requirements.

As mentioned earlier, video game developers often use a scripting language to write the game logic. This approach enables rapid prototyping and easy change—often without even needing to recompile the game.

Business systems can opt to take a similar approach to areas where changes are anticipated by allowing modules to be plugged into the system at runtime, or by creating abstractions that allow changes to be added, albeit at compile time. In functional-first programming languages like F#, this flexibility can be achieved using internal and external DSLs.

DSLs bring a number of benefits. Internal DSLs consist of types and functions that map closely to the business domain, and logic can be changed quickly as requirements change. External DSLs can be used to specify behavior or to configure the system. You can achieve properties similar to scripting in video games—you can change the configuration or behavior without recompiling (or even restarting) the application.

If restricted languages aren't enough for your use case, it's worth pointing out that F# code can also talk to scripting languages like Lua.NET, IronPython, and IronRuby. Thanks to the F# Compiler Services project (http://fsharp.github.io/FSharp.Compiler.Service), it's also easy to embed FSI itself as a scripting language in your application.

Domain-specific languages

DSLs are languages that make it easy to solve one specific problem. They can be either *external* (with their own syntax and format) or *internal* (embedded as libraries in a host language). In chapter 3, we looked at Markdown, which is an external DSL for writing documents.

Philip Wadler has described functional programming languages as domain-specific languages *for creating other domain specific languages*.[1] As a functional-first language, F# makes light work of creating internal DSLs and external DSLs. The latter is demonstrated in chapter 3. Speaking of the latter, almost any well-designed F# library will seem like a DSL to some extent. You'll see this when looking at F# testing libraries like FsUnit.

Avoiding defects early with types

It's a common belief that the earlier a defect is found, the cheaper it is to fix, with defects discovered in production being the most expensive. A combination of compile-time type checking and automated testing can help catch defects earlier during development.

F#'s strong type system can help eliminate a number of common defects found in languages like C#, Java, and JavaScript, including the prevalent null reference exception (NRE). The introduction of `null` is considered a billion-dollar mistake by its inventor, Tony Hoare;[2] and to quote Don Syme, "Friends don't let friends use `null`."[3]

One way to find out if you have a problem with NREs is to search your bug database. For me, NREs are the most common defect I find in C# code. When programming in F#, the types that are declared in F# can't be assigned `null` as a value. This doesn't prevent NREs *completely*, because you can still get a `null` value when calling .NET or C#, but it significantly reduces the number of NRE-related issues in your code. In F#, you have to be more explicit when dealing with missing values:

```let person = tryFindPersonByID(42)```
```match person with```
```| Some p -> p.Name```
```| None -> "(unknown)"```
	```var person = TryFindPersonByID(42)```
	```if (person != null) then```
	``` return person.Name;```
	```else```
	``` return "(unknown)";```

---

[1] Philip Wadler, "A Practical Theory of Language-Integrated Query," Functional Programming eXchange 2014, March 14, 2014, http://mng.bz/tN1e (video).

[2] Tony Hoare, "Null References: The Billion-Dollar Mistake," QCon London, August 25, 2009, http://mng.bz/l2MC (video).

[3] Don Syme, "Keynote: F# in the Open Source World," Progressive F# Tutorials NYC 2013, September 18, 2013, http://mng.bz/8rcO (video).

The two examples look similar, and they both return the name of the person only if the person has been found. But in F#, the function returns option<Person>, indicating that the value might be missing. In C#, this is indicated by returning a null value. The problem is that in C#, you could easily forget the null check and access person.Name right after you get the object. This would, of course, cause an NRE. The F# pattern matching is much safer. It even warns you if you've missed a case as you're writing the code.

Not your grandfather's static type system

The F# type system is in many ways stronger than that of C#. For numerical code, there is built-in support for units of measure, and conversion operations between types must be explicit. Other benefits of F# for mathematics were illustrated in chapter 4: F# can be read like mathematical notation, which means details aren't lost in translation and Mathematica and MATLAB users can work in a familiar environment.

In F#, even string formatting is type checked. For example:

```
printf "Hello: %s" 42
```

This call gives a type mismatch error, because the format specifier %s indicates that the argument should be of the type string, but we're calling it with a number instead!

Despite being *more explicit*, the F# type system is *less verbose* than the system used, for example, in C#. This is thanks to type inference, which can figure out most of the types automatically so you need to write types only when you want to be explicit.

The typical programming style in F# has other aspects that help prevent defects. By default, F# functions are typically independent and pure (free from side effects), and data structures are immutable (write-once, read many) and employ structural equality (compare by value), which makes them easier to test and less error-prone. In summary, strong typing can help avoid many defects. For other defect types, there's automated testing.

Holistic approach to testing

I like to encourage a holistic view of testing that focuses on the qualities that are important to specific areas of your application. This means starting by understanding both *functional* and *nonfunctional* requirements and then focusing on the aspects that matter:

- *Correctness* is the key nonfunctional requirement when you're implementing, for example, financial calculations where an error has potential dramatic consequences.
- *Performance* and *scalability* might be more important factors for action games and server-side services.
- *Maintainability* is often the key when developing LOB applications where requirements frequently change.

F# has all the tools you need to cover all of these aspects. Fuzz testing (using FsCheck or Pex) can be used to generate test inputs to explore the boundaries of an API and ensure correctness even in unexpected corner cases.

F# also works with all the major .NET unit-testing frameworks like NUnit, xUnit, and MSTest, as well as mocking libraries like Moq, Rhino Mocks, and FakeItEasy. It also adds its own libraries like Unquote, FsUnit, NaturalSpec, and TickSpec, which we'll explore later in this chapter. Which of the tools you'll need to use depends on your requirements and focus—whether you're testing implementation or business scenarios. Table 1 gives a brief overview of the testing techniques.

Table 1   Relative alignment (business and implementation) of various testing approaches

Technique	Business aligned	Implementation aligned	F# tools
Exploratory testing	No	Yes	Using F# Interactive is the first part of the testing story in F#.
Unit testing	No	Yes	NUnit, xUnit, FsUnit, and Unquote.
Fuzz testing	No	Yes	FsCheck, which lets you test your algorithms on sample inputs.
Performance monitoring	Yes	Yes	Using the `#time` directive in F# Interactive REPL.
Specification by example	Yes	No	BDD, which lets you capture user stories as specifications.
User interface tests	Yes	No	Canopy (http://lefthandedgoat.github.io/canopy), a library for writing user interface tests for the web.

From exploratory to unit testing

When writing code, most F# programmers start by writing their code in F# script files and running it interactively in FSI to test it on sample inputs. In the interactive mode, you can also easily check nonfunctional requirements like performance. Once the initial prototype works (on sample inputs) and is efficient enough, you can turn it into a compiled library and add systematic unit testing. In this section, we'll explore this approach using a simple function for calculating Scrabble scores as an example.

> **NOTE**   Scrabble is a board game in which players score points for placing words on a board. Each letter has a score, and placing letters on certain parts of the board multiplies either the letter or word score.

For now, we'll look at calculating the score of letters and words, but we'll get back to multipliers later in the chapter. You can see the initial prototype in the following listing.

Listing 1   Calculating the word score in Scrabble

```
let letterPoints = function
    | 'A' | 'E' | 'I' | 'L' | 'N' | 'O' | 'R' | 'S' | 'T' | 'U' -> 1
    | 'D' | 'G' -> 2
    | 'B' | 'C' | 'M' | 'P' -> 3
    | 'F' | 'H' | 'V' | 'W' | 'Y' -> 4
    | 'K' -> 5
    | 'J' | 'X' -> 8
    | 'Q' | 'Z' -> 10
    | a -> invalidOp <| sprintf "Letter %c" a
let wordPoints (word:string) =
    word |> Seq.sumBy letterPoints
```

Returns the value of an individual character ❶

Fails for unknown letters

❷ Returns the value of a whole word

Sums values returned by letterPoints

The code is simple, but it's interesting enough to demonstrate a number of testing techniques. The letterPoints function ❶ uses an elegant pattern-matching approach to return the value of a single letter, and wordPoints ❷ iterates over all letters in a word using Seq.sumBy and sums the letter values.

To get started, you don't need to create a project. All you need to do is create an F# script file (say, Scrabble.fsx) and copy the code into the file. Now you can check what your code does using FSI.

Exploratory testing

Exploratory testing will be familiar to users of most programming languages outside of the C family (C/C++, C#, Java, and so on) that provide a REPL—languages like Clojure, Erlang, LISP, OCaml, Ruby, and Python, to name a few. With a REPL, you can get quick feedback by setting up values and applying functions in the REPL environment. You're also free to quickly try out a number of different implementation options before settling on one.

> **NOTE** F# is a cross-platform language, and a number of editors provide support for running F# scripts. These include Xamarin Studio and Visual Studio, but also Emacs. In other words, you can run the same script unchanged on Windows, Mac, Linux, and OpenBSD.

In Visual Studio and Xamarin Studio, you can execute lines of code by highlighting them and sending them to the FSI window (right-click or press the keyboard shortcut Alt-Enter). F# script files (*.fsx) can be edited and run either in your IDE or at the command prompt with fsi.exe.

CHECKING FUNCTIONAL REQUIREMENTS

Once you select and evaluate the two functions from listing 1, they'll be available in FSI and you can check how they work. The following interaction shows an example. You can either type the code directly into FSI or write it in the main source code editor and send the commands to FSI using Alt-Enter:

```
> wordPoints "QUARTZ";;
val it : int = 24
```

```
> wordPoints "Hello";;
System.InvalidOperationException: Letter e
   at FSI_0002.letterPoints(Char _arg1) in C:\Scrabble\Script.fsx:line 12
   at FSI_0036.wordPoints(String word) in C:\Scrabble\Script.fsx:line 15
   at <StartupCode$FSI_0041>.$FSI_0041.main@()
```

The first command works as expected, but as you can see in the second case, the wordPoints function currently fails when called with a word that contains lowercase letters. This might or might not be the correct behavior, but thanks to exploratory testing, you can discover it early and modify the function to behave as expected.

Exercise 1

Let's say that your explorative testing has revealed an issue in your original implementation, and you want to make the wordPoints function work with lowercase as well as uppercase letters. Modify the function implementation, and check that it returns 8 when called with "Hello" as an argument.

Exercise 2

In some languages, a pair of characters is used to represent a single letter. This oddity is called *digraphs*. For example, in Czech the characters *CH* represent a single letter.[4] Although *C* and *H* are distinct, standalone letters, when *C* is followed by *H*, the pair represents a single letter. So, for example *CECH* (guild) should be counted as [C][E][CH].

As an exercise, extend the wordPoints function so that it can handle digraphs. Assuming that the value of *C* is 2, *E* is 1, *H* is 2, and *CH* is 5, the value of the word *CECH* should be 8 (instead of 7).

CHECKING NONFUNCTIONAL REQUIREMENTS

As discussed earlier, exploratory testing can be also used to check nonfunctional requirements like performance. In FSI, the #time directive turns timing of expressions on or off. You can use it to check the performance of your function:

```
> #time;;
--> Timing now on

> let s = System.String(Array.create 10000000 'Z');;
Real: 00:00:00.039, CPU: 00:00:00.046, GC gen0: 0, gen1: 0, gen2: 0
val s : System.String = "ZZZZZZZZZZ"+[9999989 chars]

> wordPoints s;;
Real: 00:00:00.097, CPU: 00:00:00.093, GC gen0: 0, gen1: 0, gen2: 0
val it : int = 100000000
```

---

[4] See "Czech," *Wikipedia*, http://en.wikipedia.org/wiki/Ch_(digraph)#Czech.

In the Scrabble application, calculating the score of a word consisting of 1 million letters in less than 100 milliseconds is certainly fast enough. But if performance was your key concern, you could easily try changing the functions to run faster. For example, you could replace the Seq.sumBy function with a mutable variable and iteration:

```
> let wordPointsMutable (word:string) =
    let mutable sum = 0
    for i = 0 to word.Length - 1 do
      sum <- sum + letterPoints(word.[i])
    sum;;
(...)

> wordPointsMutable s;;
Real: 00:00:00.032, CPU: 00:00:00.031, GC gen0: 0, gen1: 0, gen2: 0
val it : int = 100000000
```

This version of the function is longer and harder to write, but it's about three times faster. Which of the functions should you use? This is why understanding nonfunctional requirements is important. For most applications, simplicity and readability are preferred, so the original implementation is better. But if performance is your key concern, you can choose based on a simple explorative test. Now, let's look at the next step of the testing process: unit testing.

Unit testing

Unit testing is likely the most common testing approach, whether the tests are written before or after the system under test (SUT). Test-driven development or test-first development is prevalent in dynamic languages and some parts of the Java and .NET communities.

Within typed functional programming communities like F#, Scala, and Haskell, type-driven development or functional-first programming is common, where the types of data and functions are defined first. The defined types often underpin the domain model of the system under development (in a way similar to how tests underpin the behavior in dynamic languages). Adding tests is often the next step, and you can also often turn code snippets written during exploratory testing into automated unit tests. In both test-driven and type-driven development, some amount of upfront design is wise.

> ### Continuous integration
>
> For large LOB and enterprise applications, it's useful to automate the execution of a suite of unit tests triggered on submission of changes to the source control system or to run the tests overnight. This approach can help uncover regressions made by changes as they happen. Running of tests is usually done on a dedicated machine.
>
> There are a number of packages for .NET that automate application builds and running of tests, including JetBrains' TeamCity, CruiseControl.NET, and Microsoft's Team Foundation Server. These continuous integration servers typically expect unit tests to be specified using a common .NET unit-testing library like NUnit, xUnit,

(continued)

MbUnit, or MsTest; these libraries all take a similar reflection-based approach to discovering unit tests in assemblies. To install the F# runtime on a build machine without Visual Studio, download the F# tools here: http://go.microsoft.com/fwlink/?LinkId=261286.

Many F# open source projects hosted on GitHub use FAKE build scripts and the Travis continuous integration (CI) server to run tests. When you use Travis, GitHub automatically displays the build results in pull requests, and managing the open source project becomes even easier. For examples of how to set up Travis CI and FAKE build scripts, see some of the projects at https://github.com/fsharp.

In this chapter, we'll mostly run the tests in an IDE. Both Visual Studio and Xamarin Studio support running unit tests directly. You may also consider third-party runners such as TestDriven.NET and NCrunch. F# works seamlessly with all the major unit-testing frameworks, test runners, and CI suites.

TESTING SCRABBLE WITH NUNIT

This chapter mainly uses NUnit, but we'll briefly look at other testing frameworks too. NUnit is one of the first and most popular open source unit-testing frameworks for .NET. It was originally ported from JUnit, but it has evolved quite a bit on the .NET platform and has become one of the standard tools.

Setting up

To get started, you'll need to move the Scrabble code you've written so far from a script file into a library project. Here, you'll create a project containing a single F# file with a module `Scrabble` that contains the two functions you wrote earlier: `letterPoints` and `wordPoints`.

Typically you'll also create an F# library project to host your tests. Sometimes it's more convenient to create tests in the same project first and then migrate them to a separate test project afterward. NUnit (as well as other libraries) can be easily installed from inside Visual Studio using NuGet by right-clicking the project and selecting Manage NuGet Packages. On other platforms, you can download the package and install it by adding a reference to the `nunit.framework.dll` assembly.

Once you have a library, you can write tests. You already wrote two simple tests during the exploratory testing phase (calling the `wordPoints` function with "QUARTZ" and "Hello" as sample inputs), so let's start by turning them into unit tests.

In NUnit, unit tests are defined as methods of classes or functions in modules annotated with a `Test` attribute. Defining classes and methods, as shown in the next listing, will be familiar to Java and C# developers.

Listing 2   Unit tests for Scrabble, using classes and members

```
namespace Scrabble.Tests

open NUnit.Framework                          References NUnit and
open Scrabble                                 the tested library

[<TestFixture>]
type ScrabbleTests() =                      ❶ Marks the class and
    [<Test>]                                   method as tests
    member test.``Value of QUARTZ is 24`` () =
        Assert.AreEqual(24, wordPoints "QUARTZ")    Uses a nice name,
                                                   ❷ thanks to backticks
```

Note that F# members names specified with backticks ❷ can contain whitespace. Using backticks can improve the readability of your tests and lets you focus on specifying what the test does. The names also appear nicely in test runners, so they're much easier to understand.

In listing 2, the test is written as an instance method ❶ in a class marked with the TestFixture attribute. In F#, you can omit some of the ceremony. You can specify tests as functions in a module:

```
module Scrabble.Tests

open NUnit.Framework
open Scrabble
let [<Test>] ``Value of QUARTZ is 24`` () =
    Assert.AreEqual(24, wordPoints "QUARTZ")
```

For most F# projects, this is the preferred way of writing unit tests, and you'll use this style in the rest of the chapter. Functions in a module are compiled as a type with static methods, so this approach works only with testing frameworks that support static methods. One of the first to support this was xUnit.

---

xUnit

xUnit was written by the original author of NUnit as a successor. Just like with NUnit, you can install xUnit with NuGet. Again, tests can be written as both classes and modules:

```
open Xunit

let [<Fact>] ``Value of QUARTZ is 24`` () =
    Assert.AreEqual(24, wordPoints "QUARTZ")
```

For simple tests, the main difference from NUnit is that functions are annotated with the Fact attribute.

In this section, we use only simple test assertions that test whether the actual value equals the expected value. The next section looks at other ways of writing assertions.

WRITING FLUENT TESTS WITH FSUNIT

When writing assertions and tests, you can use the functionality provided by NUnit and xUnit out of the box. If you want to get more readable tests or better error messages, two interesting F# projects are available that make testing more pleasant: FsUnit and Unquote.

Let's look at FsUnit first. It provides fluent assertions with functions and is built on top of existing unit-testing frameworks, including NUnit and xUnit. The following example uses NUnit, so you'll need to add a reference to the FsUnit library for NUnit (FsUnit.NUnit.dll):

```
open FsUnit

let [<Test>] ``Value of QUARTZ is 24 (using FsUnit)`` () =
    wordPoints "QUARTZ" |> should equal 24

let [<Test>] ``Calculating value of "Hello" should throw`` () =
    TestDelegate(fun () -> wordPoints "Hello" |> ignore)
    |> should throw typeof<System.InvalidOperationException>
```

You can continue using functions in a module and using readable names of tests, thanks to the backtick notation. The new thing is the body of the functions. Rather than using the `Assert` module, you're writing the assertions using a DSL provided by FsUnit.

The key construct is the `should` assertion. It takes a predicate (such as `equal` or `throw`) followed by a parameter (the expected value or exception). The last argument (which you specify using the pipeline operator, `|>`) is the value or a function to be checked.

WRITING ASSERTIONS USING UNQUOTE

Unquote approaches the problem of writing assertions differently. Rather than writing assertions using a method call or using an F# DSL, you can write them as ordinary F# code, wrapped as an F# quotation (as usual, you can install Unquote using NuGet):

```
open Swensen.Unquote

let [<Test>] ``Value of QUARTZ is 24 (using Unquote)`` () =
    test <@ wordPoints "QUARTZ" = 24 @>
```

The API of Unquote is simple—all you need is the `test` function. When using Unquote, you write assertions as quoted expressions specified between the `<@` and `@>` symbols. This means the library is called with a *quotation* (or an *expression tree*) representing the F# predicate that should evaluate to true.

This has an interesting consequence: Unquote can provide detailed information about test failures. The reported messages are given as step-by-step F# expression evaluations. For example,

```
test <@ 2 + 2 = 5 @>
```

gives the following message:

```
Test failed:

2 + 2 = 5
4 = 5
false
```

This approach is particularly useful when you're testing code that performs numerical computations, because the error log gives you a detailed report showing which part of the computation doesn't behave as expected.

Unit-testing tips

Here are some hints that are important when you're writing tests. These are useful in F# as well as other languages:

- *Test behavior, not methods*—Each unit test should exercise a particular behavior. It's not unusual to generate multiple tests for a specific method.
- *Negate tests*—To check that the test is valid, negate the value and rerun the test. If it still fails, your test probably won't catch regressions.
- *Refactor*—If you find that your tests use a common setup, consider creating a setup function or parameterizing your tests.
- *Ensure speed*—Tests should be fast; as a rule of thumb, they should take less than 100 ms so you can get quick feedback from your test suite.

Before looking at more advanced testing topics, the following section discusses how to combine the exploratory style of testing with the usual unit-testing style.

COMBINING EXPLORATIVE AND UNIT TESTING

Exploratory testing and unit testing serve somewhat different purposes. When using exploratory testing, you can quickly call a function with different inputs created by hand to see how it works, and you can also measure nonfunctional requirements (like performance using the #time directive). You can use unit testing to encapsulate the tests and run them automatically.

In practice, having both of the options available is extremely useful. With one handy trick, you can write code that works in either compiled mode (as a unit test) or interactive mode (by running code in FSI). The trick is to use conditional code based on whether the INTERACTIVE symbol is defined. For example, you can see the setup for unit testing the Scrabble library in the following listing.

Listing 3   Setup for testing the Scrabble library

```
#if INTERACTIVE
#load "../ScrabbleLibrary/ScrabbleModule.fs"
#I "../packages/NUnit.2.6.3/lib"
#I "../packages/FsUnit.1.2.1.0/lib/net40"
#r "nunit.framework.dll"
#r @"FsUnit.NUnit.dll"
```

 Loads the Scrabble scoring implementation

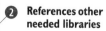 **References other needed libraries**

```
#else
module Scrabble.Tests                    ◁─┐   Defines a name for
#endif                                   ❸    the compiled code

open NUnit.Framework
open Scrabble

let [<Test>] ``Value of QUARTZ is 24`` () =
    Assert.AreEqual(wordPoints "QUARTZ", 24)
```

Listing 3 starts with a preamble that can be both compiled and run in FSI. In compiled code, it just defines the name of the module containing the tests ❸. When executed interactively, it loads the tested functionality and references all the necessary unit-testing libraries so that you can use them in FSI.

You first load the file containing the scoring functions using the #load directive ❶. This directive loads the file and compiles it on the fly so you don't need to recompile the library before testing it. This strategy works nicely for single files, but for larger libraries, it's better to reference the compiled library using #r. In listing 3, you use #r to reference NUnit and FsUnit ❷; this way, they become available in FSI, and you can run the body of the test or explore how the function behaves for other inputs. To do that, select the conditional block of code, followed by the open statements; then you can evaluate the body of the first test and modify the inputs:

```
> Assert.AreEqual(24, wordPoints "QUARTZ");;
val it : unit = ()

> Assert.AreEqual(25, wordPoints "QUARTZ");;
NUnit.Framework.AssertionException:    Expected: 25
  But was:  24
```

The great thing about this approach is that you get the best of both worlds. You can explore the API using FSI, but at the same time, you can run the tests as part of your build process as ordinary unit tests.

> **TIP** Although this chapter explains how to write F# tests for the F# library, you can use the same techniques for testing code written in C# and VB.NET. This is a risk-free way of introducing F# into the development cycle. Writing tests in F# is easy and fun, but at the same time, you're not reimplementing your key system using a language that you're learning.

Now that we've covered the basics of unit tests, let's look at how you can easily test functions on multiple inputs using parameterized tests.

Parameterized tests

When testing functions interactively, you'll often run the test on a number of sample inputs and check that the result is what you were expecting. You could turn this code into unit tests by writing a new test for each input, but that would make the code repetitive.

Both NUnit and xUnit provide a way to write parameterized tests, which let you test a function with a range of inputs to avoid repeating yourself. In NUnit, this is done using the `Values` attribute:

```
let [<Test>] ``Value of B,C,M,P should be 3``
    ([<Values('B','C','M','P')>] letter:char) =
        Assert.AreEqual(3, letterPoints letter)
```

Here, you want to check that the value of *B*, *C*, *M*, and *P* is 3. Rather than writing four separate tests for each of the letters, you can specify the letters as parameters and capture all four cases in a single test.

The previous example is easy to write because you have a number of sample inputs, but the result is always the same. What if you wanted to check the behavior for multiple different inputs and outputs? The `TestCase` attribute lets you specify multiple arguments and, optionally, the expected result:

```
[<TestCase("HELLO",Result=8)>]
[<TestCase("QUARTZ",Result=24)>]
[<TestCase("FSHARP",Result=14)>]
let ``Sample word has the expected value`` (word:string) =
    wordPoints word
```

In this example, you're checking that some property holds for three explicitly specified pairs of values (in this case, input and outputs). Sometimes, you may also want to check that a property holds for all possible combinations of inputs. In NUnit, this can be done using the `Combinatorial` attribute:

```
[<Test; Combinatorial>]
let ``Word value is not zero, minus one or max value``
      ( [<Values(Int32.MinValue, Int32.MaxValue, 0, -1)>] value:int,
        [<Values("HELLO","FSHARP","X")>] word:string) =
    Assert.AreNotEqual(value, wordPoints word)
```

In this example, the test runner will run the test for all possible combinations of `value` and `word`, covering 12 cases in total. You're checking that the `wordPoints` function doesn't return `MinValue`, `MaxValue`, 0, or -1 for any of the sample words.

Using parameterized tests, you can cover a large number of interesting cases; and if you choose your sample inputs carefully, you can also cover the usual tricky corner cases. For some problems, it's useful to take the next step from parameterized testing, which is to use *random testing*.

Writing effective unit tests

So far, we've looked at basic testing techniques that are similar in F# and other languages. The main difference has been that F# puts more emphasis on exploratory testing. Now, let's look at two advanced techniques where F# gives you interesting options that you wouldn't get otherwise. We'll start with *fuzz testing* using FsCheck and then look at functional ways of writing *test doubles*.

Fuzz testing with FsCheck

With unit tests and parameterized tests, you test against a set of manually specified inputs. For certain functionality, such as wire protocols and collection types, unexpected defects can be caught by generating random inputs, or *fuzz*.

FsCheck is a random-testing library based on QuickCheck. You specify properties that functions or methods satisfy, and it tests whether the properties hold in a large number of randomly generated cases. When using FsCheck and fuzz testing in general, the key to successful testing is to find good properties that should hold (see the following sidebar).

Finding good FsCheck properties

Most tutorials introducing FsCheck, QuickCheck, and similar tools will start with a property that checks whether reversing a list twice returns the original list:

```
let reverseTwice (input:int list) =
    List.rev (List.rev input) = input
```

This is a good example property, because it's universal (it works for any list) and it tests one specific function (`List.rev`). But it's a basic example, and you'd only need it when implementing your own lists. How do you write good properties?

- You can often take inspiration from mathematics. For example, some functions are associative (`foo a (foo b c) = foo (foo a b) c`) or commutative (`foo a b = foo b a`). Appending lists or strings is an example of the first case.
- When there are two ways to achieve the same thing, you can write a property that checks whether this is the case.
- If you're working with floating-point numbers, you can often write a property that checks whether the result is less than or greater than a certain number. This approach can help you catch errors with special values such as NaN, +Infinity, and –Infinity.
- Fuzz testing is great for testing custom data structures and collections. You can relate the state of a collection (such as length or emptiness) before and after some operation (such as adding or removing an element).
- When testing collections, you can often use *oracle*, another implementation of the same collection that has different nonfunctional properties (for example, it's slower) but implements the same functionality.

Going back to the Scrabble scoring example, here are two simple properties that you can check using FsCheck.

References the FsCheck library

```
open FsCheck

let repetitionsMultiply (repetitions:uint8) =
    let s = (String(Array.create (int repetitions) 'C'))
    wordPoints s = (int repetitions) * letterPoints 'C'
```

 Repeating the same letter gives multiples of its value.

```
let letterPositive (letter:char) =
    letterPoints letter > 0
```
⟵ ❷ **The value of any letter is positive.**

The properties are functions that take some inputs and return a Boolean value. When you pass them to FsCheck, it generates random values for the inputs.

Listing 4 defines two properties. The first ❶ checks that if you generate a word consisting of any number of repetitions of the letter *C*, the value of the word is the value of a letter *C* multiplied by the number of repetitions. Note that you take the argument as uint8. This way, you guarantee that FsCheck always gives you a non-negative, small number as an input.

The second property ❷ takes any character as an input and checks that the value returned by letterPoints is greater than 0. Let's see what happens when you let FsCheck test your properties, first using FSI:

```
> Check.Quick(repetitionsMultiply);;
Ok, passed 100 tests.
val it : unit = ()

> Check.Quick(letterPositive);;
Falsifiable, after 1 test (1 shrink) (StdGen (1752732694,295861605)):
'a'
```

For the first property, FsCheck generates 100 random inputs and reports that the property holds for all of them. For the second property, you get an error—in fact, it fails for the first input chosen by FsCheck, which is the lowercase letter *a*. This is an error in the property. When called on characters other than letters *A* to *Z*, the letterPoints function throws an exception.

To address this common problem, FsCheck provides the ==> operator. When you write cond ==> prop, the prop property is checked only when the cond condition holds. You can see this in action in the next listing, which also wraps the Check.Quick calls as NUnit tests.

Listing 5 Wrapping properties as unit tests

```
[<Test>]
let ``Value of a valid letter is positive`` () =
  Check.Quick(fun (letter:char) ->
    (letter >= 'A' && letter <= 'Z') ==>          Checks the property when
      lazy (letterPoints letter > 0))             the letter is between A and Z

[<Test>]
let ``Score of a repeated letter is multiple of its value`` () =
  Check.Quick(fun (letter:char) (repetitions:uint8) ->
    let s = (String(Array.create (int repetitions) letter))       Checks the
    (letter >= 'A' && letter <= 'Z') ==>                          property for
      lazy (wordPoints s = (int repetitions) * letterPoints letter)  valid letters
```

In both tests, you specify the property inline as a lambda function. In the first test, you check that letterPoints returns a positive number when the letter is valid. Note that the call needs to be done lazily so it's run only when the condition is true. You can wrap it with the `lazy` keyword, and FsCheck evaluates it lazily. The second test is similar, but you now take both letters to be repeated and a number of repetitions.

> **NOTE** Using the `==>` operator works nicely when the number of invalid inputs isn't too high. When you need to build more specific inputs, you can also specify custom data generators that randomly generate inputs that satisfy all your requirements.

In addition to what you've seen so far, FsCheck is useful for fuzz testing, because it can shrink the input data to the smallest set that will make the test fail. For example, it won't report that a property fails for a long list containing exotic numbers; instead, it tries to find a minimal list and usually finds one containing just a few simple values.

Avoiding dependencies with test doubles

Unit tests should test the system under test (SUT) in isolation. Assuming the SUT's dependencies are parameterized, *test doubles* can be used instead of concrete implementations, which may be inflexible or expensive to set up and tear down, particularly systems that use a network or the filesystem, like a database. Mock objects are a concrete example of test doubles; but when testing functional code, you can work at a finer-grained level and start by providing test doubles of functions.

METHOD AND FUNCTION STUBS

Let's say you have a function that, given a raw price, calculates the price with tax:

```
let CalculateTax(rawPrice) =          Simple implementation
    rawPrice * 0.25M                  for demonstration

let GetPriceWithTax (rawPrice) =
    rawPrice + CalculateTax(rawPrice)
```

In this snippet, the `CalculateTax` function is simple, but in a realistic system, it may go to a service or database to compute the value. The example introduces coupling between `GetPriceWithTax` and a concrete implementation of `CalculateTax`, which makes it difficult to test the functionality of `GetPriceWithTax` in isolation. To make the function testable, you can pass the `CalculateTax` function as an argument:

```
let GetPriceWithTax calculateTax rawPrice =
    rawPrice + calculateTax(rawPrice)
```

Now the function can be more easily tested. You can provide a method stub for `CalculateTax`, rather than using the actual, possibly hard-to-test, implementation:

```
let [<Test>] ``price with tax should include tax`` () =
    let price, tax = 100.0M, 15.0M
    let calculateTax _ = tax
    Assert.AreEqual(price+tax, GetPriceWithTax calculateTax price)
```

The snippet implements a test double for the actual `CalculateTax` function, called `calculateTax` (with a lowercase *c*). The underscore character in the function declaration signifies that the argument is ignored, so the function always returns 15.0M. The test can then easily make sure `GetPriceWithTax` adds the original price and the calculated tax.

Method and function stubs are a simple but effective technique when you're writing functions with a relatively small number of dependencies. But even with more dependencies, you don't always need the full power of mocking frameworks.

OBJECT EXPRESSIONS

Sometimes a function's or method's dependencies are defined as interfaces. For small interfaces, F# has a convenient built-in syntax called an *object expression* that lets you create an instance inline.

Say you want to test a function that supports depositing monies in a foreign currency. You may have an external currency service defined as an interface:

```
type ICurrencyService =
    abstract GetConversionRate :
        fromCurrency:string * toCurrency:string -> decimal
```

The implementation of the interface would probably be an F# object type, but when you want to write a test for a function that relies on the service, you'll need a simple implementation. For example, a stub for the currency service that always returns 10.0M can be generated with the following object expression:

```
let service =
  { new ICurrencyService with
      member service.GetConversionRate(_,_) = 10.0M }
```

Object expressions require all members to be defined, which is impractical for larger interfaces. In practice, assuming you stick to the single-responsibility principle, your interfaces should be pretty small; but not all implementers stick to this principle. In that case, F# lets you use a wide range of mocking libraries.

MOCKING LIBRARIES

A plethora of .NET mocking libraries are available for generating test doubles over larger interfaces and abstract classes. Some of the more popular ones are NSubstitute, FakeItEasy, and Moq. Going through all of them could easily require a whole chapter, so we'll look at just two. The accompanying sidebar shows a brief example of Moq, so you can see the F# syntax.

Moq

Moq provides a fluent API for setting up the subset of members you require on an interface for a test. For example, if you want to pass in an `IList<T>` instance where the `Count` property returns 0, you can write

```
open Moq
let mock = Mock<IList<int>>()
mock.SetupGet(fun x -> x.Count).Returns(0)  |> ignore
let instance = mock.Object
```

 Pipes result to ignore

(continued)

You pipe the result to ignore ❶ because in F#, return values must be ignored explicitly. For a friendlier experience with F#, try `Moq.FSharp.Extensions`, available from NuGet, which defines extension methods for this and other cases so you can write the following:

```
let instance = mock.SetupGet(fun x -> x.Count).Returns(0).End
```

Moq (as well as other .NET libraries) can be used with F#, but it doesn't use all the features that are available in F#. An alternative is to use Foq, which is a mocking library with an API similar to Moq's but written and focused on F#. Foq can be deployed via NuGet or as a single file, Foq.fs. It supports both F# quotations, as seen earlier with Unquote, as well as .NET LINQ expressions.

Foq lets you define instances of interfaces and abstract classes with one line per member or a set of methods in a way similar to object expressions. The following example builds a test double for the `IList<char>` interface.

Listing 6   Mocking the `IList` interface with Foq

```
open Foq
open System.Collections.Generic

let [<Test>] ``mock the IList interface with multiple members`` () =
    let xs =
        Mock<IList<char>>.With(fun xs ->           ❶ Count returns 2.
            <@ xs.Count --> 2
                xs.[0] --> '0'                     ❷ The indexer returns
                xs.[1] --> '1'                        two sample values.
                xs.Contains(any()) --> true
            @>                                     ❸ Contains always
        )                                             returns true.
    Assert.AreEqual(2, xs.Count)
    Assert.AreEqual('0', xs.[0])
    Assert.AreEqual('1', xs.[1])
    Assert.IsTrue(xs.Contains('0'))
```

To make it easier to specify the behavior of test double, Foq uses a combination of F# quotations with the custom operator `-->` to define the behavior. The `With` method in the example returns a quotation that represents the mapping from different properties, indexers, and methods to the expected values. Each mapping is specified using the `-->` operator, which symbolizes returning a value.

When creating the test double, Foq looks at the code quotation and creates an implementation of the interface according to the specification. In this example, the specification defines the behavior of the `Count` property ❶, the indexer ❷, and the `Contains` method ❸.

The topics discussed so far were by no means an exhaustive coverage of the options for writing unit tests in F#, but they cover the most interesting aspects, ranging from exploratory testing to powerful fuzz-testing libraries and simplified testing of test doubles. Next, we'll turn our attention from code-aligned testing to business-aligned techniques.

Acceptance testing

Up until now, we've been focusing on techniques like unit testing that ensure technical quality—that the code you've written behaves as you expect. From a business point of view, the solution should behave as the user expects. One good way to understand what the business expects is to specify example scenarios. A scenario indicates which outputs you get for given inputs. Such scenarios can be used as a form of documentation and acceptance criteria for a feature.

For high-value business features that are key to the operation of a solution, it's sometimes useful to run the example scenarios against the solution, in a way similar to unit tests, while keeping the automation close to the business language. This strategy has the advantage of making it easier to change the implementation of key features, say for performance or a new platform, without having to rewrite the scenarios.

This technique has a number of monikers, including *automated acceptance testing*, *specification by example*, and *behavior-driven development* (BDD). In this section, we'll focus on BDD.

Behavior-driven development

BDD is a relatively new (circa 2003) Agile software development approach that focuses on communication—encouraging collaboration between developers, quality assurance, and business participants. Through discussion with stakeholders, scenarios in which the software will be used are written to build a clear understanding of the desired behavior.

In a similar fashion, in order to arrange, act, and assert in unit testing, scenarios are specified in plain text in a structured form composed of these steps:

```
Given some context
When some event occurs
Then I expect some outcome
```

Developers and testers use these scenarios as acceptance criteria to drive development. Some of the acceptance tests may be automated and others checked through manual testing. A feature may be considered done when the tests pass for all its scenarios.

Many libraries exist to assist with automation of acceptance tests. Some automate execution of business-readable text files, whereas others attempt to stay close to the business language via an internal DSL (a language implemented in the host language).

> **NOTE** This section will focus on the automation side, but to effectively practice BDD, your focus should be primarily on the requirements side.

We'll begin this section with a quick overview of the tools that exist outside of the F# world and then look at TickSpec, which is a BDD library that's specifically focused on F#.

State of the art

Cucumber is probably the best known BDD framework as of 2014. It executes plain-text files written in a business-readable DSL (known as Gherkin) as automated tests. Each file describes a feature and its scenarios. During execution, steps of a scenario are matched against step definitions consisting of a regular expression and a function to execute. Cucumber is written in Ruby, and it has benefited from Ruby's light syntax and expressiveness to minimize the ceremony while defining step definitions:

```
Given /a customer buys a black jumper/ do
end
```

A number of open source BDD frameworks are available for .NET that can parse Gherkin-based text specification files. These include NBehave (http://nbehave.org), Raconteur (http://raconteur.github.io), SpecFlow (http://specflow.org), StorEvil (https://github.com/davidmfoley/storevil), and TickSpec (http://tickspec.codeplex.com).

Typically, .NET BDD frameworks take a reflection-based approach (as per unit tests). Listing 7 shows a comparison of different ways for defining a `Given` step definition that should match a Gherkin line "Given a customer buys a black jumper", written using SpecFlow, StorEvil, and TickSpec.

Listing 7 Specifying a `Given` step in SpecFlow, StorEvil, and TickSpec

```
[Given(@"a customer buys a black jumper")]           ❶  SpecFlow
public void GivenACustomerBuysABlackJumper()
{}

public void Given_a_customer_buys_a_black_jumper()   ⬅❷  StorEvil
{}

let [<Given>] ``a customer buys a black jumper`` () =  ⬅❸  TickSpec
    ()
```

In SpecFlow ❶, the step definition is defined in a `Given` attribute, which contains the regular expression to match against the Gherkin file line. StorEvil ❷ supports reflection-based pattern matching representing spaces in C# method names as underscores. In F#, you can be even nicer. TickSpec ❸ supports F# backtick method names that can contain whitespace.

A reflection-based approach requires a compile-and-run cycle to test a feature. For iterative development in larger applications, the REPL-based approach may be more appropriate for faster feedback. Matters can be improved for .NET developers by running individual tests in isolation using tools like TestDriven.NET and ReSharper, but this still doesn't mitigate the build step. For this reason, the TickSpec library also supports development in the F# REPL. Let's take a more detailed look at TickSpec.

Specifying behavior with TickSpec

I developed the TickSpec library back in 2010 to take advantage of some of the unique features of F# for testing, like backtick methods and active patterns. The library has been used successfully in many commercial settings and has been particularly popular in the finance industry. I also used it extensively during development of the open source spreadsheet project Cellz, available on CodePlex (http://cellz.codeplex.com).

In this section, you'll return to the Scrabble example and use TickSpec to specify the expected behavior of Scrabble scoring. You'll start with the simple functions implemented so far and then add support for multipliers.

SPECIFYING SCRABBLE SCORING

You can test the earlier Scrabble implementation by specifying the scoring of a number of example words. The following scenario defines that the score for the three-letter word *POW* would be 8 ($P = 3$, $O = 1$, and $W = 4$). Written in the Gherkin syntax, the scenario looks like this:

```
Scenario: POW
Given an empty scrabble board
When player 1 plays "POW" at 8E
Then she scores 8
```

To automate the scenario via reflection using TickSpec, you'll write an F# module with functions to match the three lines. You already have the wordPoints function, so the code that implements the steps just needs to add the value of each played word and check that the sum matches the expected score. Here's the definition of the steps.

Listing 8   Specification of Scrabble scoring

```
let mutable actual = 0                                       The state is kept
let [<Given>] ``an empty scrabble board`` () =         ❶   by scenario.
    actual <- 0
Initializes
the score  ❷
let [<When>] ``player (\d+) plays "([A-Z]+)" at (\d+[A-Z])``   ❸   Adds the score of
        (player:int, word:string, location:string) =              the played word
    actual <- wordPoints word
let [<Then>] ``she scores (\d+)`` (expected:int) =          Checks the
    Assert.AreEqual(expected, actual)                   ❹   expected score
```

When evaluating the scenario, you need to keep some private state ❶ that represents the score calculated so far. Individual step definitions update or check the score. For example, starting with an empty board ❷ resets the score to 0.

The last two definitions use regular expressions to match variable parameters. For example, in the When statement ❸, the sequence (\d+) signifies matching a number, in this case the player number. TickSpec automatically converts these parameters to arguments of the specified type.

As the Gherkin specification is executed, the state is set to the initial value and then updated by adding the score of the added word. Finally, the Then statement ❹ checks that the final result matches the expected value.

SPECIFYING EXAMPLES USING TABLES

To make the specification more comprehensive, you can add scenarios that specify the value of several other words. Writing these as separate scenarios would be repetitive. Fortunately, TickSpec makes it possible to parameterize the scenario with an example table. The following listing shows a scenario that checks the Scrabble scoring for a number of two-letter words.

Listing 9   Scenario specifying scoring of two-letter words

```
Scenario: 2-Letter Words
 Given an empty scrabble board
 When player 1 plays "<word>" at 8E
 Then she scores <score>
Examples:
 | word | score |
 |  AT  |   2   |
 |  DO  |   3   |
 |  BE  |   4   |
```

The scenario in listing 9 will run against the step definitions you've already defined, so you don't need to write any more code for now. The runner will execute a new scenario for each row in the example table, substituting each row's column values with the name in the scenario marked between the < and > symbols.

TickSpec also supports multiple example tables per scenario, in which case it generates a combinatorial set of values. You can also specify *shared examples*, which are applied to all scenarios in the feature file. Before extending the scoring example, check the accompanying sidebar, which lists a number of hints for writing good, business-relevant feature files.

What makes a good feature file?

- Write in the language of the business domain, not programming.
- Use plain English.
- Use active voice.
- Use short sentences.
- Use backgrounds for repeated setup.
- Use an example tables for repeating inputs.
- Test one thing at a time.

So far, the scenarios can only describe words being placed on the Scrabble board. The next step is to add support for specifying multipliers.

SPECIFYING THE BEHAVIOR OF MULTIPLIERS

The Scrabble board contains a number of special positions that affect the score. You have to deal with double-letter scores (DLS) that multiply the value of a single letter, triple-word scores (TWS) that multiply the value of the entire created word by 3, and with the center star, which multiplies the word value by 2.

Let's start by looking at the scenarios you want to implement. This example specifies three sample words with a number of additional properties on some of the letters
or the entire word.

Listing 10   Specification of Scrabble scoring with multipliers

```
Feature: Scrabble score

Scenario: QUANT
 Given an empty scrabble board
 When player 1 plays "QUANT" at 8D
 And Q is on a DLS
 And T is on the center star
 Then she scores 48

Scenario: ALIQUANT
 When player 2 prefixes "QUANT" with "ALI" at 8A
 And A is on a TWS
 Then she scores 51

Scenario: OIDIOID
 When player 2 plays "OIDIOID" at 9G
 And O is on a DLS
 And D is on a DLS
 And D is on a DLS
 And forms NO
 And O is on a DLS
 And forms TI
 Then she scores 69
```

① Player plays QUANT

In the first scenario **①**, the player plays the word *QUANT* so that the letter *Q* is on a
position that multiplies its value by 2. The letter *T* is on the center star, so the value of
the entire world is multiplied by 2 as well.

A neat way of modeling the properties of the scenario is to define an F# discriminated union type. One case of the union corresponds to one kind of step in the
specification:

```
type Property =
    | Word of string
    | DLS of char
    | TWS
    | CenterStar
```

As you execute the scenario, you'll collect the described properties. The score for a
single scenario can now be defined as a fold over properties collected, as follows.

Listing 11   Calculating the score as a fold over properties

```
let total properties =
    let sum, mult = properties |> List.fold (fun (n,m) p ->
        match p with
        | Word(word) when word.Length = 7 ->
            50 + n + wordPoints word, m
        | Word(word) -> n + wordPoints word, m
```

① 50-point bonus

Score of a plain word

```
        | DLS(letter) -> n + letterPoints letter, m
        | TWS -> (n, m*3)
        | CenterStar -> (n, m*2) ) (0,1)
    sum * mult
```

Double-word score; Double-letter score; Triple-word score; ❷ Total

When using a fold to calculate the score, you need to keep two pieces of state: the total value of letters and words placed on the board and the multiplier for the word value. The multiplier needs to be kept separate so you can first sum all the letters and then, at the end, multiply the total sum by the multiplier ❷.

The lambda function that updates the state uses pattern matching and implements the Scrabble logic. One notable new feature is that when players use all seven letters ❶, they get a 50-point bonus.

The design where you use properties to represent individual steps works nicely with the step definitions. The methods implementing individual steps add properties to a collection. As you can see in the next listing, this approach makes it easy to define the steps.

Listing 12 Step definitions for Scrabble scoring with multipliers

```
open NUnit.Framework

let mutable properties = []
let hold p = properties <- p::properties

let [<BeforeScenario>] SetupScenario () =
    properties <- []

let [<Given>] ``an empty scrabble board`` () = ()

let [<When>] ``player (\d+) plays "([A-Z]+)" at (\d+[A-Z])``
    (player:int,word:string,location:string) =
        hold(Word(word))
[<When>]
let ``player (\d+) prefixes "([A-Z]+)" with "([A-Z]+)" at (\d+[A-Z])``
    (player:int,prefix:string,word:string,location:string) =
        hold(Word(prefix+word))

let [<When>] ``forms ([A-Z]+)`` (word:string) =
    hold(Word(word))

let [<When>] ``([A-Z]) is on a DLS`` (letter:char) =
    hold(DLS(letter))

let [<When>] ``([A-Z]) is on a TWS`` (letter:char) =
    hold(TWS)

let [<When>] ``([A-Z]) is on the center star`` (letter:char) =
    hold(CenterStar)

let [<Then>] ``he scores (\d+)`` (score:int) =
    Assert.AreEqual(score, total properties)
```

Helpers to collect properties; ❶ Resets the score; ❷ Adds a standalone word; ❸ Adds a prefixed word; ❹ Adds a composed word; ❺ Collects multipliers; ❻ Checks the final score

All the step definitions follow the same pattern. As before, they use regular expressions to specify the Gherkin language line that corresponds to the step. A new attribute, `BeforeScenario`, resets the board before anything else happens ❶.

There are three ways to create a word: ❷ creates a standalone word; ❸ adds a prefix to an existing string, forming a longer word; and ❹ occurs when a word is formed because two other words are aligned. The remaining steps collect all the multipliers ❺ and check that the score matches your expectations ❻.

USING BDD IN PRACTICE

Hopefully you're now convinced that F# provides an elegant way to develop BDD step definitions. From experience, I believe this can be a good way to gain value from introducing F# to an organization.

Regardless of your language preference, given that your business specifications could outlive your current platform and programming language, I recommend choosing a framework that's based on the well-supported Gherkin business language so you're not locked in to a specific technology in the future. Businesses are reporting real business value from adopting BDD; in Gojko Adzic's *Specification by Example* (Manning, 2011) the author examines more than 50 case studies of this style of technique.

Summary

The main theme of this chapter was taking a holistic perspective of software quality. When talking about software quality, people often focus on unit testing and neglect to consider the bigger picture, which is crucial for successful software development.

We began by looking at requirements. Understanding both functional and nonfunctional requirements is crucial for choosing the indicators that matter. For example, in my experience with gaming and trading, nonfunctional requirements such as performance play an extremely important role. These requirements can often be checked during development using the exploratory development style. Of course, unit testing is crucial for checking the correctness of an implementation, and we looked at a number of elegant ways of using F# libraries (like FsCheck) and F# features (like providing a function as a test double).

Finally, we shifted our attention and looked at behavior-driven development. BDD is gaining real traction in the development community with plenty of talks at conferences and user groups on the subject, along with blog articles and books now available.

About the author

Phil Trelford is an active member of the software development community, regularly attending and speaking at user groups and conferences, blogging, and contributing to open source projects. He is a co-organizer of the London F# User Group and a founding member of the F# Foundation. He has written a number of popular F# libraries, such as Foq and TickSpec.

F# walkthrough: looking under the covers

Tomas Petricek

The purpose of this book is not to teach you F# from scratch. There are many other books that do that, including our own *Real-World Functional Programming* (Manning, 2009). Instead, this book is a collection of interesting uses of F# written by experts from the industry who are using F# to write production code and who often have unique experience that's worth sharing.

Even after using F# for some time, many people, myself included, may be surprised by some aspect of F# or a combination of features that they haven't seen before. In this appendix, we'll walk through some of the F# basics, but we'll also look at them from a more interesting perspective. You'll learn how they fit together beautifully. As you'll see, F# is remarkably simple.

Simplicity through compositionality

Most of the power of F# is achieved by *composing* simple ideas. For someone coming from a language such as C#, which was my background when learning F#, this isn't obvious. For example, you expect that GenerateRange(0, 10) is calling a function taking multiple arguments, whereas in F#, the argument (0, 10) is a tuple and you're just calling a function—the language doesn't *need* functions of multiple arguments.

Why is this a good thing? Say you also had a function called NormalizeRange that takes a pair of numbers and returns a new pair, making sure the first one is the smaller one and the second one is the larger one. In C#, you'd probably have to define a type Range at this point. Alternatively, you can return Tuple<int, int>, although that's not idiomatic. In C#, you can call the two functions as follows:

```
var corrected = NormalizeRange(10, 0)
var range = GenerateRange(corrected.Item1, corrected.Item2)
```

(continued)

You call NormalizeRange with two arguments and get back a tuple. To call Generate-Range, you need to extract the first and second elements of the tuple using Item1 and Item2 properties. In F#, you don't need that; GenerateRange takes a tuple as an argument, and NormalizeRange returns a tuple, so you can just write this:

```
let range = GenerateRange (NormalizeRange (10, 0))
```

Compositionality is one of the key principles in F#, and you'll see a number of examples throughout this appendix that demonstrate its power. But F# is also a pragmatic language that aims to interoperate with .NET libraries and the outside world (through type providers), and so it also supports ordinary .NET members that take multiple arguments as in C#. Still, understanding the compositionality will demystify many F# constructs.

The fundamental building block from which programs are built in F# is an *expression*, so let's begin by looking at expressions in the next section.

From expressions to functions

Languages like C++, Java, and C# distinguish between *statements* and *expressions*. A statement is a command that performs some action and typically changes the state of the memory (for example, assignment) or transfers the control flow (for example, a return statement). An expression is a computation that can be evaluated and gives a result.

Starting with expressions

In functional-first programming, whole programs are written as expressions that can be evaluated and yield a result, so expressions are all you need. F# isn't purely functional, meaning you can easily do useful things like printing to the console, but even that is actually an expression. Consider the famous Hello world example in F#:

```
> printfn "Hello world";;         ◄──❶
Hello world                       ◄──❷
val it : unit = ()                ◄──┐
                                     ❸
```

The snippet shows the result of entering the command in F# Interactive (FSI). In most editors, you can do that better by writing the expression (the first line without the > symbol) and pressing Alt-Enter or Ctrl-Enter.

When entered in FSI, the expression printfn "Hello world" ❶ is evaluated to a value. During the evaluation, the printfn function prints the message to the console, so this is shown on the next line ❷. Then it continues evaluating and returns a result, which the FSI console prints on the last line ❸.

The printfn function is useful for its side effects and not for its result. For such functions, F# provides a type called unit, which doesn't represent any information.

The only possible value of type unit is written as (), and you can also see this as a tuple containing zero elements. So, the line val it : unit = () means the expression has been evaluated to a value () of type unit, which FSI assigned to a temporary variable named it. If you have an expression that returns unit, you can sequentially compose it with other expressions using the semicolon operator, or by using the newline separator as shown in listing 1.

Listing 1 Sequencing expressions

```
> let answer1 = printf "Thinking deeply..."; 42          ◁──┐   Using
  ;;                                                      ❶   semicolon
Thinking deeply...
val answer1 : int = 42
> let answer2 =                                           ❹  Both do the
    printf "Thinking deeply..."                              same thing!
    42
  ;;
Thinking deeply...
val answer1 : int = 42
```

Using ❷ whitespace

No "return" keyword! ❸

Listing 1 shows the same expression written in two possible ways. First ❶ you write it using an explicit semicolon, and then ❷ you write it using indentation. In most cases, using indentation is the recommended way, but the first approach makes it more obvious what's going on.

As you've just seen, the first expression (printfn "Thinking...") returns the only value of type unit. The sequencing operator ; ignores the value (because it doesn't represent anything useful!) and evaluates the second expression (in this case, 42) and then returns the result of the second expression ❹.

When you see the second version of the code ❷, you could view it as a code block that consists of a print statement followed by a return statement, except that you don't need the return keyword ❸. But this isn't how things work! Under the covers, the code is two expressions that are sequentially composed using ;.

Getting the indentation right

F# is indentation-sensitive, which means the whitespace determines the structure of code. This reduces the syntactic noise and makes your code more readable—indenting code properly is a good practice anyway, so why should the compiler ignore the information that the indentation gives you?

In most cases, indentation is easy to see. F# requires you to use spaces (instead of tabs) to avoid ambiguity. In some cases, getting the indentation right may be tricky. For example, when you're typing code in FSI, the shell starts a line with >, but that isn't added to the next line. For example:

```
> printfn "hi"
printfn "there"
```

(continued)

Although the two lines don't look aligned, the compiler sees them as aligned, because the first two characters of the first line are not your input. The best way to avoid the problem is to write most of your code in the text editor and then select and run it. In listings that show FSI sessions, we'll add the spaces to the second (and later) lines, but note that you don't need to type them!

The other tricky situation is when you're selecting code in the editor and then sending it to FSI (using Alt+Enter or Ctrl+Enter). In that case, you need to select a full line. If your selection doesn't include spaces at the beginning of the first line, but it does includes spaces on subsequent lines, the code sent to the compiler will be incorrectly indented.

The preceding sidebar clarifies how to properly indent code. This is important, because indentation affects the meaning of code, especially when it comes to writing more complex expressions. For example, the following listing demonstrates how to write a conditional expression.

Listing 2 Writing conditional expressions

```
> let lo = 10               Defines sample
  let hi = 5 ;;             values

> if lo > hi then "Wrong"      ❶ Body doesn't
  "Good"                          behave as "return"
  ;;
error FS0001: This expression was expected to      ❷ Compiler reports
have type 'unit' but here has type 'string'           an error

> if lo > hi then "Wrong" else "Good"    ←──┐ Both branches are
  ;;                                        ❸ expressions.
→ val it : string = "Wrong"
```

Expression ❹ evaluates to "Wrong"

You first define two values representing an incorrect range. If you incorrectly treat F# programs as C# programs without the return keyword, then you might try writing something like the first expression ❶. If the range is wrong, you return "Wrong"; otherwise the evaluation continues and returns "Good". As the compiler tells you ❷, this doesn't work.

If you write an if expression with only the then clause, then the type of the body has to be unit. This way, F# knows what to do when the condition doesn't hold; it can do nothing and return the only valid unit value. This example tried returning a string, and the compiler said it expected a body of type unit (like printfn "Wrong"):

You can also fix the code by using if as a conditional expression that returns the result of one of its two branches ❸. Here, you return a string value "Wrong" or a string value "Good", depending on the value of the expression lo > hi. FSI prints the result ❹, but you could also assign it to a symbol using let (so the if expression behaves more like the conditional operator cond?e1:e2 in C#).

Exercise 1

The ; operator requires the first expression to return unit and returns the result of the second expression. See what happens when you write the following expression:

```
let res = ( 42; printf "Hello world" )
```

Exercise 2

If you're going to apply for an F# job, you need to be able to solve the FizzBuzz problem with F#. That is, you must be able to write a function that iterates over numbers from 0 to 100. For each number, write "Fizz" if it's divisible by 3 and "Buzz" if it's divisible by 5. For other numbers, just output the number.

Some more syntax you'll need is for i in 0 .. 100 do followed by a body (indented further than the for keyword); the expression a%b returns the remainder after integer division. You can also use the usual logical operators like >=, <=, =, <> (the last two test equality and inequality—in F# you don't need double equals) as well as && and ||. It's worth noting that && and || are short-circuiting, meaning they don't evaluate the expression e2 in e1 && e2 or e1 || e2 when the result is clear after evaluating e1.

Exercise 3

As a brainteaser, try writing an expression that prints the message "Hello" when the variable trick is greater than 10, but do that *without* using the if expression. You can do this using only the F# features that we covered so far in the appendix, but you'll need to use the sequencing of expressions and Boolean operators in a clever way. As a bonus, you can also implement FizzBuzz using the same trick!

As you can see, you can have a lot of fun by writing simple F# expressions. But if you're writing a serious program, you need a way to reuse parts of your expressions. This is where functions come into the picture.

Wrapping expressions in functions

Functions are first-class values in F#, which means they can be treated as any other type. Even though languages like C# support functional constructs too, they still make a visible distinction between methods and delegates like Func<T1, T2>. In F#, a function type is written using the arrow symbol. For example, a function adding 1 to an integer has a type int -> int. Following is a comparison of functions and expressions, showing the important difference:

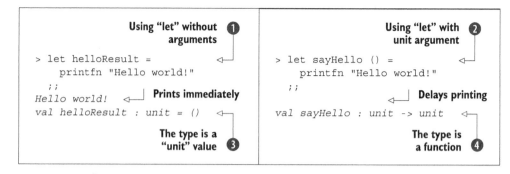

On the left ❶, you use `let` as in the previous section and define a value `helloResult`, which is the result of evaluating an expression `printfn "Hello..."`. As you can see, this prints the message when evaluating the value and returns a value of type `unit` ❸. You wouldn't normally write the code this way (because the value `helloResult` is useless), but it's interesting to contrast this with the code on the right.

On the right ❷, you add a parameter to the `let` declaration written as `()` after the name of the symbol. This makes it into a function of type `unit -> unit` ❹. Declaring the function doesn't print anything, but you can call it later:

```
> sayHello ();;                    Calls the function with a
Hello world!                       ❶ unit value as an argument
val it : unit = ()

> helloResult;;                    Displays the previously
val it : unit = ()                 ❷ evaluated value
```

The function takes a `unit` value as an argument, so if you want to call it, you need to create a `unit` value. As you already know, the only value of type `unit` is written as `()`, which explains what's happening in the first case ❶. Just out of curiosity, you can also evaluate the value `helloResult` ❷. This represents the result of the previous evaluation and so prints the `unit` value.

One more interesting thing is the declaration of the function. You add a parameter `()`, which looks like you're declaring an empty parameter list. This isn't what's going on! You could write the function differently:

```
let sayHello (u:unit) = printfn "Hello again!"
```

Here, you're declaring a function that takes an argument u. The syntax `(u:unit)` is a type annotation that explicitly specifies the type of u to be `unit`. Of course, because `unit` doesn't carry any information, you aren't going to need u anywhere in the code. For this reason, the previous version used the notation `()`, which is a pattern specifying that the parameter should be a `unit` value and should be discarded. So, you can construct a `unit` value using the expression `()`, and you can also *destruct* a `unit` value using the pattern `()`. We'll look at patterns in more detail in a moment, but let's first finish the section on functions by exploring functions that take other functions as arguments.

Using functions as values

Even though you haven't had to write a single type so far, F# is fully statically type checked. The language has a powerful type-inference algorithm that looks at the source code and infers the types of all expressions and functions. This becomes even more useful when you start writing functions that take other functions as arguments.

For example, suppose you want to write a function that will take a list of words and print them using the specified printer function. The function might print the words to a console, display them in some user interface, or even read them using a text-to-speech API. To do that, you can write the following:

```
> let sayEverything printer words =
    for word in words do
      printer word
  ;;
val sayEverything : words:seq<'a> -> printer:('a -> unit) -> unit
```

You haven't specified any type annotations, so the type inference works out the type of the function based on the code you wrote. When doing this, F# looks for *the most general* type. In the previous example, this means two things:

- The type of words is inferred as seq<'a>, which is an F# alias for IEnumerable<'a>. This means the resulting function can be used on any collection.
- More interestingly, the compiler also figures out that the type of elements can be *generalized* and turned into a generic parameter that's automatically named 'a.

How does the compiler know? You're iterating over words using a for loop, so it must support iteration. But the only thing you do with individual word values is pass them to the printer function. This means the type of elements in the collection must be the same as the type accepted by printer. Because you use printer as a function, it must be a function. Also, you use it in the body of a for loop, so it must return unit (because the body of a loop is evaluated, but its result is discarded before the next iteration). So, now you end up with a function that's even more useful than you thought!

> **NOTE** Once you understand how type inference works, it becomes a surprisingly powerful tool. The inferred type of a function lets you do basic sanity checks of your code. For example, if the type inference inferred that your sayEverything function takes a collection seq<'a> and a function 'b -> unit, it would mean you did something wrong. You're not passing values from the collection to the printer, because then the types would have to be the same. So, it can be an indication that you're probably not calling the printer as you intended.

Now let's see how you can call the function. As mentioned, you can not only use it to print strings, but also call it with a list of integers as an argument:

```
sayEverything (fun num -> printfn "%d" num) [1; 2; 3]
```

This sample uses the `fun` notation to create an anonymous function and use it as the printer. The body of the function spans as far as possible, so you need to wrap it in parentheses. The `sayEverything` function takes two arguments, which are separated by spaces. The second one is an immutable F# list containing 1, 2, and 3.

Looking under the covers

When I said that `sayEverything` takes two arguments, I was lying again. This is how it looks when you see it, and this is also the most useful way to think of the function, but you can read it differently too. When the compiler infers the type, it sees it with additional parentheses as follows:

```
sayEverything : ('a -> unit) -> (seq<'a> -> unit)
```

This is pretty subtle, but as I said in the introduction, this appendix isn't an introduction to F#. Let's see what the type means:

- `sayEverything` is a function that takes a function (`'a -> unit`) as an argument and returns a function (`seq<'a> -> unit`) as the result.
- The argument that needs to be specified when calling `sayEverything` is itself a function—that is, a printer of type (`'a -> unit`).
- The result is now a function that takes an argument of type `seq<'a>` and returns a `unit` value as the final result.

How can you then call this beast using `sayEverything printer list`? This expression can be seen as parenthesized too: `(sayEverything printer) list`. So, you first call `sayEverything` with a printer as an argument. What you get back is another function that already knows *how* to print but doesn't know *what* to print. You specify that in the second call by passing it a list.

Most of the time, you don't need to worry about the fact that functions of multiple arguments return other functions as results. But there's one situation where this becomes extremely useful. When you previously used (`fun num -> printfn "%s" num`) as the printer, you needed to create a function that takes a number and prints it. You did that by creating an anonymous function taking `num` and passing `num` to another function. There's an easier way to do this:

```
sayEverything (printfn "%s") ["hello"; "word"]
```

In this example, you're calling `printfn` with a single argument, `"%s"`. The compiler understands this and infers that the call needs one more argument of type `string`. Rather than passing a variable as an argument, you use this expression, because it has the type you need: `string -> unit`. You can check this yourself in FSI by entering `printfn "%s"` without an argument and looking at the type of the result.

You might be wondering why you use `sayEverything` so that it takes the function as the first argument and the list as the second one. This isn't an arbitrary choice. It means the function can be nicely called using the pipelining operator. To demonstrate this, let's write a fancier printer that SHOUTS the words in uppercase:

```
["hello"; "word"] |> sayEverything (fun s ->
    printfn "%s" (s.ToUpper()) )
```

The pipelining operator (|>) takes the argument on its left side (here a list of words) and passes it to the function on the right. On the right, you have a function seq<string> -> unit, which you get by passing a printer to sayEverything. As you can see, you use the fact that sayEverything is a function that returns a function again. This is called *partial function application.*

> ## Pipelining operator
>
> In F#, you can define your own custom operators. Interestingly, the pipelining operator isn't a built-in feature, but you can define it yourself using just 12 characters:
>
> ```
> let (|>) x f = f x
> ```
>
> The operator name needs to be wrapped in parentheses. It takes x and f as the left and right arguments and calls the function f with x as the argument.

Another interesting thing about the pipelining operator is that it works well with type inference. In F#, type inference propagates information from left to right. This means that in the previous example, the compiler looks at the list and sees that it contains strings. When you're writing the function and type s followed by a dot, you'll get an autocomplete list with all available members. But if you write the call without the pipeline, you'll have to specify the type of s explicitly using a type annotation written as (s:string).

> ## Exercise 4
>
> The inferred type of functions in F# can tell you a lot about what the function does. Sometimes it's more useful than the name of the function. To explore how the types work, try writing functions that have the following types:
>
> ```
> mysteryFunction1 : ('a -> bool) -> seq<'a> -> int
> mysteryFunction2 : bool -> 'a -> 'a -> 'a
> mysteryFunction3 : ('a -> 'b) -> ('b -> 'c) -> 'a -> 'c
> ```
>
> Make sure your solutions are correct by entering them in FSI and checking the inferred type. All three functions have useful implementations. Finding a useless implementation is much harder than finding the useful one!

So far, you've used basic expressions and primitive types. In any practical F# application, you'll need to use more complex data types to represent your data. In the following section, we'll look at functional types (and we'll cover object-oriented types after that).

Constructing and destructing data

Similar to functions, the F# approach to representing data structures is "less is more." There are two basic ways of constructing data structures. One is to group multiple values in a single value (for example, a person has a name and age), and the other is to combine multiple different choices (for example, a preferred contact is a phone number, email, or postal address). Let's start by looking at the first option.

Representing composite values with tuples

The basic way to combine multiple values into a single one is to use a tuple. The following snippet creates a value person that represents a person with a name and an age:

```
> let person = "Alexander", 3;;
val person : string * int = ("Alexander", 3)
```

F# uses the standard .NET type Tuple<string, float>, so you can think of this code as syntactic sugar for calling the constructor. F# also uses a shorter type alias for the name, so the inferred type is printed as string * int. Tuples are immutable, so how can you do something useful with the tuple? The following function increments the age of a person by 1 and returns the new incremented value as the result.

Listing 3   Incrementing value in a tuple

```
> let incAge person =
    let name, age = person          ←② Decomposes tuple    ←① Takes a single parameter
    name, age + 1
  ;;
val incAge : 'a * int -> 'a * int   ←③ Inferred type is generalized
```

The function in listing 4 takes a single parameter named person ①. To get values from the tuple, you use the let construct again. In its most general form, the let construct has this structure:

```
let <pat> = <expr> in <expr>
```

The in keyword is optional when you use indentation, so you wouldn't typically see it in F# code. It means let has to be followed by some other expression whose result is returned. The interesting thing here is <pat>; this represents a pattern. You've already seen two patterns. A symbol like person is a pattern that assigns any given value to a variable (because variables are immutable, *symbol* is a better name in F#). The other pattern you've seen is (), which takes a unit value and ignores it. Now you're using a pattern ② that takes a two-element tuple and assigns its two values to two symbols. You can also nest patterns and write the following:

```
let _, age = person
```

The pattern _ ignores any value, so this expression ignores the name and assigns the age of a person to a symbol, age. You can also write the following pattern:

```
let name, 3 = person
```

This is an *incomplete pattern*, meaning it won't match all possible person values. In particular, it accepts only people of age 3! This isn't a useful example, but it becomes useful when combined with match, which lets you choose between multiple patterns.

One more interesting thing about listing 4 is that the inferred type is again more general than you might've expected ❸. The code increments the second element of the tuple, but it copies the first element and doesn't restrict its type to string, which is how you happen to use the function in the following code:

```
> incAge person;;
val it : string * int = ("Alexander", 4)

> incAge ("Tomas", 29);;
val it : string * int = ("Tomas", 30)
```

In the first call, you pass to incAge an existing value that was created earlier. This works as expected, because person has a type string * int, which can be *unified* with the required type 'a * int. The function can also be called by creating a tuple explicitly as an argument. This *looks* as if you were calling a function with two arguments, but as you can now see, it's just creating a tuple and calling a function with a single argument.

For the sake of completeness, it's worth pointing out that the first version of incAge is unnecessarily long. You don't need to take person as an argument to decompose it on the next line. Patterns like name, age can appear directly in the argument list of a function, although this time the pattern needs to be parenthesized:

```
> let incAgeShort (name, age) =
    name, age + 1;;
val incAgeShort : name:'a * age:int -> 'a * int
```

Tuples are extremely useful when you're working on a small scale, but if you have a larger number of composed fields, you'll find it useful to name them. This is where records come into the picture.

Representing composite values with records

You can see records as the simplest possible kind of objects. They contain a number of fields that store data. In functional-first domain modeling, you'll often start by focusing on the data structures and records provide one key component for that. You can use records to model composite data types before you need to start thinking about the operations that you'll implement, because those can be written later as separate functions.

Unlike tuples, records need to be named and declared in advance. To make listing 5 a little more interesting, I added an overridden ToString member to the record.

Listing 4 Record with custom ToString method

```
type Person =
  { Name : string
    Age : int }                        Properties of the record
  override x.ToString() =
    sprintf "%s (%d)" x.Name x.Age      Member declarations
```

The record you create here is a simple immutable type. When you see it from C#, it looks like an ordinary .NET class with a constructor (taking Name and Age) and two read-only properties. As you'll see in the next section, records are just one small step away from the object-oriented programming features of F#. But there's one nice feature of records that's useful when you need to create modified values while keeping immutability: the with construct.

The following snippet shows a simple function that increments the age of a person, this time using the Person record:

```
> let incAgeRec person =
    { person with Age = person.Age + 1 }
 ;;
val incAgeRec : person:Person -> Person
```

The with construct is a special F# language feature that works only with records. It creates a record that's exactly the same as person, but the value of Age is calculated using the expression person.Age + 1. As you can see, the inferred type is Person -> Person. For records, the F# compiler determines the type using the fields you're accessing. This makes simple programming with records nicer, but it makes it hard to write programs that use records with field names that appear in multiple records. For public APIs of more complex systems, it's usually better to use objects. Before moving to our next topic, let's have a quick look at using the function you just wrote:

```
> let jan = { Name = "Jan"; Age = 24 };;          ◁━①
val jan : Person = { Name = "Jan"; Age = 24; }

> let older = incAgeRec jan;;                      ◁━②
val it : Person = { Name = "Jan"; Age = 25; }

> older.ToString();;                               ◁━③
val it : string = "Jan (25)"
```

To create a record, you write field assignments in curly brackets ①. The compiler makes sure you specify a value for all fields of the record, which means you don't run into problems with uninitialized fields. Then you can use it as an argument to your function ② and access its fields as well as its methods, including the overridden ToString ③.

Records are simple types, so we haven't spent much time discussing them. The real power of records comes when you use them together with tuples and discriminated unions for domain modeling.

Representing choices with unions

Records let you define new types by *combining* values of several other simpler types. In OOP terms, they correspond to classes with multiple fields. Discriminated unions let you define new types by *choosing* between values of several other simpler types. In OOP, this is usually represented by class hierarchies.

DOMAIN MODELING

For example, suppose you want to represent information about customers. Every customer has a name (which they choose when they register) and a shipping address. For this part of the model, you need a record (to combine the two values). The shipping address can be empty (before the customer proceeds to checkout) or it can be local (with an address and postcode) or international (in which case, you track the country).

To model the address, you can use a discriminated union (to provide a choice between three possible values of the address). You can see the full definition next.

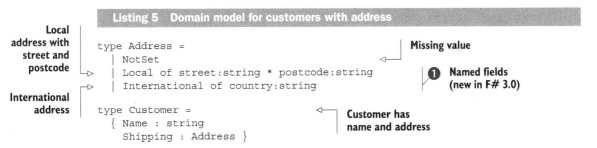

Listing 5 Domain model for customers with address

```
Local                  type Address =
address with              | NotSet                                              Missing value
street and                | Local of street:string * postcode:string
postcode                  | International of country:string           ❶ Named fields
                                                                         (new in F# 3.0)
International           type Customer =
address                   { Name : string                     Customer has
                            Shipping : Address }               name and address
```

If you haven't seen discriminated unions before, you can think of the type `Address` as a declaration of four separate classes (but on just four lines). The type name `Address` would be represented as an abstract base class, and the three *type constructors* would each correspond to a single inherited class with additional fields.

The great thing about F# type declarations is that they're direct encoding of our informal description of the domain model. We said the address is empty, local, or international, and this is *exactly* what the code says. In F# 3.0, this is even nicer thanks to the ability to add names to the fields of each case ❶.

Extensibility

Discriminated unions are similar to class hierarchies, but there's an important difference. With class hierarchies, you can easily add a new derived class, but adding new functionality is hard (you need to add a virtual method and modify all classes). With discriminated unions, you can easily add new functions (using pattern matching), but adding new cases isn't as easy (you have to modify all functions).

In functional-first programming with F#, choosing discriminated unions as your default option is a good idea for their simplicity. But as you'll see later, you can also define and use interfaces and get the object-oriented extensibility model.

In F#, you'll often start by defining the domain model (as you did in listing 6), because it lets you understand the big picture of your problem. Also, the definitions can often be explained even to nontechnical collaborators, who can verify and find holes in your understanding of the domain.

Once you have the domain model, the next step is to add some functionality. For example, let's say you want to add a function that calculates shipping price based on the address. The code in listing 7 implements the following logic:

- Shipping within New York is free.
- Shipping to other parts of the United States costs $5.
- Shipping to Canada costs $15.
- Shipping to all other countries costs $25.

Listing 6   Calculating shipping price

```
let shippingPrice address =
  match address with                                    Throw an
  | NotSet -> invalidOp "Address not set!"      <——|   exception!    Postcode
  | Local(postcode=p) when p.StartsWith("NY") -> 0.0M  <——           starts with NY
  | Local _ -> 5.0M                                         <——      All other local
  | International("Canada") -> 15.0M            <——  Country name    addresses
  | International _ -> 25.0M          <——  All other    is Canada
                                          international
```

As with the domain model, the encoding of the pricing logic using pattern matching directly follows the rules specified earlier. The match construct lets you write a number of cases (separated by |) that consist of a pattern followed by -> and an expression that will be executed if the pattern matches.

The key idea is that the patterns can be *incomplete.* You saw incomplete patterns earlier, and now you can see why they're useful. The match construct tests the cases from top to bottom, looking for the first one that matches. For example, listing 7 first tests whether the postcode of a local address starts with *NY* before the case that handles all other local addresses.

The example also uses one new feature of F# 3.0. When pattern matching on a union case with named fields, you can use the names of the fields. For example, the pattern Local(postcode=p) matches a local address and extracts the value of the postcode into a new variable named p. This not only makes the code more readable, but also makes it more extensible—adding more fields to the case won't break the code. In contrast, the pattern International("Canada") doesn't use the name and relies on the structure (the name of the country is the first and only field).

Exercise 5

Suppose you want to distinguish between personal and business addresses. To do that, modify the Address type and add another case, called Business, storing the company name, street, and postcode.

After extending Address, look at shippingPrice and try calling it with a business address as an example (you should see a warning). The shipping price for businesses is $10, except for "Manning Publications," for which the shipping should be free.

> ### Exercise 6
>
> If you want to turn this example into an online retail system, you must add order management. As an exercise, define an `OrderStatus` discriminated union that models the following three cases:
>
> - *Received*—The order has been created and received. The case carries the date when the order has been received as `System.DateTime`.
> - *Dispatched*—In this state, you'll keep the date when the order has been dispatched (`System.DateTime`) and the shipping company used (as a string).
> - *Delivered*—After the order is delivered, you'll keep the name of the person who signed for the delivery (as a `string`).
>
> Next, write a function that checks whether the order has been lost. An order has been lost if it was dispatched 14 or more days ago. It's also considered lost if it was received but hasn't been dispatched for more than 7 days. A delivered order is never lost.

If you look back at listing 7, you can see that the code can throw an exception when the parameter represents an address that hasn't been set. In C#, you might represent a missing address with `null`, so your code could easily fail unexpectedly (because of a forgotten `null` check). F# types don't have `null` as a valid value, so this isn't going to happen:

```
> let cz = International "Czech Republic"
  let customer = { Name = "Tomas"; Shipping = cz }
  shippingPrice customer.Shipping ;;
(...)

val it : decimal = 25.0M

> shippingPrice null ;;
error FS0043: The type 'Address' does not
have 'null' as a proper value
```

Uses the valid address as an argument

The null value cannot be used as an argument.

The need for an explicit check using pattern matching makes the code more error-prone, but the fact that the `shippingPrice` function can still throw an exception suggests that your domain model isn't entirely appropriate. In the next section, you'll change it slightly to avoid this problem.

IMPROVING THE DOMAIN MODEL WITH OPTIONS

In the previous section, the `NotSet` value was a valid value of type `Address`. As a result, a function that takes a value of type `Address` needs to be able to handle the `NotSet` case—even though it doesn't carry information about the shipping address, it *is* a valid address.

One of the key principles of domain modeling in F# is that invalid states shouldn't be representable. Following this idea, valid addresses should be only local and international. Whether the customer has an address or not is a separate concern. The code in listing 8 is a modified version of the previous snippet. The `Address` type now has only

Local and International cases. The fact that the customer may or may not have an address is expressed by making the Shipping field optional using the option type.

Listing 7 A better domain model

```
type Address =
    | Local of street:string * postcode:string          Represents only
    | International of country:string                    valid addresses

type Customer =
    { Name : string                        ➊  Shipping address
      Shipping : Address option }              is optional
                                                       ➋  Calculate the
let shippingPrice address =                                shipping price
    match address with
    | International("Canada") -> 20.0M
    | International _ -> 25.0M                          All cases return
    | Local(postcode=p) when p.StartsWith("NY") -> 0.0M a valid price
    | Local _ -> 5.0M
```

As mentioned already, the key change is that Address now represents only valid addresses. The Shipping property now has a type Address option ➊. Here, you're using the prefix notation rather than using the more common notation option<Address> (the prefix syntax is mainly used for built-in F# types).

In C#, you could set the field to null to represent the fact that the field is missing. If you did that, you could easily forget to add a null check and run into trouble. The option type makes this information explicit so the F# compiler can enforce that you always handle missing addresses correctly.

For example, say you want to call your new shippingPrice function ➋ on a Shipping property of a customer. To do that, you need to use pattern matching, handling both the Some case (the value is present) and the None case (the value is missing):

```
let customer = { Name = "Jan"; Shipping = None }
match customer.Shipping with              ➊  Shipping
| Some addr ->                               address is set
    printfn "Price: %A" (shippingPrice addr)
| _ ->                                                   Get and print
    printfn "Enter address!"          ➋  Catch-all        the shipping
                                          pattern         price
```

Handle a missing address

The type of customer.Shipping is Address option, whereas shippingPrice takes Address, and so the compiler forces you to use pattern matching. The first branch ➊ handles the case when the address is available, and it assigns the carried Address value to a new variable named addr that you can use later. The second ➋ is a catch-all pattern that handles all cases you haven't covered before; you tell the user that they need to enter an address first.

There are certainly more things to be said about designing functional types, and they're used extensively throughout this book. Although F# is functional-first (meaning functional style is the default), it also supports object-oriented concepts, emphasizing the good parts of the object-oriented paradigm.

It's just elementary school mathematics

When creating domain models, you have several ways to model the same thing. But how do you know whether two ways of modeling a domain are equivalent or whether one can express different states than the other?

It turns out you can do a lot by using elementary school mathematics. To make this example simpler, define three type aliases—for name, phone number, and email address—all represented using a string:

```
type Name = string
type Phone = string
type Email = string
```

Say you want to model a choice of person with a name and a phone number and a person with a name and an email address. One way to do this is to write the following:

```
type Person1 =
  | WithPhone of Name * Phone
  | WithEmail of Name * Email
```

Another way to model this is to say that a person is a record (or tuple) that always contains a name together with either a phone number or an email. In F#, this could be expressed like this:

```
type Contact = Phone of Phone | Email of Email
type Person2 = Name * Contact
```

The interesting question now is, do the types `Person1` and `Person2` represent the same thing? In F#, the tuple type is written using *, and theoreticians call it the *product* type. F# discriminated unions require explicit type definitions, but for now, let's write them using +, because theoreticians call them *sum* types. So for example, the `Contact` type could be written as `Phone + Email`. If you expand the definitions for `Person1` and `Person2` using this notation, you get this (in pseudocode):

```
type Person1 = (Name * Phone) + (Name * Email)
type Person2 =  Name * (Phone + Email)
```

The choice of + and * for the type constructors is intentional. It turns out that many properties of addition and multiplication also work for tuples and discriminated unions. For example, the distributive property says that

```
a(b + c) = ab + ac
```

Now look at the `Person2` and `Person1` types. They're *exactly* the two sides of the distributive property. Using basic mathematical reasoning, you can prove that the two types are the same. The correspondence goes further than this (for example, the `unit` type behaves as the number 1), so if you want to learn more, check out my blog post on "Reasoning about functional types" at http://tomasp.net/blog/types-and-math.aspx/.

Object-oriented programming: the good parts

Being a first-class .NET and Mono language, F# supports all the object-oriented features of the common language runtime (CLR). This means you can use libraries that require you to inherit from the base classes they provide, implement interfaces, override methods, expose .NET events, and so on.

But OOP is also useful on its own. It provides a nice way to encapsulate public functionality in libraries (be it for F# or for other CLR languages). Using interfaces, you also get a different extensibility model that's complementary to the one provided by discriminated unions.

From functions to interfaces

Say you want to check whether customer information is valid before accepting an order. You may want to check that the address is set and that the name matches some basic sanity checks. It's likely you'll want to add more validation checks later on. In the simplest form, you can represent customer validator as a function:

```
type CustomerValidator = Customer -> bool
```

This defines an F# type alias, meaning when you write `CustomerValidator` in a type annotation or definition, the compiler will interpret it as a function from `Customer` to `bool`. Using this representation, you can check whether the customer is valid, but you don't know what error message you should report. Using the object-oriented approach, you can use an interface with a `Validate` method and a `Description` property:

```
type ICustomerValidator =
  abstract Description : string              Read-only
                                       ◄──┘  property         Method of one
  abstract Validate : Customer -> bool                    ◄── argument
```

When used in a functional way, interface types are a surprisingly great fit for functional programming. As you can see here, interfaces are a natural progression from functions. A function can be called on some input. An interface groups multiple functions (or other values) together in a single type.

In this example, you have a method `Validate` and a property `Description`. The method is declared using the F# function type, but it will be compiled into an ordinary .NET method and can be easily implemented in C#. The property you're defining here is read-only (which is the default in F#), but you can also require a setter by writing `with get, set` at the end of the declaration.

Implementing interfaces

Let's stick to the idea that interface types are like function types. When you have a function type like `Customer -> bool`, you can implement it in two ways. The first way is to use an anonymous (lambda) function (such as `fun c -> true`). The second way is to write an ordinary named function using `let` binding that has the matching signature.

When implementing interfaces in F#, you have the same two options. You can use *object expressions*, which are like anonymous functions, and you can use named type

definitions. For example, listing 8 shows an object expression implementing a validator that ensures that the address is provided. This approach is often the easiest way to
implement interfaces in F#.

Listing 8 Validating addresses using object expressions

```
let hasAddress =
  { new ICustomerValidator with        ◄─┐  ❶ Returns an interface
      member x.Description =                  implementation
        "Address is required for shipment"       ❷ Implements a read-
      member x.Validate(cust) =                     only property
        cust.Shipping.IsSome }
                                              ❸ Implements a method
```

The object expression syntax ❶ consists of `new IInterface with`, followed by a number of member declarations, all wrapped in curly brackets. When you use this notation, the compiler generates a class implementing the interface behind the scenes.
But you don't need to know anything about the class, because the type of `hasAddress`
is `ICustomerValidator`.

Inside the object expression, you can use the `member` keyword to implement members of the interface. The same keyword works for properties ❷ as well as methods ❸.
F# makes it easy to write read-only properties. If you needed a getter and a setter, you
can use the notation `member x.Foo with get() = ...` and `set(value) = ...`.

Before looking at how to use the validators, let's create one more: a validator that
ensures that the name of the person is longer than a specified length. But you want to
be able to easily change the required length. For this reason, you'll use a named type
declaration. Listing 10 shows a type `NameLength` that implements the `ICustomer-
Validator` interface and has an additional mutable property, `RequiredLength`, that
specifies the length of the customer name.

Listing 9 Validating the name using object types

```
                                                                    ◄──┐  Implicit
type NameLength() =                                                        ❶ constructor
 ┌─▷ member val RequiredLength = 10 with get, set
 │      interface ICustomerValidator with        ◄────────────────────
 │        member x.Description =                           Explicit interface
 │          "The name should not be empty"       Same as in  ❸ implementation
 │        member x.Validate(cust) =              the previous
 │          cust.Name <> null &&                 example
 │          cust.Name.Length >= x.RequiredLength
```

Auto-
implemented
mutable
property ❷

The easiest way to declare classes in F# is to use the implicit constructor syntax ❶.
This means the name of the type (here `NameLength`) is followed by a list of constructor
parameters in parentheses. In this example, the constructor doesn't take any parameters, but if it took some, their values would be available in all the members of the class
(the compiler automatically generates private fields for them).

Next, you define a property, `RequiredLength` ❷. F# 3.0 supports automatically
implemented properties using the `member val` notation, meaning it generates a backing

field for the property and adds a getter and a setter. F# avoids uninitialized values, so you need to provide a default value for the property.

Finally, the declaration includes an implementation of the ICustomerValidator interface ❸. Here, you're using *explicit implementation* (similar to explicit interface implementations in C#), which means a value of type NameLength can be treated as a value of the interface type, but it doesn't automatically expose all the members of the interface.

> **NOTE** As of this writing, 3.0 was the most recent version of F# available, but the plans for future versions include support for implicit interface implementations. This means in versions after 3.0, you'll most likely be able to implement interfaces implicitly by writing inherit ICustomerValidator and providing members of the right types in the type declaration.

Now that you have two sample validators, let's briefly look at how you can do something useful with them. The FSI session in the next listing creates a list of ICustomerValidator values and then runs all of them on a given customer, printing the descriptions of failing validators.

> **Listing 10 Programming with objects interactively**

```
> let v1 = hasAddress
  let v2 = NameLength(RequiredLength=5)
  let validators = [ v1; v2 :> ICustomerValidator ];;
(...)

> let cust = { Name = "Tomas"; Shipping = None };;
val cust : Customer = (...)

> for v in validators do
    if not (v.Validate(cust)) then
      printfn "%s" v.Description;;
Address is required for shipment
val it : unit = ()
```

❶ Creates and sets the required length to 5

❷ Upcasts to the interface type

Prints descriptions of failed validators

The first code block creates a list of validators. When you create an instance of NameLength, you use the property-initialization notation to set the required name length to 5 ❶. The resulting variable, v2, has a type NameLength. When creating the list, you want to get a list of ICustomerValidator values, so you need to cast the value to the interface using the :> operator ❷. This process is called *upcasting*, and it means a type cast that always succeeds (like casting a class to an interface it implements). F# doesn't, in general, automatically perform upcasts except for a few cases—such as when you're calling a method with an object as an argument. It's also good to know that if you want to write a cast that may fail, you'd need the *downcast* operator, :?>.

Once you have a list of validators, using it is easy. The last block of code iterates over all the validators using the for loop, checks whether they fail by calling the Validate method, and then, in case of failure, prints the description.

Exercise 7

First, implement a validator for the postcode field in local addresses. To be a valid US postcode, the string needs to start with two letters, followed by an optional space and a five-digit number. Implement the validator using object expression.

Next, suppose you want to provide more flexibility and allow the user to specify the postcode format using regular expressions. Implement the `AddressRegexValidator` class that has a mutable property `FormatRegex` and checks that the postcode of an address matches the specified regex.

Exercise 8

Recall the order status discriminated union that you defined in exercise 6. Let's say that you now want to implement an extensible system for handling orders (this may not be the best approach, but it makes for a fun exercise!).

Your first task is to define an interface, `IOrderShipper`. Given an `Address`, the shipment handler decides whether it supports shipping to the specified address (USPS supports only local addresses, but FedEx can ship anywhere). Then it should provide a method that takes `Address` and `OrderStatus` as arguments and returns the new `OrderStatus`. Given a received order, it should return a dispatched order with the current date and the name of the company used.

As an example, implement a shipping handler for USPS and FedEx. Then write a function that processes an order, finding the first shipping handler that's capable of handling the address and using it to get the new order status.

As mentioned earlier, F# supports most of the object-oriented features of the CLR, so we can't cover all of them in a single chapter. Rather than trying to cover all possible features, let's focus on one object-oriented feature that's emphasized in F#: composition.

Composition over inheritance

Inheritance is an important part of OOP, but it suffers from a number of issues. One such difficulty is that by inheriting from another class, your class is inheriting all the functionality and all the complexity of the parent class. This means inheritance can only make your types more complex.

This is one of the reasons for the principle of composition over inheritance. This principle is encouraged in functional-first programming with F#. Moreover, F# provides a number of features that make it easy to compose other objects.

For example, let's say you want to have a way of composing multiple validators into a single one. Given a sequence of validators, the new validator succeeds only when all of the given validators succeed. The description is a string with descriptions of all the composed validators. The next listing implements this idea as a function using object expressions.

Listing 11   Composing validators using object expressions

Function for validator composition ❶

```
let composeValidators (validators:seq<ICustomerValidator>) =
  { new ICustomerValidator with
      member x.Description =
        [ for v in validators -> v.Description ]
        |> String.concat "\n"
      member x.Validate(cust) =
        validators
        |> Seq.forall (fun v -> v.Validate(cust)) }
```

❷ **Object expression**

❸ **Concatenates descriptions**

❹ **Checks that all validators succeed**

The listing defines a function ❶ that takes a value of type seq<ICustomValidator> as an argument (where seq<'T> is an alias for IEnumerable<'T>). It returns a single composed validator of type ICustomValidator.

To create the resulting validator, you use an object expression ❷ that creates a new implementation of the ICustomerValidator interface. The implementation is simple. The Description property concatenates all descriptions ❸, and the Validate method uses Seq.forall ❹ to check that Validate methods of all composed validators return true.

> **NOTE**   If you look just at the number of keywords available in object-oriented languages like C#, you can see that OOP is more complex than you might think. F# supports the majority of the OOP features required to interoperate with .NET, and it's impossible to cover all of them in a few pages.

Even though interoperability with .NET is an important reason for using object-oriented features in F#, the language doesn't support OOP just for interoperability. Object-oriented features are useful for structuring functional code, and we looked at some of the F# features that make it easy to use the good parts of object-oriented ideas.

Summary

This appendix serves as an F# introduction, but it's not the usual F# tutorial. Rather than looking at the features one by one, I showed you interesting examples that can offer deep insight into how F# works and how to think about it.

The recurring theme in this chapter has been *composition*. Composition is perhaps the most important concept in F#. At the expression level, you've seen that F# programs are *composed* from simple expressions. Even seemingly imperative features like printing are expressions that return the unit value as the result.

At the next level, we looked at domain modeling using functional types. Again, the type system is based on composition: you can compose the domain model from primitive types using tuples, records, and discriminated unions. These give you two basic forms of composition. You can group multiple types using records and represent a choice using discriminated unions. Finally, we looked at some of the object-oriented features of F#. Again, the focus was on composition and using interfaces, which fits extremely well with the nature of F#.

About the author

Tomas Petricek is a long-time F# enthusiast and author of the book *Real-World Functional Programming*, which explains functional programming concepts using C# 3.0 while also teaching F#. He is a frequent F# speaker and does F# and functional training in London, New York, and elsewhere worldwide.

Tomas has been a Microsoft MVP since 2004, writes a programming blog at http://tomasp.net, and is also a Stack Overflow addict. He contributed to the development of F# during two internships at Microsoft Research in Cambridge. Before starting a PhD at the University of Cambridge, he studied in Prague and worked as an independent .NET consultant.

index

Symbols

! (exclamation point) 29
** operator 28
==> operator 317
–> operator 319

A

acceptance testing
  frameworks for 321
  overview 320–321
  TickSpec library 322–326
ACID (Atomicity, Consistency,
  Isolation, Durability) 258
active patterns 14
  parsing Markdown language
    blocks 56–61
  parsing Markdown language
    spans 52–56
actor model 17
adjacency matrix 109
agent-based model 16
algorithms 16
analytical components 6
anonymous functions 344
antithetic variates. *See* AV
AppData 244
Asian options 90
assertions 311–312
async keyword 168
asynchronous programming
  I/O using 237–240
  MVC pattern and 166–168

Atomicity, Consistency,
  Isolation, Durability.
    See ACID
automated acceptance
  testing 320
AV (antithetic variates) 92
await keyword 168

B

Ballard, Chris 298
BAML (binary XAML)
  294
barrier options 91
Battocchi, Keith 150
BDD (behavior-driven
  development) 300,
  320
BeginOpenContainer 239
BeginShowSelector 239
benchmarking 256
Bigtable clones 259
binary XAML. *See* BAML
BinaryFormatter 256
BINOM.DIST function 31
business
  complexity and 14–15
  NULL references and 10
  numerical calculations
    10–11
  overview 5–9
  reducing time to market
    11–14
  scalable software 15–17

C

caching 150
Canopy 305
capital sigma 27
case studies in book 17–20
Cassandra 259
Castle.Core library 158
Cellz project 322
changing requirements 302
charting 83
Chen, Chao-Jen 97
CI (continuous
  integration) 308
client, social web application
  app 272–276
  representing game
    state 268–270
  utility functions 270–271
  XAML for 267–268
cloud computing 245,
  253–255
CLR (common language
  runtime) 344
code quotations 139–140
column databases 259
comma-separated values. *See*
  CSV
common language runtime.
  See CLR
complexity 8, 14–15, 45
composite values
  using records 337–338
  using tuples 336–337

composition over
inheritance 347–349
compositionality 327
content pipeline 216
continuations 217
continuous integration. *See* CI
continuous random
variables 76
contract parameters 84
contracts
model 249–250
request and response
objects 250–253
controller (MVC
pattern) 161–165
conversions 173–174
Couchbase 257–258
CruiseControl.NET 308
CSV (comma-separated
values) 129
CSV type provider
design strategy 133–135
implementing runtime
and type provider
138–142
inferring column types
135–138
overview 130–132
Cucumber 321
Cui, Yan 278
cumulative binomial distributions
formula for
capital sigma 27
factorials 27
overview 26–29
superscripts in 28
large number problem
36–40
overview 25–26
refactoring
creating recursive
function 42–44
eliminating common
functions in loops
41–42
eliminating cumulative
flag 40–41
testing
exposing Fact function to
unit testing 33–34
FsUnit 30
NUnit 30
processing large integers
in Binomial
function 35–36

returning large integers
from Fact function
34–35
test cases in Excel 30–33
cumulative flag 40–41

D

D3.js
overview 105–107
parameters for 107–108
daily active users. *See* DAUs
damping factor 122
dangling nodes 121
data binding
conversions 173–174
nullable values in 171–172
setting programmatically
169–170
statically typed 170
transformations 174–181
data science 13
data structures
choices, using unions
338–342
composite values
using records 337–338
using tuples 336–337
Markdown language
parsing 48–49
DataContractJsonSerializer
256
data-rich components 6
DAUs (daily active users) 244
Deedle 13
degree distribution 115–116
Delimited pattern 53
Deneux, Johann 243
derived properties 179–180
destructing unit 332
discrete random variables 76
discriminated unions 339
document processing
generating references from
hyperlinks 66–69
tree-processing patterns
64–66
domain-specific languages. *See*
DSLs
Don't Repeat Yourself. *See* DRY
downcasting 346
DrawableGameComponent
class 214
drift term 80
DRY (Don't Repeat
Yourself) 41

DSLs (domain-specific
languages) 14, 47, 299,
303
DynamoDB 258

E

Eason, Kit 44
Emacs 306
EndOpenContainer 239
EndShowSelector 239
enterprise development
client implementation
290–292
REST service
implementation 287–290
sample project
overview 281–282
user interface
making service
available 296–298
Prism shell 292–294
Prism WPF plug-in
module 294–295
using RavenDB 282–287
environment 4
equity options 74
Erlang 17
European call options 74, 92
European defense game
example 212–213,
240–243
event-based user
interfaces 210
exclamation point (!) 29
EXP (experience points) 246
expectation 76, 85
explicit implementation 346
exploratory testing
checking functional
requirements 306–307
checking nonfunctional
requirements 307–308
combining unit testing
and 312–313
overview 306
expression tree 311
expressions
overview 328–331
statements vs. 328
using functions as
values 333–335
wrapping in functions
331–332
ExprShape module 64
extensibility 339

Extensible Application Markup
    Language. *See* XML
external DSLs 47, 303

F

F#
    business uses 5–9
    environment 4
    functional-programming 2–3
    OOP and 344
    overview 2
    polyglot programming 3–4
F# Compiler Services
    project 302
F# Data package 130
F# Interactive. *See* FSI
F# Software Foundation. *See*
    FSSF
factorials 27
FakeItEasy 318
FarmVille 244
feature files 323
financial computing
    financial derivatives 74
    geometric Brownian motion
        analyzing Monte Carlo
            estimates using
            variance 88–89
        modeling stock prices
            79–84
        overview 79
        payoff function 84–88
        pricing path-dependent
            options 89–92
        variance reduction 92–96
    probability functions
        FSI configuration 74–75
        Math.NET project 75
        normal distribution 78–79
        random variables 76–78
followers, Twitter 101
Foq 319
force layout algorithm 105–106
frame-based simulation 210
Freebase type provider 130
friends, Twitter 101
FsCheck 315–317
FSharp.Charting 83
FSharp.Data.Toolbox
    provider 100
FSI (F# Interactive) 74–75
FSSF (F# Software
    Foundation) 4
FsUnit 30, 311
.fsx files 306

function keyword 62
functional programming
    business
        complexity and 14–15
        NULL references and 10
        numerical calculations
            10–11
        overview 5–9
        reducing time to
            market 11–14
        scalable software 15–17
    case studies in book 17–20
    environment 4
    overview 2–3
    polyglot programming 3–4
functional requirements 302,
    306–307
functional-first 2, 9
functions
    using as values 333–335
    wrapping expressions
        in 331–332
fuzz testing 315–317

G

Gabasova, Evelina 128
games
    asynchronous I/O 237–240
    button presses 217–223
    data modeling 223–230
    European defense game
        example 212–213, 240–243
    execution flow for
        XNA 213–215
    rendering game 230–233
    rendering scoreboard
        233–237
    state management in
        F# 210–212
    Visual Studio structure 215
    See also social web applications
Gamesys 259
generalizing types 136
general-purpose type
    providers 133
geometric Brownian motion
    analyzing Monte Carlo esti-
        mates using variance
        88–89
    modeling stock prices 79–84
    overview 79
    payoff function 84–88
    pricing path-dependent
        options 89–92
    variance reduction 92–96

Gherkin 321–322
GitHub 309
Given step definition 321
Google 119, 256, 259
graph databases 259

H

Haskell 9
HBase 259
Here Be Monsters 265
Heston model 96
Hoare, Tony 10
HTTP server 265–267
hubs 118

I

I/O (input/output) 237–240
IDE (integrated development
    environment) 131
ILSpy 284
immutable data structures 228
implicit interface
    implementations 346
incomplete patterns 337, 340
in-degrees 112–114
indentation 329
inheritance 347–349
INotifyPropertyChanged
    interface 158
input/output. *See* I/O
integrated development envi-
    ronment. *See* IDE
IntelliSense 166, 220
INTERACTIVE symbol 312
interfaces 344–347
internal DSLs 303
IronPython 302
IronRuby 302
ISessionStore interface 257
IStateRepository interface 257
ITypeProvider interface 134

J

JIT (just-in-time) compilation
    15
JSON (JavaScript Object Nota-
    tion)
    reading with type
        providers 109–112
    representing Twitter network
        in 103–105
Json.Net 256
JsonValue method 104

K

key-value stores 258
KPIs (key performance indicators) 301

L

large numbers 36–40
LINQ 132, 140
LINQ to XML library 61
#load directive 313
LOB (line of business) 299
log-log plots 116–119
Lua.NET 302

M

machine learning 13
MapReduce 123–125
Markdown language parsing
  active patterns
    parsing blocks 56–61
    parsing spans 52–56
  creating HTML 61–63
  data structures 48–49
  format overview 46–48
  processing documents
    generating references
      from hyperlinks
      66–69
    tree-processing
      patterns 64–66
  recursive functions 49–52
Math.NET project 75
matrix multiplication 113
MbUnit 309
member keyword 345
Memcached 257
Microsoft intermediate language. See MSIL
Miranda 9
ML 9
mocks 318
model (MVC pattern) 158–160, 165
Model-View-Controller pattern. See MVC pattern
Model-View-ViewModel pattern. See MVVM pattern
MongoDB 257, 259
Mono 212
Monte Carlo estimates 88–89
Moq 318
Morozovis, Dmitry 181

MSIL (Microsoft intermediate language) 179
MsTest 309
MVC (Model-View-Controller) pattern
  asynchronous programming and 166–168
  connecting components of 164–165
  controller 161–164
  data binding
    conversions 173–174
    nullable values in 171–172
    setting programmatically 169–170
    statically typed 170
    transformations 174–181
  model 158–160
  overview 155–157
  trading application and 155
  view 160–161
MVVM (Model-View-View-Model) pattern 153–154

N

NBehave 321
NCrunch 30, 309
Neo4j 259
non-dividend-paying stocks 74
nonfunctional requirements 301, 307–308
normal distribution 78–79
NoSQL databases 245, 258
NRE (null reference exception) 303
NSubstitute 318
NULL references 10
nullable values 171–172
numerical calculations 10–11
NUnit 30, 308–311

O

object expressions 344
OOP (object-oriented programming) 154
  composition over inheritance 347–349
  F# and 344
  interfaces 344–347
out-degrees 112–114

P

P&L (profit and loss) 155
PageRank algorithm
  calculating with damping factor 121–122
  mathematical formulation of 119–121
  overview 119, 125–126
  using MapReduce to compute 123–125
  visualizing important nodes 126–127
parallel model 16
parallelism 15
parameterized active patterns 52
parameterized tests 313–314
parsing Markdown language
  active patterns
    parsing blocks 56–61
    parsing spans 52–56
  creating HTML 61–63
  data structures 48–49
  format overview 46–48
  processing documents
    generating references
      from hyperlinks 66–69
    tree-processing
      patterns 64–66
  recursive functions 49–52
partial function
  application 53, 335
pattern matching 14
payoff function 84–88
performance 15, 305, 307
Petricek, Tomas 20–21, 69, 349
plot function 116
POCO (Plain Old CLR Object) 256
polyglot programming 3–4
positive part function 74
preferential attachment model 118
principle of least surprise 284
Printf.fprintf function 63
Prism
  shell using 292–294
  WPF plug-in module 294–295
probability functions
  FSI configuration 74–75
  Math.NET project 75
  normal distribution 78–79
  random variables 76–78
profiling code 75

profit and loss. *See* P&L
PropertyChanged event 158
protocol buffers 256
pure functions 304

Q

QuickCheck 315

R

R type provider 14, 115–116
Raconteur 321
random surfer model 119
random variables 76–78
RavenDB 282–287
recursive functions 42–44,
    49–52
Redis 257–258
reliability 254
REPL (read-evaluate-print-
    loop) 301, 306
Representational State Trans-
    fer. *See* REST
request-response pattern
    253
requirements, software
    301–302
ReSharper 321
REST (Representational State
    Transfer)
    client implementation
        290–292
    service implementation
        287–290
Riak 258

S

samples 76
Scala 9
scalability 8, 15–17, 244,
    254
scale-free networks 118
SDE (stochastic differential
    equation) 80
sequential model 16
serialization 256
server, social web application
    data access layer 256–260
    game engine 260–265
    HTTP server 265–267
    utility functions
        255–256
ServiceStack.Text 256
shared examples 323

SharpVille
    client
        app 272–276
        representing game
            state 268–270
        utility functions 270–271
        XAML for 267–268
    client-server
        interaction 246–248
    overview 245–246,
        276–278
    server
        data access layer 256–260
        game engine 260–265
        HTTP server 265–267
        utility functions 255–256
    UI 246
should assertion 311
side effects 304
Silverlight 153
situation, problem, implica-
    tion, need. *See* SPIN
social networks
    in-degrees 112–114
    log-log plot 116–119
    most-connected users
        114–115
    out-degrees 112–114
    PageRank algorithm
        calculating with damping
            factor 121–122
        mathematical formulation
            of 119–121
        overview 119, 125–126
        using MapReduce to
            compute 123–125
        visualizing important
            nodes 126–127
    reading JSON files with type
        providers 109–112
    representing network with
        adjacency matrix 109
    Twitter
        connecting to 100–101
        connections between
            users 102–103
        downloading @fsharporg
            network 101–102
        overview 99
        representing network in
            JSON 103–105
        requesting usernames
            102
    visualization of degree distri-
        bution using R
        provider 115–116

    visualization with D3.js
        overview 105–107
        parameters for 107–108
social web applications
    client
        app 272–276
        representing game
            state 268–270
        utility functions 270–271
        XAML for 267–268
    cloud infrastructure
        and 253–255
    contracts
        model 249–250
        request and response
            objects 250–253
    overview 244–245
    prerequisites 248
    server
        data access layer 256–260
        game engine 260–265
        HTTP server 265–267
        utility functions 255–256
    SharpVille
        client-server interaction
            246–248
        overview 245–246,
            276–278
        UI 246
software quality
    acceptance testing
        frameworks for 321
        overview 320–321
        TickSpec library 322–326
    avoiding defects early with
        types 303–304
    exploratory testing
        checking functional
            requirements 306–307
        checking nonfunctional
            requirements 307–308
        overview 306
    holistic approach to
        testing 304–305
    overview 299–301
    requirements 301–302
    unit testing
        combining explorative
            and 312–313
        fuzz testing with
            FsCheck 315–317
        overview 308–309
        parameterized tests
            313–314
        using FsUnit 311
        using NUnit 309–310

software quality *(continued)*
  using test doubles 317–320
  writing assertions using
    Unquote 311–312
SpecFlow 321
specialized type providers 133
specification by example 320
SPIN (situation, problem,
  implication, need) 5
sprintf function 174
StartImmediate method 167
state management 210–212
stateless 264
statements 328
statically typed data
  binding 170
stochastic differential equation. *See* SDE
stochastic process 79
stock data
  implementing CSV type pro-
    vider
    design strategy 133–135
    implementing runtime
      and type provider
      138–142
    inferring column
      types 135–138
  implementing Yahoo!
    Finance type provider
    generating company
      names lazily 146–147
    getting company informa-
      tion using YQL
      143–145
    overview 143, 149–150
    type provider for navigat-
      ing through
      industries 145–146
    using CSV provider
      147–149
  type providers
    advantages of 132–133
    CSV type provider
      130–132
    overview 130
stock options 74
StorageContainer 239–240
StorageDevice 238
StorEvil 321
strongly typed 2
stubs 317
SUT (system under test) 308,
  317
symbols 336
Syme, Don 20–21

T

Task Parallel Library. *See* TPL
TeamCity 308
test doubles
  defined 317
  function stubs 317–318
  mocking libraries 318–320
  object expressions 318
TestCase attribute 314
TestDriven.NET 30, 309, 321
testing
  acceptance
    frameworks for 321
    overview 320–321
    TickSpec library 322–326
  cumulative binomial distri-
    butions
    exposing Fact function to
      unit testing 33–34
    FsUnit 30
    NUnit 30
    processing large integers
      in Binomial
      function 35–36
    returning large integers
      from Fact function
      34–35
    test cases in Excel 30–33
  exploratory
    checking functional
      requirements 306–307
    checking nonfunctional
      requirements 307–308
    overview 306
  holistic approach 304–305
  unit
    combining explorative
      and 312–313
    fuzz testing with
      FsCheck 315–317
    overview 308–309
    parameterized tests
      313–314
    using FsUnit 311
    using NUnit 309–310
    using test doubles 317–320
    writing assertions using
      Unquote 311–312
TextWriter class 63
thin/thick server 247–248
TickSpec library 322–326
#time directive 305, 307
time to market 8
TPL (Task Parallel Library) 2,
  15

traditional functional
  languages 9
transformations 174–181
transition matrix 120
Travis 309
tree-processing patterns 64–66
Trelford, Phil 326
tuples 336–337
Twitter
  connecting to 100–101
  connections between
    users 102–103
  downloading @fsharporg
    network 101–102
  overview 99
  representing network in
    JSON 103–105
  requesting usernames 102
type providers
  advantages of 132–133
  caching and 150
  CSV type provider
    design strategy 133–135
    implementing runtime
      and type provider
      138–142
    inferring column
      types 135–138
    overview 130–132
  defined 13, 129
  overview 130
  portable 150
  Yahoo! Finance type provider
    generating company
      names lazily 146–147
    getting company informa-
      tion using YQL 143–145
    overview 143, 149–150
    type provider for navigat-
      ing through
      industries 145–146
    using CSV provider
      147–149
TypeProvider attribute 142
types 303–304

U

unions 338–342
unit testing
  combining explorative
    and 312–313
  fuzz testing with
    FsCheck 315–317
  overview 308–309
  parameterized tests 313–314

unit testing *(continued)*
  software quality and 300
  using FsUnit 311
  using NUnit 309–310
  using test doubles 317–320
  writing assertions using
    Unquote 311–312
unit type 328
unit vector 113
Unquote 311–312
up-and-in barrier calls 92
upcasting 346
usernames, requesting
  Twitter 102

V

variance
  analyzing Monte Carlo esti-
    mates using 88–89
  overview 77
  reduction 92–96
Vertica 259
view (MVC pattern) 160–161,
  165
Visual Studio 215, 306
visualization
  with D3.js
    overview 105–107
    parameters for 107–108

degree distribution using R
  provider 115–116
important nodes based on
  PageRank 126–127

W

waitReleased function 217
WCF (Windows Communica-
  tion Foundation) 287
WorldBank type provider
  130
WPF (Windows Presentation
  Foundation) 153
Write method 63
WriteLine method 63

X

Xamarin Studio 306
XAML (Extensible Applica-
  tion Markup
  Language) 153
XNA framework
  asynchronous I/O 237–240
  button presses 217–223
  data modeling 223–230
  European defense game
    example 212–213,
    240–243

execution flow 213–215
overview 212
rendering game 230–233
rendering scoreboard
  233–237
Visual Studio structure
  215
XNA Game Studio 212
xUnit 308, 310–311

Y

Yahoo! Finance type provider
  generating company
    names lazily 146–147
  getting company informa-
    tion using YQL 143–145
  overview 143, 149–150
  type provider for navigating
    through industries
    145–146
  using CSV provider
    147–149
yield! keyword 51
YQL (Yahoo! Query
  Language) 143

Z

Zynga 244, 259